THE LATIN AMERICAN
LITERARY BOOM
AND U.S. NATIONALISM
DURING THE COLD WAR

D1571991

THE LATIN AMERICAN LITERARY BOOM AND U.S. NATIONALISM DURING THE COLD WAR

Deborah Cohn

Vanderbilt University Press ■ Nashville

© 2012 by Vanderbilt University Press
Nashville, Tennessee 37235
All rights reserved
First printing 2012

This book is printed on acid-free paper.
Manufactured in the United States of America

Excerpt from letter by Carlos Fuentes on José Donoso's
Coronation, copyright © 1964 by Carlos Fuentes.
Reprinted by permission of Brandt and Hochman
Literary Agents Inc.

Excerpts from letter to Carlos Fuentes by Arthur Miller,
copyright © 1969 by Arthur Miller. Reprinted by
permission of The Wylie Agency LLC.

Excerpts from address by Pablo Neruda, 10 April 1972,
50th Anniversary of the American Center of PEN,
copyright © Fundación Pablo Neruda, 2011. PEN
Archives, Box 95, Folder 14. Reprinted by permission
of the Agencia Literaria Carmen Balcells SA.

Library of Congress Cataloging-in-Publication Data on file

LC control number 2011023793
LC classification PQ7081.C633 2012
Dewey class number 860.9/980904

ISBN 978-0-8265-1804-0 (cloth)
ISBN 978-0-8265-1805-7 (paperback)
ISBN 978-0-8265-1806-4 (e-book)

To my beloved boys—
Noah, Benjamin, and Daniel—
and to Peter, for giving me
the joy of his love and our family

CONTENTS

ACKNOWLEDGMENTS   ix

INTRODUCTION
Multiple Agendas: Latin American Literary
Fervor and U.S. Outreach Programs following
the Cuban Revolution   1

1   **"Catch 28":** The McCarran-Walter Immigration
Blacklist and Spanish American Writers   37

2   **PEN and the Sword:** Latin American Writers
and the 1966 PEN Congress   65

3   **Latin America and Its Literature in the
U.S. University after the Cuban Revolution**   95

4   **The "Cold War Struggle" for Latin American Literature
at the Center for Inter-American Relations**   145

CONCLUSION   193

NOTES   203

WORKS CITED   231

INDEX   243

ACKNOWLEDGMENTS

I am extremely fortunate to have had the opportunity to speak to many of the writers, translators, critics, and editors of whom I have written here. Carlos Fuentes, William Styron, and Mario Vargas Llosa provided me with important insights into the period and the dynamics covered in this book, and my interview with Mr. Vargas Llosa provided me with the seeds of my concluding thoughts. I am also very grateful to Keith Botsford, Cass Canfield Jr., Patricia Cepeda, Ronald Christ, Rita Guibert, Suzanne Jill Levine, Alfred Mac Adam, William MacLeish, John Macrae III, Rosario Peyrou, Gregory Rabassa, Alastair Reid, Rosario Santos, André Schiffrin, Saúl Sosnowski, Jane Spender, and Eliot Weinberger, for their time and their thoughtful responses to my questions. In addition to Mr. Styron, several other individuals who provided me with invaluable information died before I was able to finish this book. They include John Alexander Coleman, Arnold Del Greco, Herminia (Pipina) Prieto, and William D. Rogers. I am sorry beyond words that I am unable to thank them in person for their help with my project.

I am extremely grateful to Nick Cullather, Susan Gillman, Matt Guterl, Liam Kennedy, Caroline Levander, Robert Levine, John Macrae III, Giles Scott-Smith, and Steve Stowe for taking the time to offer important feedback on drafts of my chapters. Suzanne Jill Levine and Alfred Mac Adam, who were both involved in many of the activities that I discuss here, have given unstintingly of their time over the past few years. They have answered countless questions, suggested many leads to follow, pointed me in new directions and to new resources, and read multiple drafts of my chapters. John King has likewise generously shared his insights and his experiences through many e-mails and comments on my chapters, and I am indebted to him for his keen insights into the subjects that I discuss here. Efraín Kristal has supported me and my work in more ways than I can count, and his mentorship over the years has helped me immeasurably. I am indebted to Claire Fox for her readings and her support as we struggled with similar projects and conundrums. Over the years, Patrick Dove, Marshall Eakin, Earl Fitz, Gerald Martin, Julio Ortega, Dan Shapiro, and Maarten van Delden have responded thoughtfully—and with a timeliness that is inspiring—to my many queries. Robert Arnove, Gene Bell-Villada, Russell Cobb, and Inderjeet Parmar have also been generous with their time and their ideas, and Richard Saunders thoughtfully helped me with information on the Knopfs. The anonymous reviewer for Vanderbilt University Press gave a very careful reading to my manuscript, as well as extremely thoughtful comments. The suggestions that I received from these colleagues have transformed this manuscript and have been invaluable in helping me to articulate my ideas.

Friends such as Purnima Bose, Leigh Anne Duck, Kim Geeslin, Carl Good, George Handley, Richard King, Cathy Larson, Caroline Levander, Sophia McClennen, Alejandro Mejías-López, Jon Smith, and Steve Wagschal were terrific interlocutors and offered me a stimulating and supportive intellectual environment. Patrick Dove was always available when I needed answers, sympathy, or simply someone to vent to. Matt Guterl expanded my intellectual horizons in many ways while at the same time serving as a wonderful model of all that is possible for a scholar to accomplish.

I am extremely grateful to David Cowling and Andrea Noble at Durham University for providing me with a place—both physical and intellectual—to pull this book together during the 2009–2010 academic year. Many thanks go to Jonathan Long, Nick Roberts, Clare Zon, Seth Kunin, Santiago Fouz-Hernández, and Lucille Cairns in Durham, and María Pilar Blanco and Claire Lindsay in London, for their companionship and support. I presented my research in lectures at Durham, Oxford, Edinburgh, Sheffield, and University College London, and I wish to express my gratitude to the aforementioned Durham colleagues as well as to Phil Swanson, Edwin Williamson, Clive Griffin, Juan Carlos Conde, Fiona Mackintosh, Claire Lindsay, and María Pilar Blanco for these opportunities and for their feedback. Nancy and Giles Radford gave my husband, my children, and me both the family and the home away from home that made our year.

Several graduate research assistants have offered invaluable help and support while preparing this book. I am grateful to Laila Amine, Elaine Enríquez, Cara Kinnally, Jennifer Smith, Giovanna Urdangarain, Claudia Gervais, and Julie Gagnon-Riopel for their assistance on many different levels. Luis González, our Latin Americanist librarian at Indiana University

Bloomington, on several occasions tracked down obscure sources for me when I had despaired of ever locating them, and the staff at our Herman B. Wells Library went beyond the call of duty for me on multiple occasions. María Pilar Blanco generously reviewed my translations of archival materials while facing her own heavy workload. This book draws on materials in multiple archives, and I would like to thank in particular Elaine Engst at Cornell University's Kroch Library, Kathryn Hodson and Jacque Roethler at the University of Iowa Library, Erwin Levold at the Rockefeller Archive Center, Idelle Nissila at the Ford Foundation, AnnaLee Pauls at Princeton University Library, and Regina Rush at the University of Virginia Libraries, for both their patience and their expediency in responding to my many requests for additional documentation as I unfolded yet another leaf of this project.

I am indebted to the Robert Penn Warren Center for the Humanities at Vanderbilt University for a yearlong fellowship and an excellent research environment, both of which allowed me to lay the groundwork for this project. I am grateful to my colleagues—in particular, to Cathy Jrade, Marshall Eakin, Earl Fitz, Jane Landers, and William Luis—in the seminar on the Americas that brought us together, for both their hospitality and their feedback on my research. Mona Frederick, executive director of the center, was beyond helpful with her support and friendship and in connecting me to resources during my time at Vanderbilt. I am also indebted to Michael Ames of Vanderbilt University Press for taking an active interest in this book at that time and for his continued support and patience in the ensuing years, and to Ed Huddleston and Peg Duthie for their commitment to the clarity of this manuscript. I was additionally fortunate to receive a faculty fellowship from the National Endowment for the Humanities that gave me time to work on this book. Any views, findings, or conclusions expressed here do not necessarily reflect those of the NEH. Thanks go as well to the American Philosophical Society, the Harry Ransom Humanities Research Center, and the Rockefeller Archive Center for fellowships that supported my archival research. The Office of the Vice President for Research at Indiana University Bloomington provided me with supplemental assistance while I held the NEH fellowship, as well as summer research funding and several travel grants. The College Arts and Humanities Institute at Indiana University Bloomington also supported my research with travel grants.

Earlier versions of several chapters of this book were previously published in the following journals and are included here with permission: Chapter 2 was originally published in *Review: Literature and Arts of the Americas* (71 [2005]) as "'Ridiculous Rather than Secure': Carlos Fuentes and the McCarran-Walter Act"; "William Faulkner's Ibero-American Novel Project: The Politics of Translation and the Cold War" originally appeared in the *Southern Quarterly* (Winter 2004) and is now part of Chapter 3; and "A Tale of Two Translation Programs: Politics, the Market, and Rockefeller Funding for Latin American Literature in the United States during the 1960s and 1970s" first appeared in *Latin American Research Review* (41, no. 2 [2006]) and has become part of Chapters 3 and 4 of this book. An earlier version of Chapter 2 was published in *Hemispheric American Studies*, edited by Caroline Levander and Robert Levine (Rutgers University Press, 2008). Finally, my first article on this project, "Retracing *The Lost Steps*: The Cuban Revolution, the Cold War, and Publishing Alejo Carpentier in the United States," appeared in *CR: The New Centennial Review* 3, no. 1 (Spring 2003), and contains kernels of the ideas that appear in several different chapters of this book.

I am grateful for the love and support provided by friends such as Carrie Chorba Fross, Ruth Eberle, Erika Haber, Stephanie Merrim, and Jean O'Bryan-Knight. And, of course, for the love of my family—Tamara and Chuck Krimm, Irene Cohn, Dave Cohn and Alice Beasley, Anne Posner, Alan Posner and Gail Shor-Posner, Les Cohn, Margie and Ken Sauer and the whole Sauer family—who will now, finally, get the answer to the question of how the book is coming along that I was always too busy to give them. My husband, Peter Sauer, and I have had three children during the course of my working on this book. Noah, Ben, and Danny have grown up along with this project, and they have brought me immeasurable joy. I am grateful beyond words to Peter for his love and partnership, and the delight with which he watched over the boys as I completed this project. They are the light of my life.

Permissions

I have been granted permission to quote from materials in the following archives:

Columbia University Library, Rare Book and Manuscript Library, New York, New York

Cornell University Libraries, Division of Rare and Manuscript Collections, Ithaca, New York

Federal Bureau of Investigation (materials accessed through the Freedom of Information Act), Washington, DC

Ford Foundation Archives, New York, New York

Harry Ransom Humanities Research Center, University of Texas at Austin Library, Austin, Texas

Houghton Library, Harvard University, Cambridge, Massachusetts

Princeton University Library, Department of Rare Books and Special Collections, Princeton, New Jersey

Rockefeller Archive Center, Sleepy Hollow, New York

University of Iowa Libraries, Special Collections, Iowa City, Iowa

University of Virginia Library, Special Collections, Charlottesville, Virginia

I am extremely grateful to have been granted permission to quote from the unpublished letters and materials of the following individuals and organizations:

Richard Adams

The Carnegie Corporation of New York

Paul Engle

The Ford Foundation

Thomas Fleming

Carlos Fuentes

John King

The Knopf Doubleday Publishing Group, a division of Random House Inc.

William Koshland

Suzanne Jill Levine

Doris Meyer

Arthur Miller

Fundación Pablo Neruda

The Rockefeller Archive Center

Mario Vargas Llosa

Kurt Vonnegut

Eliot Weinberger

Herbert Weinstock

Grateful acknowledgment is also made for permission granted by the PEN American Center to quote the letters and materials from Lewis Galantière and other PEN officials concerning the 1966 PEN conference in New York. Copyright © PEN American Center, 2011. Used by permission. All rights reserved.

INTRODUCTION

Multiple Agendas

Latin American Literary Fervor

and U.S. Outreach Programs following the Cuban Revolution

In 1967, Gabriel García Márquez's *Cien años de soledad* appeared in Buenos Aires and became a runaway best seller throughout Spanish America. Printing after printing sold out, and excitement about the work coursed through the academy, the publishing world, and the general public alike. As Gerald Martin details, the novel had an unusually high first printing of eight thousand copies (almost three times the standard print run of three thousand), which was followed by three reprintings of twenty thousand each in 1967, and even larger reprintings in subsequent years (*García Márquez*, 307–8). The success of *Cien años* prompted the reissuing of García Márquez's earlier works, with larger print runs and higher sales than they had had when first released. The novel's success also stimulated interest in other contemporary Spanish American writers, and there were reprintings of the works of Julio Cortázar and others in quantities larger than their first print runs (Rama, "El 'Boom,'" 87–88). It also brought works that had been previously published—many of which had gone unnoticed—back into circulation, to a much broader reading public.

In 1970, Gregory Rabassa published his translation of the novel, *One Hundred Years of Solitude*, in the United States. It was only the second work by a Latin American writer to hit the *New York Times* best-seller list.[1] John Leonard's review in the *New York Times* declared the novel to be "marvelous . . . a recapitulation of our evolutionary and intellectual experience" ("Myth Is Alive"). For many readers, *One Hundred Years of Solitude* was their introduction to literature from Latin America, and the translation's success had a galvanizing effect on the publication, promotion, and reception of works from the region in the United States. But despite Leonard's proclamation that "with a single bound, Gabriel García Márquez leaps onto the stage with Günter Grass and Vladimir Nabokov," it would be a mistake to think that García Márquez's U.S. success had come from nowhere. By this point, Cortázar, García Márquez, José Donoso, Carlos Fuentes, and Mario Vargas Llosa were known as the members of "the Boom," the movement in which Spanish American literature had entered the international "mainstream"; throughout the 1960s, they and other Spanish American writers had carefully cultivated their reputations in Spanish America, Europe, and the United States. They had also put down strong roots in the U.S. literary and academic scenes. Rather than a beginning, then, the critical and commercial success of *One Hundred Years of Solitude* represented a turning point in the dissemination of Latin American literature in the United States.[2]

The Latin American Literary Boom and U.S. Nationalism during the Cold War situates this process—and the infrastructures that emerged to support it—within the context of the Cold War, when Spanish American writers' literary projects and political aspirations simultaneously clashed with and fed into the agendas of U.S. Cold War nationalism. During the 1960s and 1970s, fears about the Cold War in general and anxieties about revolutionary fervor in Cuba and throughout Spanish America were high in the United States. They resulted in the Alliance for Progress, the Bay of Pigs fiasco, the Cuban missile crisis, U.S. intervention in the Dominican Republic, strict enforcement of the McCarran-Walter Act's immigration blacklist, and numerous other phenomena that fostered anti-Americanism in Latin America, especially in intellectual circles. At the same time, public interest in the region translated into interest in its literature. U.S. publishers, translators, critics, and academics were excited both by the quality of the literature and, in many cases, by the politics that it represented, so they worked hand in hand with authors and one another to promote it. Their task was facilitated by the increased availability of funding and subsidies from public and private organizations seeking to cultivate positive relations with Latin American artists and intellectuals.

This book offers a multipronged examination of writers' efforts to bring their work to ever wider audiences, and of the translation subsidy programs, conferences, literary prizes, and other initiatives that assisted in this process. It examines the growing investment of U.S.-based publishers, translators, and academics in this burgeoning field, along with the Cold War dynamics that influenced the writers' efforts to establish themselves in the United States. This introduction sets the stage for my study by sketching out a general history of the publication of Latin American literature in the United States from the 1940s through the 1970s, the rise of cultural diplomacy programs and other efforts to reach out to Latin American artists and intellectuals in the years following the Cuban Revolution, and the fall of one such program that had been the beneficiary of covert CIA funding. Chapter 1 focuses on the Immigration and Nationality Act of 1952, otherwise known as the McCarran-Walter Act. The act allowed U.S. officials to base the restriction of visas on ideological grounds, and affected most of the top Latin American authors of the day, deeply marking their attitudes toward the United States. Chapter 2 presents a history of the International PEN congress that was held in New York City in 1966.[3] Conference organizers put a premium on including Latin American writers in the sessions. The participation of the writers proved to be important for establishing their reputations throughout the West, even as it revealed incipient schisms within the Latin American left. Chapter 3 explores the rising prominence of Latin American authors and Latin American literary studies at U.S. universities during the 1960s and 1970s by assessing a series of initiatives that shined spotlights on the cultural activity in the region. Finally, Chapter 4 offers a history of the Center for Inter-American Relations, an organization devoted to raising the profile of Latin America and its culture in the United States. The center's Literature program navigated the turbulent waters of supporting writers committed to the success of the Cuban Revolution while managing sponsorships by organizations and individuals opposed to Communism. The program also weathered the political rifts and polemics that fractured the community committed to Latin American literature in the 1970s and 1980s.

The approach that I take to this study is contrapuntal, moving back and forth among the perspectives of the Latin American and U.S.-based producers, publishers, and promoters of this literature. I also take into consideration hemispheric policies and political relations.[4] Consequently, the relationship between literature and the state plays a key and recurrent role in this story. My work reconfigures the way that we study Latin American literary history at the same time that it expands our understanding of the impact of Latin American authors on U.S. writers and the U.S. literary and academic scenes. I explore how the Latin Americans' aspirations of projecting their work onto a world screen benefited from the support of the top commercial and avant-garde U.S. presses of the day, which along with a number of universities developed new initiatives as means of raising both the writers' profiles and their own. U.S. authors such as William Faulkner, Arthur Miller, William Styron, and Kurt Vonnegut, among others, were also profoundly affected by their interactions with these writers and lent them their support. I further show how the state and its collaborators in the private sector participated in this process as well. While the revolutionary politics that both sparked and were sparked by the Cuban Revolution of 1959 motivated the literary production of many authors during these years, official U.S. interest in containing the spread of these politics prompted public and private organizations alike to create funding opportunities to cast the United States in a positive light for foreign intellectuals. Latin American literature's circulation in the United States thus paradoxically benefited from both hegemonic and anti-hegemonic forces—that is, from endeavors that stemmed from commitments to anti-revolutionary and revolutionary politics alike. Hence, the study of the social networks and the literary and political infrastructures through which this work circulated offers significant insights into the behind-the-scenes mechanisms and agendas that played crucial roles in the transmission and ultimate canonization of Latin American literature in the United States.

The promotion of Latin American literature in the United States had its origins in the Good Neighbor era of Franklin D. Roosevelt's administration, but it was in the years following the Cuban Revolution that the Boom reached audiences throughout the West and beyond. The rise of the Boom in the United States was both fueled and hampered by the Cuban Revolution. It was also perfectly timed to capitalize on the increasing vogue for Latin American culture in the United States. For the writers of the Boom, critical recognition of their work was indispensable to the growth of their international profile. Contemporary politics were likewise involved: the career trajectories of these writers were caught up in the dynamics of U.S.–Latin American political relations, both in terms of commercial success and the writers' ability to be physically present in the United States. The web of cultural agents, programs, and events that I study in this book thus constitutes what Gilbert Joseph characterizes as a "transnational 'contact zone'" wherein "the state's power is deployed (and contested) through a series of representations, symbolic systems, and new technologies involving agents that transcend the state," including "culture industries, educational institutions, and philanthropic foundations," among others (17).

In the end, though, it is extremely important not to lose sight of the innovativeness represented by Latin American literature at this time, or of the excitement that it generated. It is not my intention to reduce this literature to a function of contemporary institutional and political contexts. My aim, rather, is to identify the ways in which the production and distribution in the United States of this exciting new body of literature were sometimes at cross-purposes with the contemporary Cold War context, and sometimes able to take advantage of it.

The Spanish American Literary Boom and the Cold War

The Cuban Revolution sparked hopes of change and the possibility of self-determination throughout Latin America; it also ushered in a period of cultural effervescence that started in Cuba and quickly spread throughout the region.[5] Support for the revolution provided ideological coherence to the Boom through the late 1960s. The Casa de las Américas was a Cuban state-sponsored foundation committed to disseminating the new Latin American literature in tandem with its celebration of the revolution. It became a magnet for intellectuals from Latin America, Europe, and the United States who wanted to participate in this process.[6] The organization's efforts were significant beyond the revolution, affecting broader movements: as Jean Franco writes, it "celebrated the liberation struggles of the Third World, the Black Power movement in the United States, the heroic guerrilla, and the tradition of Latin American anti-imperialism epitomized by [José] Martí" (45). The Boom thus came to represent a cultural correlative of the revolution, symbolizing the region's cultural autonomy and the end of literary colonialism. Boom authors felt that their goals formed part of a larger project, and so they strove to surmount the cultural nationalism of the recent past in order to forge a pan-Spanish American cultural identity that would affirm commonalities shared by their nations rather than differences. García Márquez neatly summed this up in 1967 when he declared, "The group is writing one great novel. We're writing the first great novel of Latin American man. Fuentes is showing one side of the new Mexican bourgeoisie; Vargas Llosa, social aspects of Peru; Cortázar likewise, and so on. What's interesting to me is that we're writing several novels, but the outcome, I hope, will be a total vision of Latin America. . . . It's the first attempt to integrate this world" ("Con Gabriel García Márquez," vi). Boom authors further sought to become part of "world" literature and gain a Western audience. In Luis Harss and Barbara Dohmann's words, they made up a "cultural unit" working toward "the true birth of a Latin American novel" (32) while simultaneously considering themselves "part of the universe," with Spanish America itself representing "the center of the world, the point of fusion where all trends meet" (24).

The Boom was both a literary movement and a marketing phenomenon characterized by a dramatic increase in the publication, distribution, and translation of Spanish American works. It was also a critical construct rooted in the authors' conception of themselves as a group, their connections to the leading critics of the day, and the concomitant promotion of their work in popular and academic media. Authors and critics alike engaged in the invention of their own tradition—and the consolidation of their canonical status—by working together to promote the movement in the critical and popular spheres. Both the success of their efforts and the clear challenges they faced when trying to overturn long-standing stereotypes not just of Latin American writers but of the region itself are evident in a 1978 description in the *Chicago Tribune* of Vargas Llosa as "one of the better known of that diverse, irrepressible gang of Latin modernist writers, who are making literature a more important South American export than coffee beans and bananas" (Rexer).

The movement was at once transnational and cosmopolitan: most of the authors lived in Europe and spent time in the United States; many published their novels through the Barcelona-based publishing house Seix Barral; they participated in the juries of the Casa de las Américas; and they established close and mutually influential relationships not just among themselves but also with writers from the United States and Europe. Seix Barral gave their work unprecedented levels of publicity, its timing allowing the work to reach a new and rapidly growing middle-class readership throughout Spanish America. In the 1920s and 1930s, regionalism had dominated prose fiction, and writers such as Rómulo Gallegos, Ricardo Güiraldes, and José Eustasio Rivera had foregrounded the local. In José Donoso's words, they wrote "for [the] parish . . . cataloging the flora and fauna . . . which were unmistakably ours . . . all that which specifically makes us different [from] other countries of the continent" (11, 15). In contrast, as Lois Parkinson Zamora has observed, Boom writers participated in "an unprecedented literary conversation" in which they read and responded to one another's works, highlighting "the communal nature of their literary project . . . self-consciously engaging, and in some sense also creating, a reality shared by the many countries and cultures of their region" (20–21). Diana Sorensen adds, "At stake was a new articulation of continental identity in the production of high and low forms of cultural consumption, mediated by the emergence of critical discourses that found very strong claims for their own power and relevance in the structure of feeling energized by the Cuban Revolution and the tensions of the Cold War. Thus did Boom writers break through commercial, literary, and national boundaries that had limited the readership of their predecessors" (106–7).

Like turn-of-the-century Spanish American *modernista* authors, Boom writers and their contemporaries deliberately reached out to readers throughout the region in an effort to create and nurture a Spanish American audience and regional imaginary. They also understood their field of cultural production—the institutional framework through which their work was published, translated, marketed, and canonized—to be the West as well as Latin America. At the same time, they found themselves hindered by politics that cut across national boundaries: as Alejandro Herrero-Olaizola expertly details in *The Censorship Files*, writers who published their work in Spain in the 1960s and early 1970s were subject to significant censorship under the Franco regime; and, some writers fell victim to the infamous Cold War immigration blacklist, in spite of being courted by U.S. publishers and universities, and in spite of their works being translated thanks to subsidies from philanthropies with anti-Communist inclinations. Latin American literary production was thus closely linked to cultural sensibilities and fields of power in Latin America, Europe, and the United States, as well as to the Cold War dynamics that bound the regions to one another.

Much important work has been done on the Hispanic infrastructure supporting the Boom—e.g., the Spanish publishers, the high-visibility literary awards that brought the movement international prestige and publicity, and journals such as *Casa de las Américas* (Cuba) and *Mundo Nuevo* (Paris) that disseminated new works.[7] There has been substantial scholarship as well on the Spanish government censors who tried to rein in the writers (see Herrero-Olaizola). Much less attention has been paid to the infrastructure supporting the promotion of Latin American literature in the United States, or to the inflection of the latter by the Cold War. Jean Franco's *The Decline and Fall of the Lettered City*, Irene Rostagno's *Searching for Recognition*, and Diana Sorensen's *A Turbulent Decade Remembered* are important exceptions that do engage with a number of these issues, but as part of projects whose main emphases lie elsewhere. Claudia Gilman's *Entre la pluma y el fusil* (Between the pen and the gun) also deftly situates Latin American literature in relation to contemporary politics, although it focuses more on intra–Latin American literary and political dynamics than on the Latin American–U.S. context.

The Cold War cultural politics and diplomacy at play in U.S.–Latin American relations fundamentally shaped the promotion of the Boom in the United States, and merit more study. In recent years, scholars such as Thomas Borstelmann, David Caute, Walter Hixson, Michael Krenn, Frances Saunders, Lawrence Schwartz, Penny Von Eschen, and others have made significant contributions to documenting the Cold War background of outreach programs that supported the cultural production of foreign artists in the United States and sent U.S. intellectuals abroad. For the most part, though, their work focuses on U.S. cultural diplomacy efforts with Europe, the Middle East, and Africa, as well as within the United States, making research on Latin America, which was the subject of increasing official attention during these same years, all the more critical. Claire Fox's forthcoming study, *Creating the Hemispheric Citizen*, which examines the cultural policies of the visual arts programs of the Pan American Union from the 1940s through the 1960s, will help to fill this gap. Her work additionally shares with my own research an emphasis on the hemispheric infrastructure for the dissemination of Latin American cultural production and the political context in which it was embedded, as well as foregrounding the at times parallel, at times conflicting agendas of artists, cultural impresarios, and U.S. foreign policy.

On a broader level, my project coincides with some of the transnational tendencies of recent revisionist approaches to the Cold War. The work of Odd Arne Westad in particular has received quite a bit of attention. Westad's *The Global Cold War* studies the policies of the Cold War superpowers concerning the so-called Third World. Westad argues that the superpowers' interventions "to a very large extent shaped both the international and the domestic framework within which political, social, and cultural changes in Third World countries took place," and that "Third World elites often framed their own political agendas in conscious response to the models of development presented by the two main contenders of the Cold War [. . . and that] their choices of ideological allegiance brought them into close collaboration with one or the other of the superpowers" (3); he further studies the reverberations of events in the "Third World" back through the strategies and the trajectory of the Cold War itself. Westad's transnational, dialectical approach is useful to my own examination of the conflicting and competing agendas of cultural impresarios, opinion leaders, and political agents in the United States and Latin America. I would argue, though, that the Latin American writers whom I study here, while keenly aware of the ideological stakes and poles of the day, valued their autonomy and took care to position themselves in relation to Cuba as well as the United States, and thus their agendas did not always fit within the broader frame and goals of U.S. foreign policy during the Cold War. Also, where Westad focuses on political and economic mechanisms of intervention and response, my own research explores the cultural media through which individuals as well as public and private organizations sought to channel their aspirations for and designs on Latin America.

In *Cold War Exiles in Mexico*, Rebecca Schreiber argues that the work of the dissidents whom she studies, its "form and content . . . as well as its historical and political significance, cannot be understood in terms of any singular national context and is more than the sum of its locations of production and distribution" (xiii). My own project speaks less to the form and content of Latin American literature per se during the Cold War and more to a process of production and dissemination that, as in Schreiber's case, not only took place in multiple nations, but involved the collaboration of agents from different nations and was both enabled and hindered by the interactions of multiple fields of power in different nations. Such interactions challenge us to redefine the parameters of study of literary history during this period as fundamentally transnational.

Publishing Latin American Literature in the United States: From Bust to the Boom

Prior to World War II, Alfred A. Knopf Inc. had established itself as the premier U.S. publisher of Latin American literature. In 1942, Blanche Knopf traveled to Latin America under the aegis of the State Department. The relationships she established with writers and publishers fit nicely with the Good Neighbor agenda, as did the cultivation of the image of U.S. publishers as prestigious venues for publishing one's work. At the same time, the excursion offset her inability to travel to Europe for new prospects during the war (Balch, 50). During her travels, she contracted a number of works for the firm that, in Irene Rostagno's words, "fed the officially promoted appetite for things Latin American" (33).[8]

U.S. interest in the region waned following the war, but Alfred and Blanche Knopf's commitment to it did not, despite the fact that publishing Latin American literature was a labor-intensive and unprofitable proposition. Work from the region did not sell to a large market and was expensive to publish, for not only was greater investment in publicity needed to gain name recognition for authors who were often unknown in the United States, there was also the up-front cost of having works translated into English. However, profit was, in this case, largely beside the point for the Knopfs: over the years, and despite the losses, they remained committed to cultivating literary value and making a literary impact, all the while knowing that the works they published were more likely to become prestige items than best sellers. But if their monetary returns were disappointing, their symbolic capital was quite strong, and the couple and their firm (however unwittingly) performed an invaluable service for the United States. As public intellectuals, Latin American writers had the ability to influence public opinion in their native countries. The Knopf imprint offered them a chance to further their careers, and the publishers both fostered close relationships with them and worked with their editors to ensure that their publications were widely disseminated and positively reviewed, which helped to cultivate goodwill—and offset anti-Americanism—among the authors. Renowned Brazilian sociologist and longtime Knopf author Gilberto Freyre claimed that "the presence of Alfred A. Knopf among the Latin peoples of the continent has been that of an extra-official ambassador . . . [who brought] the United States, through the charm of his personality, closer to these same Latin peoples" (209). Translator Harriet de Onís's declaration in the 1960s that Knopf was "a one-man Alliance for Progress" was perhaps more accurate than she realized (203): the Knopfs' dedication to the promotion of Latin American literature in the United States generated a tremendous amount of positive sentiment and publicity for the nation.

The Cuban Revolution opened up an audience interested in Latin America, but the Knopfs and their fellow publishers discovered that politics and history could also be a double-edged sword. Most U.S. readers came to Latin American literature with relatively little knowledge of the region, and publishers were concerned that works with too much emphasis on the local would be too demanding and therefore less marketable. In this context, Boom novels had an advantage: although they were deeply imbued with contemporary history, their use of modern thematics and modernist techniques and their recourse to long-standing Western paradigms made them seem familiar to readers. As a result, invocations of modernism, comparisons to U.S. and European writers, and characterizations of works as "universal" in their implications—suggesting greater accessibility and, therefore, marketability—became fairly commonplace in readers' reports and published reviews, as well as in Latin American writers' assessment of their own work. Fuentes's analysis of Donoso's *Coronation* for Alfred A. Knopf Inc. offers a textbook example of this strategy:

> American readers and reviewers should be warned: José Donoso's *Coronation* is not only an analysis . . . of Chilean class structure and relations (and, as such, "interesting" to Americans who have suddenly become aware of Latin America via Fidel Castro and the Alliance for Progress). It would be meager indeed to limit Donoso's powerful literary creation to these boundaries. *Coronation*, first and foremost, is a work of universal artistic value. It meets the best work being done in the United States—Bellow, Styron, Mailer and Baldwin—in its refusal to bow down before the fragmented dead end of traditional realism as regarbed by the cold priests of the French nouveau roman and in its anguished affirmation, not of realism, but of reality.[9]

Kurt Vonnegut's blurb for *This Sunday* hit the same notes:

> I love José Donoso's new novel, *This Sunday*, with all my heart. It is a masterpiece. . . . This English version contains some of the most intricate games with language, time, and point of view that I have ever been dazzled by, *Finnegans Wake* excluded. It would be perfectly fair to present Donoso as an American writer and this book as an American book—the best American novel this year. . . . Donoso speaks English better than I do. He is an elegant product of Princeton with straw on his hair and dung on his shoes from two years of teaching at Iowa. This is a Chilean?[10]

This approach had to be taken carefully, though, for overplaying comparisons could backfire, and end up with the Latin Americans tagged as derivative or as imitators.

As Rostagno has observed, though, even Alfred Knopf and his staff expressed ambivalence toward the region and its literary production, and their concerns speak to some of the roadblocks that Latin American literature faced in the U.S. market (54). There were times when Mr. Knopf seemed to look down on literature from the region.[11] The firm declined to publish Jorge Luis Borges in the early 1950s, claiming that his work wouldn't sell in the United States, and reiterated this stance in 1963, *after* Borges had begun his rise to fame in the United States and Europe.[12] Mr. Knopf also expressed concern that the fiction of Brazilian writer Clarice Lispector (which he ultimately did publish) would be perceived by readers as too derivative of the contemporary French novel.[13] Also, as late as 1965, when translator Harriet de Onís proposed an anthology of stories to editor Herbert Weinstock, the latter's patronizing response spoke as much of his lack of enthusiasm for the volume per se as it did of the hurdles involved in publishing Latin American literature in general, despite the rising profile of the Boom at this time:

> I am not at all convinced about the desirability of an anthology of present-day Latin American short stories. I am, however, willing to be convinced. But really, Harriet, there are too many strikes against this kind of book. First of all, no one is really interested in Latin American fiction. Second, very few people are interested in reading volumes of short stories. Third, by the time we pay the various authors for rights to the stories, pay the greatest translator in the world, and carry on endless correspondence about copyrights and other details, our investment has become so huge that only a best-seller could possibly repay us. Nonetheless, as I say, if you can produce a manuscript that sets me on fire, I will burn.[14]

Even Pablo Neruda's work was met with some disdain at the firm: a 1966 reader's report on "The Heights of Macchu Picchu" felt that the poem was too political and that the poet's reputation was overstated.[15]

Correspondence from Weinstock and fellow editor Angus Cameron, as well as that of de Onís, further reveals a shared skepticism toward modernism that was particularly manifest in their assessments of Latin American writers. Weinstock at one point told Cuban writer Alejo Carpentier that Faulkner's complicated prose did not help him to be accepted by readers, and de Onís informed Donoso that while his style was similar to that of the southerner, Faulkner succeeded despite his style, not because of it (J. Donoso, 85).[16]

Cultural politics also inserted themselves into the publishing process. Weinstock in particular seemed to share with the New Critics the presumption of separate spheres for literature and politics. This could on occasion be helpful, such as when he endorsed publishing the work of Carpentier, despite the writer's high-profile support for the revolution and even after his call for a boycott of all Latin American cultural activity in the United States.[17] On the other hand, it made it difficult for Weinstock to understand the contemporary trajectory of Latin American literature, to say nothing of the activism of the writers themselves. On several occasions, he even urged writers to ignore politics and focus on the literary. In 1966, for instance, after Fuentes was publicly criticized in a letter signed by Carpentier and other Cuban intellectuals, he rescinded an agreement to write an introduction for a new edition of Carpentier's *The Lost Steps*. Weinstock unsuccessfully tried to convince Fuentes to complete the essay, arguing that literary concerns should trump political ones.[18] Likewise, when Emir Rodríguez Monegal sent Weinstock an issue of *Mundo Nuevo* that contained articles on the Vietnam War, Weinstock asked if so much political writing was necessary, as he did not want to see the journal dominated by politics.[19]

Harriet de Onís's views on literature and politics similarly affected her work. As the Knopfs were virtually the only publishers of Latin American literature in the United States through the 1950s, and de Onís was the Knopfs' primary translator—and arbiter—of literature from the region from 1950 through the late 1960s, she was in effect an extremely powerful gatekeeper: in José Donoso's words, "she controlled the sluices of the circulation of Latin American literature in the United States and, by means of the United States, throughout the whole world" (85). As a result, her preferences had an important ripple effect throughout the burgeoning field. They were not, however, always easy to pigeonhole. As Rostagno has noted, she tended to take liberties in her translations, and while her translation style was generally traditional and she harbored some skepticism toward modernism, her literary tastes were not as stodgy as critics often make them out to be (34). In fact, it was she who suggested that the firm publish Borges, as well as other experimental writers such as Carpentier, Donoso, Lispector, and João Guimarães Rosa. She also recommended several political authors, including Neruda. While strongly held, her political beliefs were not absolute, nor did they impose blinders on her literary tastes. Her correspondence with Weinstock and the Knopfs reveals that she had fairly strong anti-Communist tendencies, and that she tried to use her own work—and the Knopfs' position—to complement the government's foreign policy efforts. Soon after John F. Kennedy was elected president, for example, de Onís noted that he was cultivating relations with Brazil and suggested that the company could contribute to the process by publishing works by authors such as Guimarães Rosa and Jorge Amado.[20] She also had Weinstock send books by Amado and Freyre to Robert Kennedy prior to his 1965 trip to Brazil in order to prepare him for his visit.[21]

De Onís asked to read novels by Cuban writers Guillermo Cabrera Infante and José Lezama Lima, both of whom had distanced themselves from the revolution, but she also requested that Knopf send her works by Heberto Padilla, whose poetry in the 1960s was viewed as emblematic of the revolution's willingness to accommodate dissent from within. She had mixed feelings about Amado, though, that stemmed from his involvement until the mid-1950s with the Communist Party. When first asked by Knopf Inc. to review *Gabriela, Clove and Cinnamon* (1962), she made sure that the publisher was aware of the writer's political affiliations. She agreed to read the book despite her own reservations, and then enthusiastically recommended it.[22] Nevertheless, she never forgot Amado's background, and she often looked for clues to his shifting political inclinations as she reviewed his books for Knopf (at times, she appeared more put off by the sex in his novels than by his politics). When Knopf sought to build on the unprecedented success of *Gabriela*, de Onís waxed eloquent about the author's skill in some of his earlier novels, but expressed concern about their Communist message.[23] At the same time, she tried to conduct her own cultural diplomacy efforts in order to draw Amado toward the United States. In 1962, for example, when she asked the *Saturday Review* to review one of his novels, she stated that the work deserved good press for its quality, but she also underscored the importance of a positive reception in the United States for Amado and his fellow Latin American writers—one that could dispose them favorably toward the nation and, in turn, affect the image of it that these opinion molders conveyed to their compatriots.[24]

In the early years, despite the Knopfs' efforts, the publication of Latin American literature in the United States was largely piecemeal. Through the 1950s, there were generally four to six translations published per year; the majority of these were of works from the colonial period or the nineteenth century, but there were also a few twentieth-century novels, such as Carpentier's *The Lost Steps* (Knopf, 1956) and *The Kingdom of This World* (Knopf, 1957) and Juan Rulfo's *Pedro Páramo* (Grove, 1959), as well as the occasional collection of contemporary poetry.[25] Following the Cuban Revolution, the tide began to turn: in addition to Knopf and Grove, presses such as Dutton, Harper and Row, Pantheon, and Farrar, Straus and Giroux started to be more interested in publishing literature from Latin America, and the number of works from the region published per year began to rise steadily. The proportion of contemporary prose and poetry likewise grew.

Publishing Latin American literature remained a process of trial and error, though—of battles against the odds, and surprise successes. It required editors to be proactive and take risks. For example, Gregory Rabassa was a professor of Spanish and Portuguese at Columbia University with no formal training in literary translation when, based on some pieces he had published in *Odyssey Review* in the early 1960s (see Chapter 3), Sara Blackburn of Pantheon asked him to take on Cortázar's *Rayuela*; it was a decision that fundamentally altered the course of Latin American literature in the United States. Roger Klein at Harper and Row, in turn, was one of the few editors at the time who knew Spanish, and his interest in Latin American literature led him to reach out to Spanish publishers and agents, and to make connections that ended up bringing García Márquez and Vargas Llosa, as well as others, to the firm.[26] Editors also needed to be careful with how they did their marketing, for their job was as much about creating an audience as it was about publishing books. Some deliberately sought blurbs from well-known U.S. or British writers, as they were convinced that the public would not be impressed by endorsements written by other Latin American authors (Fuentes was an exception to this rule, but only occasionally).

Publishers additionally needed to believe enough in what they were doing to be willing to take chances and forgo their usual marketing strategies and practices. The publication history of *One Hundred Years of Solitude* offers a good example of this. Different versions of the story exist, but all agree that Harper and Row almost turned the novel down, despite the buzz associated with it even before its publication in Spanish, and despite its immediate best-seller status in Spanish America. Rostagno claims that Harper editor Cass Canfield Jr. received negative readers' reports for the novel, but that his wife, Gabriela, convinced him to publish it anyway (124). In contrast, Herminia (Pipina) Prieto maintained that the press's editorial board had previously read the Colombian's first novel, *Leaf Storm*, and not liked it, so they turned down *One Hundred Years of Solitude* without giving the matter much thought.[27] Prieto was an Argentine who had been involved with the *Sur* group in Buenos Aires and who was good friends with Gabriela Canfield; she often reviewed Spanish American works for Cass Canfield Jr., and she had pressed him to publish Cabrera Infante's *Three Trapped Tigers*.[28] According to Prieto, she urged him to take the García Márquez novel, telling the editor, "Este hombre no solamente es buen escritor, que va a ser un bestseller de la primera categoría" (This man is not just a good writer, he will be a top best seller), as he was already in Spanish.[29] Canfield did accept the novel—and Prieto's words came true, leaving Harper and Row with the highest-profile Latin American novel yet, and one that had a domino effect on the publication and sales of Latin American literature in the United States more generally, just as it had had on that of Spanish American literature published in Spanish.

Several years earlier, the awarding of the International Publishers' Prize to Jorge Luis Borges had had a similarly galvanizing effect. The prize was given to an established and influential author by an international consortium of publishers, each of which would commit to translating and publishing one work by the author.[30] Borges received the prize in 1961, the first year that it was awarded, sharing it with Samuel Beckett. Both the publicity and the publication opportunities afforded by the prize raised the Argentine's international profile significantly, opening numerous doors for him. Borges was well known in France by this time, but had published only a few short stories in the United States. Things changed quickly, though: New Directions had published two of the writer's stories in a 1949 anthology (Rostagno, 115), and in 1962 it published *Labyrinths*; Grove published *Ficciones* in 1962 and the writer's *Personal Anthology* in 1967; and in 1964, the University of Texas Press issued *Dreamtigers* and *Other Inquisitions, 1937–1952*, both subsidized with grants from the Rockefeller Foundation that were aimed at helping Latin American literature gain a foothold in the U.S. market (see Chapter 3 for a discussion of the grant program). As if to confirm that Borges had "made it," in 1967 the *Paris Review* published an interview with the writer; he also held the prestigious Charles Eliot Norton Chair of Poetry at Harvard University that year. In 1969, Alastair Reid, a translator of *Labyrinths* and a literary scout for the *New Yorker*, arranged a "first reading" contract for Borges at the magazine: it paid the author one hundred dollars for each work submitted, and it was the first contract of this type that the magazine offered to a Latin American writer.[31] The same year, Dutton issued *The Book of Imaginary*

Beings. The work did well, selling more than ten thousand copies, and Dutton was able to get Bantam, a mass-market publisher, to buy the paperback rights.[32] Suzanne Jill Levine describes Dutton's editor, John Macrae III, as the publisher who was "most interested in experimenting with unknown writers"; she also characterizes him as willing to take on books as "prestige items" that would make a "literary impact," without expecting them to be commercially successful.[33] Following the success of *The Book of Imaginary Beings*, Macrae organized a series of books by Borges that included *The Aleph and Other Stories, 1933–1969* (1970), *Doctor Brodie's Report* (1972), *A Universal History of Infamy* (1972), *In Praise of Darkness* (1974), *The Gold of the Tigers* (1976), and *Chronicles of Bustos Domecq* (with Adolfo Bioy Casares, 1976). The Argentine's fame, in turn, brought greater visibility to Latin American literature as a whole and led publishers to take more chances on works from the region. As Sorensen asserts, "Borges became a celebrity, a true cosmopolitan whose international prestige contributed to the boom's aura: here was a great precursor who was being discovered as his successors were attaining recognition. His prestige encouraged the welcome of other Latin American writers into the bookshops and colleges of the North, helping create his successors" (142).

The trajectory of Carlos Fuentes's works both reflected and furthered this movement. In 1960, Farrar, Straus and Giroux issued an English translation of his first novel, *Where the Air Is Clear*; it was followed soon thereafter by *The Good Conscience* (1961), *The Death of Artemio Cruz* (1964), and *Aura* (1965). Fuentes was a major force in bringing the Boom into the spotlight in the United States: he was a talented publicist for his own work and that of his fellow writers, and his English was nearly perfect (as was his French)—as well as much better than that of his fellow Boom writers at the time. These factors helped to make him what John King calls "an effortless communicator"—the ideal person to lead the way for his fellow writers in the United States.[34] Fuentes worked closely with his U.S. translators and with Farrar, Straus and Giroux, which took care to ensure that his novels were translated soon after they appeared in Spanish. Fuentes was contracted with Barcelona-based agent Carmen Balcells, but he was the first Latin American writer who also signed with a U.S. agent, Carl Brandt of New York, in order to increase awareness of his work in the United States as well as in Spain and in Latin America. The Mexican was, in effect, a cultural ambassador for Latin America in the West. Gerald Martin views him as "the hinge which made the entire movement swing: he would be the leading promoter and propagandist of the new wave and the one who put all the other participants in touch with one another and, in several cases, helped them with agents, translators, and even writing facilities" ("Boom of Spanish American Fiction," 480). It was Fuentes who introduced his fellow Latin American writers to authors and publishers in Latin America, Europe, and the United States, creating numerous opportunities for them; Fuentes who encouraged other writers to work with Brandt to best raise their profiles in the United States; and Fuentes who strove to create a reputation for the Boom not just through his work, but also by substantiating the movement as a literary phenomenon through critical works such as *La nueva novela hispanoamericana* (1969; The new Spanish American novel).

Emir Rodríguez Monegal, *Mundo Nuevo*, and the Congress for Cultural Freedom

Fuentes was also responsible for sending two chapters of García Márquez's *Cien años de soledad* to Emir Rodríguez Monegal to publish in the Paris-based journal *Mundo Nuevo* prior to the novel's 1967 release. Rodríguez Monegal was a prominent Uruguayan scholar and critic. He was the consummate literary insider, extremely well connected to writers, critics, and publishers in Spanish America, Europe, and the United States. He wrote prolifically on Spanish American literature of the nineteenth and twentieth centuries (with a special emphasis on Uruguayan and Argentine literature), as well as on the twentieth-century novel. He was a particularly avid scholar (and promoter) of Jorge Luis Borges, whose biography he would later write; he also wrote biographies of Andrés Bello, Pablo Neruda, and Horacio Quiroga, as well as numerous essays on French, British, and U.S. authors. Over the years, he served as an editor of journals such as *Marcha* (1943–1959), an important Uruguayan weekly, and *Mundo Nuevo* (1966–1968); his work for these journals, as well as for the Center for Inter-American Relations' *Review*, ensured the dissemination of contemporary Latin American literature throughout both North and South America.

Rodríguez Monegal was a literary ambassador who was deeply committed to promoting Latin American literature in an international arena. Throughout the 1960s and 1970s, he was frequently invited to participate on panels at international conferences showcasing writers from the region. Knopf chose him to edit the *Borzoi Anthology of Latin American Literature*, and Knopf's literary editor, Weinstock, sent him copies of all the Latin American books they published through the 1960s, knowing that the Uruguayan would have the means of generating publicity for them. Rodríguez Monegal was also seen as the "go-to" expert for the many special issues of journals and books (both Spanish-language and English-language) that featured contemporary literature from the region; a prologue or foreword from him was viewed by many as the highest imprimatur. During the 1960s and 1970s, he published articles on contemporary Latin American literature in many of the most important literary journals in Spanish America, the United States, and the United Kingdom, including *Books Abroad, Encounter, Partisan Review, Review '68, Revista Iberoamericana, TriQuarterly*, and others. A series of articles that he published in Octavio Paz's *Plural* (Mexico City) in 1972 formed the basis of his book, *El Boom de la novela latinoamericana*, which both recorded the history of "the Boom"—a term that he was among the first to publicize—and helped to establish its reputation as a movement.

The history of *Mundo Nuevo* is a microcosm of the literary dynamics of the day. It also reflects the political polemics of the era, for it reveals the tensions among Latin American intellectuals regarding support for Cuba, as well as the charged Cold War relations between Latin America and the United States. While much has been written on the journal, its history is an important part of the backdrop for my own work. It is thus worth retracing the contours of the story, though it is beyond the scope of this project to offer an exhaustive account.

As Franco has observed, *Mundo Nuevo* was founded "as a response to the Cuban Revolution's hold on the imagination of younger writers and to the influence of the Cuban journal *Casa de las Américas*" (45). In the first issue, Rodríguez Monegal described the journal's goals as "inserting Latin American culture into a context that is at once international and current, that allows voices from an entire continent that are almost always inaudible or dispersed to be heard, and that establishes a dialogue that transcends the well-known limitations of nationalisms and political parties (national or international ones)" ("Presentación," 4). Sorensen astutely describes the dialectical function of the journal's headquarters as follows: "By locating itself in Paris and interpellating the great literary capital, *Mundo Nuevo* sought consecration in the international republic of letters even as it proclaimed to its Latin American readers the universal appeal of their own culture" (117). Sorensen adds that the location similarly "attenuated the differences between center and periphery, First and Third Worlds, which had hitherto organized hierarchies of space" (119).

Mundo Nuevo served as a vehicle of both dissemination and consecration for contemporary Latin American literature: it featured new poetry and prose by established and up-and-coming authors from the region, as well as interviews, articles by renowned critics, reviews, and coverage of literary happenings in Latin America and throughout the West. The journal also engaged with contemporary Western literature and theory: it included pieces by and on such authors as Roland Barthes, Saul Bellow, Bertolt Brecht, Camilo José Cela, Eugène Ionesco, Harold Pinter, Jean-Paul Sartre, Susan Sontag, and others as a means of both laying claim to and inserting itself within the course of Western cultural heritage. Many of the articles on Western topics were reprinted from the British journal *Encounter*, as well as from other publications of the Paris-based Congress for Cultural Freedom (CCF). The connection to the CCF dogged *Mundo Nuevo* for the first two years of its existence and became a nail in the coffin of its aspirations to establish a dialogue beyond politics.

Even before the first issue was published, rumors began to circulate that the journal was subsidized by the U.S. government. Gilman situates *Mundo Nuevo*'s emergence "within the framework of a strategy aimed at seducing and financing Latin American intellectual initiatives in all contexts: plastic arts, sociology, literature" ("Las revistas," 466). Concern about efforts to co-opt their activity and compromise their autonomy led many pro-Cuban intellectuals to denounce the journal publicly, accusing it of being an arm of U.S. imperialism; several writers refused to allow their work to be published in it, including Cortázar, Mario Benedetti, and Roberto Fernández Retamar, the head of Casa de las Américas.[35] The situation was exacerbated in April 1966, when the *New York Times* published a series of articles on recipients of covert funding from the CIA, including the CCF, within which *Mundo Nuevo* had originated.

The CCF was committed to establishing an international intellectual community to promote liberal democratic values and resist the encroachment of Communism.[36] Founded in 1950, it had been planned in CIA offices by CIA officers; one of them, Michael Josselson, headed the organization's international secretariat (see P. Coleman, 40–43, in particular). The *New York Times* articles, as well as additional exposés in 1967, revealed that the CIA had not just provided leadership, it had also channeled funds to the CCF through a number of front organizations.[37] According to Frances Stonor Saunders, some funding from the agency also went to the CCF through legitimate organizations such as the Ford and Rockefeller Foundations—hence Saunders's description of the philanthropies as "integral component[s] of America's Cold War machinery" (144; see also 131–45).

The CCF had chapters around the world. It sponsored cultural events throughout Europe and the United States, and it published journals in Africa, Asia, Australia, Europe, and the Middle East. *Encounter*, edited by Stephen Spender, Irving Kristol, and later Melvin Lasky, was the organization's flagship journal. *Mundo Nuevo* was created to replace *Cuadernos*, the CCF's Latin American journal, which had been published between 1953 and 1965.[38] *Cuadernos* predated the Cuban Revolution; it was a relic that had been read more by Spanish exiles than Spanish Americans, and it had been accordingly oriented more toward fascism in Spain than toward Latin America. The CCF had tried to revitalize *Cuadernos* as part of an effort to increase its activities in the region following the revolution (P. Coleman, 194), but the journal had had little bite, and little appeal to young intellectuals committed to the Cuban cause, so it was eventually phased out. *Mundo Nuevo*, in turn, had been envisioned as bringing cutting-edge work to an international audience. In contrast to most other CCF journals, which were national in scope, *Mundo Nuevo*, like *Cuadernos*, was regional, which allowed it to capitalize on the Spanish American orientation of the Boom; at the same time, the journal's contemporary emphasis also positioned it to appeal to a broader readership.

The revelations of CIA funding for the CCF were closely followed by *Casa de las Américas* and by *Marcha*. Ángel Rama, the editor of *Marcha*, was embroiled in a long-standing, bitter feud with Rodríguez Monegal, who had been the journal's previous editor. The feud was rooted partly in politics and Rama's defense of the revolution, and partly in conflicting views of the place of politics in literature and the literary. The feud worked its way into the pages of *Marcha*, which published translations of the entire series of *Times* articles as well as additional essays by Rama and others on the topic. Both *Casa de las Américas* and *Marcha* accused *Mundo Nuevo* of being anti-Cuba and denigrated it as an instrument of U.S. imperialism whose goal was to neutralize the revolutionary impulses of Latin America's intelligentsia; both periodicals also vilified Rodríguez Monegal for his alleged complicity with U.S. policy makers and their political agendas.

Mundo Nuevo had initially been planned by the CCF and Rodríguez Monegal had been hired by the organization, so it is not surprising to find connections between the journal and the CCF in the months leading up to the former's debut. For example, before the *Mundo Nuevo* offices opened, the Uruguayan had had his mail sent to the CCF's Paris headquarters, and when the scandal erupted, he was working on a CCF-funded anthology of Latin American literature with Keith Botsford, one of the CCF's two traveling representatives in Latin America. Such connections, however, seem absent from the spring of 1966 on, as the CCF reorganized itself and, in a race to beat what seemed to be the inevitable disclosure of the organization's origins and CIA funding, Josselson urged CCF periodicals and regional centers to become independent and find private funding (P. Coleman, 221).[39]

Until his death, Rodríguez Monegal steadfastly denied that *Mundo Nuevo* had received financial support from the CCF. He claimed instead that its funding had come through the Instituto Latinoamericano de Relaciones Internacionales (ILARI), which had been founded in early 1966, and that ILARI had been fully funded by the Ford Foundation; he also seemed to believe, mistakenly, that the CCF as a whole had been fully funded by the philanthropy as of 1966. Peter Coleman's characterization of ILARI as "an independent body, which took over the work of the Congress" in Latin America points, however, to the difficulties in differentiating it from the CCF (208). ILARI continued to foster the organization's activities, including publishing some of its journals. One of these, *Aportes*, was edited by Luis Mercier Vega, the CCF's other traveling representative in Latin America, and it was he whom Rodríguez Monegal contacted immediately after the first *New York Times* story was published to find out whether there was any truth to the revelations; the Uruguayan informed Mercier Vega that if there was, he would not be able to remain affiliated with ILARI.[40] (Rodríguez Monegal wrote to Mercier Vega twice, but does not seem to have ever received a response.)

Especially given the continuity of programming, it is not certain whether ILARI actually became financially independent of the CCF. I have been unable to verify whether ILARI ever received funds directly from the Ford Foundation, for the philanthropy's annual reports for 1966 through 1969 do not list the Instituto as one of its beneficiaries; Coleman contradicts his description of ILARI as financially independent when he notes that it received almost $265,000 from the CCF in 1966—more than any other entity funded by the organization, including its own international secretariat (275).[41] Coleman does not, however, document where his information on the CCF's expenditures comes from.

In 1966, after conducting a study that concluded that the CCF was doing valuable work, and fully aware of the funding scandal in which the organization was embroiled, the Ford Foundation decided to assume the risky responsibility of funding it. In the fall of 1966, the philanthropy awarded the organization $1.5 million. At this time, in order to move out of the cloud left by the CIA funding scandal, the CCF underwent another major reorganization: several top administrators stepped down, including Josselson, as well as John Hunt of the international secretariat, whom Coleman identifies as the official responsible for managing the CCF office as well as its dealings with the CIA (173). In September 1967, the CCF changed its name to the International Association for Cultural Freedom (IACF). Soon thereafter, Ford authorized a five-year grant to the IACF that totaled more than $4.5 million; the first $1.3 million were disbursed during the 1968 fiscal year (Ford Foundation, 138).[42] While there were some differences in emphasis and priorities between the CCF and the IACF, the relationship between the two was characterized by "continuity of personnel," programming, and the "ideal of a worldwide community of intellectuals" (P. Coleman, 235). ILARI was part of this continuity: it may or may not have been independent of the CCF, but after the reorganization, the Instituto was very clearly under the umbrella of the IACF.

Mundo Nuevo was published in association with ILARI, whose imprimatur appeared in each issue. More than forty years later, the history of its funding—and its affiliations—is as difficult to pinpoint as that of the Instituto. The information available is incomplete, and the journal's records are scattered, buried in multiple archives. According to Coleman, who again does not identify the source of his information, *Mundo Nuevo* received $80,000 in funds from the CCF in 1966 (275). By late 1967, the journal was under the administrative control of the Ford Foundation-funded IACF. Funding for *Mundo Nuevo* does not seem to have been included in the philanthropy's initial grants to the IACF. According to one document, *Mundo Nuevo* "was excluded from the Foundation's general support to the Association because the journal was operated at arm's length from the Congress"; this suggests that the journal maintained some sort of connection to the CCF through 1967, although not necessarily a financial one.[43] In any case, the IACF did manage to pay the journal a $100,000 subsidy in 1967.[44] In January 1968, the organization asked several prominent Latin Americanists to "advise the Association about the future of *Mundo Nuevo*."[45] Several consultants suggested a reorganization that would change the journal's focus and move it from Paris to Buenos Aires. Rodríguez Monegal felt that the move would not be in the journal's best interests and resigned. Ford accepted the recommendations, and in the spring of 1968, it awarded *Mundo Nuevo* a three-year grant of $225,000, to be disbursed through the IACF, which had prepared the proposal (Ford Foundation, 132).

Ford funds may not have gone to the journal via ILARI, then, but they were channeled through the IACF during the second half of Rodríguez Monegal's tenure as editor. In mid-1968, the journal moved its editorial offices to Buenos Aires, where Horacio Rodríguez, the director of the Argentine affiliate of ILARI, became its editor.[46] Following the recommendations of the consultants, the journal broadened its scope to include more social sciences, but in doing so, it lost its cutting-edge focus on literature, as well as its currency, and its circulation dropped. The journal never was able to become self-sufficient, and it folded in 1971, after the last installment of funding from Ford.

When *Mundo Nuevo* arrived on the scene, anti-U.S. sentiment was running high among Spanish American intellectuals, especially those who were pro-Cuban. U.S. involvement in Vietnam—which, of course, sought to stem the spread of Communism in Asia—was escalating, and U.S. intervention in the Dominican Republic only increased tensions between Latin America and the United States. In this politically charged environment, the journal's origins in the CCF were enough to taint it in the eyes of many, as was its association with an organization that had received covert CIA funding, and the assumption that it too had benefited from the money. Thus, García Márquez, among others, broke off relations with the journal. And yet, he and Cortázar, another ardent supporter of Cuba, continued to correspond with Rodríguez Monegal, and Fuentes and Neruda also remained supportive of him.

Russell Cobb offers a nuanced view of *Mundo Nuevo* that challenges commonplace accusations of the journal as being apolitical or anti-Communist. Cobb describes the journal as championing the autonomy of the intellectual (thereby rendering it suspect to supporters of Cuba, for whom literature had an activist role) and as "freed from the doctrinaire anti-Communism typical of *Cuadernos* in particular and the early 1950s in general" (233). He also notes the journal's "political ambivalence" (235): On the one hand, it published authors whose enthusiasm for Cuba had waned, as well as political articles by CCF affiliates and liberal anti-Communists such as Theodore Draper. On the other hand, it published the work of supporters of Cuba such as García Márquez and Vargas Llosa, as well as an essay by and an interview with Juan Bosch, the deposed leader of the Dominican Republic whose hopes of regaining the presidency had been quashed by U.S. military action in 1965.[47] The journal also included other pieces critical of U.S. intervention in the Dominican Republic and the Vietnam War, as well as articles by Sartre and other critics of the CCF (P. Coleman, 194). It published both the politically revolutionary Neruda and the more conservative Borges, as well as Fuentes and Octavio Paz, both of whom, according to Peter Coleman, had quite "disliked" *Cuadernos* (207). As Cobb observes, the journal's success in attracting Fuentes and Paz is illustrative of "its significant break with the [CCF's] anti-Communist politics" (239).

Giles Scott-Smith argues that "while it is impossible to look at the formation and goals of the Congress for Cultural Freedom without addressing the impetus for its existence from American overt and covert interests, neither is it sufficient to reduce the Congress to being simply another CIA front" (*Politics*, 84). A similar case can be made for *Mundo Nuevo*. In 1965, during the journal's planning stages, Rodríguez Monegal told Fernández Retamar that he had been assured that he would have complete control of it in his capacity as editor.[48] Even if some of the journal's funding could be shown to have come from the CCF, there is no evidence in the archival materials I have seen that suggest that any pressures or constraints were placed on Rodríguez Monegal, that the CCF interfered with the journal's intellectual independence, or that it had any say in the journal's orientation or contents. This would seem to correspond with Rodríguez Monegal's editorial "La CIA y los intelectuales," in which he condemned the covert funding scheme and asserted that "if slander or deception may change the esteem in which a work or behavior is held, it cannot change its quality or independence. The CIA, or other corrupters at other banks, can pay intellectuals without their knowing it. What they cannot do is buy them."

In *The Boom: A Personal History*, Donoso writes:

> I am convinced that the history of the Boom, at the moment in which it was most united, is written in the pages of *Mundo Nuevo* up to the moment when Emir Rodríguez Monegal abandoned its directorship. Of all the literary magazines of my time, from *SUR* to *La Revista de la Casa de las Américas* . . . none has succeeded in transmitting the enthusiasm for the existence of something alive in the literature of our period and of our world with the precision and amplitude of *Mundo Nuevo* at the end of the '60s. (104)

That Rodríguez Monegal spent his two-year tenure as editor of *Mundo Nuevo* walking a political tightrope attests to the fact that it was not just the literary history of the Boom that was inscribed in the journal's pages, but the political and social fissures, too.

Latin American Literature as a Weapon in the Cold War

Gerald Martin has written, "It is no exaggeration to state that if the Southern continent was known for two things above all others in the 1960s, these were, first and foremost, the Cuban Revolution and its impact both on Latin America and the Third World generally, and secondly, the boom in Latin American fiction, whose rise and fall coincided with the rise and fall of liberal perceptions of Cuba between 1959 and 1971" ("Boom, Yes," 53).

These two phenomena were, as we have seen, linked at their very cores. Certainly, the movement was at first given ideological cohesion by the authors' support for the revolution—support that was evident in their literary work as well as in their involvement with Casa de las Américas. Like its journal, the organization responded "to the long-standing dream of the avant-garde to close the gap between life and art and to foster intellectual commitment to the cause of emancipation" (Franco, 45). Within the revolution, political commitment was at first rejected as a primary component of the literary, but nevertheless, to borrow from Vargas Llosa's famous 1967 formulation, literature was fire, and the writer's task was that of criticizing reality. Indeed, the writer was viewed as having a key role in ushering in change and, in particular, in bringing to all of Spanish America the social justice that was being implemented in Cuba.

In many ways, the Cuban Revolution caught the United States off guard. In the post-World War II years, the U.S. government had kept a close watch on the Soviet Union and Asia, which seemed to represent the primary threats to Western democracy; Latin America, in contrast, had ceased to be a strategic site for U.S. policy interests, and the aid given under the Good Neighbor policy had dwindled. In the late 1950s, official interest waxed somewhat as leftist activism and regimes in the region picked up, but the hostility with which Vice President Richard Nixon was met during his 1958 trip to Venezuela—just months before the revolution—took officials by surprise. The revolution itself was another eye-opener that brought public and official attention not just to the island, but to the region as a whole: all of a sudden, it seemed, the Cold War threat was sitting on the United States' doorstep. National security, in the government's eyes, depended on the security of the hemisphere, and so, after 1959, Cuba and Latin America as a whole became top priorities. Presidents Kennedy and Johnson fostered the image of the United States as an ally to the Latin American nations and a political model for them, and the men worked to bring the region under U.S. sway through programs such as the Alliance for Progress, which supported development and modernization projects as means of building democracy and political stability—and thereby, it was hoped, containing the spread of Communism—as well as gaining goodwill in the public sphere. But Fidel Castro's rapprochement with the Soviet Union stoked Cold War tensions, ultimately prompting the United States to use its political muscle to suspend Cuba's membership in the Organization of American States (OAS).

The Cold War was hardly a monolith, though, either in the United States or in Latin America. While the U.S. government sought to centralize its campaign against Communism throughout the 1960s and 1970s, political unrest within the nation and increasing opposition—both domestic and international—to the Vietnam War provoked growing resistance to domestic and foreign policy; the contradictions between the United States' promotion of democratic ideology abroad and its enforcement of Jim Crow policies at home played a key role in the civil rights struggles as well.[49] In Latin America, the transnational dynamics of the Cold War both complemented and exacerbated intranational political conflicts. As Gilbert Joseph writes, "The dynamics of the Latin American Cold War are embedded in a particularly ferocious dialectic linking reformist and revolutionary projects for social change and national development and the excessive counterrevolutionary responses they triggered in the years following World War II. This dialectic . . . played out in overlapping and interdependent domestic and international fields of political and social power," as, for example, when "Latin American states used a Cold War rationale, generated outside the region, to wage war against their citizens, to gain or perpetuate power, and to create or justify authoritarian military regimes" (4, 5). The revolutionary projects were themselves soon splintered: from the mid-1960s on, a number of writers and intellectuals—including Cabrera Infante, Fuentes, Paz, and others—began to express concern about the direction of the revolution, with some distancing themselves from the island. Fuentes and Neruda were publicly criticized by supporters of Cuba following the PEN congress of 1966 (see Chapter 2), and *el caso Padilla* (the Padilla affair) of 1971 revealed the revolution's refusal to tolerate internal dissent.

Starting with his publications in the early 1960s in the important literary supplement *Lunes de Revolución*, Cuban poet Heberto Padilla had written work in which dissent from the official line was evident. His 1968 collection, *Fuera del juego* (Out of the game), was published with what Gerald Martin describes as "a kind of political health warning attached" ("Boom of Spanish American Fiction," 488) after Castro tried to prevent the UNEAC (Unión de escritores y artistas cubanos) from awarding him its annual prize for poetry, but Padilla was nevertheless held up as an example of the revolution's ability to tolerate criticism from within. In 1971, however, Padilla was arrested as a "counterrevolutionary"; he was not released for more than a month, and only after he issued a public "confession" in which he recanted his dissident views and said that he had slandered the revolution to foreign intellectuals and CIA agents. Writers such as Fuentes, Vargas Llosa, Simone de Beauvoir, Juan Goytisolo, Jean-Paul Sartre, and Susan Sontag, among others, signed a public letter of protest to Fidel Castro, and many formally broke with the revolution at this time.[50]

The fallout from the PEN congress and the aftermath of the Padilla affair were just two instances of schisms that fractured the unity of the Latin American left, making enemies for Cuba and even troubling some who continued to support the revolution but were wary of what they viewed as a growing tendency toward authoritarianism. And yet, during this period, official and private U.S. agencies alike overlooked such rifts. Instead, they took a much more black and white view of Latin American politics, focusing on containing or eradicating the Communist threat they found in Cuba and other leftist activism in the region. That Cuba, in large measure because of the activities of Casa de las Américas, became a cultural center within Latin America only heightened the concern of public officials and private cold warriors alike. Thus, the State Department and the U.S. Information Agency (USIA) established a number of subsidies and centers to support both the study of the region and Latin American artistic endeavors, as did private organizations such as the Rockefeller, Ford, and Carnegie family philanthropies. Several of these programs brought intellectuals from the region to the United States, seeking in part to offset Cuba's influence by making U.S. culture attractive to them. These programs were in keeping with other contemporary initiatives that treated artists as targets for cultural diplomacy, and as vehicles through which it was to be conducted. In *Strategic Public Diplomacy and American Foreign Policy*, Jarol Manheim identifies two types of public diplomacy programs: "people-to-people" contacts that are "characterized by cultural exchanges such as the Fulbright Program" and that are "designed to explain and defend government policies and portray a nation to foreign audiences," and "government-to-people" contacts, which include "efforts by the government of one nation to influence public or elite opinion in a second nation for the purpose of turning the foreign policy of the target nation to advantage" (4). Both types of programs were deployed in the outreach to Latin American authors during this period and, in practice, their goals often blended into one another.

Cultural diplomacy programs operated on two important principles: (1) that the promotion of U.S. art abroad was a testament to U.S. cultural achievements and artistic freedom and would bring prestige to the nation, and (2) that reaching out to foreign artists and intellectuals offered a means of (to repeat Manheim's words) "influenc[ing] public or elite opinion . . . for the purpose of turning the foreign policy of the target nation to advantage," whether the outreach took place through exchange programs that brought them to the United States or in their home nations. Postwar mass communications research indicated that the diffusion of political ideas was particularly effective through so-called opinion leaders or molders—respected community members who would "exert significant influence on their peers' opinion formation" (Robin, 83), cultivating goodwill, and, it was hoped, swaying public opinion abroad toward the United States. As Robert Arnove explains, intellectuals were a key group to court not just because of their access to the means of disseminating their ideas widely, but also because they "represent an important instrumentality of cultural domination as well as potential agents of revolutionary change. They may place their expertise at the service of dominant groups, working to legitimate the social order; or they can work with underclasses to . . . assist them with different ways of viewing given social structures; and they can participate in collective struggles to transform an unjust society" (18). Strategists were also operating on the related principle that outreach could provide images of the United States that refuted "communist propaganda about the American way of life," fostering the spread of Western values and promoting alternatives to Marxism (Scott-Smith, "Building," 91).

The cultural and political leaders who lobbied for cultural diplomacy programs believed that they were a Cold War necessity that could help foster greater understanding of the nation and its cultural production as well as offsetting revolutionary fervor in developing countries. That is, the programs would contribute to the formation of what Manheim calls a "supportive symbolic environment" within which the United States would pursue its foreign policy objectives (101), and which in turn would benefit national security. Lloyd Goodrich, director of the Whitney Museum and chairman of the National Committee on Government and Art, thus urged Congress in 1962 to "consider government aid to the arts in an entirely new light, as an integral part of the defense of our civilization" (qtd. in Krenn, 1). Philip Coombs, the first assistant secretary of state for educational and cultural affairs, likewise considered cultural diplomacy to be the "fourth dimension" of foreign policy.

Foreigners were brought to the United States for varying lengths of time through official exchange programs such as the Fulbright (itself a postwar initiative), the State Department's Foreign Leaders program, and those run by the State Department's Bureau of Educational and Cultural Affairs, which had been formed as part of the Mutual Educational and Cultural Exchanges Act of 1961. There were other government-funded cultural diplomacy initiatives as well, including international tours of art exhibitions, modern dancers, jazz legends such as Louis Armstrong and Duke Ellington, and a production of *Porgy and Bess*.[51] In Michael Bérubé's words:

> In a perverse yet entirely unremarkable sense, the years of the Cold War
> were the good old days for American artists and intellectuals—the days

when . . . "the CIA was the NEA." Imagine . . . a time when the work of abstract expressionists and twelve-tone composers was considered vital to national security, a time when the establishment of the pax Americana required the funding and nourishment of a noncommunist left with high-modernist tastes in arts and letters. It is hard to tamp down a sense of nostalgia. (107)

It was, of course, not just U.S. artists and intellectuals who benefited from such programs, but those from abroad to whom the U.S. government wanted to offer a positive impression of the nation.

The government was hardly alone in its efforts. Following the Cuban Revolution, private organizations such as philanthropies also directed their resources toward Latin America. In effect, the latter worked alongside and sometimes in collaboration with government agencies, quietly carrying out the agendas of the public sphere within the private sphere. Edward Berman has argued that the Cold War "gave the foundations' overseas programs their coherence, direction, and strategic importance in the furtherance of United States foreign policy" (6). In fact, the foundations "hardly ever ventured into an area of foreign activity without prior governmental consultation and approval" (Parmar, "American Foundations"). The ties between the philanthropies and government were facilitated by the open (and sometimes revolving) door between Washington's foreign policy establishment and the philanthropic agencies: John Foster Dulles went from being chairman of the Rockefeller Foundation's board of trustees and the Carnegie Endowment for International Peace to secretary of state in 1953; McGeorge Bundy served as the White House special assistant for national security affairs from 1961 until 1966, when he became president of the Ford Foundation; and former secretary of defense Robert McNamara was a Ford trustee (see Berman, 62–63, for additional examples). Dean Rusk offers an even more extreme case: he worked at the Department of State from 1947 until 1952, when he became president of the Rockefeller Foundation, a position that he left in 1961 to return to Washington as secretary of state.

It was, additionally, standard practice for foundations to check indices of known or suspected Communists for the names of grant applicants during the 1950s and 1960s. As Inderjeet Parmar writes, when the foundations were called to appear before congressional committees, "their self-defense arguments are instructive: they denied being anti-American, un-American or pro-Marxist, stating categorically that they never awarded grants to known communists" ("Selling," 17). Parmar further notes that when Rusk was president of the Rockefeller Foundation, he similarly declared to an Un-American Activities committee that "our foundations re-frain as a matter of policy from making grants to known Communists" because that would contravene "the clearly expressed public policies of the United States" (qtd. in Parmar, "Selling," 17–18), a statement that further attests to the permeable boundary between the public and private spheres. Furthermore, whether oriented toward development or cultural exchange, the international programs supported by the philanthropies tended to pro-ject positive images of the United States while promoting liberal values such as capitalism and favoring Western—as opposed to Marxist—models of change and development (see Parmar, "Selling").

Linkages such as these form the basis of what scholars have designated the "state-private network," in which the programs and priorities of private sector organizations essentially operate in tandem with U.S. foreign policy. Liam Kennedy and Scott Lucas characterize this network as "the extensive, unprecedented collaboration between 'official' U.S. agencies and 'private' groups and individuals in the development and implementation of political, economic, and cultural programs in support of U.S. foreign policy from the early cold war period to today" (312).[52] Philanthropic agencies were particu-larly well positioned to carry out or subsidize such "stealth diplomacy": they enjoyed tremendous prestige in Latin America, as well as a reputation of po-litical independence during a period when anti-Americanism was running high, so their programs were less likely to be seen as ideologically suspect by intellectuals wary of activities sponsored by the U.S. government. In addi-tion to the philanthropies, other private entities shared the goals of the state and developed parallel programs to help realize them; these entities included (in a number of instances) the supposedly apolitical PEN, some university administrators, faculty members, and other individuals.

The promotion of Latin American literature by U.S. philanthropies emerged out of a complicated web of North American politics. The phi-lanthropies had long funded projects in Latin America, but for the most part these had been centered on public health or infrastructure. Their in-volvement with cultural projects has its roots in the 1930s, and can also be traced back to Nelson Rockefeller's official work with the region. Under the Good Neighbor policy, which viewed cultural relations as an integral part of a cooperative international order and the protection of national se-curity, the Division of Cultural Relations of the State Department had been created in 1938. The Office for the Coordination of Commercial and Cul-tural Relations between the American Republics (later, the Office of the Coordinator of Inter-American Affairs [OCIAA]), headed by Nelson Rocke-feller, followed in 1940. Both offices sponsored art exhibits, cultural conferences, educational exchanges, and speakers from Latin America, as well as subsidizing the translation of Latin American works into English. The OCIAA additionally sponsored cultural exchange programs and disseminated knowledge of U.S. culture in Latin America in an effort to cultivate cultural goodwill (see Rivas, 45–48, and Miller and Yúdice, 38–44).

The Rockefeller family had long-standing personal and business interests in Venezuela that had led to their interest in the culture of Latin America, as well as sensitizing them to its strategic importance to foreign relations and national security. Nelson Rockefeller, in fact, became a pioneer in lobbying Congress to support cultural relations as "a legitimate activity of diplomacy, particularly as an emergency program for promoting hemispheric security" (Rivas, 45). As Toby Miller and George Yúdice have observed, "Rockefeller's labors established a pattern of overseas cultural policy that dominated for fifty years and set the organizational tenor for domestic activities from the 1960s" (38). His interest in cultural diplomacy—especially his commitment to pursuing cultural exchanges as a means of improving understanding among the Americas in the service of democracy—was shared by other members of his family, most notably his oldest son, Rodman, and his brother David. Both Rodman and David were involved in inter-American affairs, as well as with organizations devoted to fostering literary and cultural relations throughout the Americas, for which they were able to secure funding commitments from the Rockefeller Foundation and the Rockefeller Brothers Fund (see Chapter 4).

In addition to the Rockefellers, there were organizations both within and outside of the state-private network that developed programs to assist in the promotion of Latin American literature in the United States. A Cold War agenda, which emanated not just from funding agencies but also at times from program administrators, played a role in implementing these initiatives as well. Time and again, the funding proposals submitted to philanthropic organizations cast programs oriented around Latin American literature as worthy of support precisely because their goals were "in the national interest": whether they were to fund visits to the United States, translation subsidies, or cultural organizations devoted to promoting this literature, such programs were seen as "portray[ing] a nation" (Manheim, 4) that was supportive of culture and the arts, and that was vastly different from the aggressive and interventionist nation that had generated such hostility in Latin America and throughout the world. The case was also frequently made that writers supported by such programs would take positive images of the United States back to their homelands, thereby becoming unofficial, native agents who extended the reach of official U.S. policy and diplomacy. It is, of course, difficult to assess the full extent to which program administrators actually believed the Cold War rhetoric that they deployed, or whether they were just making a pitch that they knew would sell. Even so, such connections reveal the Cold War subtext that underlay many programs supporting Latin American literature.

But if backing by philanthropies obscured the political agenda behind some of these programs, allowing them to remain seemingly free of (and therefore untainted by) governmental support, it offered no guarantee that the hidden agenda would be carried out. In *The Mighty Wurlitzer*, Hugh Wilford asserts that "the CIA could not always predict or control the actions of the musicians, writers, and artists it secretly patronized" (113). In other words, "the CIA might have tried to call the tune . . . but the piper did not always play it, nor the audience dance to it" (10). I too study collusions and collaborations, but as with Wilford, my intention is not to advance a conspiracy theory, in this case one that would explain the rising prominence of Latin American literature in the United States. Nor is the revelation of funding and connections from the CIA, State Department, or other governmental agencies the driving impetus behind the case studies I present here. Exposure clearly played a role in the histories of *Mundo Nuevo* and the Congress for Cultural Freedom, but one that was dynamic, with ripple effects for people, journals, and institutions that had to be dealt with over time, rather than the climactic and final moment in these histories. At the same time, the entrenched Cold War interests motivating many other programs never even came to light, for they were often sheltered deep within the correspondence between the upper management of these programs and the leaders of private organizations with their own political agendas.

I assume from the very beginning that there were Cold War figures and motives operating in the background (and foreground) of a number of the stories that I tell here. What I am most interested in, though, are the skewed lines of cause and effect that allowed Cold War operations to be turned to other uses by those who organized and participated in them, most importantly by the writers at whom they were aimed—writers who had their own literary and political agendas, and who rightly viewed themselves as agents of their own cause, rather than vehicles for transmitting official U.S. policy.[53] Penny Von Eschen demonstrates how State Department–sponsored tours of jazz artists in the 1950s and 1960s

> suggest the open-ended and unpredictable nature of cultural exchange. If policymakers grasped the possibility of appealing to emerging nations and the Eastern bloc through jazz, they never dreamed that the

musicians would bring their own agendas. Nor did they anticipate that artists and audiences would interact, generating multiple meanings and effects unanticipated by the State Department. . . . Jazz musicians didn't simply accept the way they were deployed by the State Department . . . [they] slipped into the breaks and looked around, intervening in official narratives and playing their own changes on Cold War perspectives. (24, 25)

Latin American writers similarly generated "meanings and effects unanticipated by the State Department" and "interven[ed] in official narratives" in their efforts to inscribe their shared literary and political project on a world-wide stage.

These writers were, in turn, supported in the United States by cultural agents who were not only genuinely enthusiastic about their work, but with whom Latin American politics resonated deeply. As the following chapters demonstrate, these politics were appealing to quite a few U.S.-based writers, scholars, and publishers—groups that Richard Welch Jr. counts among those that were "more attracted to Fidel and his revolution than were other subsections of the American public" in the early 1960s (138). As the 1960s and 1970s wore on, bearing witness to multiple instances of U.S. intervention in Latin America (to say nothing of the Vietnam War), the opposition of the U.S. left to domestic politics and foreign policy mounted. Involvement with Latin American writers offered cultural agents in the United States the opportunity not just to support Cuba, but to communicate their own growing disaffection with U.S. Cold War nationalism, and to forge alliances with others who shared their politics. By including writers from the region in their programs and lists, U.S.-based cultural agents promoted literature that they found exciting and challenging even as they furthered their own efforts at circumventing Cold War policies.

Other agendas played into the promotion of Latin American literature in the United States as well. There was no single piper calling the shots in this process, which involved hundreds of people and organizations, some collaborating while others worked independently. But if the agendas of Cold War nationalism in the United States and of Latin America's cultural avant-garde agreed on the importance of promoting literature from the region, the political firestorm in which *Mundo Nuevo* was embroiled attested to the fact that many writers would not have viewed themselves as collaborators in a shared endeavor. Thus, the case studies I discuss in this book reveal both the common means and the divergent causes and ends underlying the dissemination of Latin American literature in the United States.

But even as high levels of interest in Latin America led public and private entities to create programs that would engage with intellectuals from the region, the official impulse toward containment, which sought to eliminate the Communist threat in its site of origin and prevent it from spreading to and within the United States' own borders, often worked at cross-purposes with such initiatives. Most notably, Section 212(a)(28) of the McCarran-Walter Act authorized the denial of visas to enter the United States to individuals with Communist affiliations, whether documented or simply alleged. Over the years, as I discuss in Chapter 1, numerous writers, scholars, artists, and politicians from Latin America and around the world were prohibited from traveling to the United States on ideological grounds, stirring up hostility rather than tempering anti-Americanism. Here, then, is one of the great paradoxes of the period: containment policies prevented many writers who supported the revolution from entering the United States at the same time that the increase in financial support for the study of Latin America and its literature helped to disseminate their work within the United States and to underwrite their visits to the nation—that is, when visas could be had.

It was not just writers' extraliterary political pronouncements, their involvement with Cuba, or the political content of their work that made them appear politically threatening: even their use of literary modernism was potentially subversive. As Lawrence Schwartz has detailed, the late 1940s and 1950s bore witness to a depoliticization of modernism that was, in effect, part of a broader Cold War movement. During these years, formalist aesthetics and the avant-garde displaced the realism of the prewar years, and critics condemned the representation of politics in literature (201–2), focusing instead on explorations of universal themes and concerns; this approach was bolstered by structuralist literary criticism and the New Criticism, which dominated the academy during this period. Modernism was considered to be

an instrument of anti-Communism and an ideological weapon with which to battle the "totalitarianism" of the Soviet Union. In the arts, so the argument went, the United States encouraged individual expression and experimentation, while the Soviet Union accepted only the monolithic, the banal, and the propagandistic. The United States represented freedom, democratic institutions, and an open society promoting diversity and tolerating dissent; but the Soviet Union stood for fanatical authoritarianism, unquestioning obedience, and stupefying bureaucratic control. . . . In the morality play of the Cold War, American "liberalism" represented democracy; and its literature and art, cultural freedom. (201)

This dynamic was itself part of what Volker Berghahn calls the "emergent totalitarianism paradigm" (115), a struggle to defend artistic freedom—conceived of as both synecdoche and symbol of democracy—from the totalitarianism associated with Communist countries. As scholars such as Von Eschen and others have described, during the postwar years, abstract expressionism, jazz, and modern dance were celebrated—and subsidized—by government agencies and philanthropies alike because their refutation of realism and representation was seen as emblematic of the freedom of expression—and, by extension, freedom in general—enjoyed by artists in the United States.

However, in the same way that the politics of many Boom writers and their contemporaries contravened official U.S. Cold War policy, so too did their literary style. Franco writes that Spanish Americans (as well as North Americans and Europeans) "at first found in Cuba the freedom to innovate and experiment that was missing in other socialist states" (89). Their experimentation was literary as well as political. I have discussed the Boom authors' relationship with modernist authors such as William Faulkner, Virginia Woolf, and others elsewhere, so I won't belabor the point here.[54] It is important to note, however, that in the Latin American literature of the Boom years, modernism was by no means antithetical to Marxism; rather, the writers' style and content alike were imbued with the revolutionary politics and projects that were sweeping across the region. As Franco further notes:

> In the United States, modernism became institutionalized in the Cold
> War years, when the focus was on the "spiritual critique" of literature.
> In Latin America it was a time of acerbic polemics and debate as writers'
> hitherto untested claims of commitment were challenged by publics
> whose imaginations were fired by armed struggle and revolution. All
> kinds of aesthetic and political projects now appeared possible—the
> aesthetic utopias of modernism and the historical avant-garde, the
> notion of pure art and pure literature, participatory theater, liberation
> from capitalism. (2)

This had a direct and somewhat contrary effect on the experience of authors in the United States: public interest in Latin America and its writers opened up new audiences and made Latin American work increasingly marketable, but some gatekeepers were hesitant to publish these writers out of concern that they leaned too far to the left or that the political content of their work might have a negative impact on sales. For the most part, though, publishers were encouraged to sign these authors, and worked with organizations such as the Rockefeller Foundation, the Ford Foundation, and the Center for Inter-American Relations (see Chapter 4) to establish subsidies and grants that would facilitate the translation and promotion of their publications in the United States. The following chapters examine this dynamic, as well as other aspects of the paradox of containment and dissemination of Latin American literature as it played itself out in the 1960s and 1970s.

1

"Catch 28"

The McCarran-Walter Immigration Blacklist
and Spanish American Writers

In 1952, the immigration and naturalization law known as the McCarran-Walter Act was passed by Congress. President Truman vetoed the act, declaring that "seldom has a bill exhibited the distrust evidenced here for citizens and aliens alike—at a time when we need unity at home and the confidence of our friends abroad," but Congress voted overwhelmingly to override his veto (Cong. Rec. 1952, 8084). The act was a product of the McCarthy era and the Cold War, and for almost forty years, it had a major and negative impact on the attitudes of Latin American authors—as well as many others—toward the United States. One of the principal changes that it introduced to existing immigration law was the addition, in Section 212(a)(28), of provisions for denying visas to foreigners who believed in, wrote about, or were affiliated with organizations or individuals that promoted Communism; who advocated or were in any way affiliated with organizations that advocated "the economic, international, and governmental doctrines of world communism or the establishment in the United States of a totalitarian dictatorship"; and so on.[1] Section 212(a)(28) did allow an individual's ineligibility to be waived: a visa could be granted following an interview with a U.S. consular officer, who had to approve the application, after which both the State Department and the attorney general had to agree that "the admission of such alien into the United States would be in the public interest" (Immigration and Nationality Act). Securing a waiver was, however, a complex, time-consuming, and often Kafkaesque process. Many visa applications were turned down by local embassies, the Immigration and Naturalization Service (INS), the State Department, and even the attorney general's office. This generated great hostility toward the United States, as did the waiver application process: many foreigners refused to apply for visa waivers because they resented being asked whether they were members of the Communist Party, convicted felons, drug addicts, or prostitutes (among other classes of aliens ineligible under Section 212); because visas were frequently denied at the last minute; and because when visas were approved, they only allowed an individual into the country for as long as his or her commitments lasted. Moreover, the smoothest implementation of the McCarran-Walter Act depended on the collaboration of two separate government bureaucracies with different databases and different chains of command—the Department of Justice, headed by the U.S. attorney general, and the State Department, to which U.S. consular offices report—a collaboration that was often far from seamless.

The ideological exclusion clause was applied broadly. Time and again, it was used to justify denying visas to individuals who had expressed leftist or anti-American views or were simply suspected of holding them. Over the years, political figures, intellectuals, and writers were placed on a secret government list of "undesirable" aliens whose presence in the United States was deemed "contrary" or "prejudicial to the public interest." These individuals included Hortensia Allende (Salvador Allende's widow), Michel Foucault, Graham Greene, Farley Mowat, Jan Myrdal, Daniel Ortega (a former president of Nicaragua), Pierre Trudeau, and Nino Pasti (an anti-nuclear activist who had formerly served as a deputy supreme commander of NATO for nuclear affairs). The list also included several winners of the Nobel Prize in Literature: Dario Fo (as well as his wife, Franca Rame), Doris Lessing, Czeslaw Milosz, and, from Spanish America, Miguel Ángel Asturias, Gabriel García Márquez, Pablo Neruda, and Mario Vargas Llosa. Even U.S.-born writer Margaret Randall fell afoul of the act.[2] The reach of the act extended well beyond public figures: in 1964, hundreds of Eastern European athletes had to petition the State Department for visas so that they could change planes in Alaska while en route to the Tokyo Olympics ("U.S. Eases Visas"), and in 1982, three hundred antinuclear activists from Japan who wanted to attend the U.N. Disarmament Conference were denied visas ("McCarran Redux").

There was public outrage at such incidents, and concern that they violated the guarantee of freedom of expression and the free circulation of ideas in the First Amendment—and, later, concern about whether such exclusions contravened the Helsinki Accords of 1975. These issues prompted numerous efforts to modify and repeal the clause in Section 212. The McGovern Amendment of 1977 weakened it, requiring the secretary of state to recommend visa waivers for ineligible individuals unless she or he explicitly stated that an individual's activities—not just his or her presence in the United States—represented a threat to national security.

The amendment, however, was frequently circumvented. McCarran-Walter was initially, as Cheryl Shanks writes, "the first line of defense against communism," and it was viewed by supporters as an important weapon for "prevent[ing] threats by foreign ideologies" (128)—rationales that helped to keep the act in effect. As Steven Shapiro discusses, resistance to the act grew in the early 1980s (937), but the government upheld the need for the restrictions that McCarran-Walter imposed, arguing in part that (in Shapiro's words) "ideological exclusions are an indispensable tool of foreign policy in the world of realpolitik" (944); the failure of efforts to repeal or modify the act was similarly due, in large measure, to the fact that "few members of Congress [were] anxious to cast a vote that might be portrayed as soft on communism by political opponents" (939). Thus it was not until 1990, in the wake of the fall of the Berlin Wall, that adherence to Communism and the expression of so-called subversive ideologies were removed from the law as grounds for excluding foreigners from the country.

The close encounters of Spanish American writers of notably different political stances with the ideological exclusion clause began in the early 1950s, but became much more frequent—not surprisingly—in the years following the Cuban Revolution, to which, as we have seen, many of these writers were politically linked. This chapter studies these run-ins, focusing in particular on Carlos Fuentes's long-standing saga of difficulties with the act, which ultimately charted a path between a dock in Puerto Rico, the U.S. embassy in Mexico City, the State Department, the Department of Justice, and the floor of the U.S. Senate. The experiences of Fuentes and his fellow Spanish American writers were emblematic of the paradoxical nature of U.S. anti-Communist tactics that simultaneously courted and excluded Spanish American intellectuals, pitting the nation's cultural diplomacy efforts against its own immigration policy and containment efforts. Additionally, the response of writers, publishers, and politicians to these incidents offers insight into the rising prominence of Spanish American literature within U.S. literary and academic circles, and of the writers themselves within the U.S. public and political sphere.

"Catch 28": Spanish American Writers and McCarran-Walter

In the years following the Cuban Revolution, USIA, Department of State, and covert CIA programs promoting U.S. accomplishments abroad were stepped up, and the State Department also brought writers, artists, and political figures from Spanish America to the United States under the aegis of its various exchange programs in an effort to portray the United States in a positive light to them. But even as the U.S. government reached out to foreign intellectuals, the support of many Spanish American writers for the revolution and their high-profile activism on behalf of Cuba combined with generally high levels of paranoia in official circles regarding the spread of Socialism in Latin America to bring about numerous run-ins with the McCarran-Walter Act. Time after time, intellectuals and cultural leaders from the region and around the world were denied visas to enter the United States by the State Department's passport and visa offices, which one critic described as "contain[ing] the hard-core remnants of the McCarthy era" (A. Schwartz, 4). Such difficulties led many critics to comment on the hypocrisy of exchange agreements authorized by the act that automatically granted waivers to Communist Party members from Eastern Europe.

Few waivers of ineligibility were issued prior to the Kennedy administration, which took an early stance against the act. President John F. Kennedy and Attorney General Robert Kennedy believed that admitting foreigners with oppositional political views did not pose a threat to national security. On the contrary, they carefully cultivated the image of the United States as an "open society" that, in the words of one official, welcomed "visitors of every political persuasion in the conviction that we are strong enough as a democracy to sustain the expression of every belief, no matter how unpopular. . . . [The Kennedys also embraced] the principle that the more people who are exposed to democracy as we know it in the United States— and to the achievements and aspirations of this system as a free society—the more people we can hope to impress favorably" (A. Schwartz, 35). Despite the Kennedys' efforts, though, many visas were still turned down at other levels.

The language of Section 212(a)(28) was vague enough to be used to justify the exclusion from the United States of individuals who were not Communist Party members, advocates, or even sympathizers. The troubles did not start with the Cuban Revolution. At times, the results were paradoxical. Few would consider Jorge Luis Borges to be a leftist, let alone a Communist, and yet he still had difficulties getting a visa in the 1950s. Also, in 1953, within a year of the act's implementation, Colombian writer Germán Arciniegas had his first of three run-ins with McCarran-Walter, episodes that brought notoriety to the act at an early date and offered insights into the complexities and contingencies of its machinations. Arciniegas was a distinguished writer, historian, educator, and diplomat who had lived in the United States since the early 1940s. He had been a leader of his country's Liberal Party and an outspoken advocate of democracy whose criticism of military dictatorship in Colombia and throughout Latin America had led to the banning of several of his books in his homeland, as well as exile in the 1950s. Arciniegas was also critical of the U.S. government for its assistance to military regimes in the region. At the same time, he served as an officer in the American Committee for Cultural Freedom (ACCF), the U.S. branch of the Congress for Cultural Freedom, of which he was a founding member; in the early 1960s, he would assume the editorship of the latter's first Spanish-language journal, *Cuadernos*, the precursor to *Mundo Nuevo*.

Despite marked ideological differences between the two writers, Arciniegas's case eerily foreshadowed that of Fuentes in its high-profile status; in the ire and activism it provoked, as well as efforts to change the legislation; and in the ways it revealed the inconsistent and paradoxical manner in which the act was applied. Arciniegas's anti-Communist credentials granted him no immunity from the scrutiny given to foreigners living in the United States. In September 1953, on returning from Paris to New York, where he was teaching at Columbia University, Arciniegas was taken from the airport to Ellis Island, where he was held overnight for questioning "as a security case" ("U.S. Seizes"). Arciniegas had been granted a reentry permit by the U.S. consulate in Paris, which is part of the Department of State, but he was detained by the Immigration and Naturalization Service (INS), a branch of the Justice Department, thus revealing the mixed messages and procedures involved when two separate agencies, each with different information and each serving different masters, were responsible for enforcing the act. In the morning, the writer was asked by an INS official "whether he had been critical of the relations between the United States and some South American countries"—a question to which he replied in the affirmative, citing his 1952 book, *The State of Latin America*. He was then released with an apology from the officer for the inconvenience ("Professor Freed").

Arciniegas's detention made the front page of the *New York Times*. It was also the subject of a scathing editorial that decried the "reprehensible" McCarran-Walter Act, claiming that it "has injured a distinguished foreigner and humiliated all Americans who see their own traditions of democracy violated by fellow Americans" ("McCarran Act at Work"). The newspaper followed the fallout from the case over the next few weeks, focusing on proposed changes to the legislation and protests by the ACCF and American Civil Liberties Union, to which the INS responded by committing to "seek ways of avoiding unnecessary detainment of resident aliens of the United States when they re-enter the country after visits abroad" ("Rules May Be Eased"). The *Times* also printed a letter to the editor from Arciniegas in which he thanked the paper for its editorial and spoke of the outpouring of support on his behalf as examples of the freedom of expression enjoyed in the United States and an affirmation of the power of democracy.

Arciniegas traveled widely over the next few years. For the most part, he had no difficulties reentering the United States. In 1954, however, he was detained again, although with little fanfare. In 1957, he was detained when returning to New York from a trip to Panama, where—ironically—he had given a lecture titled "Problems of Democracy in the United States" ("Aide at Columbia"). He was held for two hours under what immigration officials described as "a routine policy of investigating non-citizens when they re-enter the country" (ibid.). Arciniegas, for his part, attributed his troubles this time not to U.S. policy per se but rather to his political enemies, who he speculated had put together "a dossier on him 'proving' he was a Communist" and sent it to the FBI (ibid.). Once again, there was a large public outcry. The chairman of the International League for the Rights of Man, a consulting agency for the United Nations for which Arciniegas had served as a board member, sent a telegram to Secretary of State John Foster Dulles stressing Arciniegas's anti-Communist credentials (ibid.). The *New York Times* published its second strongly worded editorial on the writer's troubles, decrying the latest incident as a "deplorable piece of stupidity" and arguing that it "harms us" rather than Arciniegas by making "the United States look ridiculous in Latin American eyes and foster[ing] the belief that Washington favors the dictators" ("Unfortunate Incident"). The commissioner of the INS responded immediately with a letter to the editor in which he admitted that the incident was "regretted" and "unfortunate," and that Arciniegas's name should have been removed from the blacklist sooner—a shortcoming for which he accepted some responsibility. He agreed with the editorial's "statement that a single such case is one too many and a poor advertisement abroad," but criticized the paper for granting the incident notoriety and, further, upheld the act as a matter of national security (Swing). The INS seems to have straightened out its records after this, and Arciniegas does not appear to have had any further troubles with the blacklist.

After the Cuban Revolution, troubles with McCarran-Walter came fast and furiously for Spanish American writers. During the 1960s, virtually every single one of the best-known writers fell prey to the act in one way or another. As the U.S. government was not required to confirm the accuracy of the information whereby an individual's name was added to the blacklist, some aliens were excluded because of wrongful suspicions or outdated information (May). Guillermo Cabrera Infante, for instance, was the first Cuban writer to break publicly with Fidel Castro, but he still needed a waiver to enter the United States for years afterward.[3] Other Spanish American writers endured frustrating and humiliating experiences at the hands of passport officials as well. On different occasions, Leopoldo Zea and Jaime García Terrés, both distinguished writers with official positions with the Mexican government, were detained by immigration authorities and almost denied entry to the United States, despite holding proper paperwork—and, in the case of García Terrés, a diplomatic passport.[4]

In early 1965, José Donoso was denied a visa when trying to enter the United States to participate in an interview and celebrate the publication of his novel *Coronation* by Alfred A. Knopf Inc. In her memoirs, Donoso's wife, María Pilar, attributes the incident to a case of vengeance: the Indian ambassador to Chile had taken offense at something that Donoso had done and had taken revenge by telling the U.S. embassy that the writer was a Communist and a member of the Instituto Chino-Chileno de Cultura, prompting the labeling of Donoso as ineligible for a visa (207). A few months later, Donoso accepted a position as writer-in-residence in the University of Iowa's renowned Writer's Workshop. This time, he did not leave the visa approval to chance, and he asked several U.S.-based contacts to lobby on his behalf. Robert Wool, president of the Inter-American Foundation for the Arts, spoke to a contact at the U.S. embassy in Mexico City. According to Wool, the official speculated that the earlier visa problem had been a bureaucratic mistake rather than a political problem, and reassured Wool about the prospects for the new application.[5] Paul Engle, the director of the Writers' Workshop, likewise reached out to a contact in the State Department, who seems to have smoothed the way for the issuing of the visa.[6] Donoso also apprised his publisher of his troubles, but Alfred Knopf was hesitant to get involved in the matter. Ultimately, his assistance was not needed, as the visa was granted without difficulty this time.

In 1968, Mario Vargas Llosa had problems with his application for a visa to hold a visiting position at Washington State University. The writer was, at the time, a vocal supporter of Cuba and other causes viewed as radical by the U.S. government. Indeed, the year before, when accepting the Rómulo Gallegos Prize for *La casa verde* (*The Green House*), he had given his widely publicized speech "La literatura es fuego" ("Literature is Fire"), in which he predicted that within a matter of years, "the hour of social justice will arrive" in Latin America, as it had already in Cuba, and that "the whole of Latin America will have freed itself from the order that despoils it" (73). While it is impossible to ascertain the effect of this speech on immigration officials, it may have caught their attention and resulted in the need for the visa waiver. The visa to go to Pullman did eventually come through, albeit only at the last minute. Mindful of this history, the organizers of a 1971 conference at Columbia University wrote a letter to the U.S. consul general of Barcelona (where Vargas Llosa was then living) prior to the gathering, urging the consulate to issue a visa to the writer in order to avoid a potential public relations disaster for the United States on top of the logistical difficulties Vargas Llosa's absence might cause for the conference.[7] The waiver was granted and the writer attended the conference without incident.

Julio Cortázar was another ardent supporter of the revolution with close ties to its cultural institutions and leaders who was denied visas on multiple occasions, making him reluctant to accept invitations to visit the United States. In 1980, he expressed his frustration in a statement to the Fund for Free Expression as part of a brief advocating the repeal of the ideological exclusion clause: he described how, when applying for his visas, "I am always informed by the Consul or some other official that I am considered a 'subversive person,' that I perform 'communist activities' and, once, that I have committed the awful crime of writing articles 'for the Communist paper published in Argentina.' To tell them that this is not true, among other things because such a paper does not exist, seems to be quite useless" (Cortázar et al., 38).[8] García Márquez, too, had numerous run-ins with Section 212(a)(28). In 1961, when he was still relatively unknown in the United States, he made a pilgrimage to the Oxford, Mississippi, home of William Faulkner, who had profoundly inspired his work. Over the next few years, though, he was denied waivers to enter the United States on multiple occasions. In 1967, in the wake of the exposure of covert CIA funding for the Congress for Cultural Freedom, García Márquez, who had published two chapters of *Cien años de soledad* in *Mundo Nuevo* in 1966, notified Emir Rodríguez Monegal that he would not contribute any additional materials to the journal. At the same time, he admitted to being amused that CIA funding was being used to help disseminate his work when he himself was considered too dangerous to be allowed into the United States.[9] García Márquez was not granted a visa to return to the country until 1971, when he was awarded an honorary degree by Columbia University. Even then, the visa had to be arranged at the highest levels. According to the writer, "Once [Secretary of State] Henry Kissinger came [to Mexico City] and ended a speech with a quote from *One Hundred Years of Solitude*. . . . Some friend asked him if he knew that the author he quoted was banned from the United States. One month later, I was told to pick up a visa at the embassy. It said, 'For lecture at Columbia University.' That is now the formula. Every time I go to the United States, the fiction is that it is 'for lecture at Columbia University'" (qtd. in Riding). After this trip, García Márquez was regularly issued waivers. Even after receiving the Nobel Prize in 1982, and despite requesting unconditional visas, he was granted only restricted and provisional visas; indeed, in 1983, Harvey and Bob Weinstein of Miramax fought to get him a visa so he could enter the United States to help publicize *Eréndira*, the film version of one of his novellas (Rosefelt). Eventually, he decided that by accepting U.S. visas, he was granting his tacit consent to the system, and he refused to return to the country without an unconditional visa.

The McCarran-Walter Act also was used to prevent so-called undesirables or subversives from staying in the country for the long term. In 1982, Uruguayan Ángel Rama, who had recently taken a position as a tenured professor at the University of Maryland, had his application for permanent residency denied. Rama was a brilliant scholar, critic, cultural journalist, and editor. In 1959, he had succeeded Rodríguez Monegal as editor of the literary section of the Uruguayan weekly journal *Marcha*; during his tenure in the position, which he held through 1968, the periodical showcased the new currents in Latin American literature, making it along with *Casa de las Américas* and *Mundo Nuevo* a crucial vehicle in the Boom's rise to fame. Rama wrote prolifically, and his books—such as *Transculturación narrativa en América Latina* (Narrative transculturation in Latin America) and *La ciudad letrada* (*The Lettered City*), among others—offer paradigms for reading Latin American literature that have been fundamental to key readings and theorizations of this work over the years. He also cofounded the Editorial Arca, where he published both Uruguayan writers and up-and-coming Spanish Americans (Peyrou, 13).

Rama considered himself a Socialist and a believer in Socialist democracy, but not a Communist. He was an early supporter of Cuba and had served on the editorial board of *Casa de las Américas*, but he had grown disillusioned with the direction taken by the revolution. He had severed his ties to Casa de las Américas and to the revolution in general after the Padilla affair of 1971. His distancing of himself from Cuba, however, seems to have been overlooked during the investigation into him for visa purposes. Instead, U.S. officials focused on his activities, writings, and editorial work from the 1960s, which they labeled as Communist and anti-American. *Marcha*, for instance, was frequently critical of U.S. Cold War politics and interventionism. In 1966, under Rama's leadership, *Marcha* had translated and published the entire set of *New York Times* exposés on the covert CIA funding for social and political organizations, as well as a number of critical essays on the funding scheme, paying particular attention to the implication of the Congress for Cultural Freedom—and, by extension, *Mundo Nuevo*—in the scandal.

In 1966, Rama had been granted a standard visa to enter the United States (Rama, "Catch 28," 9). The visa expired in April 1970, when Rama was teaching at the University of Puerto Rico. When the scholar and his wife, writer and art historian Marta Traba, applied to renew their visas in order to visit other countries and be able to return to the United States afterward, Rama was deemed ineligible for a visa under Section 212(a)(28);[10] for the rest of his life, he was able to obtain visas only through the waiver process. Like many "28"s, he was at first unaware of his status, knowing only that he needed to wait for a waiver (Rama, "Catch 28," 8). He did not learn why this was the case until 1980, when a consular official informed him that he was considered a "communist subversive."[11] While it is impossible to ascertain what triggered the denial of visas under McCarran-Walter, it seems likely that Rama's spearheading of *Marcha*'s coverage of CIA funding for U.S. organizations, as well as additional articles he had published in the journal criticizing the agency's efforts to infiltrate Latin American intelligence organizations, may have brought him to the attention of immigration officers and cinched the "undesirable" status.[12] (The documents in Rama's FBI file exhibit what the scholar dubbed "selective vision," as they make no reference to the articles he'd written against the repression of dissident intellectuals in the Soviet Union [Rama, "Catch 28," 10].)

The declassified government documents on Rama's case that I have been able to obtain under the Freedom of Information Act (FOIA) indicate that the FBI kept a file on Rama from the time of his 1970 visa application.[13] The couple's application set the bureaucratic wheels—and telexes—in motion. FBI headquarters instructed its San Juan office to conduct agency checks and consult with local informants regarding the couple; it also ordered the CIA, INS, and State Department to review their records for information on them.[14] FBI correspondence also foregrounded what it viewed as Rama's "excludable" qualities. He supposedly had "an extensive record of pro-communist and pro-Cuban activities." He was allegedly a "formerly very active socialist leader who was then separated from the Socialist Party" (he was not, in fact, ever associated with Uruguay's Socialist Party). He was characterized as "a follower of the Chinese Communist line," an accusation that Rama denied. He was identified, also incorrectly, as an editor of *El Popular*, "self-described as official organ of the Communist Party of Uruguay." His editorial position at *Marcha* was noted, the agency labeling the periodical as "a Marxist publication which consistently follows an anti-U.S. line."[15]

In June 1970, Rama was interviewed at the consular office of the U.S. embassy in Montevideo, where he was asked primarily about his travels and his writing for *Marcha*. According to an "Internal Security-Uruguay" memo issued by the FBI, during this interview, Rama confirmed that he had visited post-revolutionary Cuba, Czechoslovakia, Russia, and (Communist) China, and that he was "associated with the Uruguayan-Chinese Cultural Institute in Montevideo."[16] According to Rosario Peyrou, Rama was not in fact directly associated with the Instituto de Amistad Chino-Uruguayo.[17] Peyrou suggests that the invitation to visit China may have come from one of Rama's friends, Sarandy Cabrera, who was himself associated with the institute.[18] The FBI most likely interpreted this connection as evidence of Rama's own association with the organization being tighter than it was in actuality. The memo also claimed that Rama admitted to having "signed many 'pro-Cuba' and 'pro-other communist activities,'" although it also noted that he "described himself as a socialist and a nationalist, who does not believe in communist party discipline and has never been a member of the communist party."[19] The consular officer deemed Rama ineligible for a visa because of his writings, his association with *Marcha*, and his alleged affiliations with a number of Communist groups.[20] The officer noted, however, that the U.S. embassy in Montevideo had recommended a waiver under Section 212(d)(3)(A) of the McCarran-Walter Act "as it will further the United States' interest in cultural and educational fields," and a waiver and visa were quickly issued.[21]

In 1979, when Rama was hired by the University of Maryland as a visiting professor, he was again found ineligible for a visa under Section 212(a)(28). He was granted a twelve-month visa, with the Department of State recommending admission "in the interest of international exchange."[22] In 1981, after accepting a position as Distinguished Scholar at the university, he submitted an application for permanent residency in the United States. In July 1982, the INS notified Rama that he was "inadmissible to the United States" (Rama, "Catch 28," 8). That fall, however, Rama's application was returned without a decision by the regional commissioner of the INS to Wallace Gray, the agency's district director, for further action. Rama's lawyer, Michael Maggio, wrote to Gray, notifying him that the regional commissioner had authorized that Rama be given an explanation for the ruling of excludability, as well as an opportunity to rebut it.[23]

After this letter, there is a chronological gap in the correspondence that I received under the FOIA, which may correspond to some of the pages that were removed from the records sent to me. In any case, the bureaucracy moved slowly, although it was attended to at the highest levels. In March of the following year, Alan Nelson, the commissioner of the INS, wrote to William Webster, director of the FBI, to ask whether he could release to

Rama and his lawyer several documents that the INS had used as grounds for its decision to deny residency to Rama.[24] The FBI responded in the negative, claiming that the files still warranted classified status.[25]

At some point during this process, Rama was called to defend himself at a hearing, but the INS would not tell him what the charges were because the evidence was classified.[26] Rama was told that he would be eligible for a visa if he applied for defector status; he recalled that the FBI wanted him to "provide evidence of my repentance and my desire for atonement . . . in the form of proof 'of having been an active opponent of communism for the past five years'" (Rama, "Catch 28," 9). (As one critic of the act noted, "The Biblical procedure for the cleansing of lepers is simple in comparison" [Wardlaw, 22].) These stipulations would, however, have required him to perjure himself, for he had already sworn under oath that he had never been a Communist. It was a situation that Rama likened to that of Joseph K. in Kafka's *The Trial*, and that he often described as his "Catch 28."[27] And yet, as paradoxical as the situation was, Rama had been given a chance that few others received, for aliens who were refused visas under the act were generally not given an opportunity to challenge the decision.[28]

The PEN American Center, the Latin American Studies Association, and the Helsinki Watch Committee, among others, lobbied fruitlessly on Rama's behalf.[29] The matter was given considerable attention in the *New York Times*, the *Washington Post*, and other prominent U.S. newspapers. The case was also, as one *New York Times* article noted, "widely publicized in Latin America, and deplored as an example of Yankee crudeness" (Lewis). Belisario Betancur, president of Colombia, where Traba had lived for many years, entered the fray: when President Ronald Reagan visited Bogotá in late 1982, Betancur asked him to halt deportation proceedings against Rama; Betancur also granted Colombian citizenship to the couple (Herbers).[30] In the spring of 1983, Rama went to Europe on a Guggenheim Fellowship, unsure if he would be able to return to the United States afterward. On November 24, he expressed his resignation in a letter to his lawyer. "Since I do not have many years of life left," he wrote, "I have refused to turn myself into a man of ceaseless litigation" (Lewis). Days later, Rama died in a plane crash in Madrid, along with Traba, Mexican writer Jorge Ibargüengoitia, Peruvian novelist Manuel Scorza, and many others. The tragedy ended a story that would otherwise—most likely—have gone unresolved for years to come.

From National Security to National Embarrassment:
The Fuentes Case

While the difficulties of many Spanish American writers during the period after the Cuban Revolution were long-standing and ongoing, Carlos Fuentes's case was the most widely publicized and, ultimately, the one that brought about the greatest change in the way the ideological exclusion clause was applied. On numerous occasions during the 1960s, Fuentes was denied visas to enter the United States. His well-documented experiences perhaps best illustrate both the humiliation and the ironies entailed in being subject to the blacklist. In the early 1960s, Fuentes contracted with Farrar, Straus and Company, which issued translations of his novels soon after they were released in Spanish. To further ensure good publicity for his work, Fuentes signed with a U.S. agent, Carl Brandt, whose client list included Elizabeth Bishop, Harold Brodkey, John Dos Passos, C. Wright Mills, and Calvin Trillin, among others. Additionally, he befriended U.S. writers such as Norman Mailer, Arthur Miller, William Styron, and others, who helped him to make valuable connections to U.S. publishers and publicity opportunities.

Even as Fuentes's literary star rose in the United States, though, his difficulties with the INS escalated. Fuentes had lived in the United States as a child, when his father, a diplomat, was posted in Washington, DC. Over the years, he had returned to the United States many times, without trouble. Like his peers, Fuentes was, at first, caught up in the euphoria of the Cuban Revolution.[31] He visited the island several times and promoted the revolution's accomplishments in his fiction and journalism. His political views seem to have made a powerful enemy of Thomas Mann, a staunch anti-Communist who was then U.S. ambassador to Mexico. According to one source, "It seems [Fuentes] got into a fight with Ambassador Mann who called him a Communist which Fuentes has denied" (qtd. in Schlesinger, 454). As late as October 1961, when Fuentes went to New York to celebrate the publication of his novel, *The Good Conscience*, he had no difficulties obtaining a visa. In 1961, however, he traveled to Havana as a delegate of the Congreso de Solidaridad con Cuba, and in early 1962, he spoke out strongly against the United States at the Congreso de Intelectuales at the Universidad de Concepción in Chile; it was after these trips that his difficulties with the blacklist began (Ortega, 108). In April 1962, Fuentes was set to participate in a televised debate on Latin American development and the Alliance for Progress with Richard Goodwin, Kennedy's deputy assistant secretary of state for inter-American affairs. Goodwin had committed to the event in March, but when Fuentes applied for a temporary visa, he was turned down by the U.S. embassy in Mexico less than a week before the scheduled date of the debate. Despite the willingness of Goodwin—a high-ranking State Department official—to debate Fuentes, the department in effect sided with the decision made by its embassy and declined to request a waiver for Fuentes. One source alleged that "the State Department feared that Fuentes might be persuasive in showing that the United States was to blame for the low prices paid for Latin American products, so it instructed our Embassy in Mexico to delay granting a visa while it arranged for the debate to be cancelled" (A. Schwartz, 46). The Justice Department did ultimately issue a waiver, but not until after the debate had been canceled (Cortázar et al., 40).

As Irene Rostagno notes, the incident turned Fuentes into "a martyr of the anti-establishment" (121). Lee Baxandall, one of the editors of *Studies on the Left*, traveled to Mexico to interview Fuentes for the journal; the published feature was prefaced with a reference to the rejected application. The visa denial was also widely reported by other periodicals in the United States and Mexico.

Two letters to the editor published in the *New York Times* in the wake of the incident offer interesting insights into contemporary attitudes of U.S. scholars toward Latin America. The first ("Barring Fuentes") was written by Richard W. Weatherhead, a PhD candidate in history at Columbia University (and later a Latin Americanist scholar). On the one hand, Weatherhead criticizes the McCarran-Walter Act for countering the efforts of the Alliance for Progress and, more broadly, those of Kennedy's Latin American policies. On the other, he argues that the Alliance "is based . . . upon the noble precept of redeeming the common man of the Americas from the debasing conditions of poverty," and so forth. In many ways, his argument reflects the basic tenets of the "open society": Fuentes held "Leftist, Radical and Socialist" political views and sympathized with Castro and the Cuban Revolution, but "fear of . . . verbal attacks and critical arguments" did not constitute grounds to "deny expression to those radical dissenters who oppose us." However, while Weatherhead's argument deplored McCarran-Walter for unraveling the First Amendment's guarantee of the right of free expression, it also reflected a streak of deeply rooted paternalism toward Latin America.

Frank Tannenbaum, a distinguished historian of Latin America at Columbia, sent a letter ("Visa Policy Assailed") to the *Times* on the heels of Weatherhead's. Tannenbaum likewise noted the disconnect between the McCarran-Walter Act's effects (i.e., "The practice of denying a visa . . . has done us more harm in Latin America than any other single policy") and the goals of the Alliance for Progress. He also invoked the deleterious impact of the act on the region's intellectuals. Tannenbaum's letter does not display the implicit rejection of Fuentes's politics that is evident in Weatherhead's. However, his letter is similarly shot through with latent paternalism. On the one hand, he expresses concern about the effects of the visa denial on the intelligentsia, who had the means of shaping public opinion toward the United States in their home countries. On the other, his language draws on a stereotype of Latin Americans as driven by pride and honor rather than by reason as is evident in his characterization of them as a "sensitive and proud people" who had taken the visa denial as a "personal affront," a "gratuitous insult," and "a slap in the face." In effect, despite their respect for Fuentes and his work, both Weatherhead and Tannenbaum demonstrate tensions among competing movements in the U.S. academy following the Cuban Revolution: these included the advocacy for Latin America and its culture, a rejection of the political ideology that brought the region to the spotlight, and a vision of the region's inhabitants as governed by old codes of behavior rather than modern-day rationality and objectivity.

The State Department explained in a press release that Fuentes was "ineligible on security grounds to receive a visa" (qtd. in A. Schwartz, 46). According to several sources, the department had learned that Fuentes might be a Communist and that he had supposedly consulted with Communist leaders in Mexico while preparing for the debate (A. Schwartz, 46; Szulc). *New York Times* writer Tad Szulc, an acquaintance of Fuentes's, noted dryly in an article on the incident ("Visa Denial Bars Leftist's Debate") that the "officials would not explain why Señor Fuentes' alleged Communist connections were not known last October when he came to New York for the publication of his novel, *The Good Conscience*." The State Department also asserted that there was "no evidence available which would indicate that the granting of a waiver of his ineligibility to Mr. Fuentes would be in the national interest"—the precondition for approving such a waiver (qtd. in A. Schwartz, 46). Fuentes, for his part, attributed the denial of the visa to Ambassador Mann. Later, when he met Mann in a restaurant, he demanded to be told what the grounds of excludability were and why he had been denied a visa for being a Communist when he wasn't one. When Mann refused to explain, Fuentes retorted that this type of treatment was likely to turn him into a Communist.[32] The writer further alleged, "It seems the American Embassy sent information that I was a trained-in-Moscow agent" (qtd. in Baxandall, 56). Perhaps if he had been, he might have received the visa: in 1961, exchange agreements had authorized visas for Alexsey Adzhubi, Khruschev's son-in-law and editor of *Izvestia*, and Mikhail Kharlamov,

Khruschev's press secretary, to debate Harrison Salisbury of the *New York Times* and Kennedy's press secretary, Pierre Salinger, on *Face the Nation*.

In early 1964, the U.S. embassy in Mexico denied Fuentes's request for a waiver in order to give a lecture at Washington University. In March, he once again applied for a visa, this time to attend a party in honor of the U.S. publication of his novel, *The Death of Artemio Cruz*. According to Abba Schwartz, the embassy summarily denied Fuentes a visa and recommended against a waiver (47). Several sources attribute this decision to Mann, who had recently been appointed assistant secretary for inter-American affairs. Schwartz was a Washington lawyer and advocate of liberal immigration policies who had been appointed administrator of the Bureau of Security and Consular Affairs at the State Department by President Kennedy. He discussed the matter directly with Mann, who objected to granting Fuentes a visa because of his political views (48–49). This time, however, Fuentes's publisher and agent protested. They also contacted officials in the State Department and the attorney general's office. Robert Kennedy himself reviewed Fuentes's file with Schwartz. Both men agreed that a waiver should be authorized, but even though he knew that the attorney general would approve it, Secretary of State Dean Rusk neglected to take action. Eventually, when Rusk was out of town, Acting Secretary of State George Ball recommended the waiver.

Despite the support for Fuentes at the highest levels, the visa issued to him was restricted: the author was allowed to enter the United States for only five days, and he was not to leave the island of Manhattan. Fuentes further alleges that he was followed while in the country (see Mitgang, "On the 7th Day"). Nonetheless, Fuentes's overall impressions of the United States were profoundly improved by his visit, lending credence to immigration reform advocates who argued that an open door policy was key to courting foreign intellectuals and, through them, to sharing with the public with which they communicated a positive image of the United States. Fuentes wrote to a friend afterward that the trip had allowed him to see the nation in a different—and more congenial—light, and that he planned to write an essay on his experiences that would allow him to communicate this sentiment to a wider audience.[33]

But in December 1964, Fuentes was again denied a visa. He later laughed the matter off, claiming to have argued with consular officials that there had to be a way of removing one's name from the blacklist, and that "even the Devil, one day, would come out of Hell, or there was no God" ("Lecture," 58). At the time, though, he was infuriated at being told that according to McCarran-Walter, he would be eligible for a visa only if he demonstrated his commitment to anti-Communism for the next five years; he further decried the act for alienating Latin American intellectuals from the United States.[34] If the open door policy was useful for presenting opinion molders with a positive impression of the United States, then McCarran-Walter's exclusionary policy was equally potent in its ability to alienate the same intellectuals, creating enemies of them and fostering bad publicity for the nation.

In April 1965, President Johnson sent marines to the Dominican Republic, operating on incorrect information that suggested that former president Juan Bosch's Partido Revolucionario Dominicano was headed by Communists and had received support from Cuba. The invasion further stoked Fuentes's anger at the United States. In May, the *New York Times* asked him to write a letter to the editor on the event. Fuentes complied, submitting a draft in which he linked the intervention to the immigration blacklist, both of which, in his eyes, stemmed from what he saw as overzealous efforts at containing Communism: he argued that the U.S. government's labeling of him and other writers as Communists was symptomatic of a broader tendency that had likewise identified Bosch's oppositional movement as Communist and thereby justified its suppression. The Mexican denied that he and his fellow Latin Americans were in fact Communists, but he also denied that they were anti-Communist, for he equated this stance with U.S. support for dictatorships in the region—a tactic, he noted, that only served to push Latin Americans toward Communism.[35]

The initial draft of the letter was too long, though, and it was edited to half its original size for publication. The writer's excoriation of McCarran-Walter was deleted, but his criticism of U.S. violation of international law with the Dominican intervention was retained, as was his prediction of revolution if Latin America remained a pawn in the struggle between the United States and the Soviet Union ("Mexican Novelist Assails Intervention").

In the fall of 1965, Fuentes again returned to New York to meet with his publisher and translator. This time, he had no trouble with the INS. In February 1966, President Johnson announced that he wanted the United States to be able to host more international meetings, and he called on the secretary of state and the attorney general to "remove unnecessary hindrances" for visas to individuals ineligible to enter the United States under the ideological exclusion clause ("U.S. Eases Visas"). The State Department acknowledged that "the delays and embarrassment involved in obtaining permission to enter the United States . . . under the present procedure have caused some guests to abandon plans to attend conferences . . . and have marred this country's image as a free and open society" (ibid.). Thus, in May, the State and Justice Departments jointly implemented a significant procedural change that automatically granted group waivers to individuals traveling to international conferences or sports events in the United States, specifically when "the national interest requires a group waiver of the provision of law which would otherwise automatically exclude all persons invited to the conference who had at any time been associated with a Communist party."[36] This allowed visas to be issued more expeditiously and involved significantly less travail (and humiliation) for applicants. The change immediately benefited Fuentes, Neruda, and numerous other writers who attended the 34th congress of International PEN, which was held in New York City that June. Neruda, who had repeatedly been barred from entering the United States because of his Communist affiliations, was issued a U.S. visa for the first time in over twenty years, and Fuentes was also able to secure his without difficulty (see Chapter 2 for a discussion of the congress).

In November 1966, Fuentes was granted a waiver when he applied for a visa to visit Colorado State University as a writer-in-residence for the spring of 1967 and then teach at Dartmouth College the following academic year. According to Abba Schwartz, the waiver was issued on the grounds that "contact with American universities might advance what the Embassy regarded as Fuentes' more constructive attitude toward the United States"—a rationale that Schwartz viewed as a triumph of "open society" policies (50). That same fall, Fuentes's host at Colorado State, Nick Crome, had begun to organize high-profile events to take advantage of Fuentes's presence on campus: he had invited Margaret Randall and her husband, Sergio Mondragón, to come from Mexico to give readings, and he was planning a symposium on Latin American literature that Donoso was to attend. By mid-November, however, Crome was getting nervous: he had yet to receive the reading list for Fuentes's course, and he wrote to Carl Brandt to inquire about the writer's plans.

No sooner was the visa approved than Fuentes chose not to come to the United States. The decision was met with severe disapproval by the writer's friend and advocate, Robert Wool, who was saddled with explaining the change in plan to his State Department contacts.[37] Wool took Fuentes to task for his actions; further, he implored Fuentes not to blame the State Department or to publicly hold the act responsible for his not going to the United States, out of concern that this could backfire and alienate the official contacts Wool had had to cultivate over the years when trying to bring Latin American writers into the country.[38] Fuentes did keep quiet about the reasons behind his decision, and Brandt took care of breaking the news to Colorado

State. After several months, Fuentes wrote to Crome to apologize. He noted that he had been able to enter the United States for the PEN congress without needing a waiver, which had led him to believe that his troubles with the act were over, and that when he faced yet another questioning by consular officials, he was irate and refused to undertake the visit.[39]

In 1967, Fuentes received another invitation to visit the United States. Robert Mead, a professor of Spanish at the University of Connecticut, asked him to participate in a special forum at the 1968 Modern Language Association (MLA) convention. The panel, which the organization had asked Mead to arrange, was to focus on Latin American literature and would also feature Donoso and Rodríguez Monegal. The forum was to be two hours long, and it marked a high-profile celebration of the Boom by the U.S. academy. Mead had heard from Rodríguez Monegal about Fuentes's prior difficulties with McCarran-Walter; he assured the writer that MLA administrators were apprised of the situation and would be willing to assist with the visa application process.[40] The sting of the interrogation he had received when applying for the visa to go to Colorado State was clearly still fresh with Fuentes, though. While he was interested in participating in the event, he told Mead that he refused to go through the process again, and that he would return to the United States only if it was guaranteed that he would not have to go through the waiver process to be granted a visa.[41] In October 1967, John Hurt Fisher, the executive secretary of the MLA, wrote to Secretary of State Rusk asking if the organization could do anything to help normalize Fuentes's visa application process. He argued that the efforts of the university community to promote Latin American literature at this particular historical juncture made Fuentes's participation critical to the congress. Fisher received a reply from the head of the Domestic Services Division of the Visa Office, who outlined the standard procedure for the visa application process. The official also assured Fisher that Fuentes would "be accorded every consideration compatible with the law."[42] In other words, he promised nothing and did not accede to Fisher's request for a streamlined application process.

Fisher conveyed the information to Mead and asked him to urge Fuentes to begin the application process in order to leave enough time to go through the waiver process, should that be needed; he also offered his assurance that the MLA would appeal to the attorney general if Fuentes's application was turned down by the State Department.[43] Unable to reach Fuentes directly, Mead wrote to Rodríguez Monegal in December 1967, asking him to convey the message that the MLA would be willing to assist with his case by putting pressure on government officials.[44] Fuentes, however, felt that the official's response only bore out his belief that going through the visa process would be a humiliating process ("Letter").[45] Thus, he declined the invitation to participate in the session.

The great irony here, of course, is that Fuentes should have been issued a visa under the same policy that in 1966 had facilitated his participation in the PEN congress—that is, the policy that circumvented standard procedures by granting group waivers to conference participants. That even the high-ranking visa officer who explained the application process to Fisher did not mention this policy attests to the complexities and lack of transparency in the implementation of the act.

Ultimately, even Fuentes acknowledged that the State Department would be justified in not authorizing a waiver for him: "Although I do not belong . . . to the communist party . . . I am part of a militancy that is much broader . . . the almost universal opposition of the intellectual classes, both within and outside of the United States, to the imperialist politics of the government in Washington" ("Letter"). At the same time, Fuentes explained his refusal to enter the country as a gesture of solidarity with U.S. intellectuals who rejected their government's "politics of internal conformism and external aggression": "The best relationship with revolutionary writers and artists in the United States will not come about by visiting them silently while on bond from the Attorney General of the United States, but in encouraging them from outside, refusing, first of all, to accept the conditions, as ridiculous as they are offensive, that the North American visa offices impose" (ibid.). Fuentes did not keep quiet this time about the reasons behind his refusal to come: instead, he asked that his letter to Mead declining the invitation be published in *PMLA*, the MLA's flagship journal, as a public expression of his rejection of both McCarran-Walter and U.S. government policy in general. In the end, Donoso pulled out of the forum for health reasons, and the workshop on Spanish American literature was canceled.

Fuentes's difficulties with U.S. immigration policies reached a very public climax in 1969. On February 22, when returning from Spain to Mexico, the boat in which Fuentes was traveling docked briefly in San Juan, Puerto Rico. The writer tried to disembark, but a U.S. immigration official found his name on the INS blacklist and tore up his landing card. As Fuentes later observed, "From the docks, I saw land that is mine, part of Latin America, but an occupied land I cannot set foot on" (Raymont, "Fulbright").[46] After being denied permission to disembark, Fuentes returned to his room and wrote telegrams describing the situation to his agent, his publisher, and Norman Mailer (who he knew would soon be speaking to the PEN American Center), asking them to protest on his behalf. Mario Vargas Llosa, who was at this time a visiting professor at the University of Puerto Rico, had been waiting at the dock to meet his friend and was allowed to board the ship. Vargas Llosa took Fuentes's messages and sent them to their final destinations (Fuentes, "Lecture," 59).

An INS official later disavowed responsibility for the event by claiming that "Mr. Fuentes should have been aware from his prior experience that he requires special permission to enter the United States temporarily because of an existing ground of inadmissibility."[47] The contretemps triggered a national and international uproar. Henry Raymont, one of the *New York Times*'s chief Latin America correspondents, wrote several articles criticizing the McCarran-Walter Act. As it had done earlier with Arciniegas, the newspaper published an editorial condemning the episode: "One sure way to tarnish the United States is for some bureaucrat to decide that a writer . . . is an 'undesirable alien' because of his work or beliefs. Politicizing literature is a common practice for authoritarian governments; it should not become one for this country" ("Fuentes Incident"). The editorial further urged Congress to "re-examine and eliminate these purposeless restrictions, which make the United States ridiculous rather than secure. Literary imprimaturs by the Immigration Service or any other Government body are alien to the United States itself." Fuentes's agent, Brandt, mobilized writers, critics, and publishers to protest the incident. His publisher, Roger Straus, wrote in *Publishers Weekly* that "somehow the republic survived [the visits of Fuentes and other "28"s for the 1966 PEN meeting] and may even have benefitted from them. The session on Latin American writing was among the most productive at the PEN congress, and it forecast a new degree of inter-American harmony in the world of letters. That momentum has now been considerably jeopardized by the immigration officials' action with respect to Mr. Fuentes" (37). Straus also prepared a resolution, signed by more than two hundred writers at the National Book Awards ceremonies on March 10, that condemned the act. The resolution urged the repeal of immigration restrictions based on the expression of dissenting political views on the grounds that the United States was "secure enough in its democratic values" ("Authors Condemn").

As in 1964, Fuentes's supporters took their protests to the highest levels of the U.S. government. The PEN American Center immediately complained to the State Department (Chute, 86).[48] Straus wrote to Attorney General John Mitchell. Mitchell also heard from Columbia University administrators Frank MacShane (chair of the university's Writing Division) and Charles Wagley (director of Columbia's Institute of Latin American Studies), who had jointly invited Fuentes to speak at the university and hoped to convince him to accept an appointment there. In a letter to the *New York Times*,

MacShane and Wagley further urged Congress to change immigration law "so that we in the United States can participate in the modern intellectual world" (Wagley and MacShane). William D. Rogers, president of the Center for Inter-American Relations and a former head of the Alliance for Progress, wrote to Secretary of State William P. Rogers (no relation) that

> the notion that Fuentes's presence among us could in any sense damage our national interest is unworthy of serious discussion. To the contrary, it is his rejection which will cause us immense harm. It will be interpreted by the youth and intellectual community in Latin America as meaning that our commitment to free expression is superficial and will confirm the impression to some that we are timid and fearful of criticism of Latin-American writers. (qtd. in Raymont, "Fuentes Incident")

Thus, he urged the Nixon administration to announce "that it would welcome Fuentes and other leading Latin-American writers to our shores, regardless of their political opinions" (ibid.). In his response, the secretary of state denied that the State Department was responsible for the incident, maintaining that "on previous occasions we have sought and obtained waivers on behalf of Mr. Fuentes, as we have done for many Latin American intellectuals."[49]

Abba Schwartz and Arthur Schlesinger Jr. organized a campaign to lobby Congress to change the immigration law. Schlesinger, a former foreign policy adviser to President Kennedy, knew Fuentes through events sponsored by the Inter-American Foundation for the Arts; he declared that the Nixon administration's response to the incident would be a test of its ability to improve relations with intellectuals in the United States and internationally ("Authors Condemn"). Schwartz, in turn, sent a telegram to Senator J. W. Fulbright, then chairman of the Senate Foreign Relations Committee, asking the committee to renew efforts to repeal section 212(a)(28) in order "to prevent further senseless and embarrassing situations" in U.S. foreign relations (qtd. in Raymont, "Fuentes Incident"). In support of Schwartz, Joseph Clark, a former senator whose 1967 efforts to repeal the law had been opposed by the State Department, averred that the ideological exclusion clause "contributes nothing to the security of the United States and mainly keeps out artists and intellectuals who might become engaged in a constructive dialogue by coming here" (qtd. in Raymont, "Fulbright"). Senator Fulbright responded quickly, seeking an explanation of the visa denial from the secretary of state and the attorney general, and urging the Nixon administration to ease immigration restrictions and administer the law more flexibly. He registered his concern that such treatment of left-wing intellectuals was extremely damaging to "the image of the United States among articulate leadership groups abroad" (qtd. in Cong. Rec. 1969, 19896)—in other words, among the opinion leaders—and that "incidents of this kind . . . do nothing to protect the internal security of the United States and do a great deal to confirm the worst suspicions which are held about the United States by intellectuals abroad" (19895). He further deemed the Fuentes event "no contribution toward winning friends in the intellectual community of Latin America" (qtd. in Raymont, "Fulbright").

Although he was initially sympathetic to liberal attempts to revise the law, Fulbright ultimately decided that new legislation was unfeasible and would be met with opposition. Instead, he focused on changing the implementation of the policy for granting waivers. In a response to Fulbright on behalf of the State Department, Assistant Secretary for Congressional Relations William Macomber Jr. suggested that the situation could have been avoided if Fuentes had sought a waiver of inadmissibility, as he had done in the past (Cong. Rec. 1969, 19896). Fulbright nevertheless continued to pursue the matter, as he was deeply concerned about preventing a repetition of this type of incident. In July, Macomber reported that the Immigration and Naturalization Service had changed its procedures to allow otherwise inadmissible aliens to enter the United States while in transit to another country; it would also seek to notify all ports of entry when a "28" was granted a waiver of inadmissibility so that the authorization would be taken into consideration when future visa applications were reviewed (Cong. Rec. 1969, 22950). Satisfied with the changes in procedure, Fulbright had his correspondence with the Departments of State and Justice, along with two related *New York Times* articles, inserted into the *Congressional Record*. Fuentes was deeply grateful to the senator for taking the case to Congress and changing the implementation of the act, if not the terms of the act itself.[50]

But as the experiences of Fuentes, García Márquez, and others demonstrate, authorization of a waiver for one trip was no guarantee that one would be issued for later visits. Also, the change in implementation neither erased an individual's "28" status nor spared him or her from having to apply for a waiver. In August 1969, Senator James Scheuer introduced a bill to repeal Section 212(a)(28). Scheuer invoked Fuentes's case when he presented his bill, arguing that the writer's canceled 1962 visit

> certainly posed no more of a threat to this country than did that of the
> two well-known Communists [Adzhubi and Kharlamov] the preceding

year. Further, Mr. Fuentes himself posed no more of a threat to the security of this country in 1962 or 1969 than he did in 1961, 1964, and 1966, years when the State Department saw fit to issue him a visa. This irrationality in the State Department's treatment of Mr. Fuentes underlines the arbitrariness with which this provision is enforced. (qtd. in Cong. Rec. 1969, 22950)

His effort, too, failed.

Though the groundswell of support was not strong enough to change the law, it did ensure that after March 1969, Fuentes had no further trouble obtaining waivers to visit the United States. He returned in October of the same year without incident, and many times thereafter. Until the law was changed, though, he had to travel to Mexico City whenever he applied for a visa, as the waiver request could be filed only at the U.S. embassy there. Also, in the 1980s, his application under the Freedom of Information Act to see his file was denied, deemed "contrary to national interests" (Fuentes, "McCarran-Walter Sadomasochism").[51] In 1977, while serving as Mexico's ambassador to France, Fuentes considered settling in the United States and becoming a U.S. resident.[52] He rightly surmised that having his name on the INS blacklist could jeopardize his application for permanent residence (as Rama found out soon afterward), and he indicated that he was hesitant to move forward until his situation was resolved.[53]

William D. Rogers, the former president of the Center for Inter-American Relations, had intervened on Fuentes's behalf with the State Department after the Puerto Rico incident, and was by this time serving as U.S. counsel to Fuentes. Rogers advised Fuentes that it would be difficult to change his status or have his name removed from the blacklist. He told Fuentes to apply for an H-1 nonimmigrant visa, available to people of "distinguished merit and ability" (as the visa terms state) working for U.S. employers; he assured the writer that the Department of State would be willing to issue a waiver of excludability for this visa, which would allow him to remain in the country for several years.[54] It was a process that Fuentes characterized as "making the bureaucracy work twice: first, they refuse my application in order to abide by McCarran-Walter; immediately, they waive the undesirability because I am presented as a highly desirable professional worthy of an H-1 visa" (Fuentes, "McCarran-Walter Sadomasochism"). Once Fuentes was in the United States, Rogers would request that the INS and State Department reconsider Fuentes's status; only after his name was removed from the list of excludable aliens would he be eligible for a permanent resident visa.

With Rogers's assistance, Fuentes was issued the H-1 visa in 1977. He spent the next few years teaching in the United States, although his situation remained unresolved: sometimes he would be given an H-1 visa, but at other times he would receive the more restrictive (and less prestigious) J-1 visa—a reminder of the ongoing nature of his struggle.

McCARRAN-WALTER WAS BUT ONE FRONT in the Cold War campaigns to identify and neutralize so-called subversives and Communists. Even as foreign intellectuals were denied entry to the United States, J. Edgar Hoover was building thousands of FBI dossiers on them, as well as on U.S. writers, their publishers, professional guilds, and the like.[55] As McCarran-Walter had done with foreign authors, U.S. intellectuals were classified by the FBI as security risks not because of any activities that might have posed a direct or concrete threat to the nation, but rather because of their writings, their professional associations, and the places they visited (Mitgang, *Dangerous Dossiers*, 27). The U.S. government thus chipped away at the freedom of expression and the free circulation of ideas among citizens as well as foreigners, bringing about one of the greatest ironies of U.S. Cold War politics: constitutional guarantees thought to be fundamental differences between U.S. democracy and the Soviet system were undermined in the name of U.S. national security. As President Truman wrote in his veto of revisions to the Immigration and Nationality Act, "To punish undefined 'activities' departs from traditional American insistence on established standards of guilt. To punish an undefined 'purpose' is thought control. . . . Such powers are inconsistent with our democratic ideals" (Cong. Rec. 1952, 8084). Rogers sought throughout the 1970s and 1980s to change the legislation, and in 1980, he wrote to Theodore Hesburgh, chairman of the Select Commission on Immigration and Refugee Policy:

> If this nation is to stand for something in the eyes of the people of the
> Americas it must do so as an open, free and self-confident society; if
> we advance our model as an alternative to Marxism, we must do so in
> terms of its human values. . . . What we have done to [individuals such as
> Fuentes, Cortázar, and García Márquez], and said to the world, challenges
> our pretension to speak as the leader of the free world. For it is a denial
> of freedom, and an admission that we fear ideas, to restrain entry to this
> country on that ground alone. (Cortázar et al., 40)

Fuentes echoed this sentiment when he asserted that "it is the application of the exclusionary clause that endangers the Republic, mocks Democracy, demoralizes the true friends of the United States, and offers undeserved aces to the Soviet Union" (Fuentes, "McCarran-Walter Sadomasochism").

Even as the McCarran-Walter Act undermined democratic principles in the United States, though, it led writers and intellectuals both stateside and abroad to uphold these same principles. Thus, the literal exclusion of writers from the country paradoxically gave them a figurative entry point for inscribing themselves in the nation's democratic process. Individual writers lobbied the government to repeal the act, alongside organizations such as the American Civil Liberties Union (ACLU), the Helsinki Watch Committee, and PEN. Time and again over the years, periodicals such as the *Nation*, *Index on Censorship*, and others featured articles and editorials on the act, as well as pieces by the authors it had affected. The cases of Cortázar, Fuentes, García Márquez, and Rama in particular became touchstones for protests against the act.

In late 1983, around the time of Rama's death, the Department of State proposed an amendment that would allow "foreign policy factors" to be taken into consideration in the granting of visas (Laber). This move sparked a yearlong series of events and activism against the act. In April 1984, in conjunction with the Fund for Free Expression, the PEN American Center sponsored a public reading in New York City of the work of writers barred from entering the United States under Section 212(a)(28). Authors such as E. L. Doctorow, John Irving, Arthur Miller (a former president of International PEN and a friend of Fuentes), Susan Sontag, and William Styron (a longtime friend of both Fuentes and García Márquez) read from the work of writers such as Cortázar, Fo, García Márquez, Neruda, and Rama.[56] In June, Styron spoke on behalf of PEN at a hearing before the House Judiciary Committee's Subcommittee on Immigration, Refugees, and International Law, which was considering the State Department's resolutions to the exclusion clause. He invoked the cases of Cortázar, Fuentes, García Márquez, and Rama, as well as several others that I have discussed here, as part of his statement. So, too, did other lobbyists for the proposed changes, including Jeri Laber, executive director of the Helsinki Watch Committee, and Arthur Helton, chair of the Committee on Immigration and Nationality Law of the New York City Bar Association. That fall, the ACLU and the Fund for Free Expression, in conjunction with about thirty other organizations, hosted a conference focusing on "restrictions on the flow of information and ideas across the American border including restrictions on the right of Americans to import and export information, to travel abroad, and to receive foreign visitors," and seeking, ultimately, to repeal the ideological exclusion provisions (Benda and Halperin, 691n2). Fo and Pasti, both of whom had been victims of McCarran-Walter, participated in the conference by closed-circuit television from Canada, thereby avoiding the visa question, while Fuentes gave the plenary lecture at the event.

The momentum continued until the clause was struck down in 1990. For several years, Rose Styron (William's wife) co-chaired the PEN American Center's Freedom-to-Write Committee; she was also instrumental in the preparation of an award-winning documentary on McCarran-Walter, *Do Not Enter: The Visa War against Ideas* (1986), which featured interviews with Fuentes, García Márquez, Pasti, and others who had been affected by the act. In 1989, Larry McMurtry, a member of the executive board of the PEN American Center, testified before a House of Representatives subcommittee on behalf of PEN, decrying the ideological exclusion provision as a violation of First Amendment rights. In other words, the opinion leaders whom the State Department sought to court with its cultural diplomacy endeavors had been moved to take a very visible stance against the policy and the government that enforced it.

Steven Shapiro has argued that ideological exclusions "are symbolic gestures meant to express American displeasure with prominent individuals who have publicly disagreed with American policy" (934–35). Barring authors is tantamount to condemning the ideas in their works; in Fuentes's words, it constitutes a de facto form of "punish[ment] for our political opinions" ("McCarran-Walter Sadomasochism"). How else is it, Fuentes wondered, that the words of "undesirables" can circulate, but "only our physical persons, surely the least dangerous part of our intellectual totality, are judged dangerous" (ibid.)? Fuentes's experiences with the McCarran-Walter Act thus elucidate a primary paradox of the Boom's history in the United States: the authors' political orientation—in particular, their support for the Cuban Revolution—simultaneously rendered them attractive to the U.S. government as opinion makers who could foster goodwill toward the United States and "undesirable" as believers in "subversive" ideologies. Even as official U.S. agencies worked to establish cultural exchanges and facilitate the dissemination of work by Spanish American authors in the hope of luring them away from Communism, the denial of visas provoked in them hostility toward the United States and sympathy for rival political systems.

2

PEN and the Sword

Latin American Writers and the 1966 PEN Congress

In June 1966, International PEN held its annual conference in New York City. It was the first time in forty-two years that the United States had hosted the meeting. Arthur Miller had been elected president of the organization in 1965, and the weeklong congress, which drew more than six hundred people from fifty-six countries, marked a moment of international prestige for PEN. It also gave the PEN American Center, the local coordinator of the congress, a chance to shine a bright light on both its own efforts and the United States as a whole. Committed to promoting understanding and defending free expression, conference organizers sought to provide authors from all ideological backgrounds with an opportunity to communicate with one another and to create an environment in which Cold War politics were ostensibly put aside in favor of cultural exchange and interchange. The preceding year, the conference had taken place in Bled, Yugoslavia—the first time that the annual congress had been held in Eastern Europe since the Second World War. As Claudia Gilman observes, "The idea of a meeting behind the Iron Curtain of writers from around the world, followed by a meeting in the United States, was framed within the context of the strengthening of ties between the East and West, within the desired thawing that a good part of the world's intelligentsia had supported" (*Entre la pluma*, 124).

In 1966, PEN had seventy-six centers in fifty-five countries.[1] It had always had a strong base in Europe, where most of its congresses had been held since the organization was founded in 1921. Officials at the PEN American Center were keenly aware of the significance of holding the conference in the United States at a time when Cold War tensions were high, and they did their best to facilitate the participation of delegates from centers in Eastern Europe and Cuba. Officials also reached out to so-called peripheral writers from Africa, Asia, and Latin America, where there were few established PEN centers. Their efforts were motivated by a sincere desire to make the event a success and to use it as a means of stimulating PEN activity worldwide. At the same time, the outreach was a strategic move that reflected U.S. interest in developing nations that were vulnerable to Communist advances.

The conference marked a moment of high visibility for Latin American literature. The event became a site of competing and conflicting interests between the aspirations for Western acclaim shared by Boom writers and their Latin American contemporaries on the one hand and, on the other, the hemispheric agenda of U.S. Cold War nationalism. Following Pierre Bourdieu, I identify here the ways in which the literary activity that the conference enabled took place within and was at some level made possible by the U.S. field of power. This approach reveals how an ostensibly nonpolitical organization was not only caught up in a web of hemispheric cultural diplomacy but deliberately played to it, framing its bids for support from the State Department and philanthropic organizations in terms of the conference's contributions to the national interest. I also demonstrate how these connections facilitated the infiltration of PEN by the Congress for Cultural Freedom (CCF).

And yet, it would be misleading to study the conference solely as an unofficial hemispheric outreach program that served U.S. national interests by extending the nation's political reach and improving its international image—even if it was framed by its organizers, approved by government officials, and supported by the CCF as precisely this. Such an approach would tell only part of the story, and it would overlook a key aspect of the event's significance: the fact that Latin American writers viewed the conference as a platform for extending—through the hemisphere and beyond—the reach of a literary movement that was deeply interwoven with aspirations of regional sovereignty and solidarity. For the political and cultural forces at play in the conference to be understood, they must be studied from a vantage point that draws on the histories—literary, social, political, and otherwise—of the United States and Latin America alike. The conference's success, as well as its importance and its legacy, was inextricably linked to its status as a tug-of-war between regional goals that transcended the interests of individual Latin American nations on the one hand and U.S. national politics and hemispheric policies on the other.

As we have seen, Cold War politics played a determining role in molding U.S. cultural policy at home and abroad during the 1950s and 1960s. The 1966 PEN congress is mentioned as a turning point in almost every history of Spanish American literature that studies this period, but to date, no one has studied it from the perspective of an outreach program that courted foreign intellectuals in the service of the U.S. national interest.[2] I have chosen to focus on the conference's role in U.S.–Latin American cultural diplomacy efforts because of the tremendous opening it provided for Carlos Fuentes, Mario Vargas Llosa, and other Latin American writers at a critical moment in the history of Latin American literature.

The timing of the conference was auspicious in terms of presenting the United States with a public relations opportunity. Opposition to the Vietnam War was mounting both domestically and internationally, and anti-Americanism was on the rise, fueled in Latin America by U.S. interventions in Cuba and the Dominican Republic. The conference also allowed Latin American writers to position themselves as equals on a stage occupied by some of the world's most renowned and influential authors even as they cemented their bonds with one another. Thus, the meeting served as a venue that simultaneously enabled U.S. policy interests in Latin America and Latin American writers' designs on the U.S. and Western literary and political scenes. It also brought to the foreground the dialogic nature of the relationship between North and South during the Cold War, and the polyvalent nature of the Cold War for both regions.

Conference Organization: Invitations, Funding, and Visas

Conference organizers struggled to navigate the conflicting and even paradoxical movements in U.S. Cold War policy. On the one hand, they needed to find a way around a containment policy that, in the form of McCarran-Walter, would have prevented many potential participants from attending the conference. On the other hand, International PEN was serving as an unofficial agent of public diplomacy, actively courting foreign writers who were also public figures and molders of opinion in their own countries in the hope that their presence at the conference would be "in the national interest." In other words, PEN officials hoped that any goodwill toward the United States that the conference sparked in foreign writers would be used to sway the attitudes of their compatriots toward the nation. Thus, they walked a fine line: they insisted that the organization was nonpolitical, but it was virtually impossible to separate cultural activity from the political arena at this time. PEN's connections to the CCF only compounded the intersection of these spheres.

Organizers faced two key hurdles in planning the congress: ensuring

U.S. visas for international participants and raising funds for the conference. Both of these were subject to Cold War interests and pressures, and it was imperative to have government support in order to overcome the obstacles. In 1965, when conference planning began, the National Council on the Arts (NCA) and the National Endowment for the Arts (NEA) had only just been established, and there was little public support available to the arts. Lewis Galantière—a playwright, a translator of French literature, and the newly minted president of the PEN American Center—felt hampered by the lack of public support for cultural activities in the United States, especially since PEN conferences held abroad tended to receive large sums from national ministries of culture. He started fundraising by seeking contributions from members, U.S. publishers, and corporations. Roger Stevens, who was a special consultant on the arts to President Johnson, as well as chairman of the NCA and the NEA, was especially interested in attracting participants from Latin America; he volunteered to press his contacts in industry for funding for them.[3] The NCA itself gave funds for the conference (Chute, 81).

The CCF provided both funding and support personnel. Frances Stonor Saunders avers that it was PEN's "refusal to succumb to bias or *parti pris*, coupled with a robust defense of freedom of expression, which guaranteed the worldwide expansion of PEN during the Cold War years. But the truth is that the CIA made every effort to turn PEN into a vehicle for American government interests. And the Congress for Cultural Freedom was the designated tool" (362). International PEN and the CCF had worked together on several congresses and initiatives since 1956 (363). In 1964, the CCF sent Keith Botsford, who had been its traveling representative in Latin America, to be an assistant to David Carver, the international secretary of PEN (363). As the New York congress approached, the CCF also provided the PEN American Center with one of its affiliates as an assistant, as well as lending the services of Marion Bieber, the CCF's seminar organizer, to the center for several weeks around the time of the congress (366). Additionally, John Hunt of the CCF's international secretariat worked closely with Galantière and Carver to identify prominent writers to invite to the congress; their travel expenses were to be covered by the CCF, which wanted to ensure that top writers from Western Europe attended.[4] The initial plan, which ultimately did not materialize, was for the CCF to hold a private meeting in New York immediately prior to the congress, to be attended by distinguished foreign writers whose travel the CCF would underwrite; the writers would then participate in the PEN activities. It was a strategic move intended, according to Galantière, "to enhance the prestige of the PEN, of the New York Congress, and of the United States as a center of world literature, by ensuring that not only PEN bureaucrats but writers of great renown shall be associated with our Congress."[5] Galantière asked Hunt to facilitate the participation of Umberto Eco, Lucien Goldmann (a French intellectual and Marxist theorist), Melvin Lasky (a longtime CCF affiliate and editor of its British journal, *Encounter*), and Ignazio Silone (an Italian anti-Communist writer and active member of the CCF who was also a vice president of PEN International). He was most interested, though, in having the CCF underwrite the attendance of Graham Greene, observing that the author's attitude toward characters from the United States in his latest novel was fairly positive, inspiring Galantière to try to cultivate Greene's favorable feelings toward the United States in general.[6] Hunt, in turn, suggested the name of Emir Rodríguez Monegal, who had been at Bled the year before, and who was at this point preparing to launch *Mundo Nuevo* and collaborating on an anthology of Latin American literature with Botsford.[7]

Most of the conference's funds came from philanthropies and philanthropists, many of which earmarked their contributions for the support of delegates from the geopolitical regions corresponding to their programs' current priorities. John D. Rockefeller III, who had been involved with the post–World War II reconstruction of Japan and other philanthropic programs dedicated to the nation, gave $20,000 to bring writers from Asia to the conference.[8] The Rockefeller Brothers Fund gave $25,000.[9] According to Saunders, "The CIA also channelled money to American PEN through the Asia Foundation and the Free Europe Committee" (366). The Ford Foundation was the largest benefactor, donating $75,000 to cover travel and living expenses for delegates, interpreters, office expenses, and meeting rooms.[10] This was, significantly, the first grant that the organization had awarded to the PEN American Center, despite repeated efforts by PEN to obtain funding in the past (Chute, 81). The funds came from one of the foundation's most active—and politically strategic—sectors: the International Affairs Division. Prior to considering the center's application for funding, the Ford Foundation asked for reassurance that participants would not engage in political debates that might compromise the organization. As Kathleen McCarthy has observed, during this period, the foundation's "international arts and humanities grants were cast in ideological terms, weapons in the Cold War quest for the hearts and minds of men" ("From Cold War," 93). This was evident in Galantière's framing of his application for funds from the foundation: "Your interest in the Congress, we suggest, may be viewed under these several aspects: world understanding; the American national interest in exposing to the American scene influential men and women from thirty or more countries; and the preservation and encouragement of literary values."[11] (It seems likely that these aspects were listed in order of priority, rather than in a random order.) The proposal that Ford officers submitted to its board of trustees echoed Galantière's application, averring that "the Congress will afford an opportunity to show the richness and variety of our literary and artistic achievements and of American life in general to leading foreign writers."[12] While the Ford proposal toned down the direct emphasis on the national interest, it nevertheless stressed the importance of presenting the writers—opinion leaders at home—with a positive impression of the United States. The commitment of funds was contingent on the State Department's endorsement of the conference: the foundation asked for, and received, an official letter indicating that the department supported the conference and its goals.

PEN was also in touch with the State Department because it needed to ensure visas for conference participants from abroad. It was emblematic of the times that Galantière's invitations to foreign writers included urgent queries as to whether or not they would be able to get visas to enter the United States. Organizers knew that both the conference's success and PEN's reputation depended on their being able to circumvent section 212(a)(28) of the McCarran-Walter Act: a denial of visas would not just be damaging to the organization but could also prove embarrassing to the United States, triggering negative publicity with far-reaching political implications.[13] As Graham Greene, Pablo Neruda, and several other high-profile delegates had previously been denied U.S. visas, sparking protests around the world, this was hardly an idle concern. As we have seen, the Department of State could, if it chose, authorize a waiver for those deemed ineligible, and exchange agreements with the Soviet Union had made it easier for Russians to get U.S. visas, but visas for visitors from Cuba, East Germany, North Korea, and North Vietnam, as well as for those perceived to have Communist connections, were more difficult to arrange. In the year leading up to the conference, Galantière was in close communication with State Department officials in the Bureau of Educational and Cultural Affairs, the Soviet and East European Exchanges office, and the Cuban Affairs desk, among others, trying to drum up support for the congress and to mitigate the effects of the McCarran-Walter Act.

To make their case, Galantière and other PEN officials played up the congress's importance, framing it as an event that would serve the national interest—a quiet front for cultural diplomacy efforts. If the congress's official purpose was to serve as a crucible where foreign and U.S. writers could meet and engage in dialogue about their craft, it was also to function as a de facto venue for providing foreign intellectuals with a positive experience of the United States. Hence, John Farrar (head of Farrar, Straus and Company, and Galantière's predecessor as president of the PEN American Center) wrote to Dean Rusk, informing the secretary of state that as the words of writers abroad held sway with both their compatriots and government officials, and as literature played a powerful role in enhancing U.S. international relations, the conference would be instrumental in furthering U.S. interests.[14] Galantière likewise pressed the case of PEN as a nonpolitical organization that "nevertheless possessed a high degree of moral authority which had political consequences"; echoing Farrar, he noted that the conference would attract writers from Africa, Asia, and Latin America who were "influential molders of opinion" and whose "exposure to the American scene was deemed desirable by the Department of State."[15]

Galantière also claimed that the election of Arthur Miller as the first president of International PEN from the United States was evidence of the respect that international writers on both sides of the Iron Curtain held for the U.S. literary community, and further attested to how the latter was an asset to the national interest.[16] Miller's election, though, had also been a product of behind-the-scenes political machinations: it was Botsford who had suggested Miller for the position, and Botsford and Carver who asked him to accept the nomination (Saunders, 364).[17] Miller's own history made him a strategic choice for the position: a longtime advocate of freedom of expression, he was a critic of both the restrictions that Soviet totalitarianism placed on intellectuals and the curtailing of domestic freedoms in the United States during the Cold War. His actions had led him to be blacklisted in the entertainment business at home and abroad, to have his passport renewal denied by the U.S. State Department, and to be cited for contempt of Congress in 1957 for refusing to identify alleged Communist writers when called to testify before the House Un-American Activities Committee (the charge was overturned the following year). Miller had not previously been involved with PEN, and his response to the invitation is telling:

> I had a suspicion of being used and wondered suddenly whether our State Department or CIA or equivalent British hands might be stirring this particular stew. . . . PEN stood stuck in the concrete of what I would soon learn were its traditional Cold War anti-Soviet positions, but like the Western governments at this point, it was now trying to bend and acknowledge Eastern Europe as a stable group of societies whose writers might well be permitted new contacts with the West. (*Timebends*, 567, 568)

These moves had resulted in the organization's contemporary efforts to set up a Soviet PEN center. Miller also suspected that "the [U.S.] government might have wanted me to become president of PEN because they couldn't otherwise penetrate the Soviet Union, and they figured that traveling behind me could be their own people" (qtd. in Robins, 314).

According to Saunders, the French PEN center had previously expressed concern about Botsford's appointment as Carver's assistant out of "fear that the Americans were attempting to take over PEN" (363). It now objected to Miller's candidacy and put forth a candidate of its own: Miguel Ángel Asturias, a Guatemalan writer who was currently serving as his nation's ambassador to France. The candidacy was not well received in some quarters: Asturias was a vocal critic of the United States, and Galantière expressed concern about the Guatemalan's anti-U.S. attitudes and his connections to Communists.[18] Michael Josselson, the head of the international secretariat of the CCF, also objected to the nomination and tried to have it blocked, as did Carver (Saunders, 365).

Despite acrimonious debate, Miller was unanimously elected president of International PEN at the Bled congress. The polemics surrounding the failed nomination of Asturias may help to explain the premium put on outreach toward Spanish American writers at the New York congress, which may at some level have been intended as efforts at appeasement. But that would account for only part of PEN's efforts, for it is clear that its officials were well informed about the political and cultural fervor in Latin America and set out to draw both established and up-and-coming writers from the region. In addition to delegates from existing PEN Centers, the PEN American Center invited Neruda and Juan Bosch as headliners from the region. Both choices had obvious and significant political implications, which shall be discussed presently. The PEN American Center also worked to attract talented writers from countries where there were no PEN Centers. In late 1965, Galantière contacted experts on Latin America for the names of writers who best represented contemporary currents in literary activity; he ultimately invited more than forty of the individuals suggested to him.[19]

Concern for the national interest played a strategic role in Galantière's activism. When he wrote to Charles Frankel, assistant secretary of state for educational and cultural affairs, Galantière observed that there was a high level of anti-U.S. sentiment among Latin American intellectuals, who also of course wielded a great deal of political influence. Galantière argued that the Latin Americans who attended the conference would feel included in an international community, which would shift their attention away from more local concerns that presumably included the Cuban Revolution and the support for Socialism throughout the region.[20]

Two of the experts whom Galantière consulted for information on Latin American writers were Robert Wool, the director of the Inter-American Foundation for the Arts, and Lewis Hanke, a professor of Latin American history at Columbia. They too made the case that the participation in the congress of writers from the region could benefit the national interest. In particular, Wool felt that it was important for political reasons to invite Alejo Carpentier, president of the Cuban PEN Center and an outspoken supporter of the Cuban Revolution. Wool was even more interested, for strategic reasons, in the prospect of Bosch's and Neruda's attendance. A politician, novelist, and historian, Bosch had become president of the Dominican Republic in late 1962, following the assassination of dictator Rafael Trujillo, and he had held the position until he was deposed by military coup in September 1963. The succeeding administration had been toppled in April 1965, at which point civil war had broken out. During this tumultuous period, Bosch's supporters had tried to have him reinstated. Fearing that the Dominican Republic would follow in Cuba's footsteps, the Johnson administration had sent troops to prevent Bosch's party from returning to power. The intervention was followed by more political upheaval, although presidential elections were eventually set for June 1966. In the spring of 1966, as the PEN conference was being organized, Bosch was campaigning for reelection. Wool believed, as did Galantière, that having the writer accept the invitation would greatly benefit U.S. interests, no doubt because they believed that it would indicate reconciliation with the United States and movement away from a supposed Communist stance.[21]

Neruda, in turn, was of interest to Wool because his prominence was rising: he was one of the most widely read poets in the United States, and at least four collections of his work had been published in English since 1960. He had been a major attraction at the 1965 PEN congress. He was also an appealing prospect because he was a Communist with numerous followers—political as well as literary. According to Galantière, Wool felt that Neruda's "influence and connections were so wide that the gesture of inviting him (with assurance of a U.S. visa) was itself *politically* useful. It would itself constitute an excellent way of dissuading others from thinking of boycotting the Congress."[22]

At the same time, Wool expressed concern that some of the authors whom he had recommended might have difficulty with McCarran-Walter when trying to enter the United States. Galantière had been working on the visa question for some time and before he extended an invitation to Bosch, he made sure that the State Department had no objections to Bosch's participation in the congress. (Perhaps not surprisingly, however, Bosch never responded to the invitation.) Galantière was more concerned with Neruda, though, who had visited the United States in 1943 but had repeatedly had visa requests denied since then, turning him into an even more vocal critic of the nation. Galantière wrote to Frankel that

> strong cards would be taken out of anti-American hands, the climate in intellectual circles would change . . . if the Chilean Communist poet, Pablo Neruda . . . agreed to come and [was] granted [a visa. Neruda] would no longer be able to go about the world proclaiming that "[t]hey are afraid of me, a poet. Where else does this happen except in a fascist state?" To disarm the most widely read of all living poets in this manner, and to let him see for himself that Americans are not ogres would, I think, be in the American national interest.[23]

State Department officials seem to have been convinced by the argument that the congress and the cultural exchanges that it would enable were "in the national interest." Assistant Secretary of State Harlan Cleveland wrote Galantière that he agreed "with Mr. Farrar's remarks on the influence exerted by writers and on the mutual benefits to be derived from discussions between writers from countries of widely varying political and social backgrounds."[24] Department officials offered to assist with the arrangement of visas: Galantière's contacts in the Eastern European offices said that they were unable to prevent visa applications from being denied when initially reviewed. However, they told Galantière that if PEN provided them with the names of foreign delegates to the conference, they would notify consular officers abroad of the congress's importance to the national interest and have them assist with the visa process, including removing obstacles to approval and hastening the consideration of waivers when necessary.[25] The Cuban Affairs office had initially told Galantière that its decisions would be responses to policy matters rather than the particular individuals put forth for visas.[26] Later, though, the bureau concluded that delegates from the island would be unlikely to harm the United States in word or deed during their visit; the coordinator for Cuban Affairs indicated that the department would process visa applications from Cuban delegates in the same way that it would treat applications from other delegations, and that, in principle, the Cubans would thus be granted visas.[27] On receiving this response, Galantière immediately sent invitations to affiliates of the Cuban PEN Center, including Carpentier.

The State Department was unable to provide direct financial support to the congress, but it did agree to provide other forms of assistance as a demonstration of its commitment to PEN's goals. One officer said that the department could bring between twenty and thirty foreign delegates to the United States under the aegis of an exchange program for intellectual leaders, timing their trips to coincide with the conference. (Ultimately, PEN did not take the department up on this offer.) The United States Information Agency (USIA) agreed to provide publicity for the conference in its magazines, motion picture service, and television newsreels.[28] Finally, Secretary of State Rusk agreed to serve as an honorary sponsor of the congress, after being reassured that nothing at the conference would be said or done that would put him in a politically awkward position.[29]

In the end, a modification of U.S. visa policies made the task of facilitating access to New York City much simpler. As discussed in the preceding chapter, the State and Justice Departments announced in May 1966 that group waivers would be automatically granted to conference participants who would otherwise be denied visas under Section 212(a)(28) of the McCarran-Walter Act. The first group waiver was granted to the PEN congress. As participants confirmed their attendance, Galantiére forwarded their names to the Departments of State and Justice for the approval of waivers as needed. For the organizers of the conference and most of its participants, the group waiver was the end of the story: there is no record of conference participants being denied visas under the new policy, so if the Cuban and Soviet delegations did not attend the 1966 congress, it was because they chose—or, according to some reports, received orders from above—not to.

The State and Justice Departments, however, remained interested in several of the participants, viewing their presence as potentially "contrary" or "prejudicial to the public interest." Several weeks before the group waiver policy was approved, the U.S. embassy in Chile had recommended an advance waiver of Neruda's inadmissibility "so that the Communists would not be able to capitalize again on the portrayal of Neruda as a 'persecuted progressive.'"[30] Like Galantière, State Department officials were keenly aware that a visa denial would give Neruda an opportunity to denounce the United States publicly, so he was granted a visa in order to preempt any criticism by him of U.S. immigration policy.[31] Additionally, J. Edgar Hoover had been following Neruda's activities since the early 1950s at least, so the FBI carefully monitored his visit and continued to send reports on his activities to the director for months afterward. The Washington field office sent a biographical sketch of the poet to Hoover, FBI headquarters, and the New York office that focused on the evolution of his Communist beliefs and political activism and that deemed him "indefatigable, suave and a good speaker . . . an excellent propaganda tool for the Communists."[32] The FBI director ordered the New York office to find out the details of his itinerary, adding, "In view of the subject's Communist Party affiliations, New York should alert appropriate Latin American and Communist Party sources in order to be advised in the event subject's activities affect the security interest of the United States."[33] The FBI also alerted the White House to Neruda's presence, "in view of his prominence in the Chilean Communist Party and his easy entry into this country."[34]

From the beginning of the planning through the conference itself, then, PEN sought out and was shadowed by official (and, at times, covert) U.S. oversight. At the same time, the organization reached out to experts on Latin America in order to ensure that the region's cultural activity was accurately represented. Both interest groups agreed, for the most part, that the participation of Latin American writers would serve the U.S. national interest. Their ultimate goals were radically different, though, and both U.S. officials and conference organizers failed to take into consideration the importance of the conference to the writers themselves.

The Conference

The conference took place June 12–18 in the Loeb Student Center at New York University. The official theme was "The Writer as Independent Spirit." The topic had been proposed by a committee that included Edward Albee, Ralph Ellison, John Hersey, and several other PEN members. The committee sought a theme that would "provide a springboard for important discussion and speeches; does not enter into the political area; does not repeat previous themes, and honors the writer as a creative being" (qtd. in Chute, 82). And yet, in a climate in which art—in particular, artistic freedom— was viewed as being subordinated to a totalitarian system in the Soviet Union, the topic had obvious political implications, which PEN officials took pains both to acknowledge and deflect. Farrar, for example, wrote to Rusk that the topic was an important one in the current political climate, even as he emphasized the fact that PEN was not a political association, and that it was not treating the topic as a strictly political one.[35]

Indeed, PEN officials worried that political issues might arise that would thwart the spirit of open exchange that they hoped to foster at the conference—or that might contravene their pledges to the secretary of state and the Ford Foundation that neither would be compromised by political discussions at the conference. Organizers were also concerned that the conference would become a forum for decrying the Sinyavsky-Daniel show trial of early 1966, in which two Soviet dissident writers had been convicted of "anti-Soviet activity" and sentenced to hard labor. The incident had set off international protests and, because of the restrictions on freedom of expression that it reflected, it had become a stumbling block in contemporary negotiations to set up a PEN center in the Soviet Union. In the end, the case did not come up in the public forums (although Miller did condemn it in a business meeting) and, for the most part, people set aside their differences to allow the conference to proceed.

Despite the ideological divides among participants—according to Fuentes, even Miller confessed that "I disagree with three quarters of what has been said in this Congress" ("El P.E.N.: Entierro," 50)—only two public political interventions of note seem to have taken place. First, Valery Tarsis, a Russian writer who had been stripped of his citizenship and sent into exile for anti-Communist remarks, strongly criticized the Soviet Union and called for a "hot war" to defeat Communism, as well as for atom bombing the nation. His speech was protested by fellow participants and he was rebuked by Miller for violating the conference's goals of encouraging diversity of beliefs ("Soviet Writers"). According to Fuentes, Miller's response indicated that "this is not a platform of war, whether hot or cold. We have all been indoctrinated within a single cause. Our goal here is to restore diversity. The PEN Club is a free and open platform" ("El P.E.N.: Entierro," 57). Second, during a session titled "The Writer as Public Figure," Neruda and Silone got into a heated debate. When Silone declared the intellectual to be "the leader against the totalitarian state," Neruda felt singled out by the remark and challenged Silone's characterization of the Socialist states as totalitarian. Neruda further took Silone to task for introducing the Cold War into the discussion, and asserted that he had met more happy writers in Socialist countries than in capitalist ones (Gilroy; see also Yglesias). The exchange ended with both men conceding that they did not want to contribute further to the Cold War, although all subsequent panelists except Miller attacked Neruda for his declaration.

Latin American writers were prominent in activities throughout the week. The conference opened with an extremely successful public reading by Neruda—his first ever in the United States—at the Poetry Center of the 92nd Street Y. The *New York Times* reported that "Archibald MacLeish, who introduced the Chilean poet . . . expressed the opinion that Neruda should be considered 'an American poet' since the word 'American' belonged to both continents and since South America was too small to lay exclusive claim to such expansive myth-making" (Rodman). MacLeish also used his introduction to denounce the State Department's exclusionary visa policy. One of Neruda's translators brought the audience to its feet by declaring the Chilean the greatest living poet anywhere. Neruda read a selection of pieces that spanned his career, making certain to include several anti-U.S. and anti-imperial poems, among them "United Fruit Co." as well as others protesting the U.S. role in the Vietnam War. The reading was an event that Fuentes characterized to Neruda as "a victory to have read in the heart of the empire the verses that we heard from you[.] Is it not a victory for everyone that the writers from the North American Left stood up to their country's official bureaucracy and demanded that you be allowed to enter? . . . Is it not a victory that these honest, hounded men, friends of Latin America, feel that they are not alone, that they can count on our support?" ("Correspondance," 73). During the rest of the week, Latin American writers were well represented on the round tables that were the cornerstones of the conference—indeed, there was no round table that did not feature a writer from the region: Brazilian poet Haroldo de Campos spoke in the session called "The Writer in the Electronic Age" along with R. Buckminster Fuller, Richmond Lattimore, Marshall McLuhan, and Norman Podhoretz; Fuentes and his compatriot Ramón Parrés participated with Ralph Ellison in the session titled "Literature and the Social Sciences on the Nature of Contemporary Man"; and João Guimarães Rosa of Brazil and Victoria Ocampo of Argentina appeared with publisher William Jovanovich and Melvin Lasky of the CCF on the panel for the session "The Writer as Collaborator in Other Men's Purposes" (Ocampo was also present at the congress as a vice president of PEN International).[36] Neruda was originally scheduled to participate in the panel for "The Writer in the Electronic Age," but he protested that it was not an appropriate subject for him (according to one observer, some of the Latin Americans "thought that this was P.E.N.'s way of neutralizing Neruda") and he was reassigned to the aforementioned panel with Silone (Yglesias, 53).

But for the Latin American writers, as well as many others, the most memorable event at the congress was one that was not in the original program. Despite the rising international prominence of Latin American literature, many of the writers from the region had not yet met in person. The PEN congress provided them with a unique opportunity to do so. The conference also afforded the writers the opportunity to help PEN realize one of its own goals: opening itself up to a broader constituency. Fuentes relates how Miller proclaimed in his inaugural speech that one of PEN's goals was to universalize culture ("El P.E.N.: Entierro," 58). Fuentes, who had also attended the Bled congress, had known Miller for several years, and when the two men went out to dinner with Neruda and Mexican writers Homero Aridjis and Marco Antonio Montes de Oca, the group proposed a session on Latin American literature (ibid.). Miller agreed and asked Rodríguez Monegal to moderate.

Altogether, twenty-three Latin American writers from seven countries attended the conference, and many of them spoke at the session, which was open to all participants—provided that they spoke in either English or French, PEN's official languages.[37] The problems that each writer identified were echoed repeatedly. Writers observed that high levels of illiteracy resulted in few publishing opportunities, small print runs, and equally small markets. These factors, in turn, hampered the professionalization of writers, who were forced to support themselves with other jobs, leaving little time for writing. Speakers addressed the problem of isolation and the difficulty of fostering the pan–Latin American literary tradition that the Boom sought to cultivate when there was little circulation of works within or between the different nations. They also spoke about underdevelopment and political commitment—the writer's responsibility to make changes by challenging censorship, taking up the cause of the poor and marginalized, and fighting for justice. Vargas Llosa put forth a number of ideas that he would include in his famous speech, "La literatura es fuego," which he gave upon being awarded the Premio Rómulo Gallegos the following year. He was particularly eloquent on the marginalization of writers and literature in Peru, claiming that in his country

> the literary vocation leads, almost inexorably, to the threshold of revolution or to a political awakening. In effect, if, by virtue of being a writer, a man . . . is exiled from his society and placed on the margins of everyday life . . . he will find it difficult to be a part of that society. His natural attitude will be one of rebellion, of questioning his society. . . . This solidarity between the writer and the disenfranchised forces many writers to become politicians. (qtd. in "Papel del escritor," 28–29)

Several writers acknowledged the importance of PEN in bringing them together and helping them to overcome the obstacles that they faced. In this spirit, Neruda called on Vargas Llosa to found a PEN center on his return to Peru. Manuel Balbontín, president of the Chilean PEN club, presented several proposals to the international organization: that it lobby to have Latin American and Spanish literature included in high school and university curricula, that it urge large publishers to translate and publish selected Latin

American works in English, and that it set up a committee with representatives from Latin America to compile a collection of key literary works from the region for translation. Miller closed the session by offering PEN's services in attempting to address these issues.[38]

Though the visitors to New York hailed from different nations, the spirit of transnational camaraderie that characterized the Boom was evident throughout the conference. As Rodríguez Monegal wrote, the congress "demonstrated that at this time there is a Latin American literature that operates above national divisions and that has international force and strength" ("Diario"). Writers likewise seemed to view themselves not as representing their own nations, but as part of a Latin American delegation. PEN officials treated them as a group representing a region, too.

Latin Americans were given pride of place at the conference in other ways as well. Miller, for example, spent quite a bit of time socializing with them during the week, and he praised the impromptu round table as the most significant act of the conference when he delivered his closing speech (Rodríguez Monegal, "Diario"); years later, he singled it out as "the most encouraging and useful session" of the assembly (595). (The official history of the PEN American Center's first fifty years likewise deems the session "the most remarkable of these Round Tables" [Chute, 82].) Rodríguez Monegal wrote that the conference marked Miller's discovery of Latin American literature ("Diario"). In fact, the Latin American writers used the congress, created in the shadow of and in many ways enabled by the United States' hemispheric Cold War agenda, to open the eyes of writers around the world to their work, and to make connections that would serve them well as their fame grew over the next few years.

Backlash: Publicity and Politics

In terms of both publicity and material support for the promotion of Latin American literature in the United States, the PEN congress was a windfall. It gave writers the opportunity to meet one another, as well as colleagues from the United States and elsewhere, and to make contacts with publishers, critics, and others interested in their work. The night before Neruda's poetry recital, MacLeish hosted a party at his home to which he invited Galantière, Miller, Neruda, Neruda's translator Ben Belitt, U.S. poets Robert Lowell and Mark van Doren, and Spanish poet Jorge Guillén. Another night, Wool gave a cocktail party at his house, to which he invited U.S. critics and publishers as well as the Latin Americans. Neruda took advantage of being in the United States to visit Washington, DC, where he recorded some of his poetry for the Library of Congress collection; he also gave a reading at the University of California, Berkeley, that was attended by several Beat poets (see Conclusion).

The conference received widespread media coverage. The *New York Times* reported on it almost daily, focusing in particular on the Cold War dramas that played out at the congress, such as the Soviet delegation's last-minute pullout from the event in response to concerns that the Sinyavsky-Daniel trial would be a topic of debate, the confrontation between Silone and Neruda, and later a Soviet condemnation of PEN for allowing the anti-Soviet Tarsis to participate. The newspaper also published a feature story on Neruda in July that was no doubt prompted by his high-profile success at the conference (Rodman). The *Nation* published an article on Neruda's activities in New York as well as an essay on the conference by a Hungarian writer and PEN official (Boldiszar, "View from the East"); the journal also promised to include more articles on Latin American literature in the future, and started moving toward that goal by including a review by Alan Cheuse of two novels by Brazilian writers in the same issue as the articles on PEN. Journalists and writers alike repeatedly hailed the presence of Neruda and other authors from Latin America and Eastern Europe as a major accomplishment; they also praised PEN for having secured the necessary visas, viewing this as emblematic of the organization's commitment to upholding writers' freedom of expression. Neruda's presence in particular brought tremendous cachet to the conference. According to Chute, he "was applauded and interviewed and followed about everywhere, and to the young people in particular his presence was one of the literary events of the year" (82). Neruda himself deemed the conference "the best international meeting of writers to date" and congratulated PEN on being "the first institution to break down the Cold War boundaries between the capitalist and socialist worlds during the postwar period" (qtd. in Rodríguez Monegal, "El P.E.N. Club," 87).

The round table devoted to Latin American literature was widely publicized in U.S. media directed at Hispanic readers and in newspapers and journals throughout Latin America. Rodríguez Monegal, for example, published a chronicle of his experiences at the conference in *Mundo Nuevo* later that year ("Diario del P.E.N. Club") as well as a transcript of the round table on Latin American literature (see "Papel del escritor en América Latina"). Journalist Rita Guibert covered the conference for *"Life" en español*, the Spanish edition of *Life* magazine (which also featured Hispanic topics), as did Miller's wife, Inge Morath, a photographer with the magazine. The

August 1 issue of *"Life" en español* included an interview with Neruda by Guibert and an article by Fuentes, "El P.E.N.: Entierro de la guerra fría en la literatura" [The PEN congress: The burial of the Cold War in literature]. In the latter, Fuentes hailed the conference for allowing writers to join in productive dialogue with political consequences: "There, the practical conviction that cultural isolation and lack of communication only help international tensions, triumphed" (57). Moreover, the conference represented for Fuentes the culmination of a long process of change and rapprochement:

> Twenty years ago, only a science fiction writer would have foreseen that, in the brave new world of 1966, a Chilean Communist poet would be acclaimed by thousands of people in New York, Washington, and Berkeley, California. Another writer of stories . . . might have imagined that an exiled Russian writer would launch . . . furious anathemas against the Soviet government, but not even with H. G. Wells's imagination would he have been able to foresee that the public would protest vigorously against these warlike reprimands. A third dreamer might have located in New York a group of leftist writers who abstained from attacking the United States. And, finally, a new Jules Verne might have been able to describe the improbable spectacle of five hundred writers—conservatives, anarchists, communists, liberals, socialists—gathered together not to hurl accusations, nor underline differences, nor to announce dogmas, but, rather, to discuss concrete problems, recognize a community of spirit, and accept a diversity of intentions. . . . The difference is enormous. Twenty years ago, a leftist novelist from Latin America would have taken advantage of the occasion to launch an attack against the United States. And a North American novelist, even with—or perhaps because of—his liberal credentials, would not have passed up the opportunity to make an anti-Communist contribution to the debate. (57)

Finally, Fuentes described the conference as "a final good-bye to the late Senator McCarthy" (ibid.).

The writer also praised the conference in a less public forum: a letter to his friend José Donoso, who had been unable to attend. While Fuentes was not above making critical remarks about some of his fellow Latin American writers, he spoke in superlatives about others, noting the accomplishments of Neruda and his compatriot and fellow poet Nicanor Parra, as well as those of Vargas Llosa.[39] Fuentes further raved about his meetings with Edward Albee, Saul Bellow, and Miller. He came away from the event profoundly impressed by the support that he had found among his friends there, as well as by the literary environment in the United States, which he compared favorably to his experiences in Europe. Fuentes's article and letter alike attest to the power of the "open society" in serving as a mode of unofficial cultural diplomacy. Both texts are, additionally, examples of the process of transmission by which opinion leaders disseminate positive views of a nation both to their friends and to a wider audience.

Not all the publicity for the congress was positive, however. Fuentes's reports of the passing of Cold War tensions were exaggerated, as soon became evident. In late July, the Union of Soviet Writers—an official group—issued a public denunciation of PEN for allowing anti-Soviet and anti-Communist writers to speak at the congress ("Soviet Writers"). Their declaration suggested that the last-minute withdrawal of the Soviet delegation from the conference had not been because of concern that these writers would face challenges about the Sinyavsky-Daniel case, as was reported in the U.S. press at the time, but rather as a protest against the inclusion of Tarsis in the program (ibid.). At approximately the same time, newspapers in Havana published an open letter titled "Carta abierta de los intelectuales cubanos a Pablo Neruda" in which a number of Cuban writers, including Cuban PEN Center president Carpentier, director of Casa de las Américas Roberto Fernández Retamar, and poet Nicolás Guillén—none of whom had responded to invitations to the conference—denounced the presence of Latin American writers at the event.[40] The Cubans declared that the United States' authorization of visas for the Latin Americans and other leftists had been politically expedient. They decried intellectual exchanges between the United States and Latin America as part of a concerted "castration program" and claimed that the writers' participation in the conference could be presented as reflecting an easing up of Cold War tensions and used as a means of neutralizing opposition to U.S. politics. The Cubans further criticized Neruda for his supposed collusion with the United States' efforts to neutralize the "total revolution" that they felt was the only way left to liberate their countries from U.S. imperialism, and they excoriated him for betraying the Cuban Revolution ("Carta abierta," 31).

The letter also brought Rodríguez Monegal and Fuentes into the fray. The former was already under attack for his involvement with *Mundo Nuevo*, and the scandal surrounding the journal tainted the perception of the PEN congress in revolutionary circles. The conference took place just weeks after the *New York Times* broke the story on covert CIA funding of the CCF that implicated *Mundo Nuevo*. *Casa de las Américas* and *Marcha* took Rodríguez Monegal to task for his alleged complicity with U.S. policy makers and their political agendas—accusations that the letter from the Cubans also leveled. (Had the Cubans known the details of Neruda's post-conference trip to Washington, DC, they would no doubt have criticized him for it too: the poet had been invited to DC by Poet Laureate Stephen Spender, who was also a founder and editor of the CCF's British journal, *Encounter*.) The letter also described *"Life" en español* as an instrument of the U.S. establishment and an "organ of imperialist propaganda," and condemned the periodical for its attacks on Cuba and its support of the U.S. intervention in the Dominican Republic. The authors of the letter excoriated Fuentes for his optimism, asserting that "it is unacceptable for us to sing the praise of a supposed peaceful existence or to speak of the end of the Cold War in any field at the same time that North American troops, which have just assaulted the Congo and Santo Domingo, savagely attack Vietnam and prepare to do it anew in Cuba" ("Carta abierta," 30).

Many of the charges made in the letter were further developed in a round table featuring Fernández Retamar, Edmundo Desnoes, Lisandro Otero, and Ambrosio Fornet that was broadcast by Radio Habana Cuba on 10 August 1966, and later published in *Casa de las Américas* under the title "Sobre la penetración intelectual del imperialismo yanqui en América Latina" (On the intellectual penetration of Yankee imperialism in Latin America). Fornet also addressed these issues in "New World en español," an article in *Casa de las Américas* that accused *Mundo Nuevo* of attempting to neutralize and depoliticize Latin American intellectuals. In the article, Fornet additionally criticized Fuentes for his collaboration with *Mundo Nuevo* and further accused him of frivolity and a lack of concern for social and political issues in Latin America.

Rodríguez Monegal had been under siege for months and responded to the letter from the Cubans in an article in *Mundo Nuevo* detailing the Cold War tensions during and after the conference ("El P.E.N. Club contra la guerra fría"). The other targets of the letter, however, were unlikely ones and were taken by surprise. Neruda was not accustomed to having to defend himself against other supporters of Cuba and he was profoundly shaken. He sent the Cubans a telegram in which he reiterated his commitment to the revolution and called on them to work together with him toward "the necessary continental, anti-imperialist unity among writers and all revolutionary forces" ("Habla el poeta," 31). Fuentes, who at this time still supported the Cuban Revolution, was playing a key role in Rodríguez Monegal's networking and promotional activities in support of the Boom, and one wonders if some of the impetus behind the letter from the Cubans stemmed in part from this collaboration. In any case, the matter frustrated Fuentes greatly, for he found himself on the one hand accused of selling out the revolution and, on the other, repeatedly denied visas to enter the United States because of his support of Castro and other leftist causes. He made no public response to the letter, but he did pull out of writing an introduction for Knopf's new edition of Carpentier's *The Lost Steps*, because he believed that his contribution would be viewed by Carpentier and his compatriots as a sign of political opposition, and he did not wish to invoke their wrath again.[41] The letter from the Cuban writers and these authors' responses to it thus reflected an incipient breakdown in the political unity that had heretofore held the left together. The Padilla affair of 1971 would once and for all splinter support for the revolution among intellectuals from Latin America, the United States, and Europe. Although nowhere near as high profile, the letter and its aftermath foreshadowed the affair and the deep schism it created among supporters of Cuba.

"In the National Interest"

The Cubans' letter to Neruda in 1966 was a response to the increasingly hard line that Castro was taking toward dissent. The letter also came on the heels of criticism by Castro of the Chilean Communist Party, which was on a more "revisionist" and less "revolutionary" course at this time. Neruda was a member of the Chilean party and some suspected that the letter was directed at the party as well as at, and through, the poet.

The 1966 incident came with a price tag for the revolution, and what might have been seen as corresponding side benefits for the U.S. national interest. It marked a turning point for Fuentes, whose support of Cuba cooled significantly after this episode. Aside from feeling personally insulted, he was indignant at the attack on Neruda, expressing to a friend his disbelief that the poet's many years of advocating for leftist causes did not shield him from such criticism. He further lamented the inability of some of his fellow writers of the left to understand that isolating writers from Latin America and the United States only hurt their shared interests.[42] He vowed at this time not to return to Cuba until Fernández Retamar was no longer at the helm of cultural activities, and to this day he has kept his word, though he has continued to defend the nation's right to self-determination.[43]

Neruda had been a longtime defender of Socialist revolution, but the letter from the Cubans left him hamstrung, with his ability to support Cuba severely compromised. As his longtime friend Jorge Edwards wrote, "How could he continue as a Communist militant and at the same time direct his heavy artillery, of proven efficacy, against his colleagues, who represented a young revolution, the only one on the American continent, the only one that spoke our language?" (*Adiós*, 149). The schism had a ripple effect: Edwards further explains, "When we . . . learned of the letter, we Latin American writers felt ourselves divided between our respect and admiration for Neruda and our unconditional support of the Cuban Revolution" (*Persona*, 36). On a personal level, the poet never completely forgave the Cubans. He never again interacted with Carpentier, even though the two had been friends for years, and even though this avoidance required careful choreography later in their lives when Neruda, as Salvador Allende's ambassador to France, had to visit the Cuban embassy in Paris, where Carpentier was the cultural attaché (*Adiós*, 150). Neruda also took oblique revenge on Guillén in his memoirs, where he refers to Spanish poet Jorge Guillén as "Guillén (the good one: the Spanish one)" (*Confieso*, 165).

PEN officials carefully followed the fallout from the letter. According to a report presented to the Ford Foundation after the conference, "Cuban and other Communist Party reproaches against Neruda brought articles by other Latin Americans in his defense, and in refutation of the charges leveled against the United States in the communist press." This observation was, however, but a small part of PEN officials' efforts to spin the conference's accomplishments for the foundation in terms of their benefit to the national interest. Conference organizers complimented themselves on the attendance of foreign intellectuals whose role as public figures could be "seen in the newly developing countries where, because writers form a high proportion of the educated social stratum, they fill leading posts in diplomacy, ministries of education and information, institutions of learning, radio and television stations, and the mass as well as the quality journals." They also stated that participants saw "the fact that delegates from the East German PEN Center could be present at the first congress they had ever attended on non-communist soil, and that the world-renowned communist Chilean poet, Pablo Neruda, was able, through our intercession, to come to the United States for the first time since 1943 . . . as confirmation that the U.S. Government, though it defrayed a part of the costs, did not intervene to lend the congress a propaganda cast." Finally, they claimed that "by arranging the presence of twenty-three prominent Latin American writers . . . American P.E.N. dissipated a cloud that had long hung over U.S.-Latin-

American relations in literary and intellectual circles, at least to the extent that for those writers the United States has ceased to be symbolized exclusively by the 'big business' whipping boys of the militant anti-Yanqui."[44]

After 1966: PEN and Latin American Literature

The 1966 congress marked a turning point for Latin American writers' visibility in the United States. At the same time, International PEN itself was profoundly affected by the Latin American activity at the conference, and the organization made a commitment to prioritize matters concerning Latin American literature over the next few years. In 1967, the PEN American Center called on the organization's international executive committee to pursue the initiatives proposed at the round table in New York, focusing in particular on stimulating activity in extant Latin American centers and on founding new ones.[45] In the following months, a new center was formed in Puerto Rico, while writers in Mexico and Venezuela worked to reactivate national centers that had been inactive. In 1970, the PEN American Center organized the first conference on translation to be held in the United States, with a program featuring presentations by key figures in the Latin American literary scene such as Gregory Rabassa, whose translation of *One Hundred Years of Solitude* had just placed García Márquez on the *New York Times* best-seller list; John Macrae III, the head of Dutton publishers and an active proponent of Latin American literature; and Frank MacShane, director of the Writing Division at Columbia University, who over the years devoted considerable attention to Latin American writers and their translators (see Chapter 3 for a discussion of the Writing Division). The center also sponsored several conferences focusing specifically on Latin American literature.

One of the most interesting of the possibilities stemming from the increasing prominence of Latin American literature in the organization is what could be considered the road not taken. In 1969, Miller asked Fuentes to consider succeeding him as president of PEN International. Fuentes and Miller had known each other for a number of years, and after the New York congress, Fuentes had asked Miller on several occasions to intercede on behalf of fellow writers who were imprisoned or under pressure from their governments. Fuentes's activism mirrored Miller's own commitment to defending writers' freedom of expression, and no doubt factored into his choice of successor. So did Miller's desire to raise the profile of Latin American literature within PEN and to bring together writers from behind the Iron Curtain with those from the West. "I believe," Miller wrote, "that as time goes on it will become more and more important to maintain an arena where the three worlds can meet without being swallowed up by the ideological conflicts which will of course continue for a long time to come." Fuentes, he thought,

> would be invaluable as the President both because of what I know of your attitudes, and as well because you are multilingual and could place new emphasis on the problems of Latin America and the emerging world. I tried with some success to generate activity in Latin America, and I believe you would be the best man to enlarge it and give it direction. Also, you are a real bridge between the Old and New Worlds and this too is extremely important. The coming years will be crucial for what P.E.N. has tried to maintain in the world, especially the as yet incomplete bridge-building to the Socialist camp. I hope you will be able to accept the job.[46]

Fuentes was profoundly moved by the offer. On the one hand, he was committed to the direction toward which Miller had steered the organization. On the other, he was currently having difficulties with his own government: his opposition to the Mexican administration had recently led its leaders to crack down on both the publication of his work in Mexico and the production of films based on his novels. Fuentes had also incurred the wrath of both the Soviet Union and the United States: he had been declared *persona non grata* by the Soviet Writer's Union for his denunciation of the Czech invasion and his support for Czech writers, and the incident where he had been barred from entering Puerto Rico under McCarran-Walter had taken place just weeks before Miller wrote to him. Thus, he wondered if he would indeed be in a position to build the bridges that Miller had indicated and otherwise further PEN's interests.[47]

Fuentes's relationship to Cuba was also a concern. Clearly thinking about the open letter to Neruda following the 1966 congress, the Mexican shared with Miller his concern about the direction in which Cuba was heading. On the one hand, he believed that the situation should be denounced. On the other, he realized that this would support official U.S. anti-Cuba efforts and additionally put him in a position where he would have to take a public stance against the revolution, which he was reluctant to do.

In the end, Fuentes declined the invitation—not, at least primarily, for political reasons but rather in order to focus on his writing.[48] In his stead, he proposed Vargas Llosa, who he felt would be an outstanding choice given his fluency in English, Spanish, and French, his cosmopolitanism, and his sensitivity to the concerns of intellectuals in the developing world. This was, however, a suggestion that would have to wait. In 1969, French poet Pierre Emmanuel was elected president of the organization. The choice stirred up Cold War tensions within PEN and raised concerns about its apolitical nature among insiders and outsiders alike, for Emmanuel was at the time director of the CCF's successor, the International Association for Cultural Freedom. Even in the waning years of the CCF, its remnants managed to retain their hold on PEN International.

Another testament to the growing primacy of Latin American literature in the organization was the PEN American Center's 1972 invitation to Neruda to be the keynote speaker at a dinner celebrating its fiftieth anniversary. Thomas Fleming, president of the center, wrote to Neruda that since the 1966 congress, "the emphasis in the American P.E.N. has been on a strong desire to improve our contacts with the writers of the third world. We feel that you would have much of value to tell us, and the American public, on this subject." Fleming closed the invitation with what was no doubt a veiled reference to the poet's visa situation: "Without the least desire to pressure you, but because we feel it is important to prepare for your visit well in advance, we would appreciate hearing from you as soon as possible."[49] Neruda's acceptance of the invitation sent the center into action. PEN officials immediately began to lobby the State Department to grant the writer a visa—a task further complicated by the fact that Neruda was serving as ambassador to France for Allende's Socialist government. Kirsten Michalski, the center's executive secretary, consulted the U.S. Mission to the United Nations to ascertain the best strategy for securing the visa. She informed Fleming that she was advised "to stress that although Pablo Neruda is the Ambassador from Chile to France, he is coming here strictly on a cultural visit, and he has been invited by P.E.N., as a poet and that he is the most recent winner of the Nobel prize in literature"; she also counseled Fleming "to write a very brief, flowery note to the American Ambassador . . . trusting that His Excellency will do whatever is in his power to facilitate the obtaining of a visa. . . . I think we can then . . . say we have done whatever possible to get Mr. Neruda and his wife to these shores without any unnecessary hindrance."[50] Fleming followed her instructions to the letter, assuring officials that Neruda's "visit here will be strictly nonpolitical and totally cultural. We have invited him, as one of the great poets of our time, as well as a leading voice of the so-called 'third world' to give the main speech at our dinner. Almost certainly he will stress the purpose of P.E.N.—free communication between the writers of the world, no matter what their political orientation."[51] Responses from State Department officials were cautious: Neruda's request would be looked at quickly, but no decision could be made until an application had been received.[52] Nevertheless, the reassurance that "there seems to be no reason to believe . . . that the decision will be any different from that reached in 1966" proved true, and Neruda had no trouble receiving a visa.[53]

Neruda's visit was a great success. It was his first trip to the United States since the 1966 congress and he was very enthusiastically received. His principal commitment was the anniversary dinner, where Miller introduced the poet as "the father of contemporary Latin-American literature" (Raymont, "Neruda Opens Visit"). Fleming's promise that the man who in his official, ambassadorial capacity had publicly accused the United States just months before of attempting to overthrow Allende's government (Raymont, "Solzhenitsyn's Nobel Dispute") would be making a "strictly nonpolitical and totally cultural" visit was almost immediately voided. (Politics, were, indeed, present throughout the evening, such as when Fleming read a greeting from President Nixon to Neruda that drew boos and hisses from the audience [Raymont, "Neruda Opens Visit"].)[54] Neruda's speech did speak to PEN's support of "free communication between the writers of the world, no matter what their political orientation," and closed with a paean to the organization for bringing writers together "across political, linguistic and racial boundaries" and thus paving a path for the establishment of "one uninterrupted universal community of thought." However, the heart of his address was a pointed discussion of the obstacles that Chile's Socialist government faced. Chile, Neruda proclaimed, "is in the course of carrying out a revolutionary transformation of its social structure with true dignity, and within the strict framework of our legal constitution. . . . As a nation, we chose our path for ourselves, and for that very reason we are resolved to pursue it to the end. But secret opponents use every kind of weapon to turn our destiny aside. . . . Dollars and darts, telephone and telegraph services: each seems to serve!" He spoke of a meeting with Chile's creditors to renegotiate the nation's external debt where the creditors "seemed to be taking aim in order to bring Chile tumbling down." Invoking Samuel Taylor Coleridge's "Rime of the Ancient Mariner" and comparing Chile to the albatross, Neruda singled out the U.S. representative at the meeting for "conceal[ing] an arrow underneath his business papers—ready to aim it at the albatross's heart!" But, he cautioned, the creditor should be reminded "that the sailor who perpetrated such a crime was doomed to carry the heavy corpse of the slain albatross hanging from his neck—to all eternity."[55] His remarks touched a chord with his audience: when he finished, he received a standing ovation (Leonard, "Letter").

Nor were politics far from the poet's other New York appearances. In addition to the speech at the PEN dinner, Neruda gave poetry readings at the 92nd Street Y and the United Nations; he also spoke to MacShane's writing seminar at Columbia. Henry Raymont of the *New York Times*, who interviewed the poet and attended several of these events, published several articles on the visit. Raymont suggested that "the rather mild political content of his public appearances . . . seemed to reflect his own ambiguity about the visit, combining as it does the role of a cultural envoy with that of a Chilean diplomat" (Raymont, "Solzhenitsyn's Nobel Dispute"). The journalist noted that the poet "generally confined his remarks to general allusions to Chile's economic difficulties, which have been heightened by Washington reluctance to give his Government further credits" (ibid.). However, politically charged remarks that he made regarding Aleksandr Solzhenitsyn generated both publicity and controversy. Solzhenitsyn had won the Nobel Prize for Literature in 1970 but had not been able to receive the award out of concern that the Soviet government would not let him return if he traveled to Stockholm. When asked by a reporter about Solzhenitsyn's predicament, Neruda avowed that he had "no intention of becoming an instrument for anti-Soviet propaganda" and referred to the situation as "a big bore" (qtd. in Raymont, "Solzhenitsyn's Nobel Dispute"). His remark was condemned by the Poetry Society of America—an organization that the *New York Times* characterized as "not noted for its militancy"—whose president retorted that "no censorship or any other form of oppression of the untrammeled functioning of the literary arts anywhere in the world is a matter of indifference to writers" (Lask). The dust had yet to settle when Neruda's visit ended with a departure that was itself a political statement of sorts: from New York, he headed to Moscow, where he was to serve on the committee for the Lenin Peace Prize. In this, Neruda's final trip to the United States, we see once again the elements that had combined to make the 1966 conference such a success for Latin American writers: PEN's commitment to supporting their work, and its efforts to play to Cold War tensions when securing visas for the writers while nevertheless striving to give them a prominent platform in the United States where they could speak freely on politics and literature alike.

FOR U.S. OFFICIALS, PEN OFFICERS, and Latin American writers alike, the PEN congress had a number of unintended consequences. For the Latin

Americans, the conference was both a beginning and an end. It greatly enhanced the visibility of the writers and their work in the United States. At the same time, even as the writers attempted to create an image of a transnational movement unified by and grounded in its support for Cuba, the event brought to the foreground tensions among differences in leftism that, in turn, precipitated political rifts that forever changed several key writers' relationships with the revolution. Thus, the aftermath of the letter from the Cubans anticipated the polarization of attitudes toward the island that became more pronounced after 1971. From the perspective of Cold War cultural diplomacy, the conference was a paradox, and all parties in the tug-of-war went home declaring victory. On the one hand, the congress was one of many staging grounds in the battle for "the hearts and minds" of foreign intellectuals, and it was extremely successful in its goal of generating symbolic capital for the United States throughout the hemisphere and beyond. On the other, it functioned as a venue that allowed writers from an "at risk" region, many of whom were drawn together precisely by their support for Cuba, to deepen their relationships and pursue their ideals within the political sphere of the antagonist. Official U.S. interests saw the Latin American writers as instruments—as cultural diplomats and opinion leaders whose goodwill was to be cultivated as a means of influencing public opinion in their native lands. Despite PEN's final assessment of the conference's effects on the writers, though, the latter eluded the reach of the United States' Cold War agenda. The Latin American authors viewed themselves as ambassadors representing their region to the West, and they did their utmost at the conference to usher Latin American literature into an international mainstream, erasing once and for all the label with which PEN had previously identified them: "Peripheral Writers (Latin-America)." It is a testament to these authors' success that Vargas Llosa, who attended the conference as an up-and-coming writer from a country that did not have its own center, was nominated for the presidency of PEN International by the PEN American Center—most likely at the urging of Miller—and became president of the organization in 1976.[56]

As a case study, the PEN congress demonstrates the limitations of scholarly approaches confined to the national or regional boundaries set by area studies that are themselves products of the Cold War. It further establishes the necessity of redefining the parameters of study of Latin American—and U.S.—literature as hemispheric rather than regional or national. Latin Americanist literary criticism has traditionally emphasized the opportunities for networking and visibility that the conference afforded Latin American authors, as well as the attack on Neruda. These are important to understanding the history of the Boom, but the emphasis on them overlooks the considerable role that the hemispheric agenda of U.S. Cold War nationalism played in enabling the conference in general and the attendance of the Latin Americans in particular. However, a study that focused only on PEN's and the State Department's courting of Latin American writers as opinion molders would deny these writers the agency—and the agenda—that was clearly in evidence in their efforts to establish Latin American literature as a phenomenon worthy of international attention. The congress brought together individuals from different nations and regions in symbiotic relationships even as it laid bare both the contradictory forces at play in U.S. Cold War cultural politics and the schisms in the Latin American left.

3

Latin America and Its Literature in the U.S. University after the Cuban Revolution

The surge in attention to Latin America in the 1960s also rippled through the U.S. academy. Following World War II, government and philanthropic support for area studies programs flourished. For the most part, though, such programs were focused on regions of strategic interest to U.S. national security such as the Soviet Union, Asia, and Africa. Thus, when the Cuban Revolution took place, few universities had Latin American Studies programs—a situation that changed dramatically over the next few years. As scholars such as Mark Berger, Howard Cline, Helen Delpar, and others have discussed, the revolution brought about both awareness of the need for an institutional umbrella for the study of Latin America and the Caribbean and an influx of financial support from public and private sources that made such research possible. Since 1917, as Cline details, Latin Americanist scholars had attempted multiple times to create an organization to help coordinate and disseminate their work.[1] But this was an elusive goal: several were formed over the years, only to fold, in some cases as a result of the loss of impetus and of funding as interest in Latin America waned in the postwar years. Even the Association of Latin American Studies, which had been founded on the heels of the revolution with assistance from the Carnegie Corporation, collapsed under the weight of its own disorganization (see Cline, 62–63). In 1966, though, the Latin American Studies Association (LASA) was incorporated, and the newly formed *Latin American Research Review*, a beneficiary in its early years of funding from the Ford Foundation, became the official organ of LASA. As Cline observes, "At some point in its future career, [LASA] might well erect a monument to Fidel Castro, a remote godfather. His actions in Cuba jarred complacency in official and university circles, dramatically revealing that all was not well in Latin America, and that something must be done about it. Revived national concern with Latin America again created a climate in which serious programs could begin and even flourish" (64).

Such programs did indeed flourish, with support from private organizations such as the Carnegie Corporation, the Rockefeller Foundation, and the Ford Foundation, the last authorizing more than $11 million in grants to support Latin American studies between 1962 and 1966 alone (Cline, 65). Public funding was instrumental in this process as well. The National Defense Education Act (NDEA) of 1958 was expanded to allow for the provision of fellowships for advanced training in Latin America, while Title VI of the NDEA allocated federal funds to universities to establish area studies programs and centers.[2] As Delpar details, the rise in interest in Latin America was also evident in the established disciplines (174–83). The number of course offerings on Latin America increased substantially, particularly in literature and history. According to a survey conducted by Martin Needler and Thomas Walker, the number of courses on Latin America given at U.S. colleges and universities in 1969 was twice what had been reported in surveys from 1949 and 1958, revealing a sharp jump in offerings in the years after the revolution (133). Like Cline, Needler and Walker also attributed the difference to the "increased interest in Latin America that followed on Fidel Castro's assumption of power in Cuba," as well as to "the worsening of relations between Cuba and the United States, and the heightened emphasis put on Latin America by the Kennedy administration" (133–34).

In *Response to Revolution*, Richard Welch Jr. analyzes the early support for Castro among university students and faculty and concludes that scholars were stymied in their protests against U.S. policy toward Cuba by divided opinion about the revolution and their own poor organization. He argues, "With a single exception [i.e., C. Wright Mills's *Listen, Yankee!*], one cannot point to a speech, article, book, or open letter by an American academic and say with confidence that it influenced either public opinion or government policy" (151). This chapter challenges the assumption that the sphere of action and measure of success for U.S. academics interested in Cuba—and, more broadly, inter-American relations—lay in directly influencing public policy and opinion through traditional scholarly venues. I explore here several university-based initiatives that sprang up in the years following the Cuban Revolution and that were some of the most far-reaching of their day. These programs were dedicated to raising the profile of Latin America and its literature for an audience that extended well beyond the academy, and in some cases performing labors of unofficial cultural diplomacy.[3] This overview does not claim to be exhaustive, though: there was simply too much activity related to the region and its cultural production at universities across the country to document in a single chapter. My goal here, then, is to identify the literary goals and contexts motivating these programs while situating them within the context of literary dynamism that was the Boom, and within the political field of Cold War pressures and U.S.–Latin American tensions in the years following the Cuban Revolution.

The programs that I study here include the creation of visiting faculty positions and fellowships for Latin American authors, creative writing programs that highlighted Latin American literature, literary competitions, and translation assistance programs. I also discuss Cornell University's "Latin American Year," which took place during the 1965–1966 academic year, showcasing scholarship on Latin America and cultural activity in the region. Some of these initiatives were avenues through which Latin American writers and academics at U.S. universities could speak out about Latin America and inter-American relations even as they engaged in the task of promoting literature from the region. Diverse and decentralized, the programs did not necessarily seek to channel public opinion in specific directions; rather, they strove to create greater awareness of the region in an audience that included not just the university community, but a broad reading public, publishers, diplomats, and public officials. However, they did indeed have the potential to affect public opinion toward the United States in Latin America: by presenting the nation in a positive light to intellectuals who functioned as opinion leaders in their own countries, such programs could influence the writers' attitudes toward the United States, and through them, those of their compatriots. Thus, the programs played an important role in shaping the climate toward Latin America in the United States, and vice versa.

This chapter tells a story about networks—about how Latin American literature swept through the U.S. academy in the 1960s, leading U.S.-based scholars to develop courses, journals, and conferences for publicizing Latin American literature and, additionally, to create opportunities for the writers themselves to practice their craft and raise their profiles in the United States. Even programs that fell short of their goals contributed to the dissemination of knowledge about Latin America. This chapter is also, crucially, about Latin American writers' efforts to bring their work—inseparable, for many, from their politics and support of Cuba—to a broad audience. Some of the programs I examine became sites in which political tensions and pressures played out, and in hindsight they may be seen as microcosms of Cold War diplomacy and politics. This, then, is also a tale of the political subtexts that motivated interest in and funding for some of these projects. Thus, I follow the collisions and intersections between the Cold War politics of administrators and funding sources on the one hand and, on the other, the agendas of Latin American writers and U.S.-based academics that were visible in the implementation of the programs.

Latin American Writers in the U.S. Academy

Spanish writers such as Dámaso Alonso, Francisco García Lorca, Jorge Guillén, Juan Ramón Jiménez, Ángel del Río, and others began to take visiting positions in U.S. universities during the interwar period, many while in exile following the Spanish Civil War. It was not until the early 1960s, though, that writers from Latin America started to become a significant presence in the United States as well. Jorge Luis Borges was among the first of the modern writers to hold a visiting position in the United States. After receiving the prestigious International Publishers' Prize in 1961, he spent the fall at the University of Texas at Austin; it was his first trip to the United States, and he traveled and gave lectures throughout the country after he left Austin. Borges later returned to Harvard to hold the Norton professorship in 1967—a stay that had lasting consequences for his literary career, for it was here that he met Norman Thomas di Giovanni, who for many years was the primary translator of his works. The 1960s and 1970s also witnessed an increase in the number of critics from Spanish America with both personal and professional connections to the Boom—e.g., Roberto González Echevarría, Julio Ortega, José Miguel Oviedo, Emir Rodríguez Monegal, and others—who accepted permanent faculty positions at U.S. universities.[4] These critics also helped to boost the profile of Latin American literature at their universities by creating courses, arranging lectures by guest speakers, and organizing conferences that drew scholars and authors alike.

During these years, faculty members were able to convince administrators that inviting Latin American writers to campus was a timely and worthwhile investment that could bring prestige to their universities. At the same time, the writers' presence helped to meet the growing demand for courses in Latin American literature. In addition to survey courses on Spanish American literature, the literature courses most commonly offered in the late 1960s were on the Latin American novel and variants thereof, such as the twentieth-century novel, modern or contemporary literature, and recent prose fiction (Needler and Walker, 131). This seems to suggest that as Boom authors and their contemporaries became increasingly well known in the United States, their work was being introduced into university curricula alongside more established genres such as the novel of the Mexican Revolution and the *novela de la tierra* or regionalist novels of the 1920s and 1930s. Many writers taught in both English and Spanish, answering the need for Latin American offerings in both English and Spanish departments.

It was the rare Latin American writer who was able to support himself with the proceeds from his work at this time, so the prospect of a faculty position in the United States was quite enticing. Such an appointment offered an opportunity to write while earning a guaranteed salary and to disseminate one's work to students and scholars alike. Additionally, class sizes tended to be limited so as not to overburden the writers; courses were scheduled to accommodate the authors' need to write and travel. Moreover, working at U.S. universities allowed writers to collaborate when they were in the United States at the same time. For example, the correspondence among writers such as José Donoso, Carlos Fuentes, and Mario Vargas Llosa reveals that they coordinated the teaching of one another's work in their courses, invited one another to give lectures at their host institutions, asked one another for advice on teaching, and offered support to one another through periods of writer's block and other challenges.[5]

Writers took the visiting positions as they arose. In the mid-1960s and early 1970s, the invitations were more often from lower-profile state schools: Jorge Amado held a visiting faculty position at Penn State in 1971; José Donoso went to Colorado State in 1969; Nicanor Parra was poet-in-residence at Louisiana State University from 1965 to 1966; and Mario Vargas Llosa spent the fall of 1968 at Washington State and the spring of 1969 at the University of Puerto Rico. The invitations also came from more prestigious and private universities, especially as time went by and the writers' reputations began to soar. Donoso taught in the renowned Writers' Workshop at the University of Iowa from 1965 to 1967, and later spent time at Columbia, Dartmouth, Princeton, and New York University. Carlos Fuentes taught at Columbia, Dartmouth, Harvard, Princeton, and the University of Pennsylvania, and had a fellowship at the Woodrow Wilson International Center for Scholars.[6] Parra spent several terms at New York University and Columbia. Octavio Paz took a leave from his position as Mexican ambassador to India to be in residence at Cornell's "Latin American Year" in the spring of 1966, and later held the Charles E. Norton Professor of Poetry chair at Harvard. Manuel Puig taught at Columbia. Vargas Llosa did stints at Columbia; the University of California, Berkeley; and the Wilson Center.

In addition to visiting positions, there were numerous opportunities for writers to lecture at U.S. universities. Those who taught in the New York area often became involved with Frank MacShane's writing program at Columbia and with the Center for Inter-American Relations, which is the subject of the following chapter. Both of these programs coordinated readings and other events that brought the writers' work to a large reading audience and put them in contact with New York–based publishing firms. Additionally, the biennial Puterbaugh Conferences organized at the University of Oklahoma under the aegis of *World Literature Today* offered prime opportunities for networking and self-promotion: authors would come to the campus to participate in courses on their work, give lectures, do readings (often recorded for posterity for the Library of Congress's Archive of Hispanic Literature), meet with students, and participate in symposia on their work with papers given by some of the most distinguished scholars of Spanish American literature. Though the conferences specifically covered both francophone and hispanophone nations, Spanish American writers predominated, with Borges (1969), Paz (1971), Julio Cortázar (1975), Vargas Llosa (1977), Fuentes (1983), and Guillermo Cabrera Infante (1987) as six of the conference's first ten featured writers.[7] Many of the conference papers were subsequently published, either as proceedings by the University of Oklahoma Press or in *World Literature Today*, so the gatherings also became mechanisms for producing and disseminating scholarship on contemporary writers.

Sometimes political turmoil at home made opportunities to visit the United States both timely and attractive. For example, following the 1968 massacre at the Plaza de Tlatelolco in Mexico City, Paz resigned in protest from his position as Mexico's ambassador to India and went to Harvard. Gustavo Díaz Ordaz had been president of Mexico during the 1968 student riots and massacre; when he was appointed Mexico's ambassador to Spain in early 1977, Fuentes resigned his own position as Mexico's ambassador to France and headed almost immediately to the United States, where invitations poured in for him to teach at universities around the country. At times, however, the reverse was true, and rather than accepting visiting positions as safe harbors, writers turned them down to signal their rejection of U.S. military actions or policies such as McCarran-Walter; they also refused such offers out of concern that their presence in the United States might be interpreted as complicity with Cold War politics and policies. Fuentes, as we saw in Chapter 1, pulled out of several academic engagements to preempt being subjected to questioning under McCarran-Walter. Additionally, in the fall of 1970, he rescinded upcoming commitments to teach at New York University and Columbia in protest against the U.S. resumption of bombing in North Vietnam; he claimed that he was unable to teach literature in the face of such imperialistic actions, and he urged other Latin American writers to boycott the United States as well.[8] Cortázar similarly turned down a number of invitations to the United States, in many cases because he did not want to face the McCarran-Walter machinery and, like Fuentes, declining others for political reasons. In 1969, for example, he turned down a visiting professorship at Columbia that MacShane had offered to him, stating, "As a Latin American, I feel that I should not visit the United States so long as that country continues its imperialist policy in various regions of the world and especially in Central and South America" (qtd. in MacShane, 37). He further observed—echoing the criticism leveled against Pablo Neruda for attending the 1966 PEN congress—that his visiting the United States would have "a symbolic value in Latin America, a negative one, of course, and in the last instance it would represent a new triumph for the reactionary and imperialist forces in their 'brain drain' technique, which unfortunately continues in the field of the arts and sciences" (ibid.). In the end, then, the history of these acceptances and refusals offers insights into the creative fervor, intellectual networks, and political tensions affecting Latin American writers and the promotion of their work in the United States in the 1960s and 1970s.

A Latin American Odyssey at Columbia University

During these same years, Columbia University—like New York itself—was a hotbed of activity related to the promotion and translation of Latin American literature. During this period, the university boasted of faculty such as Gregory Rabassa and Federico de Onís (both in the Department of Spanish and Portuguese) and MacShane (in English and Writing), who became involved with efforts to translate Latin American literature and who drew on their connections to bring authors to campus and create venues for the publication and publicizing of their work. One of these initiatives was the *Odyssey Review*, a little journal that ultimately transformed the history of translation of Latin American literature. In late 1961, under the aegis of the Latin American and European Literary Society, four professors—Saul Galin and Ursula Eder of Brooklyn College and Alan Purves and Rabassa of Columbia—started publishing the journal, which showcased literature from Latin America and Europe on a quarterly basis. *Odyssey Review* boasted of an advisory board of distinguished writers, critics, and translators from the United States, Europe, and Latin America. Latin America was represented by Eugenio Florit, William Grossman, Raimundo Lida, Victoria Ocampo, Federico de Onís, Octavio Paz, Ángel del Río, Arturo Torres-Rioseco, and others. The journal's list of sponsors was equally impressive, bringing together authors and critics, including New Critics, New York intellectuals, and writers associated with Cold War liberalism and the Congress for Cultural Freedom (CCF), such as W. H. Auden, Jacques Barzun, Cleanth Brooks, Lawrence Durrell, Robert Graves, Aldous Huxley, Robert Lowell, Archibald MacLeish, Stephen Spender, Lionel Trilling, Robert Penn Warren, and René Wellek. Sponsors also included Borges, Eduardo Mallea, several U.S. ambassadors to Latin America and Europe, European and Latin American ambassadors to the United States and the United Nations, and José Mora, secretary general of the Organization of American States.

Odyssey Review was committed to publishing original translations of works that had not previously appeared in English. It also sought to "strengthen existing literary and cultural ties and to establish new ones between the United States and the countries of Latin America and Europe" ("Statement of Aims"). Each issue featured translations of twentieth-century works from two Latin American countries and two European countries. This was a remarkable project for the time. European literature was, at this point, an established discipline, so the translation of works from the continent was unlikely to raise any eyebrows. In contrast, in 1961, Latin American literature—like Latin American studies as a whole—was only beginning its upswing in the U.S. academy. While Spanish departments had a long history in the U.S. academy, peninsular literature tended to be the primary focus of their curricula and degree programs.[9] Dedicating the journal to both Latin American and European literature not only put the two fields on equal footing, it brought the Latin American works to readers interested in European literature who might not otherwise have encountered it. The editors seem to have been quite conscious of the journal's potential to valorize Latin American literature, for the layout of the issues regularly alternated the order of presentation of the sets of translations: in the first issue (December 1961), for example, translations from Argentina and Brazil preceded those from France and Holland, whereas in the second issue (March 1962), Italy and Germany preceded Peru and Puerto Rico, and so on.[10]

During its two-year, seven-issue existence, the journal published a range of work by both established and up-and-coming Latin American authors such as Demetrio Aguilera Malta, Fernando Alegría, Juan José Arreola, Miguel Ángel Asturias, Mario Benedetti, Jorge Luis Borges, Rómulo Gallegos, Clarice Lispector, Luis Palés Matos, Juan Carlos Onetti, Nicanor Parra, Samuel Ramos, Alfonso Reyes, Julio Ramón Ribeyro, Sebastián Salazar Bondy, César Vallejo, Xavier Villaurrutia, and others. The journal's life span covered the earliest years of the Boom. In fact, the September 1962 issue included a focus on Colombia, but García Márquez, who was still relatively unknown, was not featured. Rabassa, who was responsible for seeking out new literature in Spanish and Portuguese for the journal (Rabassa, *If This Be Treason*, 24), kept a close eye on contemporary literary and political developments, linking these to the choice of featured nations. The first issue of the journal included Argentina, clearly as a means of shining a spotlight on the work of Borges, who had just been awarded the International Publishers' Prize. Rabassa also tied his task to his research, parlaying his interests in Brazilian fiction into the choice of Brazil as the second nation included in the issue.[11] The December 1962 issue, which was published in the wake of the Cuban missile crisis, marked the sole exception to the journal's standard format of featuring two Latin American and two European nations: in what was clearly a nod to the contemporary political situation and an effort to transform public interest in politics into a boon for literature, the issue focused exclusively on Russia and Cuba.

The informational blurb in the first issue of the *Odyssey Review* boasted that its translations represented "the highest standards in the field" and identified Harriet de Onís, Robert Lowell, and William Grossman as among its primary translators. Rabassa soon found, though, that there was a shortage of translators of Spanish and Portuguese, so even though he had no formal training in literary translation, he frequently tried his hand at it, often using pseudonyms to give the impression of variety (Rabassa, *If This Be Treason*, 24). It was for the *Odyssey Review* that he first translated a number of authors whose work publishers would later commission him to take on, including Asturias, Lispector, and Aguilera Malta. The most lasting legacy of the *Odyssey Review* was that it brought Rabassa's skills to the attention of Sara Blackburn, an editor at Pantheon, a press "whose goal, like that of a cluster of more enlightened publishers, was to bring to American readers a select upcoming group of experimental and left-wing writers from Europe and Latin America" (Levine, "Latin American Novel," 306). Blackburn was impressed by Rabassa's work and asked him to translate Julio Cortázar's *Rayuela* (1963). *Hopscotch* was published in 1966 to tremendous critical acclaim, sharing the first National Book Award for Translation and signaling a turning point for Latin American literature in the United States.[12] As Elizabeth Lowe and Earl Fitz write, "Shattering old stereotypes about what literature 'south of the border' was like, *Hopscotch*, with its subversive, often absurdist humor, its international scope, its structural play, and its intellectually sophisticated content, ushered in a new age for the reception of Brazilian and Spanish American literature in the United States" (139). The demand for Rabassa's services immediately took off, skyrocketing even higher four years later with his translation of García Márquez's *Cien años de soledad*.

Harriet de Onís, the principal translator of Latin American literature in the United States at the time, helped with the *Odyssey Review*; Rabassa was presumably able to recruit her because they were both connected to Columbia. Harriet was married to Federico de Onís, a distinguished Hispanist who chaired the Department of Spanish and Portuguese at the university for many years; he had supervised Rabassa's dissertation and hired him as faculty. Federico de Onís bore a great deal of the responsibility for building up Hispanic Studies at Columbia, which in turn sent ripple effects throughout New York and the U.S. academy: he founded the Casa Hispánica (where the Department of Spanish and Portuguese is now housed) as a site for public and professional gatherings related to Hispanic literature and culture; he established the *Revista Hispánica Moderna*, which remains today a noted journal in Hispanic literary studies; and he was responsible for having Latin American literature approved as a field of study for the PhD in Spanish and Portuguese at Columbia. Professor de Onís also brought a steady stream of distinguished Latin American writers and critics to the university, including Germán Arciniegas, Gabriela Mistral, and Arturo Uslar Pietri, among others (see Young).

Harriet de Onís met many of these visitors, as well as her husband's colleagues and students, and these contacts gave her even greater power over the field of Latin American literature and translation. She began to recommend and translate Uslar Pietri's and Arciniegas's work for Knopf while both writers were at Columbia. She also met Rodríguez Monegal through her husband's circles and spoke highly of him to Alfred Knopf, who entrusted the critic with the *Borzoi Anthology of Latin American Literature* soon after the two men first met.

Harriet de Onís also played a role in Rabassa's nascent career in translation. In 1964, Rabassa was suggested to Knopf as a possible translator for Lispector's work. Although the recommendation came from a fellow publisher, Seymour Lawrence, and at the behest of Lispector, who had met Rabassa and been impressed by his work, Knopf was hesitant: at this point, *Hopscotch* was still a work in progress and Rabassa's only published translations were those that had appeared in the *Odyssey Review*. Knopf turned to de Onís for more information. De Onís responded that she personally disliked Rabassa, but she ultimately advised Knopf to go with him if he approved of the translation and Lispector supported the choice.[13] In the end, that is exactly what Knopf did, and starting in the mid-1960s, Rabassa translated the works of high-profile writers such as Cortázar and García Márquez for the publishing house, as well as those of quite a few Brazilians whom he lobbied Knopf to publish.

In the end, though, it was the graduate-level Writing Division in the School of the Arts at Columbia that developed the university's highest-profile and most systematically cultivated connection to contemporary Latin American literature. The Writing Division, which Frank MacShane founded in 1967 and directed until 1981, was a whirlwind of activity. MacShane was an English professor whose critical work focused on U.S. writers, but he also translated several Spanish American writers and was deeply invested in the promotion of their work, giving it pride of place in the Writing Division. MacShane traveled to Spanish America several times, and no doubt his interest in the region was also sustained by his interactions with Rabassa, who over the years recommended a number of works to him. MacShane and Rabassa seem to have been in touch regularly, even after the latter left Columbia in 1968, and both men shared information about the writing program and its activities in their correspondence with Latin American writers.

Because of the high concentration of writers in New York City, MacShane had plenty of talent at hand to draw on. But from the program's inception, he made a concerted effort to bring in writers from Spanish America, and in the mid-1970s, the university became one of five institutional hosts for professorships endowed by the Tinker Foundation.[14] The grants supported Latin American writers teaching in the United States, and allowed MacShane to bring Vargas Llosa in 1975 and Fuentes in 1978. Authors would generally come for one or two semesters at a time. The salaries were low, but on some occasions the Literature program of the Center for Inter-American Relations was able to cover the expenses. In addition to coordinating these visiting positions, MacShane arranged a steady stream of lectures, classroom visits, conferences, and short-term residencies. Over the years, he was able to bring to campus distinguished writers such as Donoso, García Márquez, Parra, Puig, and Homero Aridjis, among others. He invited translators to campus to speak about their work, contributing to the budding institutionalization of the craft. In fact, it was Suzanne Jill Levine who first brought Puig to MacShane's attention, which points to a role that translators played in helping to establish the Boom in the United States.[15] MacShane also organized a conference on the topic of "Society and the Arts" in the spring of 1971 in which Borges, Parra (who was then teaching in the Writing Division), Vargas Llosa, and others participated. Additionally, he was able to capitalize on his position and the current interest in Spanish American literature by publishing profiles of authors such as Cortázar, Fuentes, García Márquez, Neruda, and Parra in the *New York Times* in the late 1970s.

MacShane was well attuned to U.S.–Latin American relations and their bearing on the willingness and ability of writers to visit the United States. McCarran-Walter was, not surprisingly, a major impediment to his efforts. When coordinating the aforementioned conference, he had several top administrators write to the U.S. consulate in Barcelona regarding Vargas Llosa's visa (see Chapter 1). MacShane had also gained the goodwill of Fuentes in 1969 with the letter he and Charles Wagley had sent to the *New York Times* protesting the refusal to grant Fuentes entry into Puerto Rico (see Chapter 1). When Fuentes rescinded his agreement to teach at Columbia in 1971 because of the renewal of bombing in North Vietnam, MacShane tried to convince him that his presence in the United States would in fact better serve his politics by giving him a public opportunity to protest U.S. policies and be heard by sympathetic audiences.[16] Fuentes did not change his mind, but MacShane continued to invite him to Writing Division events, all the while underscoring the literary and political benefits of attending them. For instance, MacShane framed his invitation to Fuentes to participate in the 1971 conference on society and the arts as a chance for Fuentes to express his views on the war. To assure Fuentes that dissenting voices would be prominently featured at the conference, MacShane informed him that Cuban writers had been invited, and that if he did not hear from them, he would invite writers associated with the Allende government.[17]

In 1972, MacShane expanded the reach of the Writing Division in a move that had a significant impact on the development of the field of translation and translation studies. In collaboration with the PEN American Center and with funding from the National Council on the Arts, he opened a translation center within Columbia's School of the Arts. The center built on the work of the Writing Division, which already ran a weekly workshop for translators in the New York area. The center was a major undertaking: it coordinated a translation clearinghouse that put translators, writers, and publishers in touch with one another; it commissioned translations; it organized international conferences; it sponsored seminars through the School of the Arts; and it offered yearlong fellowships for the study of lesser-known languages. Its broader goals encompassed assisting with the professionalization of translators, as well as helping to establish translation as a legitimate craft and discipline. Over the years, the translation center sponsored lectures and readings by Borges, Neruda, Parra, Joseph Brodsky, and many others. In 1973, it launched a journal, *Translation*, which not only included translations of literary works but also served as a place for reflection on the craft of translation and its importance: it sponsored forums in which authors such as Arthur Miller and Thornton Wilder offered their views on the importance of translation for their work.[18] It also published dialogues between translators and authors, as well as commentaries by translators, writers, and editors, and it occasionally included suggestions for translators prepared by the PEN American Center.

In many ways, the translation center mirrored the activities of the Center for Inter-American Relations (CIAR), although the latter focused on work from Latin America, whereas the Columbia center worked with the translation of literature in all languages. Rather than rivalry or over-lap, though, there was a spirit of collaboration: the directors of both centers planned events together; when in New York, authors would often schedule engagements at both venues (in fact, teaching in MacShane's program often allowed authors to participate in CIAR activities that helped them to net-work and publicize their work); and translators such as Rabassa and Levine, among others, were involved with the activities of both centers. The trans-lation center and the CIAR alike, then, as well as the Writing Division as a whole, all found room to play important roles in the promotion of Latin American literature in the United States.

The University of Iowa's Writers' Workshop

The renowned Writers' Workshop at the University of Iowa played a criti-cal (albeit insufficiently studied) part in raising the profile of Latin Ameri-can literature in the 1960s. The Writers' Workshop has long been one of the most distinguished creative writing programs in the United States, drawing high-profile authors-in-residence to work with students enrolled in the pro-gram. Paul Engle directed the workshop from 1941 until the mid-1960s. In early 1965, no doubt influenced by the publicity afforded to Latin Ameri-can literature during the early Boom years, he invited Donoso to teach in the program. Donoso was at Iowa from 1965 to 1967, along with Nelson Algren, Irish writer Bill Murray, Philippine author Bienvenido (Ben) San-tos, Kurt Vonnegut, and others (M. P. Donoso, 211). Participation in the workshop was an important break that provided Donoso with a guaranteed income and a place both to practice and promote his craft while he was in the throes of working on *El obsceno pájaro de la noche* (*The Obscene Bird of Night*), which he struggled to finish for several years. The opportunity to work with Vonnegut was an additional boon: the two men became lifelong friends, and the U.S. writer further served as a mentor to Donoso by keep-ing a watchful eye out for opportunities and supporting him professionally on numerous occasions.

The stay in Iowa allowed Donoso to influence budding writers by exposing them to current literary developments in Spanish America. Ac-cording to María Pilar Donoso, the author's proposal of a seminar on contemporary Spanish American narrative was initially turned down by the program's director of workshops on prose on the grounds that there were very few translations available and that poetry was a more important course of study (212). Donoso prevailed, only to find that the scarcity of trans-lations of contemporary prose did indeed make the course difficult to ar-range. In 1965, the selection was limited to several collections of Borges's stories, Donoso's own *Coronation*, and novels by Juan José Arreola, Miguel Ángel Asturias, Alejo Carpentier, Rosario Castellanos, Carlos Fuentes, and Agustín Yáñez. But even the works that had been translated could be dif-ficult to get. Roger Klein, a talented young editor at Harper and Row who was known for his commitment to Latin American literature at a time when knowledge of the field was still rare among literary editors, suggested that Donoso supplement the lack of primary materials with Luis Harss and Bar-bara Dohmann's *Into the Mainstream* (Harper and Row, 1967), which in-cluded interviews with up-and-coming authors such as Borges, Cortázar, Fuentes, García Márquez, and Vargas Llosa, as well as discussions of their work.[19] And when Cortázar's *Hopscotch* was published in 1966, Donoso was able to add it to his course, to great success (M. P. Donoso, 212).

Donoso's residence in Iowa also sparked an effort to develop a writing program aimed specifically at bringing Latin Americans to the university. In January 1966, Paul Engle and Robert Wool began to plan a joint program for the Writer's Workshop and the Inter-American Foundation for the Arts. They envisioned it offering fellowships to between eight and twelve writers annually, and planned for it to be led by a distinguished Latin American writer. Such a program would give writers that rare commodity—time—as well as structured critical feedback. Engle and Wool wanted the program to start in the fall of 1966, and Donoso to be its first chair. Fuentes, with whom Donoso was in close contact, had expressed interest in participating in the program as a fellow. It was an arrangement that would have suited Fuentes by offering him time, and enhanced the program by bringing it prestige and attracting writers.[20] Rodríguez Monegal, who was at this point editing *Mundo Nuevo* and reading the work of talented new authors, agreed to suggest the names of those who he felt would benefit from the program.

Donoso was enthusiastic about the prospect because he knew how im-portant the fellowships could be to writers' careers. Engle and Wool shared Donoso's enthusiasm, and were additionally motivated to promote the program because of its potential in the field of cultural diplomacy: they believed that it could have an effect not just on Latin American literary production, but on the attitudes of Latin American writers and opinion molders toward the United States. Engle's experience had shown him that the current writing program had a "powerful effect on the impressionable minds of young writers who come here" from abroad, who, on returning home, would publish positive articles about the program and otherwise serve as ambassadors for the United States. Thus, he was "confident that we can work such a change in some potentially very important young people from Latin America" with the proposed program. But, Engle warned, the selection of fellows must be made carefully:

> We must discover in Washington what political obstacles there may be to our project. Knowing the leftish convictions of many of the world's young writers, it must be decided just how close a writer can be to what appears to be the communist line and still gain admission to the USA. It would be fatal to nominate a writer and then have his visa application rejected. That would create vast bad will in Latin America. Personally, I think it is precisely those who have harsh attitudes toward us who ought to have an authentic experience here and discover the myths they have been believing. . . . [W]e are convinced that this Program, along with all of the arts in Iowa City, could have a profound effect on the writing of Latin America, as well as a strong and persuasive impact on the attitudes toward the USA.

Indeed, Engle felt that it was imperative to start the program as soon as possible in order to offset the political turbulence and increasing anti-Americanism (some attributable to the 1965 invasion of the Dominican Republic by the United States) in Latin America. The fact that Donoso, who Engle and Wool believed would be an ideal person to spearhead the program and bring in high-profile participants, would be in his second and final year at the Writers' Workshop made an immediate start date all the more urgent.[21]

In order to finance the program, Engle suggested including a translation component as a means of convincing publishers interested in Latin American literature to contribute. There was not much money, however, to be expected from these sources. Engle and Wool directed their primary fundraising efforts at the State Department's Bureau of Educational and Cultural Affairs, the USIA, and the Guggenheim Foundation. Both men played up the political benefits of the program among potential contributors. Wool, for example, wrote to Leonard Marks, director of the USIA, that bringing writers from Latin America to the United States and thereby attempting to dispel their misconceptions about the nation might not only help to diminish their anti-U.S. tendencies but could, by extension, have a broad political benefit, given the influence they wielded at home.[22] Engle seems to have convinced Jacob Canter, the new deputy assistant secretary of state for educational and cultural affairs and an outspoken supporter of the State Department's exchange programs, to provide support for bringing at least four Latin American writers to Iowa. Canter, however, seems to have made a number of suggestions for the project that raised serious objections from Donoso and that ultimately sounded the death-knell for the proposal. I have unfortunately been unable to locate a copy of a letter that Canter seems to have sent to Engle in mid-March. Engle shared it with Donoso, though, who viewed Canter's suggestions as symptomatic of the U.S. government's clumsy interactions with intellectuals from the region, many of which had generated bad will.[23] In keeping with his negative assessment of the effects of State Department interactions with Latin American intellectuals, Donoso argued that U.S. government support for the project should be limited to assistance with visas and other administrative matters so as not to taint it and thereby condemn it to failure.[24] The Chilean did, however, share his colleagues' view of the proposed fellowship program as a way of strengthening inter-American relations and mutual understanding.

Engle and Wool agreed not to accept Canter's suggestions and to limit themselves to pursuing logistical assistance only from the State Department, but they were subsequently unable to raise sufficient funds, and the program never took shape. Donoso was clearly upset by the matter, and when Wool asked him in late 1966 to assist the Inter-American Foundation for the Arts with its efforts to find translators and publishers for Latin American works, Donoso essentially told Wool that he thought the foundation's efforts were redundant and would be better directed at funding writers themselves rather than translations.[25] Engle did not give up entirely, though. Driven by the desire to put Iowa's resources at the service of writers from around the world, he refocused his energies on a broader project, the International Writing Program (IWP), which he started in 1967. In many respects, Engle seems to have folded his ideas for the Latin American fellowship program into the IWP, which likewise sought to provide financial support and critical feedback to writers from abroad. He kept the spirit of supporting cultural exchange alive with grants from the Bureau of Educational and Cultural Exchange that covered maintenance costs for several visiting artists from abroad each year; the grants also allowed recipients to travel in the United States and "meet with other writers and with American publishers, to study American theater and drama, and to observe American life and culture in general."[26] Grantees were expected to spend several days in Washington, DC, en route to Iowa, during which they would discuss their travel plans and undergo "programming," which suggests that the State Department was eager to shape these writers' experiences in and perceptions of the United States.[27] Engle also managed to secure two $30,000 grants from the Ford Foundation (one in 1967 and one in 1968), as well as some funding from a number of U.S. embassies in Latin America, to bring in writers from Latin America to participate in the IWP.[28] Over the years, María Pilar Donoso, Jorge Ibargüengoitia, Fernando del Paso, Gustavo Sáinz, Tomás Segovia, Luisa Valenzuela, and others took advantage of the opportunity to study at Iowa. The IWP thus served as an umbrella under which Engle was able to realize, albeit on a smaller scale, many of his goals for supporting and promoting Latin American literature, and to conduct a bit of cultural diplomacy on the side.

The Association of American University Presses and the Latin American Translation Program

Up to this point, I have examined sustained efforts that focused on literary production and, to a lesser degree, on exposing Latin American writers to the United States, and vice versa. I turn now to the question of the translation and dissemination of literature from Latin America, which I will address with the study of a translation subsidy program that overlapped with the short-lived existence of the *Odyssey Review*.

The publicity generated by Borges's receipt of the International Publishers' Prize in 1961 not only benefited the author, it helped to increase the visibility of Latin American literature in general. Even with this added cachet, though, in the early 1960s U.S. publishers were still cautious about contracting works from the region. The challenges associated with publishing works by little-known Latin American authors were not insignificant, and the U.S. publishing infrastructure was ill prepared to meet them: few publishers had editors who could read Spanish manuscripts (and even fewer who could read Portuguese), and they were often at a loss to find competent readers to review them for a contract; also, as Rabassa's experience at *Odyssey Review* attests, there were relatively few translators for Spanish and Portuguese at the time.[29] Also, as I discussed in the Introduction, publishing translations entailed additional financial burdens as well. Alfred A. Knopf was the first to admit that most of his company's translations of Latin American literature had been done at a loss and that the works that he published were prestige items rather than best sellers. Unlike Knopf, though, few of his peers at this time were willing to accept symbolic capital instead of monetary returns.

In the 1950s and 1960s, several translation initiatives took shape. The Ford Foundation, for example, funded several broad-based publishing and translation programs as part of its Cold War efforts to promote international understanding (of the United States, that is) and to offset political tensions. One of these was Intercultural Publications Inc. (IPI), which received $500,000 from Ford in 1952. IPI was led by James Laughlin, publisher of the avant-garde New Directions Press, and its distinguished advisory board included authors and scholars (many of whom would later serve on the *Odyssey Review* board) such as James Agee, W. H. Auden, Jacques Barzun, Cleanth Brooks, Malcolm Cowley, Alfred Kazin, John Crowe Ransom, Arthur Schlesinger Jr., Wallace Stegner, Allen Tate, Lionel Trilling, Robert Penn Warren, and Tennessee Williams. IPI focused its efforts on a journal, *Perspectives, U.S.A.*, which was published from 1952 to 1956 in English, French, German, and Italian. The journal featured contemporary U.S. literature and arts, but also included sections on history, literary criticism, and philosophy, as well as reviews of books in these fields. Through its focus on "highbrow" cultural production, it aimed to dispel myths about U.S. cultural production being limited to mass and popular culture, to create an international audience for U.S. cultural production, to forge bridges between U.S. writers and the European intellectual community (McCarthy, "From Cold War," 95), and, not least of all, to cultivate international understanding and thereby smooth political tensions. In the first issue of *Perspectives*, Laughlin wrote:

> It is the conviction of the sponsors of this magazine that such communication on the level of cultural exchange offers one of the best methods of fostering the development of world understanding and a sense of moral community among the peoples of the world. Appreciation of the arts can act as a solvent for ideological differences of opinion. The arts can provide a meeting ground where men of conflicting political allegiances can learn to know and respect each other as human beings. Cultural exchange can create a climate favorable to the peaceful solution of some of the world's problems and troubles. (7)

"Country perspectives" were later incorporated into the journal as a means of introducing "American readers to the culture of such newly independent states as India, Indonesia, and Burma" (McCarthy, "From Cold War," 96) and ensuring, in Laughlin's words, that foreign readers would "not feel we were simply trying to ram our culture down their throats" (qtd. in McCarthy, "From Cold War," 96). In 1965, the Ford Foundation awarded a five-year grant to the National Translation Center, housed at the University of Texas at Austin and directed by Keith Botsford of the CCF. The center offered fellowships, sponsored symposia, and published a journal, *Delos*; like the translation center at Columbia described earlier in this chapter, it sought to promote the professionalization of translation as a discipline, and it was not focused on any particular language or region.

The Rockefeller Foundation (RF) took an interest in translation as well. In 1956, under the leadership of Dean Rusk, the RF started to expand its programs into the developing areas of the world, focusing on Latin America and India in particular. John Harrison, who had a PhD in Latin American history, joined the RF Humanities Division this same year and immediately began to support projects that sought to redress problems of translating and publishing Latin American literature. When the foundation's 1960 annual report observed, on the heels of the Cuban Revolution, that "recent developments in Latin America demand a long overdue revaluation of the role the region will play in future cultural and intellectual exchange among nations" (Rockefeller Foundation, 38), the Humanities Division already had several programs well underway. In 1956, a consultant suggested developing a program that would grant subsidies to publishers to assist with the cost of translation, and Harrison actively pursued the idea. In 1957, he met with the heads of several university presses to discuss this possibility. In early 1958, Frank Wardlaw, director of the University of Texas Press, informally proposed a program that would pay for the translations of fictional and scholarly works by university presses. On the one hand, Wardlaw's goals were pragmatic: as Harrison noted, Wardlaw "felt the Latin American program offered Texas an opportunity to make an important contribution which would give the Press stature and at the same time be moderately successful commercially in the distribution of Latin American writing."[30] On the other, he had hopes—rooted in the contemporary emphasis on cultural diplomacy—that the project could, in the long term, have an impact on international relations by improving inter-American understanding and mutual goodwill—hopes that became a leitmotif of the program that eventually developed.[31] In early 1960, in conjunction with August Frugé, director of the University of California Press, and two other university press directors, Wardlaw proposed a translation subsidy project to the Rockefeller Foundation that would be overseen by the Association of American University Presses (AAUP).

The program was a natural extension of the organization's interest in scholarly publishing in the Americas. The association had recently opened a central office in New York City and sought to represent not just the interests of U.S.-based university presses, but of presses throughout the Americas.[32] Frugé, who had been president of the organization in the late 1950s, had traveled throughout Latin America on several occasions and was instrumental in setting up collaborative endeavors with scholarly presses and book vendors in the region in the 1960s. Wardlaw, also a former president of the AAUP, was, in Frugé's words, "building up a fine list of regional books, and always conscious of the border near by [sic], was beating the drums for closer relations with Latin America" (*Skeptic among Scholars*, 109).

Hesitant to embark on a translation program, the chief officers of the RF asked Alfred A. Knopf to assess the proposal. According to Frugé, Knopf "recounted his own sorry experience and said that there would never be an adequate market in this country. Harrison countered with the report that Frank Wardlaw at Texas had sold twenty thousand copies of *Platero and I* . . . by the Andalusian poet Juan Ramón Jiménez, then living in Puerto Rico. In disbelief, Knopf checked the story, found that the sale had been even higher, and advised that Latin American books deserved another try" (*Skeptic among Scholars*, 121). In April 1960, the RF awarded a five-year grant of $225,000 to the AAUP. The program called for individual university presses to propose works appropriate for their lists to a national committee set up by the AAUP's executive officers. It would award approximately fifteen grants of up to $3,000 each per year, and literary works as well as recent and canonical texts in the humanities and social sciences would be eligible for the subsidies. Starting in October 1960, the committee, which consisted of three Latin Americanist scholars and two university publishers, met semiannually to consider applications. From the beginning, there was no shortage of applications to consider: the committee approved subsidies for fifteen titles during the first year of the program, and thirty-five—more than twice the annual goal—during the second.[33] Between 1960 and 1966, the program approved the publication of eighty-three books.[34] Twenty presses were involved. Together, Texas and California, both of which had a history of publishing Latin American literature and scholarship, published fifty books, including most of the literary ones subsidized by the program.[35] Titles included both scholarly works and numerous important works of literature (see Table 1), some of which had been fundamental to the development of the Boom and of Spanish America's *nueva narrativa* ("new narrative") of the 1950s and 1960s.

In 1966, as the end of RF funding for the program approached, the grantees requested a renewal of support in the amount of $240,000. The proposal urged a continuation of funding because most of the titles approved to date had been published at a loss, and sales income alone would be insufficient to sustain a program of publishing in the field. It further argued that "the value of the program to scholarship and international understanding has been far greater than sales and monetary returns would indicate." As the writers published through the program became better known, "other publishers will become interested. If the effort can be continued for another four years, we believe that the North American view of Latin American literature can be transformed."[36]

Current and past members of the selection committee sent letters of endorsement. Their assessments spoke to the program's success in creating a market for books on Latin America, to its contributions to inter-American relations, and to its effects on intellectuals, who were targeted as molders of opinion for their compatriots. For example, Richard Morse, chair of Latin American Studies at Yale, wrote that the RF program had opened up a new and broader audience for Latin American literature, and predicted that the rising interest in Latin America within the academy and in the political sphere would soon help to make the program self-sustaining.[37] Harrison, who had left the foundation in 1962 to direct the University of Texas's Institute of Latin American Studies, also lent his support, crediting the program with having been a critical factor in introducing Latin American literature to U.S. readers.[38] An audience was growing, but, he argued, support for translation was still needed before presses would be able to publish Latin American works regularly without subventions. William Sloane, then chair of the translation program's executive committee, was the only insider who voiced doubts about the program's prospects during the endorsement phase. He argued that the market (whether commercial or academic) for the translations was small and not yet self-sustaining, and therefore unlikely to become much stronger without further assistance from the RF.[39]

In weighing the decision of whether or not to renew funding, Gerald Freund, an associate director at the RF, observed that the program was not in keeping with the foundation's current priorities, even though the organization was shifting its priorities from the advancement of scientific knowledge to an emphasis on aiding cultural development and on fostering interdisciplinary projects in developing nations (Nielsen, 67). Additionally, he claimed that the program was not self-sustaining and that there was no guarantee that it could become so with continued support. However, he noted that "the program has demonstrably served the academic and intellectual institutions of Latin America directly and indirectly," and at relatively low cost.[40] He also warned of "the possibility of adverse public reactions to

Table 1. Selected literary works published through the AAUP program

Author	English title	University press	Date of publication in English
Juan José Arreola	*Confabulario and Other Inventions*	Texas	1964
Adolfo Bioy Casares	*The Invention of Morel*	Texas	1964
Jorge Luis Borges	*Dreamtigers*	Texas	1964
	Other Inquisitions, 1937–1952	Texas	1964
Concolorcorvo	*El lazarillo: A Guide for Inexperienced Travelers between Buenos Aires and Lima, 1773*	Indiana	1965
Daniel Cosío Villegas	*American Extremes*	Texas	1964
Rubén Darío	*Selected Poems of Rubén Darío*	Texas	1965
Sergio Galindo	*The Precipice*	Texas	1969
Elena Garro	*Recollections of Things to Come*	Texas	1969
Francisco López de Gómara	*Cortés: The Life of the Conqueror by His Secretary*	California	1964
William Grossman, trans.	*Modern Brazilian Short Stories*	California	1967
Martín Luis Guzmán	*Memoirs of Pancho Villa*	Texas	1965
Inca Garcilaso de la Vega	*Royal Commentaries of the Incas, and General History of Peru*	Texas	1966

Author	Title	University	Year
Joaquim Maria Machado de Assis	The Psychiatrist and Other Stories	California	1963
	Esau and Jacob	California	1965
José Carlos Mariátegui	Seven Interpretive Essays on Peruvian Reality	Texas	1971
José Martí	Martí on the U.S.A.	So. Illinois	1966
José Luis Martínez, ed.	The Modern Mexican Essay	Toronto	1965
Ezequiel Martínez Estrada	X-Ray of the Pampa	Texas	1971
	Selected Poems	Indiana	1963
Octavio Paz	The Siren and the Seashell, and Other Essays on Poets and Poetry	Texas	1976
Ricardo Pozas	Juan the Chamula: An Ethnological Re-creation of the Life of a Mexican Indian	California	1962
Rachel de Queiroz	The Three Marias	Texas	1963
Graciliano Ramos	Barren Lives	Texas	1965
Samuel Ramos	Profile of Man and Culture in Mexico	Texas	1962
Alfonso Reyes	Mexico in a Nutshell and Other Essays	California	1964
Juan Rulfo	The Burning Plain	Texas	1967
José Vasconcelos	A Mexican Ulysses: An Autobiography	Indiana	1963
Agustín Yáñez	The Edge of the Storm: A Novel	Texas	1963
	The Lean Lands	Texas	1968
Leopoldo Zea	The Latin-American Mind	Oklahoma	1963

a Rockefeller Foundation declination," referring specifically to a laudatory *Saturday Review* article on the program that had concluded with the statement that "the AAUP translation project runs until April 1, 1966. In view of the program's achievements thus far, it is unthinkable that the AAUP will not again knock on the door of the Rockefeller Foundation and that their request will not again be honored" (Clements, 61).[41]

Robert West, another associate director at the foundation, was, however, more skeptical: in addition to the program's not fitting in with contemporary RF goals, he was not convinced by the argument that "six years of subsidizing publication of Latin American literature has not succeeded in making this program self-sustaining by the economic standards of university presses but that six more years and thirty more titles will make it unnecessary to obtain a $3,000 per volume external subsidy. . . . After they have skimmed off the best 105 titles, why should we expect the 106th to command an adequate market so that the $3,000 subsidy would not be required?"[42] In June 1966, the proposal for renewal was turned down because, despite its merits, the issue of translation was considered "too tangential" to the foundation's current programs and goals.[43]

During its six-year history, the AAUP program subsidized the translation of a critical mass of classics that laid the groundwork for the rise in interest in Latin American literature among the trade presses at nearly the same time, yet without itself producing any bestsellers. The program boosted the production and profile of Latin American literature in the United States, but was not itself a financial success. Information provided by the University of California Press and the University of Texas Press, which between them published more than half of the books supported by the program, indicates that sales were modest at best.[44] According to a 1965 report, only twelve of the hardcover publications had sold over 1,000 copies, and none of them had sold over 3,000 copies, although 3,500 copies had been sold of two of the paperback books.[45] Most works brought in between $2,700 and $5,200. Martín Luis Guzmán's *Memoirs of Pancho Villa*, Agustín Yáñez's *The Edge of the Storm*, and Francisco López de Gómara's *Cortés* were the top sellers, netting between $8,200 and $14,800; perhaps not coincidentally, *Memoirs of Pancho Villa* and *Cortés* had benefited from the highest promotion and advertising budgets. However, with the sole exception of *Cortés*, which had posted a gain of $1,301, as of early 1966 California and Texas had published all their books at a net loss, for manufacturing costs, overhead, editorial fees, and other expenses significantly increased the presses' investment in each book.[46] Hence, despite heavy investment in promotion, *Memoirs of Pancho Villa* posted the highest overall loss ($6,270); in contrast, Borges's *Dreamtigers*, which had had the smallest promotional budget, had the smallest loss—a testament, it would seem, to the high literary quality of the work, as well as a reflection of the growing interest in the Argentine's work.[47]

I would argue that the sluggish sales of books in the program were at least partly related to its neglect of the contemporary fiction that was gradually rising in popularity during these years. Frugé later described the program as supporting "many current studies, [as well as] most of the classics and standard works that had long been unavailable" (125). The University of Texas Press was the only press to publish any recent fiction, namely works from the 1940s through the 1960s by Arreola, Bioy Casares, Borges, Rulfo, Yáñez, Sergio Galindo, and Elena Garro. (Borges's time at the University of Texas, in fact, served as the impetus for the press's publication of his work: after Borges left, Mildred Boyer, professor of Romance languages at the university, published translations of some of his works in *Texas Quarterly* and was convinced by her colleague Miguel Enguídanos to undertake the translation of *El hacedor*, which appeared as *Dreamtigers* in 1960 [Rostagno, 116].) The University of Texas Press also issued the translations of the most contemporary novels that were subsidized by the AAUP program, Galindo's *The Precipice* (1960) and Garro's *Recollections of Things to Come* (1963). Although these were published in Spanish during the early Boom years, neither one of them attained—even in Spanish—the high profile of Boom works. The other literary works published by the various university presses fell, for the most part, into three main categories: conquest and colonial narratives (López de Gómara's *Cortés*, el Inca Garcilaso de la Vega's *Royal Commentaries*, and Concolorcorvo's *El lazarillo*); Brazilian fiction (*Modern Brazilian Short Stories*, an anthology translated by William Grossman, and works by Joaquim Maria Machado de Assis, Rachel de Queiroz, and Graciliano Ramos); and, most of all, essays (e.g., those of Daniel Cosío Villegas, José Carlos Mariátegui, José Martí, Octavio Paz, Samuel Ramos, Alfonso Reyes, and Leopoldo Zea).[48]

University presses rely heavily on the recommendations of academics for their lists, and it seems likely that faculty were proposing titles that were currently being taught in university classrooms. The contemporary fiction may have been included in the increasing number of courses on Latin American literature in translation, while the essays and earlier texts would have been suitable for courses in both literature and history. Autobiographical works on the Mexican Revolution by Guzmán and by José Vasconcelos also would have been appropriate for courses in either discipline. Not all Latin Americanists were equally apprised (or, in some cases, approving) of the latest trends in narrative, which foregrounded the stylistically avant-garde and politically revolutionary. This may have affected the number of proposals that university presses received to translate Boom and other contemporary literature. At the same time, there was a core group of academics in the United States in the 1960s who, during the years of the AAUP program, were actively involved in promoting the Boom.[49] As Lowe and Fitz observe, there was "a small cadre of visionary teachers and scholars, many of whom . . . were themselves active, committed translators," who attended symposia such as the 1966 PEN congress or the 1967 Instituto Internacional de Literatura Iberoamericana and CIAR conferences in Venezuela in order to learn about current developments and share their knowledge with their students (177). Many of these academics had connections to the CIAR, which (as I discuss further in the following chapter) worked closely with commercial publishers to place Latin American literature. Instead of referring works to university presses, then, these academics were more inclined to send them to commercial presses by way of their contacts at the center.

The increasing professionalization of the Latin American writer during these years was also a factor hampering the ability of the AAUP program to break into the market for contemporary literature. At this time, Boom writers and their contemporaries were becoming much more market savvy in their efforts to place and promote their work. Most hired Carmen Balcells, the legendary Barcelona-based agent who was instrumental in creating the Boom's high profile, to represent them in Spain and internationally. In 1961, though, Fuentes—whom José Donoso refers to as "the first active and conscious agent of the internationalization of the Spanish American novel of the 1960s" (37), and who was undoubtedly the most professional among his peers at this time—took the recommendation of his friend C. Wright Mills, professor of sociology at Columbia and international best-selling author of *Listen, Yankee!*, and hired New York–based Carl Brandt as his agent; Donoso and Cabrera Infante soon followed suit, and Fuentes was tireless in recommending Brandt to his friends.[50] Brandt and Balcells, in turn, networked closely with the CIAR and with New York publishers. As a result, contemporary literature was more likely to be placed with commercial presses, whose marketing strategies and financial contracts (to say nothing of the quality of their better-trained and more professional translators) were more advantageous to writers than those of university presses. Plus, by the late 1960s and early 1970s, following the publication of *Hopscotch* and *One Hundred Years of Solitude*, even the commercial presses were willing to take more risks: as Levine writes, publishers such as Dutton, Harper and Row, Knopf, and Pantheon were "able to branch out into a literature that might not sell many copies but would receive great critical acclaim and have a pioneering impact on university curricula and intellectual circles" ("Latin American Novel," 306). The factors that kept the risks down for university presses included smaller print runs (for smaller and more specialized audiences) and lower costs compared to those of commercial publishers. Moreover, as nonprofit organizations, the university presses benefited from the fact that they received subsidies and were not as driven by corporate pressures to show large annual profits. These aspects made them good initial vehicles for building an audience for Latin American works, but also ultimately rendered them unsuitable to the "best-sellerism" that defined the Boom.

Starting in the early 1960s, publishers in Spain and Spanish America had ramped up their production and promotional infrastructure both to meet and to cultivate demand. This process was slower in the United States, and the Rockefeller Foundation had granted the funding for the AAUP project as a means of speeding it up and, not incidentally, tying the outcome to its own goals of promoting international understanding. Despite the RF's political motivations, however, it would be difficult to identify any direct or determining relationship between Cold War pressures and the program's results. The comments made by AAUP program organizers on the political implications of their project were equivocal. Officially, Frugé rejected any connection between the translation subsidy program and increasing tensions in inter-American relations in the wake of the Cuban Revolution. In a summary of a 1959 survey of AAUP member presses on their interest in publishing works from Latin America, he noted, "Several presses believe that books . . . should be chosen for their merit as works of literature or scholarship and not for noble reasons connected with international relations. (This is also the opinion of the Executive Committee and of all who are working on the project.)."[51] The proposal for the translation subsidy project submitted to the RF in 1960 similarly declared that "there is no disposition on the part of the Association of University Presses to embark upon a translation program for the sake of international relations."[52]

It is clear, however, that the organizers were sensitive to the political arena, as well as to the RF's priorities, and to what the AAUP program might mean to hemispheric relations, for the proposal also noted that "many significant developments in Latin America will inevitably call for a reorientation of U.S. thinking. . . . All of these trends are of high significance to the United States, not least of all to the role it may play in the future in cultural and intellectual exchange among the nations of the Americas."[53] Frugé's co-organizer, Wardlaw, for his part, spoke of the group's conviction that the program would both cultivate connections between the United States and Latin America and provide a means for helping the United States to understand Latin America's culture and history.[54] The Rockefeller Foundation acknowledged this benefit in its approval of the program by stating that one of the functions of university presses is the exploration of new areas of scholarly need; the foundation also echoed the proposal's language on international relations when it observed that university presses "now appear ready to act on the belief that significant recent developments in Latin America call for a reorientation of thought in regard to the role this area will play in the future of cultural and intellectual exchange among nations."[55] Harrison, who had initially set the project in motion, later wrote to a colleague that the AAUP was the organization that he felt had been most attentive to issues relating to the national interest during his time at the RF.[56]

As Harrison's assessment attests, both RF officers and those coordinating the AAUP program were well aware of its potential to improve mutual understanding, provide opportunities for exchange between the United States and Latin America, and benefit the national interest. As Lawrence Schwartz (among others) has detailed, the RF channeled a significant amount of funds in the 1950s to journals and programs that sought to promote Western liberal democratic and anti-Communist values.[57] Like other philanthropies at the time, the RF paid close attention to the history and politics of the organizations and projects that it funded, and Communist or Socialist affiliations were often used to justify denying support to applicants for funding. Hence in 1958, when Harrison was asked about the foundation's attitude toward including a piece by the openly Communist Neruda in an issue of *New World Writing* on recent Latin American literature that the RF was subsidizing, he responded that "as long as Rockefeller Foundation funds were being used to pay the translator, and not Neruda, he saw no objection, but as this small number of poems did not pretend to be an anthology it might be just as well to omit any poems of Neruda."[58] ("Ode to Laziness" was nevertheless included in the collection.) While RF priorities may have influenced the initial decision to fund the AAUP subsidy program, the program itself operated with autonomy, with no evidence of political interference in the decision-making process. Neither the foundation nor the AAUP had control over the choice of book proposals presented by individual presses, and the recommendations made by the scholars on the program's executive committee were respected. It would seem that although the AAUP program was developed and funded with an eye to improving hemispheric relations, in the end its actions and decisions were not subject to political pressures from the RF.

William Faulkner's Ibero-American Novel Project

Much more local in scale—albeit not in ambition or resonance—was the Ibero-American Novel Project, a literary competition and translation assistance endeavor set up by William Faulkner in 1961 at the University of Virginia. As I have discussed elsewhere, Faulkner traveled to Latin America as goodwill ambassador for the Department of State in 1954 and 1961.[59] He returned from his travels vowing to study Spanish and return to the region. During his 1961 trip to Venezuela, he met with numerous writers, including the nation's past and current presidents—Rómulo Gallegos and Rómulo Betancourt, respectively—all of whom told him stories about the difficulties of publishing in Latin America. Out of a desire to ease these challenges and build on the friendships he had made, Faulkner set up the Ibero-American Novel Project (IANP) on his return to Charlottesville. The project was a literary competition administered by the Faulkner Foundation at the University of Virginia and directed by Arnold Del Greco, an associate professor of Romance languages. There was no cash prize involved; rather, project officials were to use the prestige associated with Faulkner's name to convince presses to publish the novels selected by the project.

The IANP was one of many competitions to shine an international spotlight on Latin American literature at this time. For instance, Borges received the International Publishers' Prize the year the IANP was launched. As Alejandro Herrero-Olaizola details, the Premio Biblioteca Breve was likewise an important "springboard for the international success of the Latin American Boom novels" (18): sponsored annually by Spain's Seix Barral, it launched the career of Vargas Llosa, whose *La ciudad y los perros* (*The Time of the Hero*) received the award in 1962, and it enhanced the international success of Guillermo Cabrera Infante's *Tres tristes tigres* (1964; *Three Trapped Tigers*) and Fuentes's *Cambio de piel* (1967; *Change of Skin*). Even Donoso's *Obsceno pájaro de la noche* (1970) benefited from the publicity associated with the prize; it had been selected for the 1969 award but did not receive it because of upheaval within Seix Barral (see Herrero-Olaizola, 23–24). The Premio Biblioteca Breve offered consecration in the European metropolis that, in turn, brought Latin American writers greater fame in their homelands (Sorensen, 133). The Neustadt Prize administered by *World Literature Today* at the University of Oklahoma also singled out Latin American literature with its honoring of García Márquez in 1972, the second time that the prize was awarded. None of these, however, was as much of a cultural phenomenon as the literary prizes administered by Cuba's Casa de las Américas, the recipients of which, Jean Franco notes, were "published and distributed throughout Latin America" (45). Whereas the International Publishers' Prize and the Premio Biblioteca Breve both had their roots in Europe, Casa de las Américas was the cultural epicenter for Latin America in the 1960s and 1970s and "represented a new cultural geography, one whose center had drastically shifted from Europe" (ibid.). Intellectuals from throughout the region as well as Europe gathered in Cuba to judge the organization's competitions, in effect celebrating the Cuban Revolution through both their efforts and their very presence on the island.

A one-shot deal with a shoestring budget administered out of a faculty office at the University of Virginia, the IANP had a much lower profile than these other prizes, which benefited both from professional support and infrastructure. Nevertheless, Del Greco and his collaborators shared the goal of encouraging the publication of Latin American literature as well as its dissemination in the United States. Faulkner's association with the prize brought it cachet and goodwill both nationally and internationally, thereby garnering the support of writers and scholars that was necessary to carry out the work of the competition. At some level, then, the IANP was, like Faulkner's overseas missions, an informal player in inter-American cultural diplomacy; according to Del Greco, it was a means of promoting cultural exchange and improving mutual understanding within the Americas.[60]

When the project was announced in May 1961, the story was picked up immediately by the *New York Times* and *Washington Post*, among other papers, generating quite a bit of publicity. Flyers explaining the competition in English, Spanish, and Portuguese were distributed throughout the United States and Latin America. The plan was to choose from each Latin American country the best novel written since 1945, of the ones not yet translated to English. One of these novels, in turn, would subsequently be chosen as the best Latin American novel overall, for which it would be honored with a plaque from the Faulkner Foundation. For each nation, Del Greco tried to put together a panel of three judges, preferably from the country whose novels were being judged; ideally, the judges would be less than twenty-five years old, for Faulkner believed that his own success had come from this demographic group and that it was the best qualified to assess the contemporary literature emerging from Latin America.[61] Del Greco chose the judges based on consultations with colleagues at the University of Virginia, as well as professors and critics throughout the United States and Latin America. The prestige of the competition was so great that Del Greco was able to recruit some of the most renowned writers and scholars of the day to serve as judges: Rodríguez Monegal and novelist Carlos Martínez Moreno served on the Uruguay committee; Ernesto Cardenal judged the Nicaraguan competition; Cedomil Goić and Jorge Edwards evaluated the submissions from Chile; and Fernando Alegría, Eugenio Florit, and Roberto Esquenazi Mayo sat on the Cuban panel. The plan was for each panel to choose the best novel at the national level by the end of 1961; copies of the prize-winning novels from each nation would then be sent to Del Greco for the next stage of the competition.[62]

Correspondence traveled remarkably quickly within the United States and to and from Latin America, but lost and delayed missives, as well as the difficulty of acquiring books—even in the original language, part of the problem that the IANP sought to redress—slowed the process down significantly and eliminated some countries from the competition altogether. It was not until February 1963 that the prize-winning novels from fourteen different nations (of the twenty originally included in the competition) were announced.[63] The novels chosen included both avant-garde and traditional styles and politics. The best known of these today, in both Latin America and the United States, are: *Los ríos profundos* (*Deep Rivers*), by José María Arguedas (Peru); *El señor presidente* (translated with the same title), by Asturias (Guatemala); Donoso's *Coronación* (*Coronation*; Chile); *El astillero* (*The Shipyard*), by Onetti (Uruguay); *Vidas Secas* (*Barren Lives*), by Graciliano Ramos (Brazil); and *Hijo de hombre* (*Son of Man*), by Augusto Roa Bastos (Paraguay). The other works chosen were *Gamboa Road Gang: Los forzados de Gamboa*, by Joaquín Beleño (Panama); *Cumboto* (translated with the same title), by Ramón Díaz Sánchez (Venezuela); *Marcos Ramírez*, by Carlos Luis Fallas Sibaja (Costa Rica); *Érase un hombre pentafácico* (There once was a pentaphasic man), by Emma Godoy (Mexico); *Los enemigos del alma* (The enemies of the soul), by Eduardo Mallea (Argentina); *La víspera del hombre* (The eve of man), by René Marqués (Puerto Rico); *Los deshabitados* (The uninhabited ones), by Marcelo Quiroga Santa Cruz (Bolivia); and *El buen ladrón* (The good thief), by Marcio Veloz Maggiolo (Dominican Republic).

The results of the competition were broadcast throughout the United States and Latin America on Voice of America, in coordination with the State Department. The project then entered the next phase: the selection of the best novel overall from those already chosen. The committee in charge of this stage was based at the University of Virginia: in order to respect the age limit as much as possible, Del Greco appointed six doctoral students and two assistant professors to the committee; he himself served as an ex officio member. Several other critics from Spanish America and Spain were consulted as well.[64] In August 1964, *Cumboto* (1950), which is about a rural black community and the problems of race relations and *mestizaje* in Venezuela, was awarded the top honor.

Cumboto's odyssey toward translation and publication offers a heartbreaking demonstration of the program's shortcomings, despite all the effort invested in its success. Díaz Sánchez was a respected author, journalist, and politician. He was a member of the Academia Venezolana de la Lengua and the Academia Nacional de la Historia and a recipient of the Premio Nacional de Literatura; he also held several government positions, had worked in the Ministry of Education, and had served as cultural attaché for Venezuelan embassies in Europe. Soon after *Cumboto* was named the best novel overall, the University of Virginia Press and Alfred A. Knopf Inc. considered—and rejected—it for publication. Over the next few years, Del Greco offered the manuscript to more than twenty publishers.[65] Some rejected it based on their readers' active dislike of the novel. In November 1965, for example, Wardlaw refused to consider the novel for the University of Texas Press, even though he was at this time spearheading the AAUP translation program and might have been able to arrange for a subsidy. Wardlaw explained that it had already been reviewed by readers who had had a poor opinion of the novel and its translation alike.[66] Other publishers simply declined, stating that it would be difficult to find a market for it in the United States.

None of the publishers indicated why they felt the novel would not be marketable to readers in the United States. Two simply wrote that they did not think that its publication would be successful.[67] Eric Swenson, vice president and executive editor of Norton, told Del Greco that he felt that the novel would not appeal to a wide audience and that it was therefore not worth the investment that it would require.[68] Other prize-winning novels generated a similar response. In 1964, William Koshland at Knopf wrote to Del Greco that they were still deciding whether or not to publish Mallea's *Los enemigos del alma*. He explained that they had had several reports offering a variety of opinions on the novel and its potential appeal to U.S. readers, and that they were undecided about whether or not they would publish it.[69] He later wrote, "With very few exceptions, we have examined the greater part of the books you have listed and have in most cases decided not to undertake their translation into English in this country. Many of them, we felt, did not measure up to the particular standards we require for presenting books in translation in English; others we felt would not make their way with the American public."[70]

Díaz Sánchez anxiously followed his novel's peripatetic trajectory over the years. In 1965, he wrote to José Antonio Cordido-Freytes, a compatriot who was a member of the Faulkner Foundation, to express his frustration with the competition's outcome. He noted that U.S. publishers were reluctant to publish Spanish American literature and attributed this attitude to a more generalized disdain for the region as a whole. He also expressed his disillusionment with the competition, which he thought had been established as a means of eroding this disdain and improving cultural relations between the United States and Spanish America, and he asserted that the true prize would be publication, not just a metal plaque.[71] It is ironic that he should mention the plaque: because of a series of thwarted plans (for Díaz Sánchez to accept the prize on a visit to the United States, for Cordido-Freytes to give him the award in Caracas, and so forth), Díaz Sánchez never received his plaque, and it is still in the files at the University of Virginia.[72]

In late 1965, the Faulkner Foundation authorized a $2,000 subvention to subsidize the English publication of *Cumboto*, but this did not, at first, help to place the novel. In August of the following year, however, the University of Texas Press inexplicably consented to review the novel again. Perhaps Wardlaw was convinced by the subsidy, although it was less than the $3,000 to which he might have had access through the AAUP program. In any case, in early 1967, he authorized the novel's publication, using the subvention to commission a new translation. Díaz Sánchez was pleased to hear that his novel was finally going to be released in the United States, but he died in late 1968, just months before it was published. *Cumboto* was one of five finalists for the National Book Award for Translation that year, but is out of print today.

The success of the Boom writers in the United States both paved the way for the publication of other Latin American works and, in turn, was facilitated by the publicity surrounding the Faulkner Prize. The selection of *Cumboto* as the best Latin American novel was a bit surprising, however, and more than twenty years too late, for the literary tide in the region had turned. I would speculate that the selection of *Cumboto* may, in part, have reflected Del Greco's tastes, which were those of an older generation. In an interview that I conducted with Del Greco, he revealed his distaste for the work of Gabriel García Márquez and other contemporary novelists. Del Greco, who was in his midfifties when he ran the competition, published on the Nicaraguan modernista poet Rubén Darío, the presence of nineteenth-century Italian poet Giacomo Leopardi in Spanish American literature, and other aspects of nineteenth- and early twentieth-century Spanish American and European literature. His research interests thus tended more toward the traditional and classical, rather than toward more experimental fiction. His disinclination for modern writers may have come across in deliberations over which novel would receive the top honor, swaying the graduate students and young faculty members on the committee, which he had chaired. I have also wondered if the link between avant-garde literature and radical politics during the Boom years played a role in this decision.

In addition to the literary dimension of the IANP's history, it is important to note how the project was inflected by the contemporary field of power. Cold War cultural politics influenced not just literary taste but the dynamics of the competition itself. The IANP took place against the backdrop of heightened U.S. interest in Latin America. It was conceived during the Kennedy years, and it would be wise not to overlook Charlottesville's proximity to Washington, DC. Del Greco coordinated different stages of the project with State Department and government officials from the USIA and other agencies, and he met with Edward Kennedy at least once to discuss the IANP. Del Greco was also sensitive to the project's potential to benefit the national interest as a vehicle for cultural diplomacy with Latin American opinion molders. This seemed to reflect his own political inclinations—namely, his investment in Cold War efforts at containment. These were evident in his involvement with a State Department–funded program in Bolivia, where the Movimiento Nacionalista Revolucionario, a radical reformist movement, was in power from 1952 to 1964: during this period, he traveled to Bolivia several times, recruiting students to spend six weeks participating in the Bolivian Seminar at the University of Virginia Law School in order to get them away from being indoctrinated, and—in his words—to "convert" them from Communism.[73] In the interview with me, he noted that bookstores in La Paz sold plenty of Russian literature, but no translations of U.S. literature.[74] Thus, in addition to his commitment to the IANP's goals, Del Greco sought to have the competition help in its own way to promote international relations. In 1963, he proposed to Muna Lee, then cultural coordinator of the State Department's Office of Public Affairs of the Bureau of Inter-American Affairs, that the department organize and fund a symposium to bring the prize-winning authors together in the United States. He argued that the symposium would generate goodwill among the writers toward the host country, and that this attitude would be communicated to their readers, swaying their opinions about inter-American relations and ultimately benefiting the nation.[75] In 1964, Del Greco arranged for Quiroga Santa Cruz (Bolivia) and Veloz Maggiolo (Dominican Republic) to visit the United States under the aegis of the State Department's Foreign Leaders program. It is unlikely to have been a coincidence that both writers hailed from nations where radical politics were in the ascendance (and, in the case of the Dominican Republic, where tensions with the United States were increasing).

This is not to say, though, that Cold War politics held sway over the general procedures or the ultimate outcome of the competition. Some administrators and judges acknowledged the pressures in various ways, but these pressures did not determine the final outcome of the contest. For the most part, the judging was conducted independently by writers in each nation, with Del Greco hearing back from the panels only after a decision had been made. Indeed, the leftist sympathies of Asturias, Fallas Sibaja, and Graciliano Ramos were well known at the time and clearly did not prevent their novels from being chosen by individual panels. But the ripple effects of national and regional politics did surface in various ways, to the extent that several of the national competitions can be studied as microcosms of the political turmoil affecting the individual nations and even the hemisphere as a whole. The panel from the Dominican Republic, for example, notified Del Greco that they had been unable to complete their task because of political turmoil in the nation.[76] Instead, they narrowed the field down to two works: Ramón Emilio Reyes's *El testimonio* (The testimony) and Veloz Maggiolo's *El buen ladrón*, which was selected by two of the three judges (Veloz Maggiolo was also a judge on the panel, and he voted for Reyes's novel).[77] Politics also took a toll on the career trajectory of the winning novelist from Costa Rica. Fallas Sibaja was a political activist, labor organizer, and member of the Communist Party who in the 1930s had led a strike protesting the poor labor conditions of United Fruit Company workers. The author expressed his concern to Del Greco that U.S. publishers might have turned down the opportunity to translate his novel for nefarious reasons. He alleged that his mail was being illegally inspected and asked Del Greco to take over the job of placing his novel so that publishers would not have to correspond directly with him.[78] (Del Greco declined to take on this task.) In 1973, a translator working with Fallas Sibaja's widow wrote to Del Greco that they believed that *Marcos Ramírez* had been turned down earlier because of the author's leftist political beliefs; now, however, they felt that the political climate had changed and that publishers might be more amenable to accepting the work.[79] However, they too were ultimately unsuccessful in their quest.

Cold War politics also played a key role in the selection process for the Cuban novel, which was conducted by a panel made up entirely of Spanish American author-critics on faculty at U.S. universities: Esquenazi Mayo, a Cuban writer and literary critic at the University of Nebraska who also worked in the cultural division at the Pan American Union and was a founding editor of "*Life*" *en español*; Florit, a Cuban poet and literary critic at Barnard; and, at least nominally, Alegría, a Chilean critic and novelist at the University of California, Berkeley. Esquenazi Mayo, who headed the panel and was a determining political force in the deliberations, was politically conservative and fervently opposed to the Cuban Revolution. For several years, he had been on the editorial board of *Cuadernos*, the CCF's first Latin American journal, and in his later years he would describe Castro as a tyrant (19) and Cuba as a "Marxist tyranny" (6).

In March 1962, Esquenazi Mayo wrote to Del Greco that while there were a number of very good novels from Cuba, many of the writers were associated with Castro and the revolution, of which he disapproved.[80] Del Greco agreed that the Cuban situation was tricky, and while he admitted that he too would prefer an author who was not involved with the revolutionary government, he acknowledged that contest rules did not prohibit the selection of political novels and that judges had complete freedom to choose as they saw fit.[81] In June, Esquenazi Mayo informed Del Greco that Florit had chosen Alejo Carpentier's *The Lost Steps*, but that they had not had any word from Alegría, the committee's third member. Esquenazi Mayo recognized the high quality of Carpentier's novel, but also noted that the author was actively involved with the Cuban government; using the fact that the committee had not yet heard from Alegría, he suggested closing the competition without choosing a winner.[82] Del Greco avoided the political question, but agreed to the suggestion on the grounds that Alegría had not weighed in.[83] He did ask, though, to be notified if the committee heard from Alegría.[84] As they never did, no Cuban novel ever received the award. Ultimately, this exchange was as ironic as it was interesting from a political perspective, for it need never have happened: Alfred A. Knopf Inc. had actually published *The Lost Steps* in 1956, to positive reviews but disappointingly low sales (and, clearly, little publicity).[85] Had Del Greco known this, he could have disqualified the novel on these grounds and avoided the political debate altogether.

The absence of Cuba from the final list of novels was singled out by Linton Massey, president of the Faulkner Foundation. After the first stage of the competition was completed, Massey wrote to Edgar Shannon, president of the University of Virginia, commending Del Greco for his work. He noted in particular that the latter had been able to organize committees that were not driven by Communist agendas, and had moreover managed to avoid including Cuba in the contest.[86] This was, of course, a misreading of what had transpired, but it reflects the attentiveness of university administrators to Cold War questions, and it was a misperception that went uncorrected and thus had the last word.

Perhaps the ramifications of these cultural politics are small. For, in many respects, despite the prestige associated with Faulkner's name, the award ultimately failed in its main objective. Only seven of the award-winning novels have to this day been published in the United States, and most of these were published without the assistance of the competition. *Cumboto* was a key exception, of course, as was *Barren Lives*, which was published by the University of Texas Press in 1965, with a subsidy from the AAUP translation program. *Coronation* and *El señor presidente*, however, were already under contract by the time the awards were announced, and *Deep Rivers* and *Son of Man* did not come out until years later, without the assistance of the Faulkner Foundation.[87] The authors whose prize-winning novels were published in English later had other works translated; Mallea and Marqués likewise saw several works appear in English, although not the ones that had been finalists in the IANP competition.[88] However, to the best of my knowledge, very few works by any of the other authors have ever been published in English, despite initial interest in Godoy's and Fallas Sibaja's novels.[89] Less than half of the prize-winning novels are still in print—let alone read or studied—in either English or Spanish. These shortcomings were not due to any lack of effort or goodwill on the part of project participants: Del Greco worked tirelessly and without remuneration to coordinate the competition and publicity, and to match the award-winning novels with publishers; and Latin American judges, critics, and authors repeatedly indicated their belief that the IANP would be instrumental in bringing their work to the North, which they felt was ignorant of their culture, and that it had the potential to improve relations between Latin America and the United States.

I believe that the reasons for the project's failure lie elsewhere. The IANP was timely, and it should have been well positioned to capitalize on the incipient surge in translation of Latin American works in the United States in the early 1960s. During this time, Harper and Row created an International Division to focus on several areas, most notably Latin American literature. In 1964, Seymour Lawrence, then editor of the Atlantic Monthly Press, wrote to Del Greco that his company was undertaking an effort to promote works in translation and that they were especially interested in publishing works from Latin America as part of the program.[90] Several other publishers contacted Del Greco, saying that they would like to consider the award-winning novels for their lists. But when presses requested descriptions of the works, which Del Greco did not have on hand, he referred them to the novels' dust jackets (which were, of course, in Spanish and which the publishers would presumably have to acquire on their own) for plot summaries.[91] Nor did he have information on the works' publication history or, ironically, translation status, so he referred inquiries to the original Latin American publishers, giving the U.S. representatives a task that could be difficult to pursue. Additionally, U.S. presses were expected to contact prize-winning authors and their publishers directly in order to arrange rights to the works in English.

These logistics, however, account for only part of the outcome. I would suggest that *Cumboto*'s fate, as well as that of several of the works that were never translated, was in many respects a question of style and timing. The novels chosen by the project's judges were evenly split: almost half were avant-garde in style or theme, while the rest were regionalist in scope and realist (or social realist) in style. The regionalist novel, of which *Cumboto* could be said to be an exemplar, was a genre that had had its heyday in Spanish America in the 1920s and 1930s, but that had receded to the background in the region as the *nueva narrativa* emerged in the 1940s and 1950s. José Donoso once described regionalism as reinforcing the "frontiers between one region and the next, between one country and another" (14–15). If the emphasis on so-called local color was unlikely to appeal to Latin American readers outside of an author's homeland, it was even less likely to be of interest to a U.S. audience; the use of an outmoded style rendered the works even less marketable. And yet, thanks in large measure to the lobbying of Harriet de Onís, Knopf's lists were dominated by regionalist works, even through the early 1960s. Rostagno speculates that the poor sales of Latin American literature at Knopf may have been because, "lacking the necessary background, readers of South American works faced a particularly strenuous effort" (33). Thus, I would read the aforementioned assessments by publishers that *Cumboto* and the other IANP-endorsed novels did not meet their standards or were unlikely to appeal to a wide audience in the United States as code for this.

With the exception of *Cumboto*, the prize-winning novels that were translated and published in the United States were at least marked—if not defined—by a more experimental style and modern world view. Indeed, the fact that *Cumboto* was published is a testament to Del Greco's commitment to the novel and to his persistence: even de Onís was at this point translating the work of writers such as Guimarães Rosa and Carpentier, and there was very little audience for regionalist fiction in the United States at this time. *Cumboto* was, in fact, one of the few regionalist novels published in the United States during the 1960s and 1970s. While the prize-winning novels other than *Cumboto* that were published in the United States also addressed local issues, settings, and history, I would speculate that their questioning of reality, use of modern and urban settings, and treatment of themes such as dictatorship were seen by publishers as more appealing to the sensibilities of a broader audience. Indeed, the judges responsible for selecting these novels often commented on what they viewed as the works' "universality" and further sought to differentiate them from regionalist works. These qualities and themes additionally dovetailed with those exhibited in the work of the Boom authors who did not—other than Donoso—even compete in the project, which began just before they wrote the works that shot them into the international spotlight. Ultimately, then, the project's results—however sad, when one considers its unfulfilled potential—were caught between the old and the new, reflecting the transition between literary generations.

Cornell University's "Latin American Year"

The final university-sponsored initiative that I will examine is Cornell's "Latin American Year" (CLAY). CLAY was a series of events focusing on Latin America that was held at the university and several other sites between October 1965 and June 1966. It was an intensive effort to draw attention to the university's involvement with the region, and in turn to increase interest on campus and throughout the nation in Latin American affairs. To administer the project, University officers chose as its director William MacLeish, who had spent several years at *Visión*, a highly successful Spanish-language newsmagazine based in New York City and distributed throughout Latin America. MacLeish was assisted by a coordinating committee that included Latin Americanist faculty and staff from the arts, humanities, social sciences, law, business, international studies, the library, and university administration.

CLAY was the brainchild of James Perkins, an expert on education and government who had become president of Cornell in 1963, after serving as a vice president at the Carnegie Corporation of New York for thirteen years. The 1960s were, of course, a time of turbulence in the United States that resonated well beyond the Cold War and inter-American relations and that made its way into university settings. In particular, the demonstrations at the University of California, Berkeley, starting with the Free Speech Movement in 1964, sent ripples of concern through university administrations across the country. At this time as well, increasing disciplinary specialization was prompting experts in higher education to wonder about the fate of the university as a community. At Cornell, Perkins sought to stem the trend toward atomization by proposing projects with centralizing themes structured around curricular and extracurricular activities that would attract the efforts of many departments and thereby help to integrate the university.[92]

The choice of Latin America as the focus of the first such exercise stemmed from the university's long history of research, teaching, and training projects in the region, as well as its involvement in efforts to promote the improvement of universities there. It also reflected Perkins's own interests, for he had been a founder and a longtime leader of the Council on Higher Education in the American Republics. Additionally, Cornell's Latin American Studies program, founded in 1961, had been one of the earlier programs to spring up in the wake of the Cuban Revolution, and it had grown rapidly: by 1965, there were forty students enrolled in its PhD minor, and it coordinated numerous activities in Latin America.[93]

To fund the endeavor, Perkins requested a $150,000 grant from his former employer, the Carnegie Corporation, whose mission was the "advancement and diffusion of knowledge and understanding." His proposal for six conferences stressed the benefit of CLAY as a test case for redressing the dispersal of focus in U.S. universities by arguing that the program offered Cornell an opportunity to "re-achieve internal communication and coordination, to regain the sense that each major new dimension of academic effort is the business of the whole University and—above all—to share within Cornell and within the whole American community of higher education the challenge and the gain resulting from the work of specialists collaborating in a single and novel academic program."[94] For Perkins, CLAY represented both "a new initiative in the self-improvement of the American University and . . . a major contribution . . . to improved understanding of Latin American society and its problems."[95]

Perkins was, however, careful to downplay contemporary interest in the region and its politics as a rationale for the choice of topic. This was evident in his proposal, which acknowledged that "there are valid reasons to single out the area of Latin American Studies" for such an initiative, but that "ultimately the choice is necessarily also incidental."[96] There was some confusion on this point at first, though. Carnegie officers reported that Perkins initially framed the importance of the conferences in terms of "their relevance to our international program rather than in terms of their collective significance as an attempt at solving a general problem of higher education in America."[97] The officers met with Perkins and reported that the president had reassured them that "the entire objective of the project is . . . entirely unifying of the Cornell campus and has nothing to do with U.S.–Latin American relations, at any rate as far as he is concerned."[98] The final proposal submitted to the Carnegie Corporation accordingly foregrounded "the community-building aspects of the Year."[99] The officers felt that if CLAY was successful, Perkins "would have made a major contribution to alleviating a problem which faces all large institutions in this country."[100] In contrast to the political subtexts motivating the Rockefeller and Ford Foundations' support of grants (as discussed earlier in this book), the Carnegie Corporation's funding of CLAY reflected its prioritization of the mission of supporting higher education. And, in this instance, the corporation itself seemed genuinely to be much less interested in Cold War politics per se.

In March 1965, Carnegie approved the grant with a resolution that highlighted the project's potential to offer a solution to contemporary challenges in higher education:

> One of the important issues facing the university today is whether it can regain a sense of community or whether it must inevitably become a loosely affiliated set of unrelated activities. (Needless to say all questions concerning the social coherence of the university have gained a new urgency as a result of the Berkeley riots.) . . . Whether Mr. Perkins will succeed in his effort to recreate a sense of community is hard to predict. But it is a timely move, and worthy of support.[101]

The president's office at Cornell also put $30,000 toward CLAY. Event organizers were additionally able to tap into the current largesse toward Latin American programming at philanthropies and public agencies for the remainder of the estimated $300,000 budget: large sums came from the Agency for International Development ($55,000 for partial support of the conferences) and Ford Foundation ($75,000 for foreign travel, visiting professorships, and publication of CLAY materials), and smaller contributions from the Rockefeller Foundation (for the conference on tropical agricultural development) and the Bureau of Educational and Cultural Affairs (ECA) at the Department of State (for the student seminar, as detailed below).[102]

The high public profile of CLAY was evident from the very beginning. The opening ceremonies drew the most distinguished Latin Americanists in the country, as well as top government officials and philanthropy officers. Numerous directors of NDEA-sponsored Latin American Studies centers attended, as did Lyman Legters, the director of the Language and Area Centers Section of the Department of Education, and Howard Cline, the director of the Hispanic Foundation of the Library of Congress. Three of the Rockefeller Foundation's highest-ranking administrators were present, as were directors of two of the Ford Foundation's international programs and officers from the Carnegie Corporation and the Social Sciences Research Council. The event also drew Jacob Canter, who was at this point director of the Office of Inter-American Programs of the ECA; Representative Howard Robison; and Elinor Halle of the Latin American office at the USIA. Also present was Thomas Messer, the director of the Guggenheim Museum, which with CLAY had co-sponsored an art exhibition, *The Emergent Decade*, featuring contemporary paintings by forty artists from nine Latin American countries; the show opened at the university's White Museum, traveled to Dallas and Ottawa, and ended its tour at the Guggenheim Museum. The Cornell Glee Club gave a joint concert with the Coro de Cámara de Valparaíso, a well-known student choral group from the Universidad de Valparaíso in Chile.

The star power present at the opening ceremonies was in evidence throughout the year, as CLAY organizers kept up a breakneck pace of activities, many focused on the social sciences. The six conferences all featured top scholars and high-ranking diplomats. They focused on modernization and the city, the tropics and rural development, race and class, economic development, U.S. university involvement in Latin American development, and highland communities. Additional lectures were given throughout the year by high-profile personages such as Messer; Felipe Herrera, president of the Inter-American Development Bank; Juscelino Kubitschek, the former president of Brazil; Carlos Sanz de Santamaría, the chairman of the Inter-American Committee on the Alliance for Progress; Radomiro Tomic, the Chilean ambassador to the United States; and Brazilian writer Erico Verissimo. Directors of NDEA-funded Latin American Studies centers met with U.S. Department of Education officials, and the board of the newly formed *Latin American Research Review* convened in Ithaca as well (its chair was Tom Davis, an economist who was also a member of the CLAY coordinating committee and the director of Cornell's Latin American Studies program); during the *Review* meeting, recommendations for the organization of the Latin American Studies Association, which was founded soon after the gathering, were discussed.

There were also a number of events in the humanities and arts. Octavio Paz took a leave of absence from his duties as Mexico's ambassador to India to spend the spring term at Cornell, where he taught courses on poetry (in both English and Spanish, allowing him to reach a broader selection of students), met with students, and gave a reading from his work.[103] The stay at Cornell also allowed Paz to further his own literary agenda, for he gave lectures at various universities and appeared at the Guggenheim Museum in an event organized by the Academy of American Poets. In April, the Cornell Dramatic Club put on a performance in English of Mexican playwright Emilio Carballido's *Medusa*; additionally, the author, who attended the performance, gave a lecture on Mexican theater. Distinguished Chilean composer Juan Orrego-Salas, a student of Aaron Copland and founder of the Latin American Music Center at Indiana University Bloomington, was commissioned to write a composition for CLAY: *América, no en vano invocamos tu nombre* (America, we do not invoke your name in vain), a cantata based on the work of Pablo Neruda, premiered during the year. In the visual arts, the White Museum planned several smaller exhibits on Latin American art in addition to the co-sponsored exhibition with the Guggenheim. Also, Peruvian painter Fernando de Szyszlo gave a lecture on campus, and several schools hired renowned artists and architects to serve as artists-in-residence and visiting teachers.

CLAY organizers strove for balance in the representation of participants from the United States and Latin America: the majority of lectures were given by Latin Americans, and the representation of conference participants from both regions was almost equal. This was significant, for it meant that Latin Americans were actively involved in the image of their region that was coming out of CLAY activities, and that the program as a whole was less vulnerable to criticism of it as an imperialist endeavor. Equally important was the respect that CLAY organizers demonstrated for political positions that were generally unwelcome in the Cold War United States at that time. According to MacLeish, the steering committee resisted any ideological bias against Socialism and sought to make CLAY an "even playing field."[104] The opening ceremonies set the tone, indicating that CLAY was open not just to ideas about inter-American exchange, but also to critique of U.S. policy in Latin America. George Harrar, president of the Rockefeller Foundation, gave a politically neutral speech, "Reciprocity in Education in the Americas," on the former theme. In contrast, Risieri Frondizi, former rector of the Universidad de Buenos Aires, gave a lecture titled "A Latin American View of U.S. Policy in Latin America" in which he accused President Johnson of switching U.S. policy toward Latin America from its "Good Neighbor" praxis back toward the "Big Stick" diplomacy of the early twentieth century, in effect alienating the region's politicians and pushing them away from viewing the United States as a viable political model. Invoking an event that was fresh in everyone's minds, he declared that "intervention in the Dominican Republic earlier in 1965 by United States armed forces made more people join the Communist Party in one week than the sum total of all Communist propaganda did during the preceding year" (Frondizi, 23). He also spoke directly about the "failure of United States policy in Latin America," which he attributed to "the tendency to transfer North American values and problems to an area which has a completely different historical and cultural background—different needs, different values and different concerns" (ibid.). In other words, "Communism may be a menace in Latin America. But starvation, ignorance, prejudice, endemic diseases, dictatorships and economic instability are daily facts of life. How can one expect a Latin American to be more concerned about a potential and unseen threat than about a dramatic reality of his daily life?" (ibid.). To redress the situation, Frondizi urged the State Department to pay more attention to academics and less to the military, hoping that the values he viewed as underpinning higher education in the United States might have a beneficial effect when translated into foreign policy.[105] His speech provided a powerful opening to the year's activities.

The concern about presenting the political perspectives of both Latin Americans and U.S. citizens was in evidence in the debates surrounding the planning of the student-organized conference, "The University Student and National Development," which took place from February 22 to 26. The conference was organized by Gail Richardson, a senior majoring in arts and the president of the student committee for CLAY, with assistance from George Irvin, a graduate student in government.[106] It was a closed event, conducted as a workshop in Spanish, where sixteen student leaders from Latin American universities met with twenty-four Cornell students from the United States and Latin America to discuss "the role of student political groups in helping to fulfill the university's responsibility to its country" as well as the place of politics in the university, and the role of the university in national affairs and development.[107] Germán Arciniegas and Kalman Silvert, a distinguished professor of government at Dartmouth, gave lectures on related topics that were open to the public.

Participating students from Cornell were chosen "on the basis of their knowledge of Spanish and knowledge of and interest in Latin America."[108] The initial selection of potential participants from Latin America was made by the U.S. Department of State, which also provided funding for the travel of the delegates (the costs of the seminar itself came from funds from the Ford and Carnegie Foundations). Richardson and Irvin traveled to Latin America in the summer of 1965, where they interviewed the candidates and made a final selection, which then had to be approved by the local embassies. I have found no documents that explain how the State Department selected students for its initial list. As they hailed almost exclusively from the larger universities in the capital cities of Argentina, Bolivia, Chile, Colombia, Mexico, Peru, and Uruguay, the department seems to have been targeting students who would have influence over large numbers of peers in urban settings, many of which had borne witness to rising tides of leftist activism. The State Department no doubt viewed this as an opportunity to offset the students' exposure to leftism in their native countries and present the United States and its democratic system to student leaders—opinion molders within their own universities—in the hope that they would share their positive impressions of the nation on their return home. Thus, the department not only paid for the students to visit Cornell for ten days, but also covered travel in the United States for an additional three weeks, presumably as a means of further exposing them to the nation's culture and politics.

The student-organized conference caused the CLAY steering committee no small amount of consternation over the course of the year. Committee members were concerned from the start that they had little information about how it was being planned, and further felt that it needed to have an experienced director.[109] These concerns only multiplied when the student organizers reported to the committee in late November. When presented with the final set of students chosen by Richardson and Irvin, committee members complained that the group had two "deficiencies." First, there were no Brazilian students included, because the State Department "would not mix Portuguese with Spanish."[110] There were also no Marxists and no students from Cuba. This was unlikely to have come as a surprise: while the State Department did sponsor programs that brought students from Latin America to the United States in order to remove them from leftist indoctrination and expose them to U.S. liberal democratic values (e.g., the Bolivian Seminar that Del Greco participated in), officials may well have been less inclined to bring outspoken Marxist student leaders to the United States for a highly publicized event involving close interactions with U.S. students. The steering committee considered redressing the lacunae, noting that "it might be possible to find a Marxist in other institutions in the United States," as well as Brazilians who might be able to step in.[111] In the end, though, no additions were made to the list of students, perhaps because the conference was entirely run by students and the steering committee may have wished to respect their autonomy. In any case, the radical perspective was far from absent among the students selected from the State Department list. The conference featured sessions titled "Revolución violenta: Las implicaciones de Cuba" (Violent revolution: The implications of Cuba) and "Relaciones entre América Latina y América del Norte" (Relations between Latin America and North America) and debate was reportedly heated. Also, throughout the conference, the students from Latin America "stressed the inevitability of revolution in their countries, but said they recognized the accompanying need for agricultural development and increased productivity. The students also called for the reintegration of Cuba into the Latin American family of nations [reversing its expulsion from the OAS] regardless of its form of government."[112]

The conference seems to have been quite successful—and its organizers figured out a way of incorporating another radical voice into the debate, albeit outside of the conference proper. On February 28, two days after the student conference ended, Emmanuel Espinal gave a public lecture at Cornell, "The Dominican Crisis: Past, Present and Future," that was sponsored by the CLAY Student Committee. Espinal was identified in the minutes of a steering committee meeting held just prior to the event as simply "a student in New York," and he appears just as a "lecturer" on the list of participants included in MacLeish's final report on CLAY.[113] The report's list of lecturers for the year, however, properly identified him as the head of the Juventud Revolucionaria Dominicana, the youth section of the Partido Revolucionario Dominicano (PRD). The Juventud Revolucionaria Dominicana was the more radical branch of the PRD—its leaders had been influenced by Marx, Lenin, and Che (Kryzanek, 132)—which was supported by former president Juan Bosch. As noted in Chapter 2, Bosch was campaigning for reelection at this time; however, he made very few public appearances out of fear of reprisal (Kryzanek, 120). Perhaps Espinal, too, was protecting himself by pursuing studies in New York during this period. In any case, scheduling Espinal's lecture to follow the student conference seems to have offset an apparent lack of Marxist representation among conference participants and granted a public forum to a revolutionary political perspective. As the Latin American students were to spend at least ten days at Cornell, most were probably still on campus for Espinal's lecture, providing an opportunity for interaction and exchange of perspectives. At the same time, by not including Espinal in the official conference program, organizers managed to avoid confrontation with the State Department, which no doubt would have been loath to have the perspective of the political party it had so recently deposed from power share the stage with the students it had so carefully selected.

In the end, all involved in Cornell's Latin American Year programming felt that it had been a success. Close to four hundred scholars, artists, statesmen, and others participated in the programs, and most of the conferences, lectures, and performances had drawn full crowds.[114] The proceedings of several of the conferences were published by Cornell University Press. Publicity was widespread, with press releases sent regularly to both U.S. and large Latin American periodicals, generating broad national and international awareness of CLAY activities. On the downside, organizers felt that they had not been as successful reaching out to non-academic audiences who were not already interested in the region, and that coverage by the national press had been "disappointing."[115] They were pleased, however, that "the academic community and those with diplomatic, trade, and journalistic interests were made aware of the coming events," and that participants, Latin Americans (including many Cornell alumni), and academics and diplomats were able to disseminate information on CLAY to interested parties in the United States and Latin America.[116] Latin Americanists on Cornell's faculty reported to MacLeish on returning from trips to the region that "the reaction to CLAY has been quite favorable and that as a result, interest in the University and willingness to cooperate with it are generally on the increase."[117]

Certainly, Paz's time at the university was widely—and positively— covered for Latin American readers: "*Life*" *en español* published an article, "Octavio Paz enseña y aprende en Cornell" (Octavio Paz teaches and learns at Cornell), which *Mundo Nuevo* featured as "Octavio Paz en Cornell," summarizing and quoting heavily from the original article while offering its own gloss on the importance of the poet's visit.[118] Both versions discussed Paz's impressions of the students and their concerns, and also took advantage of the opportunity to shine a spotlight on his assessments of the growing international reputation of Latin American writers, such as his declaration that "Spanish American literature has something to say to the world. Thus it is not strange that Spanish American writers are beginning to be known in Europe and the United States" (qtd. in "Octavio Paz en Cornell," 73). The *Mundo Nuevo* feature concluded that the presence in the United States of the writers who attended the 1966 PEN conference—as well as that of Donoso (University of Iowa), Parra (Louisiana State University), and Paz— signaled an important breakthrough not just for their own work but for the possibilities of international understanding: "The contact of these great writers, men of open spirit and independent opinions, with North American reality can be very beneficial for the dialogue that must necessarily get more intense if the two Americas are ever to truly understand each other" ("Octavio Paz en Cornell," 73–74).

CLAY programming had an important effect within the university as well. In MacLeish's opinion, "The CLAY conferences had their greatest impact outside the University whereas the arts and humanities projects had their greatest impact inside. . . . The students who associated with the artists in residence will remember the experience for years to come. Those who took on the hard work of making a new composition come alive or of staging a complex theatrical production shared a rare sense of accomplishment."[119] The writer- and artist-in-residence programs were extremely successful, and attracted more students than the conferences or other activities. The arts programs in general reached a wide public.[120] Following the conference, the number of faculty and students focusing on Latin America, already on the rise, was expected to increase dramatically; the projected growth in the Latin American Studies program, in turn, was expected to attract more Latin American scholars to the university, as well as resulting in expanded library holdings in the field.[121] Thus, MacLeish concluded his final report on the year by saying that "CLAY will go far toward achieving its first two goals—those of helping to increase interest in this country in Latin American affairs and of underscoring Cornell's commitment to the area."[122] CLAY also seemed to bolster a sense of community among the faculty and students who had participated in its events.

Despite the program's success, though, it did not set a precedent for future theme-driven years, an idea that seemed to fall by the wayside. Perkins instead devoted the next few years of his presidency to developing new departments and spearheading major capital campaigns at the university.[123] Additionally, Perkins, who had been chair of the board of trustees of the United Negro College Fund, set up programs to increase the enrollment of African American students and to provide greater support to them while at the same time trying to quell the tensions and demonstrations on campus relating to issues of race and social justice. It was a combination of these circumstances that led to his resignation from the presidency in 1969, when he came under fire for his handling of the occupation of the student union by armed African American students—a protest that sparked confrontations elsewhere, was one of the most widely publicized of its day, and left deep wounds at Cornell that to this day still generate sharp feelings.[124] Thus, the president who began his term seeking to unite and integrate the university ended up himself becoming a casualty of the turbulence of the times.

EVEN WHEN TAKEN TOGETHER, these case studies barely scratch the surface of contemporary activity in this area. Nevertheless, they give an idea of both the possibilities and the political exigencies of the time. Several of these projects fizzled out, having realized some of their goals, but with a more limited long-term impact than their organizers had aspired to. CLAY attracted high-level participants and generated publicity within and outside of academia, but after the year's activities were over, its impact was circumscribed within the university. Faulkner's novel competition brought visibility to Latin American literature and its growing importance, as well as earning goodwill in the very fact of the endeavor, but didn't actually manage to get many of the prizewinning works published. The literary works subsidized by the AAUP program likewise gained some press but earned little revenue, and were destined to become prestige items rather than best sellers—if they were lucky. The Latin American workshop at Iowa never materialized, but the International Writing Program at least succeeded in realizing its work of cultural diplomacy—and, of course, cultivating writing skills—with a broader scope that included Latin American writers.

Ultimately, I would argue that the *Odyssey Review* (despite its short life span) and the Writing Division at Columbia University left the most lasting legacies, for they were both predicated on successful and lasting collaborations among writers, academics, translators, and publishers, and built on them.[125] Rabassa, MacShane, and others involved in these two endeavors also worked with the Center for Inter-American Relations in joint efforts that further benefited from the presence of Latin American writers in visiting academic positions during these years. Together, these efforts were fundamental to establishing Latin American literature's reputation in the United States, and constitute an important example of academia and the trade publishing sector successfully joining forces.

In *Under Northern Eyes*, Mark Berger demonstrates how the discipline of Latin American studies in effect operated in collusion with U.S. Cold War policy.[126] Cline's statement that the Cuban Revolution showed that "all was not well in Latin America, and that something must be done about it"—that "something" being the development of Latin American studies and its professional organization—speaks directly to this inclination (64). While Cold War policy and pressures left a clear imprint on the programs I have discussed in this chapter, the degree to which they were driven by "doing something about" Cuba or the spread of Marxism through Latin America varies widely. Across the country, scholars in English and Spanish departments alike were caught up in a wave of enthusiasm for the Boom and for contemporary literature from Latin America, and they found the interest in the region to be timely for their endeavors. Given the support of many Latin American writers for Cuba, at least during the 1960s, the promotion of this literature in the United States carried an inherent political charge. This did not go unnoticed by the State Department or U.S. philanthropies, which provided funding for a number of programs as venues for cultural outreach, although time and again the levels of mediation between philanthropy administrators and those who implemented the individual programs brought home the lesson that funding was no guarantee of a political outcome. The academics involved in these projects and others walked a fine line: a number of them played to the Cold War context in their framing of their projects and the fundraising for them. However, some of them also took active roles in resisting Cold War policies and interventions, and in ensuring that voices oppositional to U.S. policy were heard in their programs.

4

The "Cold War Struggle" for Latin American Literature at the Center for Inter-American Relations

Just days after the end of the Cuban missile crisis, a group of artists, scholars, journalists, publishers, and politicians from Latin America and the United States gathered on Paradise Island in the Bahamas to discuss inter-American cultural and political relations. The symposium, which was aimed at improving mutual understanding and communication between artists and intellectuals from both regions, was the brainchild of Robert Wool, editor in chief of *Show: The Magazine of the Performing Arts*, who had traveled to Latin America on numerous occasions and frequently wrote on the region. In attendance from Latin America were Chilean writer and critic Fernando Alegría; Chilean painter and art historian Jorge Elliott; Argentine critic Rafael Squirru, who was also director of the Museum of Modern Art in Buenos Aires (and soon to become director of cultural affairs at the Pan American Union); Peruvian artist Fernando Szyszlo; Peruvian writer and diplomat Carlos Zavaleta; and several others. U.S. participants included writers Edward Albee, Peter Matthiessen, William Styron, and Gore Vidal; composer Aaron Copland; Richard Goodwin, deputy assistant secretary of state for inter-American affairs; John Harrison, director of the Institute of Latin American Studies at the University of Texas at Austin; Richard Morse, chair of the Council on Latin American Studies at Yale; Norman Podhoretz, editor of *Commentary*; Arthur Schlesinger Jr., a historian and special assistant to President Kennedy; and John Thompson, executive director of the Farfield Foundation. After the symposium, the Latin American participants flew to New York, where Wool had set up meetings with publishers in the hopes of assisting them with the dissemination of their work in the United States. From Manhattan, the Latin Americans traveled to Washington, DC, where they met with President Kennedy; Robert Kennedy; Hubert Humphrey; Lucius Battle, assistant secretary of state for educational and cultural affairs; Teodoro Moscoso, coordinator for the Alliance for Progress; and numerous other White House and State Department officials.[1]

The idea behind the symposium seems to have percolated among *Show* editors for some time. In April 1962, while preparing a special issue on contemporary Latin American culture and arts, they published an article on the importance of cultural diplomacy as a front in the Cold War.[2] The article took a clear anti-Soviet stance, lamenting that the Department of State's newly formed Bureau of Educational and Cultural Affairs had a much smaller budget than the Soviet Ministry of Culture and was therefore unable to project an image of the United States and its democratic values as effectively. The article was followed by an "immodest proposal" from the magazine's editors that strongly criticized the bureau for promoting programs that were "stodgy" and "establishment" ("Immodest Proposal," 55). Instead, the editors lobbied for "the young and experimental" to be included in cultural diplomacy programs because students were an increasingly powerful constituency and "from the standpoint of our national interest, put in cold-war terms, it is these young who must be reached" (55). *Show* editors also argued for an "artistic Peace Corps" that would send U.S. artists to live abroad and interact with their counterparts in order to "further the exchange of ideas and alter some dangerous international false impressions" (55). This "immodest proposal" in effect functioned as a blueprint for the Paradise Island symposium, which brought together both young and established artists and intellectuals from the United States and Latin America in dialogues aimed at increasing participants' understanding of inter-American relations and, just as importantly, one another.

The response to the symposium was so enthusiastic that participants clamored for more. In early 1963, Wool left *Show* to found the Inter-American Committee (IAC), a nonprofit organization dedicated to promoting cultural exchange between Latin America and the United States. The organization, based in New York, was envisioned as a counterpart to the Asia Society, founded in 1956 by John D. Rockefeller III, which sought to build awareness of Asia in the United States and to foster relationships and mutual understanding between the Asian countries and the United States. And, also like the Asia Society, the IAC originated in a Cold War political context. The battle between democracy and Communism was inscribed in the organization's origins with the rhetoric of what Volker Berghahn has labeled the "emergent totalitarianism paradigm" (115). This was a struggle to defend artistic freedom—conceived of as both an extension and emblem of democracy—from what U.S. citizens viewed as the "subjugating [of] art to the dreary dictates of a totalitarian political ideology" in the Communist countries (Wilford, *Mighty Wurlitzer*, 101). Thus, President Kennedy declared to symposium participants, "We don't want to see the artistic and intellectual life used as a weapon in a cold war struggle, but we do feel that it is an essential part of the whole democratic spirit. . . . The artist necessarily must be a free man."[3]

The "cold war struggle" to which Kennedy referred had, of course, moved closer to home with the Cuban Revolution and the spread of leftist activism throughout Latin America. The IAC's origins as a facilitator of cultural exchange that could make U.S. cultural activity—and the political form with which it was seen to be coextensive—attractive to Latin American artists was inextricably tied to these political tensions. That committee programs were initially planned as "supplements to existing governmental programs" speaks, as we shall see, to the high degree of overlap between official Cold War politics and policy on the one hand and the cultural exchange programs sponsored by private organizations in the United States on the other.[4]

The IAC, which later became the Inter-American Foundation for the Arts (IAFA) and eventually part of the Center for Inter-American Relations (CIAR), is the focus of this chapter. I review the history of the organization and its efforts to promote Latin American cultural production in the United States, exploring the role played by market forces in establishing a place for Latin American arts in the United States. I also study the organization's relationship to the contemporary U.S. field of power, examining the politics operating behind the scenes and the organization's role in the cultural Cold War while paying particular attention to its direct and indirect links to government officials and institutions. It would not be difficult to identify parallels between the IAC and the Congress for Cultural Freedom (CCF): both entities were conceived as venues for conducting cultural diplomacy, facilitators of cultural exchange that held out the hope of improving international understanding and, at some level, luring artists and intellectuals away from Communism. The geographical scope of the IAC was, of course, narrower. And while the organization was tightly connected to the U.S. foreign policy establishment, as I detail, it was not a recipient of CIA funds. Hugh Wilford has observed, though, that the many "links between the worlds of intelligence and art . . . meant that the CIA did not always have to foot the bill in the Cold War promotion of American art" (*Mighty Wurlitzer*, 107). Wilford is specifically interested in "joint public-private venture[s]" between the CIA and "privately owned and internationally famous institutions behind which it could conceal its interest in artistic patronage," such as the collaborations between the CCF and the Rockefeller-led Museum of Modern Art (ibid.). The CIA was neither footing the bill nor operating behind the scenes at the IAC, but the history of the latter provides another example of an unofficial "public-private venture" in which private institutions took on the work of the state, funding cultural exchanges and other projects set up to serve Cold War priorities and public interests. Instead of the CIA, though, it was philanthropies such as the Ford Foundation and the Rockefeller Brothers Fund that sought to bring the committee into alignment with the public sector's priorities by providing the IAC and its successors with the great majority of their funding, for they viewed the organization as playing a critical role in the private sector's battle against Communism.

This chapter traces the operations of the state-private network in the history of the IAC and its successors. The IAC reached out to Latin American intellectuals, many of whom supported the Cuban Revolution and were hostile toward U.S. foreign policy interests in the region. It was committed to improving mutual understanding among the American nations, promoting a more favorable opinion of the United States in the hemisphere, and ultimately strengthening U.S. relations with Latin America—goals that tied in closely with those of the Fulbright Act of 1946 and the Information and Educational Exchange Act (Smith-Mundt Act) of 1948. The IAC presented itself as apolitical and was, in fact, perceived as such by many of the people involved in its programs. It was also, however, caught up in a web of political relations that linked its supposedly private activities tightly to U.S. foreign policy interests.

And yet, just as Wilford demonstrates in his study of CIA sponsorship of the cultural Cold War that "intellectuals as well as government officials were capable of determining political outcomes" (*Mighty Wurlitzer*, 116), the IAC was not confined by the politics of its leaders and backers. In fact, the political ideology of the authors involved with the organization often deviated significantly from official U.S. Cold War ideology. Thus, I study the dynamics and political tensions stemming from the competing impulses that marked the operations of the IAC and its successors. As Cold War figures and motives were involved throughout the history of the organization, I identify its sponsors and the political agendas that accompanied the funds from them. I also trace the political motivations and machinations that came into play as the IAC became the IAFA and subsequently part of the CIAR, of which David Rockefeller assumed the leadership and set the political course. But this is only part of the story: I reveal how what was in many ways a Cold War operation was not limited to serving strategic interests and, instead, was put to other uses and even turned around by its supposed targets. The literary programming of the CIAR and its predecessors represents one of the great paradoxes of the period: Cold War efforts to neutralize the Communist threat motivated public and private support for the cultural production of a region of great political interest to the United States, creating a space for authors associated with the rising tide of Marxism in Latin America and, by extension, for the expression and dissemination in their works of the ideology that the state was trying to eradicate. Finally, I examine how the history of the CIAR and its predecessors complicates a binary understanding of Cold War dialectics by revealing the internal political rifts of this period: the Boom may well have been unified by support for the Cuban Revolution at first, but leftism among Latin American writers and their promoters in the United States was, as we have seen, far from monolithic, and, moreover, changed over time, resulting in fissures that profoundly shook the organization.

This is a story that maps the interweaving of and disjunctions between multiple political and cultural histories. For the State Department and various cold warriors, the cultural "value" motivating the establishment of programs such as the IAC was rooted in the potential political use value of Latin American intellectuals and the literature that they created. For the writers, such programs provided invaluable opportunities for them to boost the profile of their work. The agendas of these two parties cannot be reduced to each other's, and the complexities of the different stories told here are not always resolvable; no doubt, too, there are parts of the tale that are not captured here. Nonetheless, the story of the IAC and its successors offers critical insights into both the cultural dynamics and the political pressures involved in promoting Latin American literature in the United States during the 1960s and 1970s.

History and Fundraising: From the Inter-American Committee to the Center for Inter-American Relations

Wool, who became the IAC's first president, recruited prominent community leaders, businessmen, and scholars to serve on the board of directors. Academics Harrison and Morse, as well as Albee, Styron, and Vidal, all of whom had participated in the Paradise Island symposium, were joined by Andrew Heiskell, chairman of Time Inc.; Flavián Levine, a Chilean economist; Rodman Rockefeller, Nelson Rockefeller's oldest son; and Argentine filmmaker Leopoldo Torre Nilsson.[5] Over the years, many other luminaries sat on the board, including actors Kitty Carlisle Hart and Paul Newman; philanthropists such as Julius Fleischmann and Joan Heinz (Mrs. H. J. Heinz II); publishers Alfred A. Knopf, Roger Straus, and William Barlow; Thomas Messer, director of the Guggenheim Museum; Hans Neumann, a Venezuelan industrialist and patron of the arts; Arthur Taylor, president of CBS; and Ramón de Zubiría, rector of the Universidad de los Andes in Bogotá. The board brought together strange bedfellows, including ardent leftist Lillian Hellman, who had been blacklisted in the 1950s; Secretary of State (and anti-Communist) Dean Rusk; and Fleischmann, whom Hugh Wilford labels "the CIA's principal front man in the cultural Cold War" (108), for he was the head of the Farfield Foundation, a philanthropy that was one of the CIA's primary front organizations for funneling money to the CCF. (Despite the obvious red flags that Fleischmann's presence on the board raises concerning the IAFA's connections and funding—i.e., whether or not it, too, was a front for carrying out official agendas covertly—I do not make more of his involvement in the organization because there is little documentation of his active participation in it beyond some small financial contributions in the early years, which may well have come from "tainted" sources.)

In early 1964, the Inter-American Committee was renamed the Inter-American Foundation for the Arts, presumably to differentiate it from the Inter-American Committee of the Alliance for Progress, a multilateral organization coordinating the alliance's activities that also had been founded in 1963; the new name additionally served to foreground the IAFA's focus on cultural activity. Like its previous incarnation, the IAFA sought to implement a broader cultural exchange system that would assist in dispelling cultural stereotypes and political antipathies between the United States and Latin America. Priorities included developing translation programs, setting up bi-national cultural institutes in Latin America with which to coordinate activities and exchanges, and establishing a journal about the arts of the Americas. Wool continued his efforts to encourage New York publishers to become more proactive in publishing literature from Latin America. To further the organization's goals of promoting mutual understanding and fostering dialogue, the IAFA organized additional symposia in 1963 and 1964. The topic of the 1963 conference, held in Puerto Rico in November, was "The Individual as Artist and Citizen in the Americas Today." A number of participants from the first symposium attended, but there were also quite a few new faces, including writer James Baldwin; Jaime Benítez, chancellor of the Universidad de Puerto Rico; Mexican painter José Luis Cuevas; designer Charles Eames; Mexican theater director Juan José Gurrola; Mexican writers Juan García Ponce and Jaime García Terrés; Argentine writer Er-

nesto Sábato; Colombian writer and art critic Marta Traba; and IAC affiliates such as Fleischmann, Hellman, Messer, and Rodman Rockefeller. Once
again, the Latin American participants traveled to New York and Washington, DC, following the conference to meet with publishers and politicians,
including President Kennedy himself on November 20; it was the last public
function the president held. Wool had arranged for the Latin Americans to
give lectures at various U.S. universities following the DC trip, but several
were so distraught by the president's assassination that they canceled their
plans and returned home.[6]

García Terrés and other Mexican participants in the Puerto Rico symposium were instrumental in organizing the 1964 conference in Mexico.
They brought the IAFA to the attention of President Adolfo López Mateos,
who underwrote the costs of the symposium.[7] Fifty-two participants from
the United States and Latin America met to discuss two topics: "The Human and Aesthetic Problems of Urbanism" and "U.S. Elections and Inter-
American Relations." The symposium was followed by an Inter-American
Festival of the Arts and several shows and performances in Mexico City.[8]
The event seemed to have the desired effect among the writers and publishers who participated in it. James Laughlin, for example, became quite involved with publishing literature from Latin America and participating in
cultural exchanges with the region over the next few years as a result of the
interests and contacts that he developed at the symposium.[9]

By 1965, though, the IAFA was floundering and its future was uncertain. Wool had not been able to secure continuous funding for the organization and his administrative skills came under question from a number of
board members. Several candidates for partnerships with the IAFA came on
the scene. The first was the Council on Latin America (today, the Council
of the Americas), which was founded by David Rockefeller in 1965. The
council was a pro-market, pro-business organization that sought to facilitate
the development of broader investment contacts with companies in Latin
America and to improve business relations with the region. Through his
work with the council, David Rockefeller continued the family tradition
of fostering U.S.–Latin American collaborations, patronizing cultural exchange, and promoting cultural diplomacy with the region. As chairman of
the council, he generated significant interest in the organization within the
U.S. business community.

Several IAFA board members thought that a merger of the IAFA and
the Council on Latin America would be beneficial to both parties, granting the foundation stability and respectability and bringing to the council
"experience in cultural interchange and an important network of friends

and contacts in the intellectual and cultural field throughout most of the countries of Latin America" as well as "a reputation for non-partizanship [sic], and 'simpatia' [sic] with the Latins."[10] Members of both organizations were concerned, though, that the arrangement would present significant challenges, for it would bring together intellectuals with Marxist sympathies participating in the IAFA with the more conservative, often anti-Communist businessmen and industrialists associated with the council. These tensions had implications not just for daily coexistence but for programming and fundraising as well. In a memo summarizing the ideas of IAFA board member Heiskell, James Hyde noted that the "notion of supporting an organization which does show an interest in Marxists is a sophisticated idea to peddle more widely in fund raising."[11] This assessment was borne out in the response of one of the council's backers, a leading industrialist who asked, "Why should we support these fellows who spend all their time criticizing American industry, free enterprise and the American way!"[12]

Another potential partner for the IAFA emerged during this period. In 1965, David Rockefeller also founded the nonprofit Center for Inter-American Relations, which worked with businessmen and government officials from both parties. According to its founding documents, the CIAR's programs sought

> to improve communication among those concerned with the process of political, economic and social development in the hemisphere, and to stimulate appreciation in the United States of the artistic accomplishments and cultural traditions of Latin America, the Caribbean area and Canada. . . . [The CIAR's] intention is to become for North Americans a prime catalyst and coordinator of private endeavors related to Latin America and inter-American relations [. . . and] to develop the goodwill and respect of leading Latin Americans as the sensitive interpreter in the United States of their desires for understanding and recognition, both of themselves and of their countries' problems and aspirations.[13]

Barlow, the founder and publisher of the U.S.-based Spanish newsmagazine *Visión*, took charge of planning the center's operations. At his suggestion, William MacLeish, who had worked with him at *Visión* and who was just finishing his contract at Cornell, was named executive director of the center in 1966. William D. Rogers, a prominent Washington, DC, lawyer who had been coordinator of the Alliance for Progress from 1963 to 1965, became president of the center at David Rockefeller's request. Rockefeller also put together a board of directors with prominent figures from the arts, publishing, and government, including Barlow; Heiskell; René d'Harnoncourt, director of the Museum of Modern Art; Lincoln Gordon, former assistant secretary of state for inter-American affairs; poet (and William MacLeish's father) Archibald MacLeish; Assistant Secretary of State Thomas Mann; Arthur Ochs Sulzberger, president and publisher of the *New York Times*; and writer and philanthropist Edward Larocque Tinker, among others. Statesmen Hubert Humphrey, Jacob Javits, Robert Kennedy, John Lindsay, Covey Oliver, and Nelson Rockefeller served as honorary trustees.[14]

Margaret Rockefeller Strong de Larraín, the Marquesa de Cuevas, was also named an honorary trustee, in gratitude for her gift of the building in which the center would be housed. A granddaughter of John D. Rockefeller Sr., she had purchased three adjoining historic townhouses on Park Avenue in 1965 to prevent them from being demolished. The center was given the corner mansion, 680 Park Avenue, which had, ironically, previously housed the Chinese delegation to the United Nations, the Soviet consulate, and, most recently, the Soviet Mission at the United Nations.[15] Interior demolition had already begun when she purchased the building, and it was not until September 1967, when extensive renovations were finally complete, that the center officially opened its doors to the public.

The history of the building might seem superfluous to a study of the CIAR, but in fact, it provides insights into the center's history and the difficulties it faced. The balcony where Khrushchev had given press conferences and the front steps where, in 1960, he had famously embraced Fidel Castro became entryways to the center and to its efforts to improve Cold War relations between Latin America and the United States, suggesting a political transition that many would have liked to see in effect on a broader level. The building is also relevant because it contributed to the organization's monetary plight: an attractive showcase for hosting activities, the mansion was also a tremendous financial drain—at once the center's greatest asset and its largest problem. During the early years, the building, designated a landmark in 1970 by the New York City preservation commission, commanded much of the attention and the fundraising efforts of administrators: of the $1.7 million that the center raised in its initial campaigns, $1.6 million went toward renovations. Donors and granting organizations needed to be convinced that the building itself was a worthy cause to support, for time and again over the years, funds that might otherwise have been earmarked for programming or operating expenses were channeled toward building maintenance and mortgage expenses. This put the center, which was entirely dependent on private funds, in an extremely precarious financial position.

The history of the organization's fundraising efforts, in turn, provides additional insight into the Cold War politics at work behind its operations. Documentation of the efforts by the IAFA and the CIAR in the 1960s and 1970s reveals that the ability to raise money depended on several criteria, including donors believing that the center's goals were in keeping with their Cold War agenda of promoting democratic values and improving inter-American relations through outreach to Latin American intellectuals. For the most part, the IAFA's and CIAR's leaders declined to seek support from political government agencies such as the USIA and the U.S. Agency for International Development (USAID) out of concern that Latin American affiliates would consider the money—and, by extension, the organization itself—to be tainted. (Given the fallout from the revelations of CIA funding for the CCF, this proved to be a wise move.) The board of directors sought support from private sources, and some gave from their own pockets: Albee and Styron, for example, donated their Latin American royalties to the association, while Newman contributed $5,000 for a brochure to be used for fundraising purposes.[16] But the bulk of the center's funding came from philanthropies whose support was directly tied to the belief that the organization fulfilled Cold War imperatives. As Kathleen McCarthy has observed, "The events of the Second World War combined with [a] new sensitivity to contemporary international concerns to raise the humanities from the vacuum of personal interest to the center of the policymaking arena" ("Short and Simple," 5). As we have already seen, the sensitivity to the potential political "use value" of the arts and humanities increased exponentially during the Cold War and, following the Cuban Revolution, many U.S.-based philanthropies implemented programs targeted specifically at Latin America.[17]

The IAFA and the CIAR, which absorbed the former in late 1966, offered the philanthropies attractive and timely opportunities to reach Latin American opinion molders. The foundation and the center cultivated relationships with writers and assisted with the dissemination of their work—and, by extension, the cementing of their reputations—in the United States. In these efforts, which were designed to have a collateral effect of fostering in the writers a positive attitude toward the United States, the organizations were in fact engaging in cultural diplomacy. CIAR leaders played this up in their applications to funding agencies, identifying one of the organization's primary goals as the fostering of "serious communication among leaders in the political and cultural life of the Americas. In inter-American relations, cultural and political interests are so often intertwined that the politician may also be an artist or a musician."[18] And the philanthropies took note of the center's awareness of the artists' potential as agents of cultural diplomacy. One officer singled out Heiskell, a driving force in the IAFA and the CIAR, for his sensitivity to

> the fact that the intellectual in Latin America plays a more important role than the intellectual here as a member of the Establishment. Also, [Heiskell] was impressed that most of the intellectuals in Latin America, including the journalists, are likely to be Marxists, although he was very clear to point out that in saying this he did not mean to suggest that they were Soviet communists. Therefore, he felt there were various reasons why contacts between the intellectual communities of Latin America and the United States are important.[19]

The center's de facto role as a counterweight to the Casa de las Américas further increased the value of its programming in the eyes of funding officers.

Wool spent much of his tenure at the IAFA trying to secure funding for the organization. Between 1962 and 1967, he submitted several proposals to the Ford Foundation. Since the 1950s, Ford had made international programs a top priority, devoting considerable resources—including several large grants to the CCF—to cultural activities with Europe, the Soviet bloc, and Communist China. In 1959, on the heels of the Cuban Revolution, Ford's Overseas Development program named a director for Latin America (Cline, 64). And by the early 1960s, with decolonization in developing nations looming large, the activities of Ford's International Affairs program had "expanded increasingly into Third World countries," where the foundation's Overseas Development Division was also active (Berghahn, 194). In the mid-1960s, the International Affairs program's mandate was revised to focus more directly on the role of intellectuals in cultural diplomacy efforts. Accordingly, the program turned its attention to "increas[ing] cultural cooperation within the Western Hemisphere" by encouraging "the artists and intellectuals who play a large role in the economic, social, and political activities of their own countries . . . to participate in general international relations and development projects of the Western Hemisphere."[20]

It is not surprising, then, that Ford officers saw IAFA programs as effective media for carrying out their mandate: "While we have, and undoubtedly will continue to have, political differences within the hemisphere, differences which tend to contribute to disunity, the field of the arts can be a force for more understanding and cohesion between the countries of the Americas. While this force may not be able to transcend the political differences, it can at least counter-balance them."[21] Ford officers responded favorably to the IAFA's efforts to increase mutual understanding and respect between intellectuals from the United States and Latin America, noting the implications of these efforts for improving hemispheric relations. The IAFA found an ally in Joseph Slater, who had just moved to Ford's International Affairs Division from the Department of State, where he had been deeply involved in cultural diplomacy efforts as deputy assistant secretary of state in the Bureau of Educational and Cultural Affairs. Ford officers also found it difficult to ignore the big guns that Wool drew on for support: Kennedy advisor (and IAFA symposium participant) Schlesinger wrote to the director of International Affairs that he was impressed by the IAC's potential for improving relations among intellectuals in the Americas, while Edward R. Murrow, then head of the USIA, also strongly endorsed Wool's bid for support.[22]

Ford officials nevertheless moved cautiously. They had heard complaints from board members about Wool's management skills and wanted to assess them. There were also institutional constraints, such as resistance to supporting initiatives in the arts and humanities at a time when the foundation's priorities leaned toward industrial and agricultural development. Time after time, the foundation declined to fund Wool's proposals.[23] The situation seemed to look up for the IAFA in 1966, when the newly formed National Council of the Arts (NCA) awarded one of its first grants, for $150,000, to the organization. Wool's proposal to the NCA explicitly positioned the IAFA as an adjunct to official diplomacy efforts: as much as the application touted the organization's accomplishments in promoting cultural activity and helping to cultivate cultural connections among intellectuals in the Americas, it also stressed the benefits to the national interest from increased understanding in the Americas.[24] The grant proposal asserted that the IAFA was nonpartisan, and as such was able to foster communication among writers and intellectuals from different nations and ideological backgrounds, improving international relations without itself being subject to restrictions from any government.[25]

The NCA grant required Wool to raise matching funds, and he again turned to the Ford Foundation. The foundation initially seemed inclined to commit funds to the IAFA, and in October 1966, a motion was drafted for approval of a $100,000 grant. However, McNeil Lowry, vice president of Ford's Division of Humanities and the Arts, refused to support the proposal, saying only, according to a colleague, "that he thinks the National Council on the Arts probably did not do adequate staff work in arriving at a decision to support" the organization.[26] Wool's proposal was tabled at the end of 1966. Within days, however, the CIAR submitted a request for $2.5 million for start-up costs, an endowment, and program support. Wool later recalled that the IAFA was subsumed into the CIAR in December 1966.[27] The tabling of his proposal, which had probably represented the IAFA's last chance for independent survival, coincided with the merger. The center ultimately took on the IAFA's NCA grant, but its proposal to Ford makes no mention of the IAFA. The center's emphasis on policy, public affairs, and international relations, in addition to cultural exchange, was attractive to Ford officers, who foresaw opportunities for collaboration. Officers also believed that the center was well positioned to be influential in determining actions and policies in both the private and public sectors. In the spring of 1967, the Ford Foundation approved a $1.5 million grant to support the center in its efforts to become "an important force in the United States for progressive policies toward Latin America."[28]

Rockefeller leadership in the IAFA and the CIAR, as well as the family's long-standing ties to Latin America, also made Rockefeller philanthropies a logical source of funding for the organizations.[29] In 1963, when Rodman Rockefeller, a founding member and director of the IAFA, presented a proposal for funding to the Rockefeller Brothers Fund (RBF), the latter's response reflected the tight web of connections among private foundations, public institutions, and public policy interests. RBF officers were interested in the cultural activities supported by the IAFA. Prior to committing any funding, though, Laurance Rockefeller (then chairman of the RBF) and other RBF officers consulted with personnel in the Bureau of Educational and Cultural Affairs to see if "there is a need for such a cultural foundation and if the project is well regarded by the State Department."[30] Their contacts endorsed Wool's plans on the grounds that they "could result in a much needed foundation which would perform a role similar to that of The Asia Society."[31] Although Wool's difficulties securing funding for the organization caused some concern, as did questions about his administrative skills, RBF officers were swayed by the organization's potential contribution to improving inter-American relations through its relations with Latin American opinion makers. In late 1963, the RBF granted $30,000 to the IAFA for administrative expenses, with the condition that Rodman Rockefeller stay closely involved with it.[32] In May 1965, Rockefeller requested another $35,000. RBF officers met with IAFA board members Heiskell and Barlow to assess the organization's prospects. Both men expressed doubts about Wool's management skills but foresaw a merger with the CIAR or the Council on Latin America that would allow for the continuation of the IAFA's work under new leadership; both also made the case that the IAFA needed support in the interim.[33] This time, though, the RBF took no action.

Things changed after the IAFA-CIAR merger. In May 1967, the CIAR submitted a proposal to the RBF requesting $100,000; with the assurance of $1.5 million from the Ford Foundation and $150,000 from the NCA, the RBF approved the grant.[34] Over the next few years, the RBF was one of the center's largest supporters, contributing over $800,000 in general and special assistance; in 1976, it committed another $1 million to the center's capital fund. Rockefeller family members also contributed close to $2 million to the center between the late 1960s and mid-1970s; David Rockefeller alone invested more than $1 million of his own money in the restoration of the center's premises and repayment of the mortgage loan and other deficits, in addition to allowing the center to overdraw its account at the Chase Manhattan Bank, of which he was CEO.[35] New York City's Museum of Modern Art is often referred to as "Mother's museum," for Abby Aldrich Rockefeller (wife of John D. Rockefeller Jr.) was one of the museum's founders and greatest supporters. The center, too, was in many ways a family organization.

Politics and Policy Programming at the Center

The links between the private and state networks that mark the CIAR's fundraising history are also evident in the organization's structure, operations, and programming. The Rockefellers were members of the East Coast establishment and drew on their close ties to Washington while setting up the center. In 1965, for example, David Rockefeller and incoming CIAR president William D. Rogers met with Assistant Secretary of State Mann, who, as we saw in Chapter 1, repeatedly blocked Carlos Fuentes's visa applications for ideological reasons. According to Rogers, Rockefeller arranged the meeting to secure State Department approval for the venture.[36] The act suggests tacit agreement that the center would work within current Cold War policy toward Latin America. The choice of high-ranking public officials such as Hubert Humphrey and Robert Kennedy to serve as honorary trustees, as well as Mann's own position on the board of directors, likewise would seem to signal both the CIAR's deference to the state and the approval of these politicians (who, admittedly, did not hold a monolithic view of international relations during the Cold War) of the organization's mission. The center's ties to Washington, and the permeability between the public and private spheres that they implied, raised questions for some. As María Eugenia Mudrovcic has observed, the emphasis that the IAFA "placed on inter-American dialogue . . . led many Latin Americans to the conclusion that the Foundation was the artistic wing of the Alliance for Progress" ("Reading Latin American Literature," 133); this suspicion held true for the CIAR as well. (Indeed, the abbreviation CIAR—its first three letters in particular—did little to allay these concerns, especially during its early years, which coincided with the revelations of covert CIA funding for the CCF.)[37] The organization's leadership provoked similar concerns: as I've already noted, Rogers came to it after heading the Alliance for Progress, and several former State Department officials—including David Bronheim (a former deputy U.S. coordinator of the Alliance for Progress under Rogers), John Cates, Emilio Collado, and David Smith—served in positions of leadership over the years. The center's invitation-only membership also included numerous government officials from all ranks.

It would, however, be facile to characterize the center merely as a vehicle for disseminating U.S. foreign policy toward Latin America in the private sphere. In the early years in particular, CIAR leaders shared a vision of the organization as a center for cultural activities and exchange across the political spectrum. William MacLeish, the organization's first executive director, came to the center after directing the 1965–1966 Latin American Year at Cornell, where he had made sure, as we have seen, to include diverse political perspectives, and he brought this approach to his work at the CIAR. Rogers, the center's first president, had started his law career fighting McCarthy and the Red Scare; he also lobbied for years for normalization of relations with Cuba, and later engaged in secret negotiations with the Castro regime as undersecretary of state for economic affairs under President Ford. During his tenure as president of the CIAR, he ignored political tensions stemming from businessmen who complained about the high profile of leftist artists participating in the center's activities.[38] Until the late 1970s, as I discuss presently, prominent writers from the Latin American left—including Fuentes, Gabriel García Márquez, and Pablo Neruda, among others—maintained close ties to the center, while publishers considered the organization to be beyond politics.

The line between playing an adjunctive role in the process of improving inter-American relations and directly enabling Cold War agendas in Latin America was, however, a fine one, and the center's ties to government did indeed have a direct bearing on a number of its activities. This was evident at its inaugural dinner, when U.S. Vice President (and honorary trustee) Hubert Humphrey gave a speech that was deeply imbued with Cold War rhetoric. Even as he spoke of U.S. interest in Latin America in recent years and the need to develop greater knowledge of and respect for the region's inhabitants, Humphrey's words conveyed the official hard line toward Cuba—a position that ran counter to the center's stated intent of fostering dialogue and mutual understanding. "Given our special and historic concern with the Caribbean," Humphrey declared, "we will not be able to envision its stability so long as one nation remains not only outside the inter-American system, but intent on that system's destruction. . . . Until Cuba is prepared to leave her neighbors alone, to suspend the activities and the connections that led to her expulsion from the American family [that is, from the OAS], there can be no return to participation in the inter-American system."[39]

Over the years, the political inclinations of the center's leaders influenced the organization's activities in different ways and to different degrees. Together, the center's four departments—Public Affairs, Literature, Music, and Visual Arts—worked to spread information about Latin America, operating on the belief that this would help to dismantle negative attitudes toward the region and foster "a better context in which to shape policy."[40] CIAR leaders were keenly aware that there were strategies to pursue beyond actual programming: "Through informal contacts . . . it may frequently be possible to influence government officials in the direction of policies or programs likely to improve inter-American relations. Such opportunities should not be overlooked."[41] And, indeed, they were not, as was demonstrated by the Public Affairs Department, its efforts to shape policy, and the links between its political programming and Cold War politics and policies.

Public Affairs at the CIAR

The Public Affairs program organized a wide range of activities, including lectures, study groups, and forums on current events in Latin America; it also sponsored workshops to assist the media in expanding coverage of news from the region. With programs open to academics, public officials, journalists, and the general public, the Public Affairs Department was an important instrument for broadcasting information on Latin America. Politicians and intellectuals from the region were aware of the center's ability to command a wide and powerful audience, and for years (and, indeed, to the present day), dignitaries coming to the United States for consultations in Washington or at the United Nations made sure to include an appearance at the center in their itineraries. In 1969 alone, speakers at the center included Juscelino Kubitschek, the former president of Brazil; Arnulfo Arias, the recently deposed president of Panama; and Carlos Lleras Restrepo, then president of Colombia; during its early years, the program also hosted a number of representatives of the Inter-American Development Bank, Latin American ambassadors to the United States, and Latin American economists and bankers.

A great deal of the unit's programming drew on sources closely related to the U.S. government and allied institutions. At some level, this was to be expected: a significant number of the center's board members and affiliates were statesmen. They were invited to give lectures there, and other board members drew on their extensive connections in government to attract speakers. Many of these speakers would have held perspectives on Latin America that would not have strayed far from official Cold War anti-Communism. A review of the annual report on the center's first year (1967–1968) shows that the Public Affairs program hosted quite a few speakers from the Department of State and the military who addressed sensitive subjects such as the role of the U.S. military in Latin America, the Alliance for Progress, and Latin American economic integration. The vision of Latin America that emerged from the department's programming thus incorporated both the perspective of experts from the region and from official institutions in the United States that were determined to contain the spread of the ideology behind some of Latin America's important political and economic activity. Public Affairs also organized study groups and lecture series that drew in academics along with politicians and government officials to explore Cold War hot-button topics such as U.S. military assistance and economic strategies in Latin America, U.S.-Cuban relations, Russian policy in Latin America, and Chinese relations with Latin America and their effects on U.S.–Latin American relations, among others. Transcripts of these sessions do not exist, so it is impossible to know the exact content of the information presented, but in a fair percentage of cases the choice of speakers and the perspectives and institutions they represented would seem to reflect a bias toward official U.S. points of view.

The politics behind the participation of Luigi Einaudi in the Public Affairs Department's programming are difficult to read. A social scientist at the Rand Corporation, Einaudi served as an advisor to the Department of State and an expert witness on Latin American affairs before Congress in the late 1960s and early 1970s; in 1974, he entered the foreign service full time, working on the policy planning staff of the secretary of state. During these years, neither Congress nor the State Department was likely to have sought the input of a scholar on Latin America—however well credentialed—who was sympathetic to the revolutionary activism in the region. Over the years, Einaudi gave several lectures at the center and authored a monograph on Marxism in Latin America for a study group focusing on ideologies influencing Latin American policies. And yet Einaudi's contemporary publications are fairly moderate: while not pro-Marxist or reflective of the perspective of the Latin American left (which was certainly not over-represented in the Public Affairs Department over the years), neither did they espouse a clear anti-revolutionary or anti-Cuba slant, as would have been in line with official foreign policy at the time.

The unit's ties to Washington's foreign policy establishment also played out at a deeper, structural level, with David Rockefeller making repeated efforts to link Public Affairs programming to Latin American policy initiatives. In 1969, for example, he met with Secretary of State William P. Rogers (not to be confused with the center's president, William D. Rogers) to discuss whether the CIAR might be able to assist the secretary with addressing issues pertinent to inter-American relations.[42] To facilitate the collaboration, he proposed to Charles Meyer, assistant secretary of state for inter-American affairs, that the center host a conference of the hemisphere's leaders that would at once bring together and advance the goals of both the assistant secretary's projects and the 1969 journey to Latin America of Nelson Rockefeller, the governor of New York (and David Rockefeller's brother).[43] The governor's trip was not politically neutral. After his return, he authored the *Rockefeller Report on the Americas*, which Mark Berger describes as being "central to the shift from the Cold War liberalism of the Kennedy and Johnson era and its apparent emphasis on economic aid, the middle sectors and democratization, to military modernization with its concern with order as the key to development and progress" (104–5). Berger further characterizes the report as "sanction[ing] military regimes and contribut[ing] to the legitimacy of the authoritarian and technocratic regimes in Brazil and elsewhere in the 1970s" (105). David Rockefeller's efforts to coordinate plans and strategies with the State Department would seem to undercut the apolitical image of the center and, instead, suggest complicity with official policies toward Latin America at the highest echelons of the organization.

Indeed, Richard Adams, president of the Latin American Studies Association, cited similar concerns as early as 1968 when he protested the Ford Foundation's $1.5 million grant to the center. While he was worried that the allocation would draw funds away from scholars who had limited resources to pursue their work, he was even more incensed "that a study grant of this proportion should be given to a center which is clearly run by people whose major orientation must be one which stands so closely to that of the United States Government and not that of a disinterested, or at least multi-interested, scholarly community."[44] Adams quoted a colleague who characterized publications stemming from a policy meeting on Haiti held at the center as "clear-cut State Department business."[45] He argued that such programs cast grave doubt on the supposed neutrality of academic scholarship and had significant implications for academic work on Latin America:

> American scholarship has sufficient problems in Latin America and is so heavily dependent upon Ford Foundation that the identification of Ford with the kind of business that Bronheim [then executive director of the CIAR] is apparently sponsoring at the Center can have very unfortunate consequences. . . . [The CIAR] seems to set itself up in a position where it wishes to pass itself off as an organization with scholarly credentials and yet promote its activities on the basis of State Department interest and within a State Department intellectual framework.[46]

Adams also stated, "It would have seemed to me infinitely better to have had people not so closely associated with our own government policies in Latin America" in the top leadership positions at the center.[47] Ford officers downplayed the accusations of the center's collusion with the public sector. An internal response titled "Don Quijote vs. the Windmill" disagreed with the claims and cited a CIAR brochure that "makes clear that the Center is neither an agent of the U.S. government nor a scholarly enterprise"; the official who drafted it suggested that Adams be informed that "we have no reason to imagine the Center is anything other than it purports to be."[48]

Adams's concerns, which were rather facilely dismissed by Ford officials, were rooted in the deep linkages between the public and private sectors that characterized public affairs programming at the center. At the same time, though, it would be a mistake to view the department solely as a vehicle for circulating U.S. policy, for organizers made efforts to acknowledge multiple political perspectives with many of their events.[49] In 1972, for example, the center sponsored two meetings on the status of the Panama Canal negotiations, one with the U.S. negotiators and the other with the team from Panama. The program's coverage of Cuba in the 1970s included radical voices. This was evident in a 1972 panel on prospects for U.S.-Cuban relations following President Nixon's rapprochement with China and the Soviet Union. While the panel, like quite a few others in the program, did not include scholars hailing from the island (or even Latin America), it did feature a wide range of political opinions.[50] The participants included Richard Barnet, a cofounder of the progressive Institute for Policy Study, on the one hand, and on the other, James Theberge, director of Latin American Studies at Georgetown's Center for Strategic and International Studies, whose work at the time was strongly anti-Marxist and anti-Soviet, as well as several economists and State Department officials.[51] Public Affairs also sponsored a lecture that year by Frank McDonald, a journalist studying revolutionary Cuba who had been imprisoned by Castro's government for several months under suspicion of espionage, and whose work reflected both praise for what the revolution had accomplished and criticism of its injustices.

Nor does the program's active coverage of the rise and destruction of Salvador Allende's Socialist government in the early 1970s offer a clear picture of a monolithic anti-Communist ideology—a significant accomplishment, given that the organization's leader was chief executive of the Chase Manhattan Bank: Rockefeller had consulted with Henry Kissinger on several occasions regarding the bank's interests and what he viewed as the threat to those interests posed by Allende's policies.[52] Early in Allende's presidency, the legal advisor to the Chilean embassy spoke at the center in a session titled "Nationalization Policy of the Chilean Government." A 1972 panel on the prospects and meaning of Socialism in Chile included Alegría, an early participant in IAFA activities who was now Allende's cultural attaché to the United States; Laurence Birns, a professor at the New School for Social Research who would later become a vocal critic of Pinochet and the coup; and several other speakers. Birns later returned to the center to give a lecture titled "Contemporary Chile: Some Reflections on its Relevance to Latin America's Economics and Politics." In early 1973, before the coup, there was a panel on forthcoming elections that featured Radomiro Tomic, a progressive social scientist at the Universidad de Chile who was the 1970 Partido Democrático Cristiano candidate for president and whose platform had coincided with that of Allende on several key points. Following the coup, the center organized panels titled "Recent Events in Chile" and "Chile: A Road to Tragedy" that featured Allende sympathizers and critics of the destruction of Chilean democracy represented by the coup (e.g., Arturo Valenzuela, a political scientist then at Duke University, and Andrew Zimbalist, then a graduate student at Harvard) as well as individuals who were less likely to support Allende (e.g., Jaime Ravinet, a Christian Democrat who was at the time on a Fulbright at Johns Hopkins). In 1976, French sociologist Alain Touraine, who had lived and taught in Chile and married a Chilean, spoke at a CIAR meeting on the theme of "The Nature of Counter Revolution in Chile," where his remarks were objected to by Chile's special representative to the United Nations. And in 1977, Clodomiro Almeyda, Allende's first foreign minister and a high-ranking member of Chile's Socialist Party, spoke to a group of Chilean members of the Unidad Popular and U.S. specialists who were discussing the situation in Chile.[53]

On the other hand, in 1974, the program sponsored a lecture, "The Current Chilean Situation," by General Walter Heitman, the Chilean ambassador to the United States, who had been appointed by Pinochet immediately after the coup. While sponsoring a visitor does not necessarily mean endorsing that person's opinion, the center did not offset Heitman's lecture by, say, having a respondent or scheduling presentations by speakers with other points of view. By having Heitman alone represent the "Chilean situation" in the aftermath of the coup, the center in this instance allowed the perspective of the Pinochet government to affirm itself, while not opening up space for alternative perspectives at a time when the regime was being criticized for its repression of its citizens and its human rights violations.

It should be noted that through its connections to Washington's foreign policy circles, the Public Affairs program played a significant role in reshaping U.S. policy toward Latin America. This can be seen in the unit's sponsorship of the Commission on U.S.–Latin American Relations, which was headed by Sol Linowitz, a member of the center's board of directors as well as a former U.S. ambassador to the OAS and an Alliance for Progress official. The commission also included longtime CIAR affiliates such as Heiskell, Messer, Harrar, and others.[54] In 1974, the commission published a report that challenged a history of U.S. interventionism in the region and urged the United States to "adopt a new approach toward Latin America and the Caribbean, respectful of the sovereignty of the countries of the region, and tolerant of a wide range of political and economic forms" (*Americas in a Changing World*, 12). Future U.S. actions needed to acknowledge that "the countries of Latin America and the Caribbean are not our 'sphere of influence,' to be insulated from extra-hemispheric relationships," while recognizing that "our mutual concerns in the hemisphere center not on military security, but rather on the critical issues of economic and political security in an uncertain world" (62). Thus, the commission issued a series of thirty-three recommendations for changes in U.S. policy on Latin America, including: "the United States should refrain from unilateral military interventions in Latin America, and covert U.S. interventions in the internal affairs of Latin American countries should be ended"; "the United States should expand its emergency immigration program for political refugees, whether those refugees flee oppression of the left or right"; "the United States should take the initiative in seeking a more normal relationship with Cuba"; "the United States should abandon the threat of application of unilateral measures of economic coercion in its relations with the countries of Latin America"; and "U.S. immigration legislation should be reviewed systematically with the aim of eliminating restrictions barring travel and migration on purely political grounds" (the latter being a challenge, of course, to the McCarran-Walter Act). The timing of the report's release was hardly coincidental: it came out on the eve of a meeting of foreign ministers from the Americas, in effect urging the U.S. delegates to normalize relations with Cuba and support repeal of the sanctions imposed by the OAS in 1964.

The report received quite a bit of attention. An editorial in the *New York Times* claimed, "It would be hard to produce a better blueprint for the 'new era' and 'mature partnership' in inter-American relations that Secretary of State Kissinger has promised" ("Inter-American Blueprint"). It was presented to President Ford, the secretary of state, and Congress, and it prompted hearings in both the House and Senate (*United States and Latin America*, i). In late 1976, on the heels of President Carter's election, the commission issued a second report, *The United States and Latin America: Next Steps*. This report noted changes in the global political climate and stated that with the possible exception of Panama, which was identified as "the most urgent issue" (7), Latin America and the Caribbean no longer represented the urgent threats to U.S. national security that they had in the 1960s (2). Consequently, it suggested that "the new administration should focus early attention on improving U.S. relations with Latin America not because of hidden dangers but because of latent opportunities" (3). It further urged the administration to "reject outmoded policies based on domination and paternalism and . . . show instead its respect for all the countries of the Western Hemisphere and for their political and economic aims," and to "make an early and explicit announcement of its intent to respect fully the national sovereignty of all the states of Latin America and the Caribbean (regardless of their size or ideology)" (4). Even as the commission offered constructive suggestions for the Carter administration, it severely criticized the outgoing Ford administration. The report identified dealing with human rights violations in Latin America as a top priority; it praised Congress for taking measures to address such violations, but excoriated the executive branch not only for "fail[ing] to respond promptly and effectively" to violations in Chile, Brazil, and Uruguay, but for working at cross-purposes to the measures taken by Congress to contain the problems (7).

The report also devoted attention to the matter of cultural relations and exchanges between the United States and Latin America—a move that was not surprising given the commission's ties to the CIAR and the participants' awareness of the impact of cultural exchanges within the Americas. The tone of the commission's recommendations, though, marked a significant departure from the prevalent rhetoric of Cold War cultural diplomacy. The report noted that cultural attachés at U.S. embassies, who bore responsibility for publicizing information about the United States abroad, were often structurally subordinate to public affairs officers who were themselves representatives of the U.S. Information Agency, "an agency of government whose mission is predominantly propagandistic and political" (24). The report argued that this alignment compromised the credibility of the attachés and their ability to cultivate exchanges that might otherwise lead to better cultural relations. Thus, the report lobbied for the clear separation of "the cultural relations and policy advocacy functions in U.S. diplomacy," as well as recommending significant increases in funding for programs that would increase knowledge of Latin America among U.S. citizens (26). President Carter took the committee's suggestions to heart. In order to implement the recommendation that "the new President . . . exercise prompt, vigorous, and decisive leadership in negotiating an acceptable compromise with the Panamanian Government while serving our own interest in the Canal" (6), he tapped Linowitz to spearhead negotiations for a treaty. He also incorporated other suggestions from the report in his 1977 Pan American Day address to the OAS.[55]

Before Cold War fears were heightened anew by the Sandinista Revolution in Nicaragua in 1979, the commission took advantage of a moment of lessened tensions in the mid-1970s to try to move the United States away from its interventionism and its black-and-white anti-Communist rhetoric, with some success. The commission pushed the limits of contemporary policy toward Latin America at this time, and its activities offer a pointed challenge to readings of the Center for Inter-American Relations as simply a link in the state-private network. It seems clear that David Rockefeller, in his capacity as founder and man behind the scenes at the center, worked carefully—at least during its early days—to weave the organization's activities into official programs and policies. But the range of presentations sponsored by the CIAR's Public Affairs Department, if not always balanced or apolitical (as the center liked to consider itself), included both what Richard Adams deemed apologists for "clear-cut State Department business" and more dissonant voices. It was the Literature Department, however, that served as an important venue for opening the center to pro-Marxist writers from the region.

The Literature Department at the Center

The tensions between official anti-Communism and the radical cultural and political activity in Latin America played out very differently in the CIAR's

Literature Department. The 1960s and 1970s, when the program was extremely active in its efforts to promote Latin American literature, were, of course, the Boom years. The writers' support of Cuba and of Socialism in general did bring about conflicts with the center's administration, as well as with other Latin American writers and Literature Department affiliates, as I shall detail. But politics are just part of this story: the department's dynamism was a function of the enthusiasm of its affiliates—staff, translators, and critics alike—who believed that they were working to promote the most interesting writers of the day, regardless of their politics.[56] The center's music and art programs were also very busy, sponsoring visits and exhibitions by Latin America's top performers, composers, and artists, such as Fernando Botero, David Alfaro Siqueiros, Fernando Szyszlo (a participant in the IAFA's symposia), Joaquín Torres García, Juan Orrego-Salas, and Mercedes Sosa. The guests represented a range of political orientations. The Music and Visual Arts units often coordinated their events with some of the nation's most prominent artistic venues, such as the Guggenheim Museum, the Museum of Modern Art, Carnegie Hall, Alice Tully Hall at Lincoln Center, the Corcoran Gallery in Washington, DC, the Field Museum of Natural History in Chicago, and others.[57] But it was the Literature Department that was the cornerstone of the center's cultural programs. In 1970, the center's executive director noted the success of its outreach initiatives:

> We are making a significant impact on publishing and academic circles. . . . We are carrying out in an effective manner a well thought through plan for reaching students, professors, critics, publishers and the public at large. Latin American writers respect us . . . Latin American literature contains its political thought. This program is a vital ingredient in any well rounded program designed to educate about Latin America. Additionally, we have learned that the literature from Latin America is one of the most effective vehicles that we have for getting students interested in the area.[58]

Programming, Networking, and Translation

Wool left at the time of the merger of the CIAR and the IAFA, and José Guillermo Castillo, a Venezuelan who had worked with Wool in the IAFA, took charge of the Literature Department, which he directed until 1972; he also co-directed the center's Visual Arts Department during these years. The Literature program, which thrived under Castillo's leadership, supported all aspects of the translation, publication, and promotion of Latin American literature: early descriptions of the program note that it "recommends new books, commissions objective critical commentary and sample translations, acts as informal agent for the author in question if needed, and helps a young author establish the necessary contacts which in many cases lead to translation and eventual publication" (Center for Inter-American Relations [1969], 14–15). The centerpiece of the department was the translation program, which supported the translation into English of several books per year, generally splitting the cost with publishers; it also subsidized special issues of journals focusing on Latin American literature.[59] As Irene Rostagno details, Castillo assembled an all-star committee of U.S.-based academics, critics, and translators—including John Alexander Coleman, Suzanne Jill Levine, Gregory Rabassa, and Alastair Reid, poet Mark Strand, and Argentine critics Omar del Carlo and María Luisa Bastos—to select works for translation subsidies (107). Emir Rodríguez Monegal also joined forces with the Literature Department, and his numerous connections to Latin American writers were extremely useful in drawing them into the department's activities.

The Literature Department was a full-service, centralized networking and publicity program.[60] A number of the more established authors at this time used professional agents (e.g., Carl Brandt and Carmen Balcells), but the department acted informally as an agent for many writers, regardless of whether their works had received support from the translation program: it introduced writers to North American critics, writers, publishers, and scholars; it placed works in the *New Yorker* and other literary journals (in this the program was assisted by an inside connection, Alastair Reid, who in addition to his translation work was a literary scout for the *New Yorker*); it arranged public readings at cultural centers such as the 92nd Street Y; it organized conferences on Latin American literature and translation; it sponsored receptions and press conferences; and it arranged for writers to give lectures throughout the country, often coordinating plans with Frank MacShane's writing program at Columbia University. Thus, the program created a high-profile space for Latin American literary activity in New York City and throughout the United States. The department's reach expanded even further when it began, in the 1970s, to offer literature courses to the public: in 1972, for example, Coleman, a professor of Spanish at New York University, gave a televised course on *Sunrise Semester*, a long-standing New York University program that broadcast courses for credit through eighty-five CBS affiliates across the nation.[61] Rodríguez Monegal and Levine gave lectures in center-sponsored courses on Latin American literature at the New School for Social Research, and translator and Literature program assistant Gregory Kolovakos offered a translation workshop in cooperation with Brooklyn College.

In 1968, the center began publishing a journal, *Review*, which was instrumental in publicizing new works by Latin American authors.[62] The journal's inception coincided with the demise of *Mundo Nuevo*, at which point Rodríguez Monegal moved to the United States. He first took a faculty position at Harvard and then went to Yale; during his tenure at Yale, he became involved with the center and was tapped to edit the first issue of *Review*. The new journal was by no means made in *Mundo Nuevo*'s image or likeness, though: whereas the Paris-based journal had included literature, literary criticism, and commentaries on current affairs, *Review* began simply as an annual compendium of reviews, covering books on Latin America that had been published in the United States. Its goal was to bring these works to the attention of librarians and scholars in a systematic manner. During the early 1970s, *Review* underwent a number of changes that reflected the editors' desire to present information that would be useful to teachers as well as to readers unfamiliar with Latin American literature, including: sections on specific authors and works timed to coincide with the publication of translations sponsored by the center; autobiographical pieces commissioned from authors; selections from forthcoming books; and original criticism on literature, music, and the arts. The journal targeted both professors and students, for studies were showing increasing levels of interest in college-level Latin American literature courses in the 1960s and 1970s; it was received by quite a few university libraries in the United States. *Review* received positive coverage in periodicals such as *Publishers Weekly* and *Library Journal*. As Irene Rostagno has written, "By making available in English articles written for Latin audiences . . . and by encouraging U.S. critics to write about Hispanic authors . . . *Review* reached out to a wider American audience, showing that readers did not need to know Spanish to appreciate Latin American culture. . . . It communicated with the larger American intellectual community and advanced the idea that Latin America was producing genuinely innovative literature" (109).

The Literature Department also supported a new wave of translators, which both played a role in the success of the works it subsidized and improved the quality of translation available overall. Whereas university presses often hired graduate students in order to keep their costs down, not infrequently resulting in mediocre translations (Levine, "Latin American Novel," 304), the CIAR program matched its authors with experienced translators such as Rabassa and Reid. It also assisted with the development of younger translators such as Levine and Eliot Weinberger. And, over the years, it supported the training of new translators through its programs. The fees that translators received at this time were modest at best—a standard rule of thumb was to pay five dollars per thousand words, with translators receiving no royalties or subsidiary rights—so translating was very much a labor of love rather than a vocation that translators could rely on to support themselves.

Translators affiliated with the center brought to the table a new style. From 1950 until her death in 1969, as we have seen, Harriet de Onís exercised a great deal of power over the translation of Latin American literature in the United States. While some of her projects were poorly received, she was nevertheless widely respected as a translator, and she received the PEN Translation Prize in 1967 for her translation of João Guimarães Rosa's *Sagarana*.[63] Although she championed several experimental writers, her tastes leaned heavily toward the regional and folkloric, which meant that Knopf's lists ultimately reflected similar biases. In contrast, the translators connected to the center—many of them a generation or two younger than de Onís (Levine and Weinberger were only in their twenties when they started translating)—were more open to the cosmopolitan and playful inclinations of modern writers, and they often worked closely with authors to capture the spirit of the original texts. In many ways, the generation gap between de Onís and the center-affiliated translators paralleled the shift from realism to modernism as the dominant mode in the works that they translated. The quality of the work of these up-and-coming translators was recognized by the public and critics alike: Rabassa, for example, received a National Book Award for Translation for *Hopscotch* in 1967, and Cortázar himself was so satisfied with the result that he urged García Márquez to wait until Rabassa was available to take on the translation of *Cien años de soledad*. The influence of the translators associated with the center extended far beyond their work in translation: along with agents and editors, they too became advocates who lobbied both the Literature Department and publishers to take on new authors.

Between 1967 and 1983, the Literature Department ran a translation subsidy program that supported more than fifty translations, including many important contemporary literary works (see Table 2), as well as critical works, journal issues, textbooks, anthologies, and bibliographies of works in translation.[64] The program sought to assist with the translation of six to eight books per year, as well as with the annual publication of a special issue of a journal focusing on Latin American literature and aimed at a university audience.[65] The center generally split the cost of translation with publishers, contributing up to $2,500 per work, although in several cases it subsidized

Table 2. Selected literary works published through the CIAR translation program

Author	English title	Publisher	Date of first publication in English
Demetrio Aguilera Malta	Seven Serpents and Seven Moons	U. Texas Press	1979
José María Arguedas	Deep Rivers	U. Texas Press	1978
Miguel Ángel Asturias	Strong Wind	Delacorte	1968
	The Green Pope	Delacorte	1971
Adolfo Bioy Casares	Plan for Escape	Dutton	1975
	Asleep in the Sun	Persea	1978
Jorge Luis Borges	The Book of Imaginary Beings	Dutton	1969
	Selected Poems, 1923–1967	Delacorte	1972
Guillermo Cabrera Infante	Three Trapped Tigers	Harper and Row	1971
Julio Cortázar	62: A Model Kit	Pantheon	1972
	All Fires the Fire	Pantheon	1973
	A Manual for Manuel	Pantheon	1978
José Donoso	The Obscene Bird of Night	Knopf	1973
	The Charleston and Other Stories	Godine	1977
	Sacred Families	Knopf	1977

José Donoso, Carlos Fuentes, and Severo Sarduy	Triple Cross (three novellas)	Dutton	1972
Gabriel García Márquez	One Hundred Years of Solitude	Harper and Row	1970
José Lezama Lima	Paradiso	Farrar, Straus and Giroux	1974
Pablo Neruda	Selected Poems	Delacorte	1972
Juan Carlos Onetti	A Brief Life	Grossman	1976
Nicanor Parra	Emergency Poems	New Directions	1972
Octavio Paz	Eagle or Sun?	October House	1970
	Eagle or Sun? (rev. ed.)	New Directions	1976
	Configurations	New Directions	1971
Manuel Puig	Betrayed by Rita Hayworth	Dutton	1971
	Heartbreak Tango	Dutton	1973
	The Buenos Aires Affair	Dutton	1976
	Kiss of the Spider Woman	Knopf	1979
Ernesto Sábato	On Heroes and Tombs	Godine	1981
Luis Rafael Sánchez	Macho Camacho's Beat	Pantheon	1980
Severo Sarduy	Cobra	Dutton	1975

the entire translation. By underwriting the translation of literary works, many of which had already achieved best-seller status in Spanish America and Spain, the Literature program paved the way for the Boom's success in the United States (Mac Adam, 186).

The publication of *One Hundred Years of Solitude* marked a watershed moment in this process. García Márquez's *No One Writes to the Colonel* had been published in English in 1968, but it had attracted little attention. In contrast, *One Hundred Years of Solitude* cemented the author's reputation in the United States: the Spanish-language original had been a runaway best seller throughout Spanish America, and the English-language version landed on both the *New York Times* and the *Publishers Weekly* best-seller lists in April 1970; it was also named one of the year's Notable Books by the American Library Association (ALA). The Colombian novel marked the breakthrough of Latin American literary translation in the United States, opening up a market that the program continued to feed.

While *One Hundred Years of Solitude* was the only work subsidized by the program to make the *New York Times* and the *Publishers Weekly* lists, three novels by Manuel Puig that the program had supported—*Betrayed by Rita Hayworth*, *Heartbreak Tango*, and *Kiss of the Spider Woman*—also made the ALA Notable Books lists for the years in which they were published (*50 Years*). In 1971, four of the program's translations appeared in the *New York Times*'s annual selection of noteworthy titles: Jorge Luis Borges's *The Aleph and Other Stories, 1933–1969*; Guillermo Cabrera Infante's *Three Trapped Tigers*; Octavio Paz's *Configurations*; and Puig's *Betrayed by Rita Hayworth* ("1971: A Selection"). José Donoso's *The Obscene Bird of Night* received the same honor in 1973, while its translators, Hardie St. Martin and Leonard Mades, earned a PEN Translation Prize for their efforts.

In the long run, the center's program was instrumental in transforming the conditions for publishing Latin American literature in the United States: it helped to establish an infrastructure for communication between authors and publishers at a critical moment in the history of Latin American literature, and it was directly responsible for the growth of Latin American lists at U.S. publishing houses.

Creating Best Sellers

Studying the commercial presence of the works subsidized by the translation program provides critical insights into the development of the market for Latin American literature in the United States during the 1960s and 1970s. So, too, does the contrast between the high profile of works supported by the center and the relative invisibility of those subsidized by the Rockefeller-funded AAUP translation subsidy program that was discussed in Chapter 3. The latter program did inspire a number of university presses to publish works without subsidies, and as the 1960s progressed and the reputation of Latin American literature grew in the West, commercial presses signed authors such as Borges, Cortázar, Fuentes, García Márquez, Neruda, Paz, and Vargas Llosa. Publishing Latin American literature was not a profitable enterprise, but it was on the rise, and the number of Spanish American translations (not including those of Brazilian literature) published in 1963 and 1964 was double the highest figures for the 1950s.[66] The market for these works was increasing rapidly at universities, too, where the number of courses offered in Latin American literature doubled between the late 1950s and the late 1960s, and the number of courses in translation also rose dramatically (Needler and Walker, 133). The high profile of *One Hundred Years of Solitude* further contributed to this process, bringing Latin American literature to the attention of a broad audience and ushering in a new wave of translations.

The books subsidized by the AAUP program accounted for approximately half of the Latin American translations published in any given year during the 1960s. The program thus single-handedly increased the amount of Latin American literature on the market. But as I have already discussed, it was unable to get higher-profile, contemporary literary works for its lists. Starting in the 1960s, authors such as Fuentes relied increasingly on networking to get visibility for their work. University presses may thus have missed out on the opportunity to publish current literature because mediators—not only agents, but also Castillo at the CIAR's Literature Department—had begun to market new works to commercial publishers. Additionally, for-profit presses had themselves become more proactive, seeking out "stars" and critically acclaimed works even when subsidies were not available from the center. The AAUP program may also have suffered because university presses rely heavily on the recommendations of academics for their lists, but scholars affiliated with the center steered the writers with whom they were in contact toward the center and toward commercial publishers instead. These specialists included Ronald Christ, who directed the Literature Department from 1973 to 1977; Coleman; Levine; Rabassa; Rodríguez Monegal; and Alfred Mac Adam. Even Harrison—an initiator of the AAUP program, and one of its most ardent supporters in its early days—seems to have lent more support to the IAFA, where he was on the board of directors, after he left the Rockefeller Foundation in 1962. And, while not an academic, center affiliate Thomas Colchie was a triple threat: he translated the work of Brazilian writers, served as a freelance agent for them, and used his connections to the center to try to place them with publishers (Levine, "Latin American Novel," 309).

While the groundwork for the burgeoning market for Latin American translations in the United States was laid during the early 1960s, when the AAUP program was at its peak, it was not university presses but rather commercial presses and the center's Literature Department that were able to take advantage of the momentum. The Literature Department, which took off in the late 1960s, further benefited from the high quality of the books, authors, and translators that it supported, and from its deft use of market forces to promote them. Virtually all the literary works subsidized by the center were contemporary, first appearing in the 1960s and 1970s as part of the rising tide of Latin American literature. In contrast, the AAUP program tended to subsidize literary works that had been published earlier, and while many of them had played a formative role in the development of the Latin American literary tradition, they were less likely to have as much commercial appeal; moreover, the subsidized works included only two novels from the 1960s (Elena Garro's *Recollections of Things to Come* and Sergio Galindo's *The Precipice*) and relatively few from the 1950s.

Also, the AAUP program was focused only on subsidizing the translation of titles put forth by individual university presses; it was not involved with the promotion and sale of the works. In contrast, the CIAR program planned a full slate of publicity events for the literary works that it subsidized—as well as for those it did not—and worked tirelessly to build an infrastructure that would maximize the public visibility of Latin American literature. The program's directors, for example, ensured the placement of book reviews in major periodicals, often in conjunction with publishers. As Richard Ohmann has noted, during this period "the single most important boost a novel could get was a prominent review in the Sunday *New York Times*" (202). Program directors were keenly aware of this. Thus, affiliates of the Literature Department such as Christ, Coleman, Levine, and Rodríguez Monegal, who could be counted on for positive evaluations, were frequently picked to do reviews for the periodical. Well-known writers and critics such as William Kennedy, Mark Strand, and Michael Wood, some of whom had connections to the center, were also tapped to lend authority to high-visibility reviews.

In general, reviews of center-sponsored books appeared in a timely fashion in the publications that "carried special weight in forming cultural judgments" among elite intellectuals and cultural leaders (Ohmann, 204), including the *New Republic*, the *New York Review of Books*, the *New York Times*, the *New Yorker*, *Partisan Review*, and *Saturday Review*. They also appeared in academic and popular periodicals such as *Choice, Christian Science Monitor, Kenyon Review, Library Journal*, the *Nation, Publishers Weekly*, and *Time*. Prose works were frequently reviewed in anywhere from ten to twenty periodicals.[67] Books by rising authors and those whom the center was particularly interested in promoting received even better coverage: Borges's *Book of Imaginary Beings*, for example, was reviewed in thirty-one periodicals; Donoso's *Obscene Bird of Night* in twenty-four; and reviews of the first edition of *One Hundred Years of Solitude* appeared in thirty-three magazines and journals. In contrast, literary works published through the AAUP program, where marketing was left to individual university presses, received significantly less fanfare. For the most part, each book received between one and seven reviews. There was only one literary work published through the AAUP translation program that received publicity comparable to what was regularly afforded the center's works: Brazilian writer Joaquim Maria Machado de Assis's *Esau and Jacob* (1965) was reviewed in nineteen periodicals, in both popular and elite high-circulation venues such as the *New York Times*, the *New Yorker, Newsweek, Saturday Review*, and *Time*. The attention lavished on the novel may be attributed to the perception articulated by University of California Press director August Frugé that the writer was "thought by many to be the finest fiction writer of all Latin America and the only one before Jorge Luis Borges to bear comparison with the best European writers" (112). Otherwise, AAUP-sponsored books were reviewed primarily in trade and academic journals such as *Choice, Hispania*, and *Library Journal*, which reach smaller and more specialized audiences. Finally, as some of the academic journals had slow turnaround times, reviews often did not appear until two to four years after a book was published. (AAUP-sponsored books in fields other than literature fared no better.) In the end, the AAUP program sponsored the publication of a number of classic literary works, but unlike the center's Literature Department, it was not designed to garner for them the publicity or scholarly attention that would have given them a higher public profile.

The Politics of Literature

A close look at the Literature Department reveals an openness to political orientations that deviated markedly from those of the U.S. foreign policy establishment and the CIAR's own administration. The department was not alone at the center in its efforts to include diverse political viewpoints in its programming, although it was the unit to do so most successfully. Over the years, the Visual Arts Department exhibited work by Mexican muralists Diego Rivera, José Clemente Orozco, and David Alfaro Siqueiros, whose politics strongly leaned to the left. (Anna Indych-López describes the Siqueiros exhibit as a "landmark event" at the CIAR, and the artist himself as "an unlikely candidate for a one-person exhibition at an institution founded by David Rockefeller" [87].) But in 1971, the program was shaken when several New York–based Latin American artists criticized the organization's connections to government. The work of the artists had been scheduled to appear at the center in an exhibition organized to "position Latin American art in the New York marketplace" (B. Adams, 28).[68] As a condition for their participation in the exhibition and other activities at the CIAR, the artists demanded the removal of several of its directors, including Gordon, Linowitz, and George Meany, who were decried as "symboliz[ing] United States imperialist activity in our hemisphere" ("Show Is Suspended"). The artists further insisted that the center cease its relations with public and private organizations that serve "as instruments of repression against social, political, economic and cultural liberation of our countries" (ibid.). The CIAR responded by postponing the show—in fact, it never took place—and scheduling a "substitute" exhibition for later that year, while the artists moved from boycotting the center to forming the Museo Latinoamericano as an alternative site through which they could publicize their work (B. Adams, 29).

In general, the CIAR's cultural programs sought to uphold the freedom of expression of the individual artist, which was touted during this period as a benefit of democracy and contrasted with the Soviet Union's restrictions on intellectuals' liberties. With some exceptions, directors of the Literature program seem to have worked with few constraints. No explicit ideological restrictions were placed on the program, which over the years subsidized the visits and publications of numerous Marxist and pro-Cuba authors, quite a few of whom were critical of the United States, including Asturias, Cardenal, Cortázar, Fuentes, García Márquez, Neruda, and Vargas Llosa. *Strong Wind* (1968), by Asturias, was in fact the first work subsidized by the translation program, and there was considerable interest in bringing the author to New York when he toured the United States after receiving the Nobel Prize in 1967. Archibald MacLeish, a proponent of the idea, was concerned that the proposal might meet with resistance on political grounds—not from the CIAR, but rather from Asturias himself, whose anti-American sentiment had marked his career.[69] To try to circumvent this possibility, MacLeish suggested extending the invitation through other leftist writers with whom the Literature program enjoyed good relations, but I can find no record of a visit having taken place.[70] The center's willingness to support the alternative perspectives represented within the Literature Department was also evident in 1969 when, as we have seen, Rogers and other CIAR leaders lobbied the highest levels of U.S. government on behalf of Fuentes following his being denied a visa to enter Puerto Rico. Additionally, the Literature program sponsored a series of lectures and poetry readings by Cardenal in the mid-1970s, as well as agreeing to subsidize a translation of his poetry through New Directions. While the latter project does not seem to have been completed, the center did provide a $500 subvention for a motion picture being made about Cardenal.

But while the Literature Department worked closely with writers and intellectuals regardless of their political beliefs, and while it was far from a simple vehicle of Cold War policy interests, it nevertheless faced several political conflicts with the CIAR's leadership, with its own staff and contributors, with Latin American writers, and even with the center's members and the audience at which it directed its programming. These conflicts are telling, for they reveal growing political rifts among Latin American writers and center affiliates alike, and some additionally attest to the schisms within the left in the 1970s. The department's support of Neruda provides an early example of political tensions within the center as a whole. Over the years, the department was an active advocate for the poet and his work: in addition to subsidizing the preparation of *Selected Poems* in 1972, it hosted a showing of the film *I Am Pablo Neruda*; it organized a panel discussion of the poet's work when he received the Nobel Prize; it was a sponsor of his 1972 visit to the United States; it co-organized a memorial service held at the Poetry Center of the 92nd Street Y in late 1973; and it subsidized the translation of Neruda's *Memoirs* [*Confieso que he vivido*], by Hardie St. Martin.[71] And yet John Cates, president of the center from 1971 to 1975, refused to allow the poet's name to appear on the front cover of the Spring 1974 issue of *Review*, even though the issue was to showcase the recent translation of *Residence on Earth*; ultimately, only the title of the featured translation appeared on the cover, with no other reference to the poet.[72] (Cates had been careful to keep up appearances publicly, though, and had sent a telegram of condolence on behalf of the center to Neruda's widow following the poet's death.) It should be noted that Neruda's name had figured prominently alongside those of Borges, Cabrera Infante, García Márquez, and Paz on the cover of the Winter 1971–Spring 1972 issue of *Review*, which was published soon after Cates began his tenure as president, and there was also a later issue highlighting the work of Cortázar, whose support of Cuba was well known. The difference seems to be that the issue on *Residence on Earth* was prepared in early 1974, in the wake of the Chilean coup. Neruda's death several days after the coup was equated symbolically by many with that of

Allende and the end of the Unidad Popular, and the poet came to be viewed as a martyr. John King suggests that drawing attention to Neruda, even just by mentioning his name, "at that moment could only connote resistance to/condemnation of the coup" and that it is likely that Cates censored the cover of the Spring 1974 issue because he viewed it as conveying an anti-Pinochet line.[73]

In the end, though, the greatest political crisis the Literature Department faced was not one where the unit found itself at odds with the center's politics, but where heightened tensions surrounding official U.S. cultural exchange with Pinochet's Chile caused a complete breakdown of relations within the program's inner circle. In 1976, Ronald Christ, the director of the Literature program, traveled to Chile on an exchange program that was sponsored by the State Department's Bureau of Educational and Cultural Affairs (ECA) and hosted by the U.S. embassy in Santiago. Christ was not the only U.S.-based Latin Americanist to go to Chile at this time. Columbia University's MacShane, with whom Christ was in regular contact, visited the country in the spring of 1976 in order to check on friends and see for himself what the situation was like, and it seems likely that his trip inspired Christ's. Christ's first visit set off a small stir among CIAR affiliates when the Literature Department's newsletter published a letter from the cultural attaché of the U.S. embassy, which stated that the visit had helped to promote goodwill and further cultural and diplomatic relations between the United States and Chile. John Alexander Coleman wrote to Roger Stone, the center's executive director, protesting the publication of the letter as a violation of the center's apolitical nature.[74] But it was Christ's return to Chile in 1977 that threatened to destroy the department altogether. He accepted an American Specialist grant from the ECA and, in May, went to teach at the Universidad Católica in Santiago; during the trip, he took a leave of absence from his faculty position at Rutgers University and his directorship of the Literature Department. In June, most of the program's advisory board quit in protest: Coleman and Colchie, *Review*'s advisory editors, resigned from their positions and forbade the journal from publishing any of their work in the future; Rodríguez Monegal similarly dissociated himself from the CIAR and withdrew permission for his work to appear in the journal; and Reid, who had been guest editing a section of a forthcoming issue of *Review*, resigned and withdrew his support from the center, while Colchie, Levine, and Weinberger, the translators with whom Reid had been working for the issue, stopped their work. Many additional consulting editors for *Review* also severed their affiliation with the CIAR.[75]

Several factors seemed to contribute to the strong reaction to Christ's visit. It might have been possible—if not necessarily easy—for him to go to Chile without causing a furor.[76] MacShane had in fact been able to do so the previous year, but he had made his trip privately, and does not seem to have allied himself with any official institutions. In contrast, Christ's funding came from the U.S. government, which had opposed Allende from the very beginning, helped to destabilize the Chilean economy, and sabotaged the Allende government in many other ways, creating the conditions that had made the coup possible. And, as the letter from the U.S. cultural attaché the preceding year had demonstrated, an officially sponsored visit to Chile could be used by U.S. officials as a sign of goodwill and good relations between the two nations at a time when more was becoming known about the torture and repression taking place under the Pinochet regime. Literature Department affiliates also felt that Christ's connections not just to the U.S. government but to the Chilean government would prevent him from establishing any meaningful contact with dissidents. They further believed that his position teaching at a "sanitized" university whose students and faculty must of necessity be supporters of the Pinochet regime gave the appearance of his support for the junta. Most importantly, people worried that as he was director of the Literature program, his visit would appear to be an endorsement by the center of the Pinochet government.

Christ avowed that he had traveled as a private individual and that his trip did not in any way indicate his support for the junta. However, his colleagues claimed that it was impossible for him to separate himself from his position and therefore to avoid giving the appearance of representing the CIAR officially. They were extremely concerned that his actions jeopardized the center's appearance of political neutrality, as well as its programs and the reputations of those associated with the organization.[77] Reid notified Stone that he and other CIAR affiliates had been contacted by Latin American friends who were concerned that the organization seemed to be collaborating with the Pinochet regime, which was in turn leading them to feel uncomfortable about participating in center activities. He confessed that he himself was anxious about whether his work for the CIAR would compromise his own personal and professional aspirations, including his plan to move to Latin America.[78] Rodríguez Monegal wrote that traveling to Chile with U.S. government sponsorship was, in effect, tantamount to receiving funding from the government that had undermined Allende's presidency and enabled the coup, and that Christ's trip therefore would be interpreted as evidence of the center's support for the Pinochet regime.[79] Affiliates also feared the repercussions that the visit might have for Latin Americans who worked with the center. Weinberger wrote to Laughlin that as "the merest hint of collaboration with the junta is enough to permanently damage anyone's reputation," Christ's visit put every writer in danger of being labeled a "yanqui puppet" by other intellectuals.[80]

Stone prepared an official response in which he affirmed the center's apolitical stance. He also stressed the importance of travel by CIAR staff as a means of gaining information and assisting the center in conducting its business. Stone further asserted that Christ's trip offered a chance for cultural and intellectual exchanges that might not otherwise be possible under the current regime. Stone emphasized that although Christ had traveled to Chile independently of his position at the center, it would have been impossible for him to divest himself altogether of his connection to the organization, which in turn had been helpful to the center; it was Stone's support for this that Christ's colleagues in the Literature Department found unsettling.[81]

These colleagues, former advisory board members, and other affiliates took further action. Weinberger wrote to *Review* contributors and supporters on behalf of the group, urging them to condemn Christ's visit, while Levine circulated a letter describing the Christ visit and the hazards that many felt it posed for the center. Weinberger wrote to colleagues that Stone's support of Christ could not "help but give the appearance of approbation on the part of the center toward the junta's policies" and he asked them to sign a letter to the CIAR's board that claimed that this support "jeopardized the Center's avowed position of political neutrality by creating the general impression that the Center is cooperating to a degree with the present regime in Chile."[82] The letter to the board further indicated that its signatories were severing ties with the CIAR in order to avoid "compromis[ing] our individual efforts toward cultural exchange between the Americas."[83] More than thirty people, representing a range of political positions, signed the letter, including the aforementioned affiliates, as well as writers, critics, and translators such as Homero Aridjis, Sara Blackburn, Clayton Eshelman, Juan Goytisolo, José Emilio Pacheco, Octavio Paz, Severo Sarduy, Moacyr Scliar, Mark Strand, and Nathaniel Tarn; Dutton editors John Macrae III and Marian Skedgell; academics such as Jean Franco, Alfred Mac Adam, Joseph Sommers, Hugo Verani, and Luis Yglesias; and Richard Howell, president of the PEN American Center.[84]

Christ cut his trip to Chile short and reached out to writers, collaborators, and publishers in an effort to keep the Literature Department from collapsing. His task was made more difficult by articles in the *New York Times* and *Washington Post* that publicized the matter much more widely.[85] In Mexico, Paz's journal, *Vuelta*, which was widely read by Spanish American writers and intellectuals, published a note, "Escándalo en el Center for Inter-American Relations," that took the side of Christ's detractors: "*Vuelta* thinks that it is regrettable that an institution committed to cultural goals has supported Christ in his mission. It is not possible to speak in an elegiac manner of T. S. Eliot in a country without liberty and at a university where, since 1973, the director has been a military man with the same high moral and intellectual qualities as Professor Pinochet" (55).[86] The *Wall Street Journal* was alone in siding with Christ in a strongly worded editorial in which it denounced the attacks on Christ as part of a worldwide "campaign . . . against the present Chilean regime" (a denunciation that spoke tellingly of the paper's political leanings) and declared that "any effort to stop him [from teaching in Chile] goes beyond a mere protest against the Chilean regime and becomes an assault on American academic freedom" ("Assault on Mr. Christ").[87] Christ issued a personal statement in which he stressed that in making the trip he had acted as an individual, neither representing the CIAR nor collaborating with the Chilean government. He argued instead that he was attempting to gather dissident literature and to communicate with dissenting writers and artists, an endeavor that he felt was worth undertaking despite the blockade.[88]

Several people stood apart from the fray. Cortázar wrote a letter to the center protesting the trip, but did not dissociate himself from the organization.[89] Rabassa declined to sign the group letter and instead wrote to Stone directly. While he agreed that many would interpret Christ's trip as indicative of the CIAR's support for the military regime, he attributed the visit to bad judgment rather than viewing it as a statement of political principles, and he was one of very few affiliates who asked to hear Christ's side of the story.[90] Frederick Martin at New Directions remained quietly supportive, offering encouragement but stopping short of taking a public stand for Christ.[91] Doris Meyer, a center member and a professor of Spanish at Brooklyn College, supported Christ's decision to teach in Chile. She wrote to Stone: "I feel that what Mr. Christ was trying to do in Chile is an essential form of cultural communication among members of the world academic community. Were those who protest his trip to have their way, the lines of communication would be broken entirely, and by inference, not only with Chile but with other countries of Latin America with right-wing military regimes."[92]

Donoso and Fuentes also declined to sign the letter to the board, and correspondence between the two authors reveals a sense of distance from both the politics and agents behind the letter.[93] Fuentes held Rodríguez Monegal responsible for the campaign against Christ: Weinberger and

Levine had written to many of the program's supporters, but Rodríguez Monegal was the one who contacted Latin American writers—some, such as Vargas Llosa, repeatedly, and despite the Peruvian's clearly stated difference of opinion on the matter—to try to convince them to join the protest.[94] It may appear ironic that Rodríguez Monegal, who had been terribly upset by the negative characterizations of *Mundo Nuevo* and of himself in the wake of the revelations of CIA funding, was one of Christ's principal detractors. Rodríguez Monegal may have been at least partly motivated by his own feelings of despair at what was going on in Uruguay, which was also experiencing brutal repression in the wake of its 1973 military coup. But there were other displacements as well: the tensions between Christ and Rodríguez Monegal were rooted more deeply than those caused by the visit to Chile and stemmed, at least in part, from a struggle for control of the Literature Department. Rodríguez Monegal had been deeply involved with the program from the beginning, using his connections to bring Latin American authors to the center. He had edited *Review* during its first few years of publication, and he had stayed on the journal's editorial board until March 1977, when Christ relieved him of his responsibilities, claiming that the Uruguayan's work commitments had made it impossible for him to continue to perform his duties.[95] Levine also had been involved with the center from its inception and was close to Rodríguez Monegal; she has suggested that the latter's mobilizing was in response not just to the trip to Chile, but also because at some level he viewed Christ as a composite of several antagonists who, over the years, had pushed him out of positions where his work had been meaningful to him and to others. These positions would have included his role on *Review*'s editorial board, which Christ had terminated just weeks before the trip, as well as the editorship of *Mundo Nuevo* and, prior to that, his post at *Marcha*.[96]

Rodríguez Monegal contacted Fuentes about Christ's trip to Chile. The two men had worked together closely over the years: they were both living in Paris when the Uruguayan was editing *Mundo Nuevo*, and as both were viewed as ambassadors of Latin American literature in the West, they often found themselves working together on projects and at symposia. But for Fuentes, the Christ affair seemed to be symptomatic of deeply rooted political and aesthetic differences. As King argues, in the 1970s, Fuentes became "increasingly distanced from Monegal's interpretations of modern Latin American literature, especially the espousal at Yale of Sarduy as the touchstone for literary experimentation" (120). Fuentes's reaction to the scandal seems to have been a part of this process. In fact, he associated the impetus behind the Uruguayan's campaign against Christ with his praise for writers such as Cabrera Infante, who had broken with the revolution, and Sarduy, who was also alienated from Cuba, attributing both to an underlying conservative politics and aesthetics.[97] (This association is tenuous, for the Uruguayan and others were in effect accusing Christ of aligning himself with Pinochet's authoritarian regime.)

Christ found his strongest supporter in Vargas Llosa, who was then president of International PEN, and whose *Pantaleón y las visitadoras* (*Captain Pantoja and the Special Service*) he was translating at the time. PEN's commitment to supporting the freedom of expression of writers living under repressive conditions dovetailed with the writer's strong personal convictions: as Herrero-Olaizola details in chapter 2 of *The Censorship Files*, the Peruvian had struggled with the Franco regime's censorship of his work during the 1960s and 1970s, and he had definitively broken with Castro and the Cuban Revolution following the Padilla affair of 1971.[98] Vargas Llosa rebuffed Rodríguez Monegal's efforts to convince him to sign the letter to the center's board, noting that he himself had taught at the Universidad de Barcelona during franquismo and asking if that made him a collaborator with the Franco regime.[99] Vargas Llosa also contacted Stone directly to voice his disagreement with the movement against Christ:

Pienso que es un error gravísimo confundir a los gobiernos con los pueblos . . . y considerar a la cultura como una mera repartición de la política. Proponer un cordón sanitario cultural en torno a los países donde hay una tiranía militar, como en Chile, es castigar al pueblo chileno. . . . Una manera como los intelectuales extranjeros pueden ayudarnos es manteniendo, con los sectores universitarios, intelectuales y artísticos de nuestros países, un diálogo constante. Ellos, muchas veces, pueden, cuando nos [here he is referring to his own experience under dictatorship in Lima] visitan . . . hablar con más libertad que los nativos. . . . Mi parecer es que esa oportunidad debe ser aprovechada al máximo y que esa es una manera más efectiva, más real, de combatir a las dictaduras que tendiendo un tabú o satanizando y cortando toda relación con las víctimas de la opresión.

(I think that it is a grave error to confuse governments with people . . . and to consider culture to be a mere division of politics. To propose to culturally cordon off countries where there is military tyranny, as in Chile, is to punish the Chilean people. . . . One way that foreign intellectuals can help us is by maintaining a constant dialogue with the university, intellectual, and artistic sectors of our countries. They can, often, when they visit us [here he is referring to his own experience under dictatorship in Lima] . . . speak with greater freedom than natives. . . . My view is that this opportunity should be embraced as much as possible—it is a more effective, more realistic way of fighting dictatorships than making taboos or demonizing and cutting off all relations with the oppressed.)[100]

Additionally, Vargas Llosa drew on his position at PEN to help Christ try to contain the international fallout from the situation: he notified Christ that Latin American writers in the Netherlands had asked the local PEN club to publish the letter of protest against Christ's visit, and he offered suggestions on how to defuse the situation; he also wrote directly to the head of the Dutch PEN center, explaining Christ's rationale behind his visit and urging her to read the documentation representing Christ's side of the story prior to taking any action.[101]

The damage was beyond repair, however, and Christ soon stepped down as director, passing the baton to Rosario Santos, a Bolivian who had been hired as MacLeish's executive assistant in the early days of the CIAR and who had also been Castillo's assistant and an assistant editor of *Review*. Christ stayed on for a time as a consultant, assisting with the preparation of several additional issues of *Review*.[102] Santos was very competent and well connected as a result of her years at the CIAR. However, within a few months, Stone invited Christ to resume directing the program; Christ declined, though, and resigned from the program altogether in 1979 (Rostagno, 110).

Luis Harss, the compiler of *Into the Mainstream* (1967), a timely collection of interviews with and commentary on Borges, Cortázar, Fuentes, García Márquez, Vargas Llosa, and other writers that had been an important vehicle for publicizing the rise of Latin American literature, took over editing *Review* in 1980. The respite for the program, however, was brief: issue 30 in late 1981 prompted another firestorm that threw the Literature program back into turmoil, this time facing accusations of a pro-Cuba and pro-Marxist bias. The theme of the issue was "Literature and Exile." It focused exclusively on "writers alienated from the military dictatorships of Latin America's 'southern cone,'" although Harss noted that "in other issues we will hear other voices testifying to the situation in other parts of the continent, under other types of government" ("Editor's Note"). The issue featured essays by Alegría (Chile), Cortázar (Argentina), Rama (Uruguay), and Roa Bastos (Paraguay), each of whom spoke of both personal and collective experiences of exile.

Authors alienated from Cuba and members of the center's board alike took umbrage at the issue. Their rationale seems to have been that the focus on the Southern Cone, where military dictators had brutally repressed oppositional, generally leftist, politics, allowed the issue to showcase writers whom the critics identified as leftists. The focus on the Southern Cone was further read by protesters as a means of avoiding criticism of Cuba, which writers such as Cabrera Infante and Reinaldo Arenas, among others, had left following persecution or repression that had turned them away from the revolution in particular and from the left in general. After the issue was published, Arenas wrote directly to Rama, who had been a contributing editor for the feature. On the one hand, Arenas was amicable and proposed the inclusion of one of Rama's articles for a forthcoming issue of *Review* devoted to the Cuban's work. On the other, Arenas attacked what he believed to be Rama's deliberate silence on the political brutality and oppression in Cuba; he further accused the Uruguayan of following (Communist) Party lines by not mentioning in the article Arenas's critiques of Castro and his regime.[103]

Rama, who had been a friend and a benefactor of Arenas, and who had published several of his works, wrote a sharply worded response. He affirmed his Socialist beliefs but explained his own disillusionment with Cuba and Communism. He also reminded Arenas of his own support of those—including Arenas himself—whose dissidence had incurred the wrath of the revolutionary regime, and noted that this support had in turn brought recriminations on himself from intellectuals supportive of Castro and from other quarters.[104] (Immediately after this exchange, Rama wrote to Santos to rescind his authorization for inclusion of his article on Arenas in the special issue of *Review*, although he still felt—at least at the time of the letter—that the issue was an important idea.[105])

In the fall of 1982, the matter resurfaced when Arenas and several other Cuban writers published an open letter to the CIAR in *El Universal* (Caracas), where Rama had long been a contributor.[106] The letter accused Rama and the other contributors to the issue on exile of being "communist oriented writers"; it also criticized the issue for "coddl[ing] Castroism and some of its most noted agents" and exhibiting "tendentious propaganda in favor of international communism and an obvious silencing of writers opposed to Marxism" ("Open Letter to the Center," 1). The letter further denounced what it cast as *Review*'s support of Communist writers and Cuban functionaries. It concluded that the Literature program's activities "are not designed to promote and facilitate relations between Latin American writers in general, but specifically among communists," and that the center itself "seems to follow the line of the Communist Party" (ibid.).

Prompted by a complaint from one of the center's Venezuelan members,

the board of directors also sent a letter to *El Universal*.[107] Also, in a sting-
ing (and ad hominem) article, "Las malandanzas de Reinaldo Arenas," that
appeared in the same periodical, Rama defended the *Review* issue: he dis-
counted Arenas's accusations by arguing that the Cuban himself had been
supported by the Literature program as a resident writer, that *Review* often
featured dissident Cuban writers and was in fact planning a future issue on
Arenas, and that Cabrera Infante also collaborated with the journal. Arenas,
in turn, continued the polemic, republishing the open letter in a special issue of a small New York–based journal, *Noticias de arte*. Alongside the letter, he published two additional essays. The first was a short piece in which
he deemed Rama a "subversive agent" for previously supporting, in Arenas's words, "the destruction of the United States and the proclamation of
a continental Marxist revolution led by Cuba" (as advocated by Casa de las
Américas), and then seeking to establish permanent residency in the United
States ("Ángel Rama," 2; as discussed in Chapter 1, Rama was in the midst
of his visa difficulties at this time). The second, much longer piece was a
repudiation of Rama's claims that was likewise not free of ad hominem attacks ("Una Rama").

Protests against the exile issue were heard in other quarters, too, and
continued to fan out over time. After the issue appeared, staff members involved with it were accused of being Communists in a letter sent to the
CIAR's board of directors.[108] Santos later told Rama that the board had her
draft a report that ultimately convinced them that the program was not
abetting Communists.[109] In 1983, Paz canceled a talk at the center—though
he gave a lecture elsewhere on the same visit to New York—making it clear
to Santos that the reason for his decision was that he viewed the program as
leaning too far to the left.[110]

This incident came at a time where the Literature program's budget
was already tight. In late 1981, the Center for Inter-American Relations had
merged with another David Rockefeller organization, the Council of the
Americas, and formed the Americas Society.[111] As the new organization got
off the ground during the early Reagan years, it was plagued by financial
challenges, as well as a difficult and more conservative economy. There were
cuts to the budgets of its more expensive programs, such as the Literature
Department; according to Santos, tensions between the department and the
CIAR administration that stemmed from the exile issue brought about a
decrease in funding to the unit.[112] Santos and Harss managed to publish
one more issue of the journal (no. 31, January–April 1982), motivated in
part by the fracas over the exile issue and a desire to prevent detractors from
attributing the journal's demise to their criticism.[113] After this issue, Harss

stepped down as editor and the journal's editorial board was dissolved. While Santos continued directing the Literature Department's activities, there followed a two-year hiatus for *Review*; not surprisingly, the planned issue on Arenas never materialized. During this period, the journal was reorganized and the translation subsidy program was permanently discontinued; the Literature Department was able to continue a number of its other activities, though, supported by grants from the New York State Council on the Arts (among other sources) and by revenues generated by fundraising dinners with authors such as Borges and Vargas Llosa.[114] *Review* started up again with issue 32 (January–May 1984) and a new editorial board that included Coleman and Reid (both now reconciled with the center), Rabassa, writers William Kennedy and Luisa Valenzuela, and academics Jo Anne Engelbert and Mac Adam, the latter of whom served as the journal's editor. After this point, the department's efforts were focused less on translation and more broadly on *Review* and the promotion of Latin American literature in the United States.

In some ways, perhaps the fracas surrounding the "Literature and Exile" issue of *Review* was the culmination of the conflicting politics and ideologies that set the Literature Department apart from the center in which it was housed. Most of the issue's contributors were longtime advocates of the left: Cortázar was an avid supporter of the Cuban Revolution, and he had done important work for the Russell Tribunal II as well; Alegría had been a diplomat under Allende; and Rama's Socialist beliefs, as we have seen, resulted in his troubles with the McCarran-Walter Act, which in fact flared up soon after the issue was published. In the end, the emphasis placed on the experiences of these writers at the apparent expense of those who had been forcibly exiled from Cuba because of their dissent from the Castro regime seems to have been too much, both for the fragile peace reestablished at the Literature Department and for the more conservative politics of the CIAR. The incident prompted unprecedented interventions of the organization's leadership both into the public debate on the matter and into the department's operations.

Despite Paz's (second) disavowal of the program, though, the fallout among Latin American writers and the U.S.-based academics and publishers affiliated with the Literature Department was minimal: there were no lasting effects and, surprisingly, no further backlash against the center's administration, and no protests against the department's affiliation with an organization that had tried to discount the appearance of leftism within. This, of course, stands in stark contrast to the aftermath of Christ's visit to Chile, which did such damage to the image of the center's political neutrality. But perhaps the idea of the center's neutrality that was held by affiliates of the Literature program needs, in this instance, to be nuanced. Christ's critics objected both to his association with the Pinochet regime and to his acceptance of U.S. government funding for the trip, given U.S. involvement in the fall of Allende's administration. Their response thus stemmed both from a stance against fascism and a perspective that was extremely critical of U.S. foreign policy. But while they were right to be concerned that by way of Christ, the association of the center with the Chilean regime could compromise Latin American writers and Literature Department affiliates alike, their position left room neither for the opinion that making the trip was an issue of intellectual freedom, nor for the argument—articulated by Christ and a number of his supporters—that the visit could grant opponents of the regime, many of whom would have been active in the left prior to the coup, an outlet for communicating dissent that the repressive regime was not permitting.

IRENE ROSTAGNO HAS AFFIRMED THAT *Review* "did what *Mundo Nuevo* had hoped to accomplish years earlier. It communicated with the larger American intellectual community and advanced the idea that Latin America was producing genuinely innovative literature" (109). The comparison that she draws between the two journals is a fraught one, however—one weighed down by other, presumably unintended, parallels. Both journals were, of course, plagued by their connections to the public and private sectors: under Rodríguez Monegal's editorship, *Mundo Nuevo* was tainted by the accusations of CIA funding, while *Review* and the Literature Department, as part of the CIAR, were first troubled by the center's association with the foreign policy establishment—albeit not the CIA—and later debilitated by the internecine strife resulting from Christ's trip to Chile and the issue on exile. The difficulties confronted by these two journals attest to the political minefields facing those who were committed to cultural exchange and to increasing inter-American understanding at a time when the Cold War polarization of democracy and Communism was extreme. The Literature Department also suffered because this polarization obscured the variety and complexity of opinion among Latin American writers, including the effects of the movement away from Cuba in the years following the Padilla affair.

It is important to take into consideration the full extent of the accomplishments of both *Mundo Nuevo* and the CIAR's Literature Department. *Mundo Nuevo* disseminated Boom texts and criticism widely as part of Rodríguez Monegal's strategy to bring the movement to an international audience. The Literature Department was indispensable in furthering this process. Mudrovcic has criticized what she views as the department's monopoly of the production and circulation of Latin American literature. She argues that the CIAR's financial and structural assistance created "a solid web of professional and nonprofessional loyalties that linked the Center to 'its' writers, critics, and translators" ("Reading Latin American Literature," 137)—a web of loyalties that from her perspective was also one of control, resulting in the suppression of criticism of the program because of its power over the translation market (138). Mudrovcic concludes that as a result,

> It is difficult to imagine what Latin American literature in the United States might have looked like today without the Center's intervention and patronage throughout the sixties and early seventies. What would have happened, for instance, if the United States had followed the horizontal pattern of diffusion and consecration, such as the one followed in the French cultural field? . . . Arguably, the Latin American canon would likely be a more heterogeneous, diverse, and more open body of texts (and authors). It would also be a more unstable, and perhaps even more flexible canon than it actually has turned out to be for the U.S. readership. (139)

Hugh Wilford has similarly asked in his study of CIA sponsorship of the Congress for Cultural Freedom "how writing might have developed in Cold War America without the 'umbilical cord of gold' that united spy and artist" (*Mighty Wurlitzer*, 116). These questions are legitimate ones. And yet, it is difficult to see what the mechanisms for the horizontal dissemination that Mudrovcic hypothesizes would have been.

It is worth returning to the results of the AAUP translation subsidy program once again as a point of comparison. The low profile of the literary works sponsored by the latter would seem to challenge Mudrovcic's speculation: the AAUP program lacked a centralized publicity mechanism, and individual university presses either did not have or did not commit significant resources to publicizing their translations, which for the most part received little attention in mainstream periodicals and provided disappointing sales revenues. During the mid-1950s, commercial publishers had begun releasing works by authors who were building reputations in the United States, but sales of their books were often quite low. In contrast, from the early 1960s on, the Literature Department of the CIAR and its predecessors were instrumental not just in promoting Latin American literature in the United States but in carving out a space for it, both by convincing publishers to sign new authors and by establishing an infrastructure that brought their work to the public's attention. While both the AAUP and CIAR translation pro-

grams targeted academic audiences, through which books could be introduced into university curricula and thereby achieve the status of "literature"
(see Ohmann, 205–6), only the center's program made a concerted effort to
reach a broader reading public. Ohmann has argued that during this period,
canon formation "took place in the interaction between large audiences and
gatekeeper intellectuals" (207): that is, books made their mark on the U.S.
literary scene by attaining *both* high sales and "the right kind of critical attention" (206)—in Bourdieu's terminology, by involving both the field of
large-scale production and the field of restricted production. The CIAR's
Literature program had a profound and lasting effect, then, on literary tastes
in the United States—a measure of success that eluded the Congress for
Cultural Freedom, which was better at reaching the cultural elite than the
popular masses. Without the center, it would have been much more difficult
for Latin American literature to gain the foothold that it did in the United
States.[115] It seems unlikely, then, that a "horizontal pattern of diffusion and
consecration" would on its own have provided sufficient momentum to
create a canon of Latin American literature in the United States.

In the end, of course, the Literature Department went far beyond its
stated goals of promoting Latin American literature. The program did indeed establish a foothold for Latin American writers in the U.S. literary
scene. From the very first days of the IAC, though, it was not just the organization's publicity efforts but its networking—the personal connections
and friendships that it made possible for Latin American writers—that had
a profound impact on their attitude toward the United States. For the most
part, the Literature Department maintained a high degree of cultural and
intellectual autonomy from the politics of the center and the agencies that
supported it. Nevertheless, its humanistic motives were at some level also directly tied to geopolitical concerns, including an interest in promoting inter-
American exchange for the sake of improving international relations in the
hemisphere. For years, then, the program carefully navigated competing and
conflicting agendas by taking advantage of the Cold War interest in Latin
America while simultaneously supporting authors whose politics ran counter
to those of the center's sponsors.

CONCLUSION

After the 1966 PEN congress ended, Pablo Neruda traveled to California, where he gave a poetry reading at the University of California, Berkeley. The reading was attended by Mario Vargas Llosa, Juan Carlos Onetti, and Carlos Martínez Moreno, who were traveling together at PEN's expense—visiting universities, attending writers' workshops, and otherwise establishing connections with the U.S. literary community. The Spanish American writers traveled to the recital with Allen Ginsberg and Lawrence Ferlinghetti, along with numerous Beatniks, in a bus that set out from Ferlinghetti's legendary San Francisco bookstore, City Lights, the heart of the Beat movement.[1] The auditorium was packed, and Vargas Llosa describes Neruda's success at the reading as "absolutamente apoteósico . . . fue uno de los momentos digamos de gran promoción de América Latina desde el punto de vista literario" (absolutely tremendous . . . it was a moment of great promotion of Latin America from a literary standpoint).[2] After the recital, Ferlinghetti and Neruda talked for a while at a reception at the home of Chilean writer (and Berkeley faculty member) Fernando Alegría, and the Beat poets spent the next few days showing Vargas Llosa, his wife, Patricia, Martínez Moreno, and Onetti around San Francisco.[3] It was a meeting of profoundly different movements, the counterculture of the Beats a contrast to the aspirations of Western acclaim of the Latin Americans. At the same time, though, both groups of authors shared a deep interest in crossing American boundaries (understood hemispherically) in literary experimentation, and in Cuba's revolutionary politics. This moment of contact thus stands as a touchstone—a testament to the increasingly frequent intertwining of the lives and the work of writers from different parts of the hemisphere.

The 1966 meeting was but one of many points of intersection between

Spanish American writers and Beat poets that had taken place since the late 1950s. Such moments cumulatively tell a tale of social networks and networking—of mutual interests and the reciprocal influence of writers and regions alike—that further attests to the connections between U.S. and Latin American literary spheres within the context of the Cold War. This is a story of authors crisscrossing paths in the South and North who were joined together in part by an interest in Cuba and social justice, but also by their interest in one another as poets. As the infrastructure for publishing and promoting Latin American literature in the United States grew, and as it weathered the political storms of the Cold War, the circles of Beat and Spanish American poets intersected time and again as the authors met, read, translated, published, and influenced one another's work.

Personal relations between the two groups were established in 1959, when Chilean writer Gonzalo Rojas traveled to the United States. While in San Francisco, Rojas went to City Lights and invited several of the Beat writers to attend the "Primer Encuentro de Escritores Americanos" (First meeting of American writers) that he was organizing as part of the Escuela Internacional de Verano (International summer school) at the Universidad de Concepción ("Gonzalo Rojas: Cronología"). The invitation was attractive, for a number of the Beat poets had traveled to Mexico and elsewhere in Spanish America in the 1950s, and were additionally supportive of the Cuban Revolution. Ferlinghetti and Ginsberg accepted the invitation and traveled to Chile, where they met Martínez Moreno, Alegría and fellow Chilean writer Nicanor Parra, Peruvian Sebastián Salazar Bondy, and others. Many of the writers present were caught up in the euphoria of the revolutionary period; accordingly, discussions at the workshop revolved around the social functions of literature and its importance in the process of creating a new America, as well as the political responsibilities of the writer-intellectual (Gilman, *Entre la pluma*, 71, 80). But there was also time for sharing one another's work. Alegría had recently translated "Howl," and at the conference Ginsberg read from the work in English while the Chilean read simultaneously from the translation. Ferlinghetti also presented some of his poetry, and when he read "Overpopulation," a member of the audience commented on similarities between the poem and Parra's work. Ferlinghetti acknowledged these, explaining that he had been translating some of Parra's antipoems when he wrote "Overpopulation": "Given my admiration for the Chilean, it's not strange that something of him would be transmitted to me" (qtd. in Véjar). Ferlinghetti's admiration seems to have been rooted in Parra's experimentation with form, his use of humor and satire, his rebelliousness, and his criticism of injustice and social institutions (Silesky, 100).

After the conference, Ginsberg stayed at Parra's home in Chile for several weeks, and then spent a few months traveling through Chile, Bolivia, the Amazon, and Peru. He sought out indigenous sites as well as hallucinogenics that had been recommended to him; he slept among the ruins at Machu Picchu and later claimed that the landscape of southern Chile influenced the poetry he wrote after the trip ("El aullido," 39). In Lima, he gave a recital to a packed audience at the Instituto de Arte Contemporáneo, then directed by Salazar Bondy, whom he had befriended in Concepción. Carlos Zavaleta, a writer and former Fulbright fellow who had served as William Faulkner's translator during the latter's brief visit to Peru in 1954, was tapped to do simultaneous translation for Ginsberg. During his stay in Lima, Ginsberg also met Martín Adán, a Peruvian avant-garde poet who became the subject of his poem "To an old poet in Peru," which was published in the Peruvian journal *Amaru* as well as in *Reality Sandwiches* (1963).

Ferlinghetti also traveled through the Andean nations following the conference. He overlapped with Ginsberg in Lima, and then traveled to Cuzco and Machu Picchu, where he wrote "Hidden Door," which he describes as influenced by Pablo Neruda's "The Heights of Macchu Picchu" ("Lawrence Ferlinghetti").[4] He then headed north through Central America and Mexico. Soon after his return to the United States, he released an edition of Parra's *Antipoems*, translated by Chilean critic Jorge Elliott. The inclusion of Parra's collection on the City Lights lists alongside Ginsberg's *Howl* and other Beat texts in effect brought the work into the circle of Beat writers as well as to their readers.

Later in 1960, Ferlinghetti traveled to Cuba for a celebration of the first anniversary of the Cuban Revolution.[5] It was here that he and Neruda first met. The latter gave a reading to Castro's supporters in an atmosphere that Ferlinghetti describes as "a revolutionary euphoria, the early days of any revolution. And in this one, it was fantastic. The whole place was throbbing with this vitality" ("Legendary Beat Generation Bookseller"). Both Neruda and Ferlinghetti met with Castro, and the trip worked its way into Ferlinghetti's writings, most notably his 1961 poem "One Thousand Fearful Words for Fidel Castro." Ferlinghetti and Neruda were also, not surprisingly, drawn to each other by literature as well as politics. According to Ferlinghetti, the Chilean declared to him, "I love your wide-open poetry," to which Ferlinghetti responded, "You opened the door" (Ferlinghetti, xv). Ferlinghetti believed that Neruda was referring to "the poetry of the Beat Generation that we had published in San Francisco and some of which had been published in translation in *Lunes de Revolución*" (ibid.); the bookseller would later use the phrase "wide-open poetry" to describe his own work, preferring it to the label of "Beat poetry" (Benson).

Over the years, Ferlinghetti has often revisited his connection to Neruda: in 1975, he wrote a poem about Neruda's death titled "The General Song of Humanity" (a title that deliberately invokes Neruda's *Canto general* [General song]); poem twelve in his 1997 collection, *A Far Rockaway of the Heart*, recalls his initial meeting with the poet in Cuba; and in 2004, to commemorate the one hundredth anniversary of Neruda's birth, City Lights published *The Essential Neruda*. In a way, the edition marked the fulfillment of a dream deferred: according to Barry Silesky, Ferlinghetti had wanted to convince Neruda to publish in the City Lights Pocket Poets series when they first met in 1960, but this had not come about (108). In his preface to *The Essential Neruda*, Ferlinghetti expressed his desire that the work "open the door for the greater American public," echoing his earlier declaration to the Chilean that his work had opened the door for the poetry of the Beat Generation (xv). Ferlinghetti also continued to pursue his interest in Parra: his own translations of the antipoet, along with efforts by Ginsberg, Alegría, W. S. Merwin, William Carlos Williams (to whom the Beats are also indebted for his promoting their work), and others, appeared in a 1967 bilingual anthology, *Poems and Antipoems*. Its publisher, New Directions, also produced editions of work by Neruda and the Beat poets.

Ginsberg also had a near-encounter with Neruda, but it was nowhere near as fruitful or reciprocal as Ferlinghetti's. Instead, it reflected differences and tensions between the movements and generations. Silesky recounts that Ferlinghetti, Ginsberg, and Neruda, among others, were invited to an international poetry festival in 1965, but when Neruda heard that Ginsberg planned to perform naked, he refused to attend the latter's show (139). Ginsberg, who seems to have been unaware of this non-meeting, admired the Chilean's work, and acknowledged the influence of both the political and interior dimensions of *Canto General* on his own *The Fall of America: Poems of These States, 1965–1971* ("El aullido," 39).

Like Ferlinghetti, Ginsberg was drawn to Cuba for political reasons. Ginsberg was a poet of rebellion whose mother had been an active member of the Communist Party, and his own radicalism extended to politics and political activism. In 1965, he traveled to Cuba to participate in the judging of the annual Casa de las Américas prizes. Ginsberg went to the island eager to learn what he could about life in the revolution: Jean-Paul Sartre had asked him for an article on his experiences in Cuba, and he was interested as well in putting together an anthology of post-revolutionary writing to be published by City Lights (Rodríguez, 48, 49). Ginsberg spent much of his free time with young writers, asking them about the policies of the revolutionary government on homosexuality, marijuana, and other social issues. He was concerned by their stories of repressive practices, detentions, and purges, and his anxiety mounted as several of his interlocutors were detained for "interacting with foreigners," some receiving threats of additional detention, surveillance, being brought to trial, interference with their professional lives, and other harassment if they were to meet with Ginsberg again (see Rodríguez).

Just days before the poet was to leave the island, he was expelled by government officials. According to Ginsberg, he was expelled for "fighting the Communists, for denouncing Castro's antigay policy, for hanging around with younger writers, for criticizing Cuba's monolithic press, for talking 'strange,' and for saying I thought Che Guevara was *cute*, and that Raul Castro was gay" (qtd. in Robins, 338; emphasis in the original). It seems that the poet was one thing that the revolutionary state and the U.S. government in its state of high Cold War alert could agree on: after the Cuba incident, as Herbert Mitgang details, J. Edgar Hoover labeled Ginsberg "an 'Internal Security—Cuba' case, and a potential threat to the president of the United States" (*Dangerous Dossiers*, 261). Over the years, the FBI amassed a file on Ginsberg that was more than 900 pages long, and he was the subject of records maintained at the CIA, the Drug Enforcement Agency, and other official organizations.[6] His actions in Cuba, then, paradoxically both brought on him the ire of the Cuban revolutionary state and resulted in his being deemed a threat to national security in the United States—a position that calls to mind the experiences of Carlos Fuentes in the 1960s.

The Spanish American poets, in turn, kept up their friendships with the Beat poets as they pursued opportunities in the United States. Alegría's proximity to San Francisco, with faculty positions at Berkeley and later Stanford, allowed him to stay connected to Ferlinghetti and to participate in City Lights activities over the years. Parra, in turn, made a number of trips to the United States in the 1960s and 1970s, including spending time on faculty at Louisiana State University in Baton Rouge, Columbia University, and New York University. During several public appearances, he read from his poetry in Spanish while Ginsberg read the English translations. In 1986, Ginsberg invited Parra to present his work at the Naropa Institute in Boulder, Colorado, where several of the Beat poets had studied, and where they had founded the Jack Kerouac School of Disembodied Poetics. Parra did not attend the gathering, but Ginsberg, Ferlinghetti, and others organized a tribute to him that they recorded and sent to the poet (Véjar).

In April 1970, Parra was one of eight foreign poets to participate in the Library of Congress's International Poetry Festival. The festival marked a moment of tremendous acclaim for Parra, but it was followed by a fall into a political quagmire with the Latin American left. On the last day of the festival, the participants had tea at the White House with Mrs. Nixon. Although Parra explained afterward that he had been unaware that he would be meeting the president's wife—he had thought that he would be simply taking a tour of the White House—Cuban writers criticized him for betraying the Socialist cause and removed him from the jury of the Casa de las Américas prizes. Also, the extreme left took him to task in Chile, which was gearing up for presidential elections—tight elections in which, according to Frank MacShane, Parra's actions had a ripple effect, moving some votes away from Salvador Allende (37).

At least in the United States, the pendulum swung back for Parra. Just weeks after the White House incident, he gave a poetry reading in Bryant Park in New York City as part of a series sponsored by the Academy of American Poets. He was introduced, appropriately enough, with verses from Federico García Lorca's *Poeta en Nueva York* (Oyarzún). Parra read his poems in Spanish, while Pulitzer Prize–winning poet Stanley Kunitz read them in English translation. Kunitz apologized for "a parochial convention" that prevented him from speaking of Parra as "an American poet," and then declared Parra to be "a poet of the Americas, one of the very finest" (qtd. in Phillips). His words echoed—no doubt unwittingly—Archibald MacLeish's transcontinental identification during the PEN festivities four years earlier of Parra's compatriot Neruda as "an American poet" (Rodman). Clearly, Kunitz and MacLeish each felt that the work of their Chilean guest transcended and interrogated national boundaries, laying the groundwork for a hemispheric conception of poetic accomplishment.

Scholars such as Glenn Sheldon (*South of Our Selves*) and Rachel Adams ("Hipsters and *jipitecas*") have examined the role of Mexico in the Beat poets' writings and worldviews, while Adams and Roland Greene ("Inter-American Obversals"), among others, have used comparative methods to study the Beat alongside literary movements in Latin America. As these scholars demonstrate, and as my own work also illustrates, there is a web of connections that links writers from the South and North and that demands that we too cross borders in order to best understand their poetry, their publishing histories, and their politics. Adams concludes that her comparative study of writers associated with two unconnected movements, the Beat and Mexico's countercultural *la Onda*, "attests to the inevitable but unpredictable circulation of culture across national boundaries. At the same time, it underscores the formative impact of the nation state and foreign policy on cultural production" (80). The tension that she identifies between borders that are at once easier to cross and ever more constricting on cultural production speaks to some of the paradoxes that I have found in my own study of the promotion of Latin American literature in the United States during the Cold War.

And, of course, writers circulate, too. The Beat writers construed Mexico—and Spanish America more broadly—as sites of "otherness" to which they traveled to learn about themselves. As Sheldon argues, the work emerging from their journeys interrogates notions of "Americanness" (2–3).[7] At the same time, these were real sites where the writers were able to work out their political beliefs and social values. Cuba in particular came to represent for them an example of a society where social injustices were being redressed—except for Ginsberg, who ran up against the limits of the change the nation offered, and found that his enforced crossing of borders (his expulsion from the island) also revealed the limits of U.S. citizenship in the hardening of his own nation's attitude toward him. For writers from Latin America, Cuba was a touchstone for a transnational community of writers and the formation of a regional identity that was at once cultural and political. The United States, in turn, offered these writers the opportunity to strengthen their friendships with one another and to raise their literary profiles in the international sphere, with their ties to Cuba serving to facilitate this process and, at times, to undermine it.

This conclusion has spoken of connections between individuals and of mutually influential friendships between writers from the South and North. Further, these connections and friendships assisted the dissemination of these writers' works in both regions. As in the previous chapters, I have described here a hemispheric web of relations and influences that can be accounted for only in literary histories that take a transnational approach. If Beat writers opened a number of doors, as it were, for Spanish American writers, so too was their own work affected not just by their travels through Spanish America but by their connections—literary and personal alike—to writers from the region. In his study of the Beat poets' representations of Mexico, Sheldon argues that "by looking at Mexico through the eyes of American [i.e., "U.S."] poets, the reader is forced to reconsider the greater world, one outside our local 'borders.' Mexico, as part of the 'Hispanic' world . . . helps construct the United States and its own ideas of political and cultural borders" (4). The travels of writers from both regions to the North and through the South reverberated both through their work and through the invention of their own traditions, including the notion of transnational and hemispheric literary communities. The infrastructure through which their work circulated likewise consisted of a transnational network of people and institutions that were responsible not just for its dissemination but for its canonization, both at home and abroad.

The writers whom I have examined in this book must be studied as individuals, as parts of regional (or, in the case of the Beat poets, national) cohorts, and as participants in transnational communities and infrastructures that were inflected by Cold War–era hemispheric relations. These transnational communities and infrastructures shaped their work as well as affecting its promotion and reception. The experiences of the writers speak to what Rachel Adams has described, in a related context, as a "juncture where national myths collide with foreign policy changes and the transnational circulation of culture" (59), for even as some of them ran into the bureaucratic walls imposed and enforced by nationalism, the circulation of the writers and their work alike crossed—and, in many ways, fundamentally challenged—borders that were at once literary and political. Thus, Latin America helped to construct the United States, as well as vice versa, and this synergy in turn helps to expand our understanding of what is "America," and what, in the end, is an "American" writer.

The hemispheric web of relations sketched out in this conclusion also offers insights into the complex and dialectical nature of the Cold War in the Americas, and speaks to the importance of studying what Gilbert Joseph has labeled "transnational 'contact zones'" (17). The story of the connections between Spanish American and Beat writers in the 1960s and 1970s once again brings to the fore the deep schisms within the left in Latin America, as well as the surprising points of contact that cut across both national and political boundaries—making strange bedfellows, for example, of Cuba's revolutionary government and the FBI, even if for just a moment.

In his contribution to *In from the Cold*, Joseph asserts that one of the book's principal goals was "to foment a more sustained dialogue between foreign relations (or diplomatic) historians of the Cold War . . . who have largely been preoccupied with grand strategy and the determinants of U.S. policy, and those who approach the conflict from the standpoint of the periphery . . . using the tools of area studies, social and cultural history, and cultural studies" (8). He also speaks of the recognition by scholars who take a transnational approach to the study of the Cold War in Latin America that "Cold War history should be properly fixed on the exercise of power, but [such scholars also] appreciate that power does not flow only from the policies and interventions of states; it also works through language and symbolic systems and manifests itself in identities and everyday practices" (17). Throughout this book, I too have striven to weave together the study of "grand strategy" and cultural history, and to identify the competing, conflicting, and occasionally complementary agendas through which power was both exercised and thwarted by parties both private and public in the process of disseminating Latin American literature in the United States during the Cold War.

NOTES

Note on translations: Quotations from texts published in Spanish are given in English. Whenever possible, I have quoted from published English translations; when these do not exist, the translations are my own. When quoting from archival materials and interviews that have not been published, I include both the Spanish and my own translations.

INTRODUCTION

1. Jorge Amado's *Gabriela, Clove and Cinnamon* had stayed on the list for six weeks in 1962.

2. It is important to clarify up front what I mean by "Spanish America(n)" and "Latin America(n)." I follow standard practice in my use of "Spanish America" to refer to the Central American, South American, and Caribbean nations that were formerly under Spanish colonial rule. "Latin America," in turn, refers to the region that includes both Spanish America and Brazil. "The Boom" per se was a Spanish American movement, but the profile of Latin American literature as a whole became much more visible internationally in the 1960s and 1970s, and thus this book speaks of the promotion of the work of both Brazilian and Spanish American writers in the United States. I have tried to use these terms consistently throughout this book so that the reader may have an accurate sense of the scope of my assessments of different programs and movements. However, many authors and critics from Spanish America and the United States alike use "Latin America" interchangeably with "Spanish America." When quoting and translating, I follow the usage in the original texts.

3. "PEN" stands for "poets, playwrights, essayists, editors, and novelists."

4. I am grateful to Susan Gillman for helping me to articulate this.

5. My discussion of the revolution and its impact focuses primarily on the years following Castro's identification in 1961 of the revolution as a Socialist one.

6. The foundation's eponymous journal also played an important role in the transmission of Boom literature, as I discuss later in this chapter. *Casa de las Américas* built upon the success and drew upon many of the strategies of *Lunes de Revolución*, a popular literary supplement from the earliest days of the revolution that ultimately came into conflict with the latter. *Lunes de Revolución* falls outside of the scope of this study, but more information on the supplement and its history may be found in William Luis's *"Lunes de Revolución": Literatura y cultura en los primeros años de la Revolución Cubana*.

7. See, for example, works by Susan Frenk, Claudia Gilman ("Las revistas"), Nadia Lie, María Eugenia Mudrovcic, Luz Rodríguez-Carranza, Mario Santana, and Judith Weiss.

8. See Rostagno, 31–58, for a detailed discussion of Knopf's trip and, more broadly, the Knopfs' activities on behalf of Latin American literature in general.

9. Letter by Carlos Fuentes on José Donoso's *Coronation*, copyright © 1964 by Carlos Fuentes. Qtd. in a letter from Angus Cameron, 28 December 1964, in the Alfred A. Knopf Inc. Records of the Harry Ransom Humanities Research Center (HRHRC) in the University of Texas at Austin Library, Box 1341, Folder 4. Used by permission of Brandt and Hochman Literary Agents, Inc. Materials in the Knopf Records collection will be identified subsequently as "KR" followed by box and file numbers (e.g., "KR 1341.4").

10. Letter, Vonnegut to Angus Cameron, 20 August 1967, KR 482.6, HRHRC.

11. See, for example, his letter to de Onís, 6 May 1965, KR 536.1, HRHRC.

12. See, for example, letter from Knopf to de Onís, 21 May 1965, KR 599.1, HRHRC.

13. See letter, Knopf to de Onís, 19 August 1963, KR 599.1, HRHRC.

14. Letter, Weinstock to de Onís, 31 August 1965, KR 441.8, HRHRC. This would not have been a new undertaking for de Onís, who had previously edited several anthologies for Knopf (e.g., *The Golden Land: An Anthology of Latin American Folklore in Literature* [1948] and *Spanish Stories and Tales* [1954]), as well as translating Germán Arciniegas's *The Green Continent: A Comprehensive View of Latin America by Its Leading Writers* (1944) for the company. The selections in her anthologies leaned toward the idiosyncratic: *Spanish Stories and Tales* included Spanish medieval works as well as contemporary writers from Spain and Spanish America, while *The Golden Land* emphasized "local color" in works from the conquerors through the chroniclers of the New World and up through twentieth-century (and often regionally oriented) Spanish American authors such as Ciro Alegría, Ricardo Güiraldes, Rómulo Gallegos, Martín Luis Guzmán, Alfonso Reyes, and Arturo Uslar Pietri.

15. Reader's report, Patrick Gregory to William Koshland, 23 August 1966, KR 469.7, HRHRC.

16. Letter, Weinstock to Carpentier, 31 August 1956, KR 203.1, HRHRC.

17. See my article, "Retracing *The Lost Steps*," for more information on this incident.

18. Letter, Weinstock to Fuentes, 17 October 1966, KR 452.5, HRHRC.

19. Letter, Weinstock to Rodríguez Monegal, 2 August 1966, KR 473.5, HRHRC. Rodríguez Monegal, who was then embroiled in the midst of the Congress for Cultural Freedom funding scandal, responded that the political articles were a matter of expediency, given the situation, but also underscored the importance of politics to Latin American writers more generally (letter, 21 September 1966, KR 473.5, HRHRC).

20. Letter, de Onís to Koshland, 19 November 1960, KR 295.1, HRHRC.

21. Letter, de Onís to Weinstock, 28 August 1965, KR 441.8, HRHRC.

22. Letter, de Onís to Alfred A. Knopf, 9 July 1960, KR 295.1, HRHRC.

23. Letter, de Onís to Koshland, 9 December 1961, KR 339.5, HRHRC.

24. Letter, de Onís to W. D. Patterson, 2 April 1962, KR 361.3, HRHRC.

25. Based on Bradley A. Shaw's *Latin American Literature in English Translation*. See also Suzanne Jill Levine's critical bibliography, *Latin America: Fiction and Poetry in Translation*.

26. Vargas Llosa's first novel, *The Time of the Hero*, had been published by Grove in 1966. According to Cass Canfield Jr., Klein was able to convince the Peruvian's agent, Carmen Balcells, who wanted more visibility for her client's work, to have Vargas Llosa switch publishers and sign with Harper and Row (interview by author, tape recording, May 2001, New York City).

27. Prieto, interview by author, tape recording, July 2001, Santa Barbara, CA.

28. Ibid.

29. Ibid. Alastair Reid, a longtime friend of Prieto's, tells a similar version of the story (interview by author by telephone, 30 June 2005).

30. The publishers were Einaudi (Italy), Gallimard (France), Grove (United States), Rowohlt (Germany), Seix Barral (Spain), and Weidenfeld and Nicolson (England). For more details, see Edwin Williamson's discussion of the prize and its consequences for Borges (345–46).

31. Reid, interview. Reid later arranged a similar agreement for Guillermo Cabrera Infante as well. The Cuban and Borges were the only two Spanish American writers to have such a contract with the magazine (Reid, interview).

32. John Macrae III, interview by author by telephone, 21 June 2005.

33. Suzanne Jill Levine, interview by author, tape recording, July 2001, Santa Barbara, CA. Macrae is now special projects editor at Henry Holt.

34. E-mail, King to author, 24 July 2010.

35. In fact, Cortázar consulted with Fernández Retamar before declining to publish in *Mundo Nuevo*. However, he later agreed to an interview with Rita Guibert for *"Life" en español*, which he considered to be a servant of "the cause of North American imperialism, which in turn serves the cause of capitalism by every possible means," because he viewed the inclusion of his politics and ideology in the magazine as subversion from within—"a raid into enemy territory" (qtd. in Guibert, 282). Ironically, the interview was later reprinted in Guibert's *Seven Voices: Seven*

Latin American Writers Talk to Rita Guibert, the introduction to which was written by Rodríguez Monegal.

36. See works by P. Coleman and Saunders for the history of the CCF.

37. One of the most notorious of these was the Farfield Foundation.

38. See Russell Cobb's "Promoting Literature" for a detailed history of the emergence of the journal.

39. *Encounter*, for example, ceased to receive funds from the CCF in the early 1960s; nevertheless, the revelations of covert funding damaged the journal and caused considerable upset among the editors (see P. Coleman, 59–79, for a history of *Encounter* and the fallout it faced).

40. Letter, Rodríguez Monegal to Mercier Vega, 2 May 1966, Emir Rodríguez Monegal Papers (C0652; henceforth identified as "Rodríguez Monegal Papers"), Box 8, Folder 10, Department of Rare Books and Special Collections (henceforth "RBSC"), Princeton University Library.

41. I cannot rule out the possibility that the Ford Foundation channeled funding to ILARI through a "cut-out" or intermediary organization, as it did for other projects, which would mean that no direct line of funding would be visible from the annual reports (thanks to Giles Scott-Smith for suggesting this). I do not, however, view this as likely.

42. The grant was awarded in September 1967 (letter, Shepard Stone to Howard Dressner, 13 October 1967, Reel R1900, Grant 68-335, Section IV, Ford Foundation Archives [henceforth "FFA"]), just prior to the end of the 1967 fiscal year, so the CCF did not begin to draw on it until the 1968 fiscal year.

43. Grant Action Request for International Association for Cultural Freedom, David Bell to McGeorge Bundy, 28 March 1968, Reel R1900, Grant 68-335, Section 1, FFA.

44. Letter, Shepard Stone to Harry Wilhelm, 30 January 1968, Reel R1900, Grant 68-335, Section 1, FFA.

45. Grant Action Request for International Association for Cultural Freedom, David Bell to McGeorge Bundy, 28 March 1968, Reel R1900, Grant 68-335, Section 1, FFA.

46. The publishing offices remained in Paris as a means of avoiding censorship in Argentina.

47. Vargas Llosa's allegiance would turn away from the revolution after 1971.

48. Letter, Rodríguez Monegal to Fernández Retamar, 1 November 1965, Rodríguez Monegal Papers, Box 7, Folder 6.

49. See Mary Dudziak's *Cold War Civil Rights* and Thomas Borstelmann's *The Cold War and the Color Line* for excellent discussions of the links between "domestic civil rights crises" and "international crises" (Dudziak, 6).

50. García Márquez's and Cortázar's signatures also appeared on the letter, though the former later claimed that he had not consented to having his name included and the latter retracted his protest and affirmed his support of Castro.

51. See Penny Von Eschen's impressive study, *Satchmo Blows Up the World*, for more information on the tours by Armstrong and Ellington.

52. The work of scholars such as Robert Arnove, Edward Berman, Helen Laville and Hugh Wilford, and Inderjeet Parmar is also useful for understanding the state-private network.

53. I am grateful to Nick Cullather for his comments on my work, which have helped me to articulate this aspect of my research.

54. See Cohn, "He Was One of Us."

CHAPTER 1

1. See Shanks, chapter 5, and Shapiro for the history and implications of the McCarran-Walter Act.

2. In the 1960s, Randall became a Mexican citizen in order to find better employment with which to support her family. Heeding flawed legal advice, she gave up her U.S. citizenship. When she returned to the United States in the mid-1980s, her application for permanent residency was denied solely on grounds that she had authored works deemed "subversive" and that her writings—some from more than a decade earlier—"advocate[d] the doctrines of world communism" (Randall, "Threatened," 473). Randall was given twenty-eight days to leave the country or face deportation. She chose, instead, to "stay and fight," both for her citizenship, and as an act in defense of freedom of expression. Randall filed a civil action against the U.S. attorney general and several immigration officers in 1985. The PEN American Center, along with writers such as Norman Mailer, Arthur Miller, Toni Morrison, Adrienne Rich, Rose Styron, William Styron, Kurt Vonnegut, and Alice Walker, and a number of high-ranking government officials, joined her as plaintiffs (see Randall, "Imagination of the Writer"). In 1989, her citizenship was reinstated.

3. Alejandro Herrero-Olaizola has observed how Cabrera Infante's earlier support for the revolution likewise caused him difficulties with Spanish censorship, despite his renunciation of Castro and the revolution in the 1960s (73).

4. According to Ángel Rama, Zea was put on the blacklist because he published an article condemning the U.S. intervention in the Dominican Republic in 1965—although, as Rama notes, "following this criterion it would have been necessary to classify almost all Latin American writers as communists" (Rama, "Catch 28," 8).

5. Letter, Wool to Donoso, 23 July 1965, José Donoso Papers (Manuscript Collection 340; henceforth "Donoso Papers, Iowa"), Box 12, Special Collections, University of Iowa Libraries.

6. Letter, Engle to Donoso, 6 August 1965, Donoso Papers, Iowa.

7. Letter, Kempton Webb, director of the Institute for Latin American Studies, and Andreas Cordier, dean of the School of International Affairs, to consul general of the United States in Barcelona, 5 April 1971, Mario Vargas Llosa Papers (C0641;

henceforth "Vargas Llosa Papers"), Box 6, Folder 16, RBSC, Princeton University Library.

8. Gregory Rabassa has claimed that he intervened on Cortázar's behalf with Leonard Garment, a consultant for and counsel to President Nixon (interview by author, tape recording, May 2001, New York City). According to Rabassa, Garment interceded with the consulate in Paris, where Cortázar was living, and the author never had troubles with McCarran-Walter again. (I have seen at least one instance in the mid-1970s, however, when Cortázar did have difficulties getting a visa and his U.S. sponsors had to step in and assist with the process [letter from Rabassa to Vargas Llosa, 21 June 1974, Box 18, Folder 4, Vargas Llosa Papers])

9. Letter, García Márquez to Rodríguez Monegal, 24 May 1967, Rodríguez Monegal Papers, Box 7, Folder 12.

10. Puerto Rico is subject to U.S. immigration laws—a fact that, as I will discuss presently, brought about Fuentes's final confrontation with the McCarran-Walter Act.

11. See Rama ("Catch 28," 10) for further details on the incident.

12. Rama himself reached a similar conclusion several months before his death.

13. In 2007, two years after my original request for Rama's files, I received a heavily censored set of papers from the FBI: twenty out of sixty-four pages in Rama's files were deleted under the National Security Act of 1947 and the CIA Act of 1949; of the pages that I did receive, quite a few had large passages blacked out.

14. Memorandum, FBI director to SAC (Special Agent in Charge), San Juan, re Ángel Rama Facal, 27 July 1970. Obtained from the FBI under the Freedom of Information Act (subsequent references to these materials will be identified as "FOIA papers").

15. Ibid.

16. Memorandum from SAC, WFO (Washington Field Office), to FBI director, re Ángel Rama Facal, 29 September 1970, FOIA papers.

17. E-mail, Peyrou to author, 7 January 2010.

18. Ibid.

19. Memorandum from SAC, WFO, to FBI director, re Ángel Rama Facal, 29 September 1970, FOIA papers.

20. A later memo perpetuates this misapprehension, noting that Rama and Traba had needed to apply for waivers "inasmuch as they were apparently members of the Communist Party in their respective countries" (Confidential memorandum, FBI, San Juan office, n.d. [stamped 24 September 1970], FOIA papers).

21. Memorandum from SAC, WFO, to FBI director, re Ángel Rama Facal, 29 September 1970, FOIA papers. How this interest was to be furthered was not specified. Curiously, an earlier document offered a slightly yet significantly different rationale for granting the waiver, noting that the latter was authorized "since such action is consistent with United States policy aims and interests"

(application for temporary admission to the United States for Ángel Rama, 30 July 1970, FOIA papers). While this document was also scarce on details, the rationale it offered cleaved more closely to the language of the requirement that such exceptions "be in the public interest" (Immigration and Nationality Act).

22. Application for temporary admission to the United States, Immigration and Naturalization Service (Miami office), 27 June 1979, FOIA papers.

23. Letter, Maggio to Gray, re Ángel Rama, 9 September 1982, FOIA papers.

24. Letter, Nelson to Webster, n.d. (stamped 10 March 1983), FOIA papers.

25. Letter, FBI (name of sender blacked out) to Nelson, 5 May 1983, FOIA papers.

26. To this day, as my own experience with heavily censored materials received under the FOIA attests, the information on Rama's case remains classified, to say nothing of difficult to get.

27. On being told that Rama would have "his day in court to prove he didn't do it," Maggio responded, "How can you prove you didn't do something when you don't know what 'it' is?" (Lewis).

28. Only U.S. citizens interested in meeting with the individuals denied visas could file suit against the proceedings.

29. Like its parent organization, International PEN, the PEN American Center was and is committed to lobbying on behalf of authors fighting censorship and the curtailment of First Amendment rights.

30. As a result of Colombia's interest in the couple, the U.S. embassy in Bogotá closely monitored the coverage of the two writers in local papers around this time, sending translations of articles to the State Department that foregrounded stories of their troubles with McCarran-Walter and their criticism of the United States for these difficulties.

31. See van Delden (41–50) for a discussion of the evolution of Fuentes's position toward Cuba.

32. Cortázar et al., 40; Fuentes, interview by author by telephone, 13 October 2009.

33. Letter, Fuentes to Robert Wool, 27 May 1964, Carlos Fuentes Papers (C0790; henceforth "Fuentes Papers"), Box 134, Folder 1, RBSC, Princeton University Library.

34. Letter, Fuentes to Ted Yates, 20 December 1964, Fuentes Papers, Box 117, Folder 13A.

35. Letter, Fuentes to Arthur Ochs Sulzberger, 7 May 1965, Fuentes Papers, Box 118, Folder 4.

36. Quotations from Department of State press release, Joint Statement by the Departments of State and Justice, 3 May 1966, PEN American Center Records (C0760; henceforth "PEN Archives"), Box 160, Folder 6, RBSC, Princeton University Library.

37. Letter, Wool to Fuentes, 29 November 1966, Fuentes Papers, Box 134, Folder 1.

38. Ibid.

39. Letter, Fuentes to Crome, 5 February 1966, Fuentes Papers, Box 98, Folder 7.

40. Letter, Mead to Fuentes, 8 August 1967, Fuentes Papers, Box 116, Folder 16.

41. Letter, Fuentes to Mead, 17 August 1967, Fuentes Papers, Box 116, Folder 16.

42. Letter, Harry Grossman to John Hurt Fisher, n.d., Fuentes Papers, Box 116, Folder 16.

43. Letter, Fisher to Mead, 13 November 1967, Fuentes Papers, Box 116, Folder 16.

44. Letter, Mead to Rodríguez Monegal, 7 December 1967, Fuentes Papers, Box 116, Folder 16.

45. The original letter to Mead, dated 1 February 1968, is housed at Princeton University Library (Fuentes Papers, Box 116, Folder 16).

46. Arciniegas made a similar remark after his first brush with McCarran-Walter, stating, "For a man who has fought for democracy and freedom throughout his life . . . the most unpleasant of his experiences is to see the Statue of Liberty through a window in Ellis Island" ("Public Opinion").

47. Letter, James Greene to Frank MacShane, 10 March 1969, *Review: Latin American Literature and Arts* Author Files (C0812; henceforth "*Review* Files"), Box 13, Folder 1, RBSC, Princeton University Library.

48. Fuentes later expressed his "profound gratitude" to the center, declaring that "once more P.E.N. has proved its immense value as an active force in defense of the freedom of writers" (qtd. in Chute, 86).

49. In other words, without pointing a finger directly, he was implicating the Department of Justice, to which the INS reports. Letter, William P. Rogers to William D. Rogers, 17 March 1969, *Review* Files, Box 13, Folder 1.

50. Letter, Fuentes to Donoso, 27 August 1969, José Donoso Papers (C0099; henceforth "Donoso Papers at Princeton"), Box 2, Folder 11, RBSC, Princeton University Library.

51. Fuentes did eventually receive some of the contents of his file, but many of the pages were partially (or largely) blacked out to hide information still deemed classified (Fuentes, interview).

52. The hypothetical possibility soon became a reality. In April of the same year, Gustavo Díaz Ordaz, Mexico's president during the 1968 student massacre, was named Mexico's ambassador to Spain. Fuentes resigned his own position as ambassador in protest and headed almost immediately to the United States.

53. Letter, Fuentes to William D. Rogers, 26 January 1977, Fuentes Papers, Box 88, Folder 4.

54. Letter, Rogers to Fuentes, 8 March 1977, Fuentes Papers, Box 88, Folder 4.

55. See Mitgang, *Dangerous Dossiers*, and Robins, *Alien Ink*.

56. See Laber.

CHAPTER 2

1. Preliminary docket, F. F. Hill to Henry T. Heald, 11 October 1965, PA0600-0051, FFA.

2. Most studies treat the conference as but one facet of the larger story of the rising profile of Latin American literature in the West and focus primarily on the political fallout afterwards (which I shall also detail).

3. Letter, Galantière to William MacLeish, 22 March 1966, PEN Archives, Box 157, Folder 12.

4. Letter, Galantière to Hunt, 1 February 1966, PEN Archives, Box 160, Folder 1.

5. Memorandum, Galantière to PEN files, 21 October 1965, PEN Archives, Box 156, Folder 2.

6. Letter, Galantière to Hunt, 1 February 1966.

7. Letter, Hunt to Galantière, 19 April 1966, PEN Archives, Box 156, Folder 2.

8. Memorandum, Richard M. Catalano to Shepard Stone, 1 April 1966, PA0600-0051, FFA.

9. Letter, Galantière to Hunt, 1 February 1966.

10. Preliminary docket, Hill to Heald.

11. Proposal, Galantière to Ford Foundation, 23 June 1965, PA0600-0051, FFA.

12. Preliminary docket, Hill to Heald.

13. The immigration blacklist and the difficulties that it would pose for getting visas for delegates had in fact been one of the reasons that the congress had not been held in the United States earlier. According to Marchette Chute, when John Steinbeck was made aware of this hurdle in 1957, he "amused himself by drawing up a list of the great men of history who would have been refused entry, from King David ('revolution') to Socrates ('contributing to the moral delinquency of minors') . . . even the signers of the Declaration of Independence would not be welcome, since they would have to admit to rebellion and treason" (78).

14. Letter, Farrar to Rusk, 12 April 1965, PEN Archives, Box 160, Folder 6.

15. Confidential memorandum from Galantière, 20 September 1965, PEN Archives, Box 160, Folder 6.

16. Ibid.

17. For Botsford's recommendation of Miller, see his letter to Daniel Bell, 26 May 1967, Rodríguez Monegal Papers, Box 2, Folder 23.

18. Confidential memorandum from Galantière, 20 September 1965.

19. The experts included the top scholars of Latin American literature in the United States: Lewis Hanke of Columbia University, who had been a powerful force in the founding of Latin American studies as a discipline in the United States; John P. Harrison, director of the Institute of Latin American Studies at the University of Texas at Austin; Richard Morse, chair of Latin American Studies at Yale; and José Vázquez Amaral of Rutgers, a prominent literary scholar who had been active in promoting Latin American literature in the United States and had contributed several articles on the field to the *New York Times*. Galantière also solicited names

from writers and other individuals at the forefront of efforts to promote Latin American culture and arts in the United States and abroad: Homero Aridjis, a talented young Mexican writer; John L. Brown, a former editor for Houghton Mifflin and *New York Times* literary correspondent who was Cultural Affairs Officer at the U.S. embassy in Mexico City; translator Harriet de Onís; William MacLeish, a writer for *Visión* and the director of the Cornell Latin American Year program (see Chapter 3); Victoria Ocampo, the force behind the Argentine literary magazine *Sur* and a vice president of International PEN; writer Margaret Randall, who was then living in Mexico City and co-editing *El corno emplumado*, an avant-garde literary magazine; Emir Rodríguez Monegal; and Robert Wool, the director of the Inter-American Foundation for the Arts. Information from list of authorities consulted, n.d., PEN Archives, Box 157, Folder 12.

20. Letter, Galantière to Frankel, 2 March 1966, PEN Archives, Box 160, Folder 6.

21. Memorandum, Galantière to Congress File—Peripheral Writers, 6 April 1966, PEN Archives, Box 157, Folder 12.

22. Emphasis in the original. Memorandum, Galantière to Congress File—Peripheral Writers (Latin-America), 14 February 1966, PEN Archives, Box 157, Folder 12.

23. Letter, Galantière to Frankel, 2 March 1966.

24. Letter, Cleveland to Galantière, 28 April 1965, PEN Archives, Box 160, Folder 6.

25. Confidential memorandum from Galantière, 20 September 1965.

26. Memorandum, Galantière to Steering Committee, 5 April 1965, PEN Archives, Box 160, Folder 6.

27. Confidential memorandum from Galantière, 18 June 1965, PEN Archives, Box 160, Folder 6; also, letter, John Crimmins to Galantière, June 22, 1965, PEN Archives, Box 160, Folder 6.

28. Confidential memorandum from Galantière, 18 June 1965.

29. Memorandum, Galantière to Congress File—U.S. State Department, 3 February 1966, PEN Archives, Box 160, Folder 6.

30. Biographical sketch of Ricardo Neftali Reyes Basoalto from FBI (Washington, DC), 23 August 1966, 100-HQ-163706, Serials 1-49, Section 1, FOIA papers.

31. Memorandum, W. R. Wannall to W. C. Sullivan, 23 June 1966, 100-HQ-163706, Serials 1-49, Section 1, FOIA papers.

32. Biographical sketch, 100-HQ-163706, Serials 1-49, Section 1, FOIA papers.

33. Airtel, J. Edgar Hoover to SAC, New York, 17 June 1966, 100-HQ-163706, Serials 1-49, Section 1, FOIA papers.

34. Memorandum, J. Edgar Hoover to SAC, New York, 5 August 1966, 100-HQ-163706, Serials 1-49, Section 1, FOIA papers.

35. Letter, Farrar to Rusk, 12 April 1965, PEN Archives, Box 160, Folder 6.

36. List of round tables and participants, PEN Archives, Box 160, Folder 1.

37. "Some Results of the XXXIV International PEN Congress," report from PEN to the Ford Foundation, n.d., PA0600-0051, FFA. Some conference participants boycotted the session because of the language stipulation, claiming to be unable to speak well in either English or French (Rodríguez Monegal, "Diario"). Spanish was approved as the organization's third official language in 1998, during the presidency of Mexican writer Aridjis (e-mail, Jane Spender to author, 12 June 2006).

38. See "Papel del escritor en América Latina" for a transcript of the session.

39. Letter, Fuentes to Donoso, 24 July 1966, Donoso Papers, Iowa, Box 12.

40. Some of the signatories subsequently claimed that their name had been added to the letter without their knowledge.

41. Letter, Fuentes to Herbert Weinstock, 16 November 1966, KR 918.13, HRHRC.

42. Letter, Fuentes to Alberto Cellario, 28 July 1966, PEN Archives, Box 112, Folder 12.

43. Fuentes, interview by author, and Fuentes, "Chronologie," 319. Despite Fuentes's frustration with the letter, he did not publicly criticize Cuba, nor did he fully withdraw his support from the revolution; he also continued to correspond and collaborate with Carpentier long after he signed the letter. Meanwhile, Julio Cortázar and Vargas Llosa, both of whom were active in revolutionary politics at this time, interceded with Casa de las Américas on Fuentes's behalf. At a meeting of the editorial board of *Casa de las Américas* in early 1967, both writers criticized the aforementioned article by Fornet for its attacks on Fuentes. According to Vargas Llosa, the Cuban writers admitted that they had been unfair to Fuentes and they offered him the chance to respond in *Casa de las Américas* to Fornet's article, or to comment there on the polemics about *Mundo Nuevo* or the PEN conference (letter, Vargas Llosa to Fuentes, 10 February 1967, Fuentes Papers, Box 131, Folder 23). Fuentes declined to do so, telling Vargas Llosa that he wanted to avoid any appearance of conflict with the Cubans out of concern that anti-Cuban parties could use signs of discord to their advantage (letter, Fuentes to Vargas Llosa, 22 February 1967, Fuentes Papers, Box 131, Folder 23).

44. All quotations from "Some Results of the XXXIV International PEN Congress."

45. "PEN American Center: Proposed Resolution," 22 May 1967, PEN Archives, Box 157, Folder 12.

46. Letter, Miller to Fuentes, 28 February 1969, Fuentes Papers, Box 116, Folder 11. Copyright © 1969 by Arthur Miller, reprinted by permission of The Wylie Agency LLC.

47. Letter, Fuentes to Miller, 24 March 1969, Fuentes Papers, Box 116, Folder 11.

48. Letter, Fuentes to Miller, 16 June 1969, Fuentes Papers, Box 116, Folder 11.

49. Letter, Fleming to Neruda, 17 December 1971, PEN Archives, Box 95, Folder 14.

50. Letter, Michalski to Fleming, 10 February 1972, PEN Archives, Box 95, Folder 14.

51. Letter, Fleming to John Richardson, 14 February 1972, PEN Archives, Box 95, Folder 14.

52. Letter, Richardson to Fleming, 6 March 1972, PEN Archives, Box 95, Folder 14.

53. Ibid.

54. According to Fleming, the reaction greatly perturbed Neruda, who afterward confessed to his host that he had thought that all present would be arrested for the display (personal communication to author, 14 March 2011).

55. Address by Pablo Neruda, 10 April 1972, 50th Anniversary of the American Center of PEN. Copyright © Fundación Pablo Neruda, 2011. PEN Archives, Box 95, Folder 14. Reprinted by permission of the Agencia Literaria Carmen Balcells SA.

56. He remained president until 1979 and is now a vice president of the organization, a position that he holds for life.

CHAPTER 3

1. Out of this process came other organizations, such as the American Association of Teachers of Spanish and Portuguese and its journal, *Hispania*; the Instituto Internacional de Literatura Iberoamericana and its companion journal, *Revista Iberoamericana*; the Hispanic Foundation of the Library of Congress and the library's journal, the *Handbook of Latin American Studies*; and the *Hispanic American Historical Review*.

2. For more information on the rise of Latin American studies in the United States during the 1960s and 1970s, see Delpar (153–83) and Berger (66–152).

3. I focus primarily on activities related to literature because this is a story that has not yet been told. Berger and Delpar have done an excellent job of documenting in their books the rise of Latin American studies—an important sphere of university activity related to Latin America in the 1960s and 1970s.

4. González Echevarría was a young graduate student when Rodríguez Monegal arrived at Yale, and he initially came to the Boom through his connection to the Uruguayan, who introduced him to the many writers whom he brought to campus.

5. See letters from the 1960s housed in RBSC, Princeton University Library.

6. In the early 1990s, Fuentes became Brown University's first professor-at-large—a position arranged for him by Julio Ortega, a longtime friend who had been writing about the Boom since the 1960s.

7. *World Literature Today* also organized a posthumous conference on Puig in 1991.

8. Telegram (typed draft), Fuentes to MacShane, with a notation indicating a date range of January–July 1972 (based on a telegram from MacShane to Fuentes

dated November 1970, in which the Columbia professor quotes Fuentes's telegram; the latter seems to have been written between October and November 1970), Fuentes Papers, Box 113, Folder 4.

9. Spanish departments often include the study of Portuguese and Brazilian literature; the latter field has tended to be smaller, though, and has not always benefited from the same visibility afforded to Spanish American literature, though it is gradually receiving greater prominence in the U.S. academy.

10. The continued alternation of the regions through the next few issues demonstrates that the logic of the order is not, despite the appearances of this sample, a function of alphabetical order.

11. In fact, Rabassa would soon return to Brazil to do more literary scouting, and he would champion the translation of literature from the nation for years to come. "The Crime of the Mathematics Professor" was, for example, the first translation of Lispector's work to appear in the United States, and by the mid-1960s, Rabassa was translating her novels for Knopf.

12. The other winner of the 1967 National Book Award for Translation was Willard Trask's rendering of Casanova's *History of My Life*.

13. Letter, de Onís to Knopf, 25 August 1964, KR 421.11, HRHRC.

14. The other institutions endowed with these chairs were Stanford University, the University of Chicago, the University of Texas at Austin, and the University of Wisconsin–Madison.

15. E-mail, Levine to author, 6 November 2009.

16. Letter, MacShane to Fuentes, November 1970, Fuentes Papers, Box 113, Folder 4.

17. Ibid.

18. MacShane invited Fuentes to contribute to the issue in which Miller and Wilder's opinions appeared, but he ultimately did not submit an essay for it.

19. Letter, Klein to Donoso, 19 May 1966, Donoso Papers, Iowa, Box 12.

20. Letter, Engle to Wool, 27 February 1966, Donoso Papers, Iowa, Box 12.

21. Letter, Engle to Wool, 27 January 1966, Donoso Papers, Iowa, Box 12.

22. Letter, Wool to Marks, 2 February 1966, Donoso Papers, Iowa, Box 12.

23. Letter, Donoso to Engle, 17 March 1966, Donoso Papers, Iowa, Box 12.

24. Ibid.

25. Letter, Donoso to Wool, 11 November 1966, *Review* Files, Box 10, Folder 17.

26. Unclassified document on University of Iowa International Writing Project (CA-2457), n.d., Papers of Paul Engle (MSC 514), Box 26, Special Collections, University of Iowa Libraries.

27. Memorandum, Ruth Skartvedt to Margaret Kleinman, 19 July 1971, Papers of Paul Engle.

28. Ford Foundation annual reports for 1967–1968 and 1968–1969; letter, Engle to Donoso, 28 October 1968, Donoso Papers at Princeton, Box 1, Folder 12.

29. Cass Canfield Jr. of Harper and Row was well positioned: for assistance with assessing works for publication, he relied on his editor, Roger Klein; Pipina Prieto;

and his translator, Alastair Reid. Knopf looked primarily to Harriet de Onís at first, and later came to rely on Rabassa and Rodríguez Monegal as well.

30. Quoted from the notes of an interview between John P. Harrison and Frank Wardlaw, dated 29 January 1958, Rockefeller Foundation (RF) Archives, RG 1.2, Series 200r, Box 292, Folder 2737, Rockefeller Archive Center (RAC).

31. Letter, Wardlaw to Harrison, 6 January 1958, RF Archives, RG 1.2, Series 200r, Box 292, Folder 2737, RAC.

32. In an effort to demonstrate this interest and inter-American reach, the association split its 1959 meeting between Austin, Texas, and Mexico City. The university press of the Universidad Autónoma Nacional de México soon became the association's first non-U.S. member.

33. "Report on the Latin American Translation Program" (1 April 1960–31 March 1962), RF Archives, RG 1.2, Series 200r, Box 292, Folder 2741, RAC.

34. Not all of the titles proposed, however, made it into print.

35. The Ibero-Americana series at the University of California Press was started in 1932. By the late 1950s, according to Frugé, it had issued more than forty books, most of which focused on Mexico (*Skeptic among Scholars*, 105).

36. "A Proposal to the Rockefeller Foundation for Renewal of the Latin American Translation Program," 4 February 1966, RF Archives, RG 1.2, Series 200r, Box 293, Folder 2743, RAC.

37. Letter, Morse to Dana Pratt, 4 February 1966, RF Archives, RG 1.2, Series 200r, Box 293, Folder 2743, RAC.

38. This was not entirely true, but it was not a significant (or, I would guess, intentional) exaggeration.

39. Sloane, "Report of the Latin American Translation Program Committee," May 1965, RF Archives, RG 1.2, Series 200r, Box 293, Folder 2743, RAC.

40. Memorandum, Freund to Joseph E. Black, 24 March 1966, RF Archives, RG 1.2, Series 200r, Box 293, Folder 2743, RAC.

41. Freund's warning is quoted from his memo to Black, ibid.

42. Interoffice correspondence between West and Freund, 15 January 1965, RF Archives, RG 1.2, Series 200r, Box 293, Folder 2742, RAC.

43. Letter, Black to Chester Kerr, 13 June 1966, RF Archives, RG 1.2, Series 200r, Box 293, Folder 2743, RAC.

44. The directors of these presses, Frugé and Wardlaw, provided confidential sales figures for first printings and information on advertising and promotion budgets for fourteen of their publications in order to assist with the proposal requesting renewal of funding of the program.

45. Sloane, "Report of the Latin American Translation Program Committee."

46. "A Proposal to the Rockefeller Foundation for Renewal of the Latin American Translation Program," Appendix 1.

47. Ibid.

48. The clear predominance of literary works from Mexico in the program's lists indicates widespread interest in Mexican letters. Frugé observes that most of

the forty works published in California's Ibero-Americana series by the late 1950s were on Mexican topics (*Skeptic among Scholars*, 105), a fact that he ascribed to the presence of distinguished Hispanists on the Berkeley faculty, including Lesley Byrd Simpson, whose research focused on the nation's history and culture. The AAUP program was thus not anomalous in its emphasis on Mexico, and seems instead to reflect steady interest in the nation among U.S.-based academics.

49. These academics included MacShane, Rabassa, Julio Ortega, and Joseph Sommers, among others.

50. See Lucille Kerr's article "Writing Donoso behind the Scenes," on Donoso's relationship with Brandt and their eventual split.

51. Frugé, "Summary of Answers to the Questionnaire," 5 January 1960, RF Archives, RG 1.2, Series 200r, Box 292, Folder 2738, RAC.

52. Frugé, "General Statement and Justification," 16 February 1960, RF Archives, RG 1.2, Series 200r, Box 292, Folder 2738, RAC.

53. "A Translation Program for Latin American Books Proposed by the Association of American University Presses," 16 February 1960, RF Archives, RG 1.2, Series 200r, Box 292, Folder 2738, RAC.

54. Letter, Wardlaw to Harrison, 11 March 1959, RF Archives, RG 1.2, Series 200r, Box 292, Folder 2737, RAC.

55. Resolution on "Yale University Press—Latin American Translations," 6 April 1960, RF Archives, RG 1.2, Series 200r, Box 292, Folder 2738, RAC.

56. Letter, Harrison to Kenneth Thompson, 8 October 1962, RF Archives, RG 1.2, Series 323, Box 24, Folder 169, RAC.

57. See Schwartz's *Creating Faulkner's Reputation*.

58. Notes of an interview between Harrison and José Vasquez [sic] Amaral, 27 March 1958, RF Archives, RG 1.2, Series 200r, Box 411, Folder 3543, RAC.

59. See Cohn, "Combatting Anti-Americanism," for details on the trips.

60. Arnold Del Greco, summary of the Ibero-American Novel Project, n.d., MSS 10677, Box 3, William Faulkner Foundation Ibero-American Novel Project (henceforth "IANP Collection"), Special Collections, University of Virginia Library.

61. The age criterion often complicated Del Greco's task. Although he waived it several times, at least one country, Colombia, ended up with no panel because one of his contacts felt that the country in question had no established critics in that age group (letter from Antonio Puerto Jr. to Del Greco, 19 October 1961, MSS 10677, Box 2, IANP Collection), and the others whom he invited to participate either declined or did not respond.

62. In the event that the judges could not come to an agreement, the panel was allowed to submit two nominations; when this happened, Del Greco either went for the choice of the majority or for the novel listed first as the prizewinner.

63. There was no nomination from Colombia, where García Márquez had only recently begun to make a name for himself (by 1960, when the competition began, he had only published *La hojarasca* [*Leaf Storm*]; *El coronel no tiene quien le escriba* [*No One Writes the Colonel*] and *Los funerales de la mamá grande* [*Big Mama's*

Funerals] came out in 1961 and 1962, respectively). Del Greco wrote to a contact that the Colombian judges did not select a prize-winning novel, but it is unsure whether or not a panel was ever formed for the country (see note 61 in this chapter; letter, Del Greco to Robert Kingsley, 22 August 1963, MSS 10677, Box 2, IANP Collection).

64. These included Ernesto DaCal from Spain, then chair of Spanish at New York University; Raúl Horacio Bottaro, director of la Cámara Argentina del Libro; Roberto Giusti of Argentina; and Idel Becker of Brazil (Del Greco, Ibero-American Project report for April 1963–June 1964, July 1964, MSS 10677, Box 3, IANP Collection).

65. See correspondence between Del Greco and various publishers, MSS 10677, Box 1, IANP Collection.

66. Letter, Frank Wardlaw to Del Greco, 2 November 1965, MSS 10677, Box 1, IANP Collection.

67. See letter, Robert Giroux to Del Greco, 21 September 1966, MSS 10677, Box 1, and letter, H. I. Rainey to Del Greco, 28 August 1966, MSS 10677, Box 1, IANP Collection.

68. Letter, Swenson to Del Greco, 1 July 1966, MSS 10677, Box 1, IANP Collection.

69. Letter, Koshland to Del Greco, 28 May 1963, MSS 10677, Box 2, IANP Collection.

70. Letter, Koshland to Del Greco, 2 March 1964, MSS 10677, Box 2, IANP Collection.

71. Letter, Díaz Sánchez to Cordido-Freytes, 7 July 1965, MSS 10677, Box 1, IANP Collection.

72. This episode later threatened to set the Faulkner family at odds with the foundation. When William Fielden, who was married to Faulkner's stepdaughter, Victoria, was invited by Massey to join the foundation in 1967, he was hesitant to accept. He had lived in Venezuela for several years and was acquainted with the saga and so before accepting he asked a number of piercing questions in order to ensure that his participation would be part of an endeavor that was genuinely helpful and supportive of writers (letter to Linton Massey, 4 December 1967, MSS 10677, Box 1, IANP Collection).

73. Del Greco, interview by author, Charlottesville, VA, 9 May 2001.

74. Ibid.

75. Letter, Del Greco to Muna Lee, 1 April 1963, Papers regarding William Faulkner's travels for the U.S. State Department, MSS 7258-a, Special Collections, University of Virginia Library.

76. Rafael Trujillo, the nation's long-standing dictator, was assassinated in May 1961, an event followed by several years of considerable political upheaval.

77. Letter, delegation from the Dominican Republic (Veloz Maggiolo, Estéban Deive, Henríquez y Gratereaux) to Del Greco, 15 February 1962, MSS 10677, Box 1, IANP Collection.

78. Letter, Fallas Sibaja to Del Greco, 9 November 1963, MSS 10677, Box 1, IANP Collection.

79. Letter, Susan Seligson to Del Greco, 19 August 1973, MSS 10677, Box 2, IANP Collection.

80. Letter, Esquenazi Mayo to Del Greco, 22 March 1962, MSS 10677, Box 1, IANP Collection.

81. Letter, Del Greco to Esquenazi Mayo, 27 March 1962, MSS 10677, Box 1, IANP Collection.

82. Letter, Esquenazi Mayo to Del Greco, 9 June 1962, MSS 10677, Box 1, IANP Collection.

83. Letter, Del Greco to Esquenazi Mayo, 12 June 1962, MSS 10677, Box 1, IANP Collection.

84. Ibid.

85. I discuss *The Lost Steps'* publishing history with Knopf in "Retracing *The Lost Steps*."

86. Letter, Massey to Edgar Shannon, 16 March 1963, MSS 10677, Box 2, IANP Collection.

87. The translation history of *Coronación*, in fact, attests to the increasing agency and professionalization of the Latin American writer: Donoso's novel was placed at Knopf by Brandt, at Fuentes's suggestion (J. Donoso, 51–52). Arguedas's *Deep Rivers* was published in 1978 with a subsidy from the translation program of the Center for Inter-American Relations, which will be discussed in the next chapter. Roa Bastos's *Son of Man* was published by Victor Gollancz (London) in 1965, but did not come out in English in the United States until 1988.

88. Levine describes how Blanche Knopf eagerly picked up Mallea during her 1942 visit to Argentina, feeling that it was a coup "to attach the most prominent Argentine novelist of the time to her husband's press" ("Latin American Novel," 299). Knopf Inc. published *The Bay of Silence* in 1944 and *All Green Shall Perish* in 1966, but was not interested in *Los enemigos*. Calder and Boyars (London) published *Fiesta in November* in 1969 and *Chaves and Other Stories* in 1970.

89. Díaz Sánchez's *Mene: A Venezuelan Novel* was translated by Jesse Noel, a Trinidadian writer, and was published by the University of West Indies Press in the 1980s. Beleño's prize-winning novel seems to have been published in English in Panama as *Gamboa Road Gang*. Godoy's *Caín, el hombre* was published in English in 1968 by her Mexican publisher, Editorial Jus. In all these cases, distribution was negligible. I should note that the prestige associated with the IANP was so great that the cover of a 1988 (Spanish) edition of Godoy's novel prominently displayed a seal that announced that the novel had received the Faulkner prize.

90. Letter, Lawrence to Del Greco, 6 January 1964, MSS 10677, Box 1, William Faulkner Foundation IANP Collection.

91. The descriptions were eventually prepared, but as there is no date on the papers, it is impossible to tell when this was done (as Del Greco was referring interested publishers to the original publishers and bookjackets through early 1964,

it was presumably some time after this; these papers are titled "Brief Information Concerning the Novels Designated as Notable in the Faulkner Foundation Ibero-American Project" [MSS 10677, Box 2, IANP Collection]). These were, additionally, written in Spanish—and, in the case of Ramos, Portuguese—which would have been of relatively little use to publishers who at this point in time had few (if any) Spanish-speaking editors or readers on staff.

92. Approval of $150,000 grant to Cornell University, n.d., Carnegie Corporation of New York Papers, Series III.A., Box 524, Folder 9, Rare Book and Manuscript Library (RBML), Columbia University Library (henceforth "CCNY-A"). Materials used with permission of the Carnegie Corporation of New York.

93. "Cornell Latin American Year Progress Report No. 1" (page 1), 10 May 1965, Archives 3/10/1022, Box 43, Folder 36, Division of Rare and Manuscript Collections (RMC), Cornell University Libraries.

94. "Cornell Latin American Year, A Grant Request to the Carnegie Corporation of New York," January 1965, CCNY-A.

95. Ibid.

96. Ibid.

97. Memorandum, FM and LM to JG and AP, regarding Cornell University—Latin American year, 17 February 1965, CCNY-A.

98. Record of interview between AP and Perkins, 15 February 1965, CCNY-A.

99. Memorandum, FM and LM to JG and AP.

100. Ibid.

101. Approval of $150,000 grant to Cornell University, n.d., CCNY-A.

102. "Cornell Latin American Year 1965–66, Final Report" (pages 7–8), 30 June 1966, CCNY papers, Series III.B, Box 43, Folder 4, RBML, Columbia University Library (henceforth "CCNY-B").

103. Information on activities detailed here from "Cornell Latin American Year 1965–1966, A Brief Review and Evaluation," Archives 3/11/1665, Box 6, RMC, Cornell University Libraries.

104. MacLeish, interview by author by telephone, 29 May 2007.

105. The values Frondizi spoke of were "persistence, fairness, objectivity, tolerance, self-criticism and freedom" (23).

106. "Cornell Latin American Year 1965–1966, Final Report"; conference program, Archives 3/11/1665, Box 6, RMC, Cornell University Libraries.

107. "Cornell Latin American Year Progress Report No. 1" (page 5).

108. Minutes of CLAY Steering Committee, 2 November 1965, Archives 47/4/1006, Box 1, RMC, Cornell University Libraries.

109. Ibid.

110. Minutes of CLAY Steering Committee, 22 November 1965, Archives 47/4/1006, Box 1, RMC, Cornell University Libraries.

111. Ibid.

112. "Cornell Latin American Year 1965–1966, A Brief Review and Evaluation."

113. Minutes of CLAY Steering Committee, 22 February 1966, Archives 47/4/1006, Box 1, RMC, Cornell University Libraries; "Cornell Latin American Year 1965–1966, Final Report" (Appendix B, List of Participants, p. 9).

114. "Cornell Latin American Year 1965–1966, Final Report."

115. "Cornell Latin American Year 1965–1966, A Brief Review and Evaluation" (page 15).

116. Ibid.

117. "Cornell Latin American Year 1965–1966, Final Report" (pages 25–26).

118. The article appeared in the 4 July 1966 issue of *"Life" en español. Mundo Nuevo* featured it in issue 3 (September 1966).

119. "Cornell Latin American Year 1965–1966, Final Report" (page 27).

120. "Cornell Latin American Year 1965–1966, A Brief Review and Evaluation" (page 17).

121. Ibid. (page 18).

122. "Cornell Latin American Year 1965–1966, Final Report" (page 26).

123. The Center for International Studies, which had been the base of operations for the CLAY Steering Committee, was in fact one of the units that had been created under Perkins's leadership.

124. See Donald Downs's *Cornell '69* for a detailed—though not impartial—description of the takeover and its aftermath.

125. I am thankful to Claire Fox for her assistance in helping me to formulate this.

126. Similar arguments have, of course, been made about area studies in general. Others have likewise asserted that the growing strength of U.S. American studies (and the corresponding rise in funding available to it from philanthropic organizations including the Carnegie Foundation, the Coe Foundation, and the Rockefeller Foundation) starting in the postwar years was predicated in part on the discipline's efforts to deflect Communism, and bolstered by its collusion with official foreign policy and its blindness to the fact of U.S. empire (see Kaplan, 11–19; Shumway, 312).

CHAPTER 4

1. The president was an avid supporter of cultural exchange programs, and in early 1961 he created a new position, assistant secretary of state for educational and cultural affairs, in order to strengthen the effects and effectiveness of existing programs in these fields. My information on symposium participants and the conference itself is from "The Inter-American Committee Inc.," founding documents, n.d., Rockefeller Brothers Fund (RBF) Archives, RG 3.1, Box 436, Folder 2671, RAC.

2. See Bendiner.

3. "The Inter-American Committee Inc.," founding documents. Kennedy's speech can be found online at the American Presidency Project at UC Santa

Barbara (established by John T. Woolley and Gerhard Peters), *www.presidency.ucsb* *.edu/ws/?pid=9018.*

4. Ibid.

5. "The Inter-American Committee Inc., A Fact Sheet," n.d., RBF Archives, RG 3.1, Box 436, Folder 2671, RAC.

6. Information on the symposium is found in "A Special Report on the Second Inter-American Foundation Symposium," n.d., and "The Second Inter-American Committee Symposium," n.d. Both documents are in the RBF Archives, RG 3.1, Box 436, Folder 2672, RAC.

7. Information in report to the board of directors from Wool, handwritten date of 28 May 1964, RBF Archives, RG 3.1, Box 436, Folder 2672, RAC.

8. Information from special progress report, February 1965, RBF Archives, RG 3.1, Box 436, Folder 2672, RAC.

9. Letter, Laughlin to Zea, 8 December 1964, Inter-American Foundation for the Arts, New Directions Publishing Corp. Records (MS Am 2077 [839]), Houghton Library, Harvard University.

10. Rodman Rockefeller, "Possible Areas of Collaboration between the Inter-American Foundation for the Arts and the Council for Latin America," handwritten date of 9 August 1965, RBF Archives, RG 3.1, Box 436, Folder 2672, RAC.

11. Memorandum, James Hyde to the RBF files, 12 May 1965, RBF Archives, RG 3.1, Box 436, Folder 2672, RAC.

12. Quoted from untitled document written by Lindsley Kimball, 30 November 1971, RBF Archives, RG 3.1, Box 192, Folder 1241, RAC.

13. "Program and Budget 1968–1971," section A, 15 March 1968, RBF Archives, RG 3.1, Box 192, Folder 1239, RAC.

14. Ibid.

15. Information on the history of the house and related expenses is found in an untitled draft report, 8 January 1976, and a report on the house from the Landmarks Preservation Commission, 10 November 1970, both in the RBF Archives, RG 3.1, Box 193, Folder 1245, RAC.

16. List of contributors to the IAFA in materials enclosed with letter from Rodman Rockefeller to James Hyde, 19 May 1965, RBF Archives, RG 3.1, Box 436, Folder 2672, RAC.

17. The Ford Foundation alone had at least three divisions that funded work on the region: International Affairs, Overseas Development, and Latin America.

18. "Grant Request for $100,000 for CIAR," approved at RBF Annual Meeting, 18 May 1967, RBF Archives, RG 3.1, Box 191, Folder 1238, RAC (Appendix 1).

19. Memorandum, James Hyde to the RBF files, 12 May 1965.

20. Memorandum, Shepard Stone to McGeorge Bundy, 28 July 1966, Grant 65-379, FFA.

21. Memorandum, H. P. Mettger to Joseph Slater, 30 June 1966, Grant 65-379, FFA.

22. For Schlesinger's endorsement, See letter, Schlesinger to Stone, 21 February

1963, Grant 63-177, FFA. For Murrow's endorsement, see letter, Murrow to John McCloy, 5 August 1963, Grant 63-177, FFA.

23. Ford officers nevertheless suggested various outside funding possibilities and offered their support through other channels by, for example, putting Wool in touch with the director of the Museum of Modern Art to discuss art exhibition exchange programs.

24. Proposal submitted by Inter-American Foundation for the Arts to the National Council on the Arts, n.d. Grant 65-379, FFA.

25. Ibid.

26. Memorandum, Harry Wilhelm to Slater, 29 December 1966, Grant 65-379, FFA.

27. Letter, Wool to Fuentes, 19 December 1967, Fuentes Papers, Box 134, Folder 1.

28. Request for grant actions, 24 April 1967, Grant 67-285, FFA.

29. The family's ties to Latin America are well documented in the work of Elizabeth Cobbs and Darlene Rivas.

30. Quoted in memorandum, Hyde to Dana Creel, 19 November 1963, RBF Archives, RG 3.1, Box 436, Folder 2671, RAC.

31. Memorandum, Creel to Laurance Rockefeller, 17 October 1963, RBF Archives, RG 3.1, Box 436, Folder 2671, RAC.

32. Docket memorandum, 9 December 1963, RBF Archives, RG 3.1, Box 436, Folder 2671, RAC.

33. Memorandum from Hyde to the RBF files, 12 May 1965, and memorandum from Hyde to the RBF files, 3 June 1965, RBF Archives, RG 3.1, Box 436, Folder 2672, RAC.

34. The RBF funds, along with $500,000 raised from corporate sources and $850,000 from Rockefeller family sources, went toward renovating the building in which the center was housed rather than toward programs and activities ("Grant Request for $100,000 for CIAR").

35. As the Rockefeller brothers maintained individual programs of charitable giving in addition to those implemented through the RBF, David Rockefeller's significant contributions to the center beyond those of the RBF were not unusual. Financial information taken from an excerpt from "Agenda and Docket for RBF Fall Meeting—10/28/76," RBF Archives, RG 3.1, Box 193, Folder 1245, RAC.

36. William D. Rogers, interview by author by telephone, 12 June 2007.

37. Thanks to Alfred Mac Adam for bringing the concerns about the abbreviation to my attention.

38. Rogers, interview.

39. Text of Humphrey's speech at the CIAR inaugural dinner, 18 September 1967, Grant 67-285, FFA. In a phone interview (12 June 2007), I read these remarks to William D. Rogers. Although he had been present at the event, he did not remember the speech and was in fact taken by surprise by its content, claiming that they did not reflect his views or those of the center.

40. "Rationale for the Center," 3 August 1976, RBF Archives, RG 3.1, Box 193, Folder 1245, RAC.

41. "Center for Inter-American Relations 1976–1980 Long Range Plan," 22 October 1975, RBF Archives, RG 3.1, Box 193, Folder 1244, RAC.

42. Letter, Rockefeller to Meyer, 24 March 1969, Grant 67-285, FFA.

43. Ibid.

44. Letter, Adams to Bundy, 15 November 1968, Grant 67-285, FFA.

45. Letter, Adams to Harry Wilhelm, 19 December 1968, Grant 67-285, FFA.

46. Ibid.

47. Ibid.

48. Memorandum, Nita Manitzas to Harry Wilhelm, 31 December 1968, Grant 67-285, FFA.

49. All information on the program's activities has been gathered from the center's annual reports from 1967 to 1980.

50. My review of the annual reports does show that Public Affairs hosted relatively few Latin American speakers with Marxist affiliations, instead inviting left-leaning academics from the United States, many of whom were recent PhDs who held faculty positions in the Northeast and North Atlantic coast region.

51. For examples of Theberge's anti-Marxist and anti-Soviet views, see *The Soviet Presence in Latin America* as well as his remarks (representative of the majority of the speakers) in the panel titled "Understanding the Allende Revolution and the Fall of Chilean Democracy" (Theberge, *Conference Report*).

52. See Rockefeller's *Memoirs* (432–33) for his negative assessment of Allende's presidency.

53. Both events are mentioned in Roger Stone's statement regarding the Ronald Christ uproar detailed later in this chapter, 30 June 1977, Donoso Papers at Princeton, Box 8, Folder 4.

54. Faculty members of the commission included Harrison Brown (Science and Government, California Institute of Technology), Albert Fishlow (Economics, University of California, Berkeley), Richard Gardner (Law and International Organization, Columbia), Alexander Heard (chancellor, Vanderbilt University), Theodore Hesburgh (president, University of Notre Dame), Samuel Huntington (Government, Harvard University), George Lodge (Business Administration, Harvard), Arturo Morales-Carrión (president, University of Puerto Rico, and deputy assistant secretary of state for inter-American affairs under President Kennedy), and Clifton Wharton Jr. (president, Michigan State University). Participants from the corporate sector included W. Michael Blumenthal (chairman, Bendix Corporation), Rita Hauser (attorney), Lee Hills (chairman, Knight Newspapers Inc.), Nicholas deB. Katzenback (corporate vice president, IBM Corporation), Charles Meyer (vice president, Sears, Roebuck, and Co., and former assistant secretary of state for inter-American affairs), Peter Peterson (chairman, Lehman Brothers), and Nathaniel Samuels (chairman, Louis Dreyfus Holding Company Inc.). There were some

changes in membership between the release of the first and second reports. (All information from the list of members in *The Americas in a Changing World*.)

55. The full text of the address may be found at the American Presidency Project, *www.presidency.ucsb.edu/ws/index.php?pid=7347*.

56. E-mail, Suzanne Jill Levine to author, 11 June 2009.

57. The ties between the Rockefellers and the Museum of Modern Art, which counted on the RBF as a primary source of funding, no doubt facilitated the collaborations between the museum and the center.

58. Report on the center, David Bronheim to David Rockefeller, 12 October 1970, RBF Archives, RG 3.1, Box 193, Folder 1241, RAC.

59. Letter, Bronheim to James Hyde, 17 February 1970, RBF Archives, RG 3.1, Box 193, Folder 1241, RAC.

60. This perhaps explains why the center never subsidized any works by Fuentes, who had already begun to establish a reputation for himself in the United States by the time the program started up. The program did, however, support three works by Cortázar—*62: A Model Kit, A Manual for Manuel*, and *All Fires the Fire*. Cortázar's masterpiece, *Hopscotch*, had been published to significant critical acclaim in 1966 (its honors included the National Book Award for Translation), but its sales were disappointing, so the center subsidized the three later works in an effort to build his U.S. reputation. It declined, however, to fund any additional works beyond the three.

61. See Coleman's "Sunrise with Borges et al." for a firsthand description of the course.

62. See Mac Adam (198 200) and Rostagno (108–11) for further discussions of the journal's history.

63. An example of a project that received negative evaluations was her translation of Guimarães Rosa's *The Devil to Pay in the Backlands*, which was criticized by numerous scholars and reviewers for being sloppy and simplistic.

64. Examples of critical works and textbooks include Ronald Christ's *The Narrow Act*, Edith Grossman's *The Antipoetry of Nicanor Parra*, and Jo Anne Englebert's *Macedonio Fernández and the Spanish American New Novel*. Examples of journal issues include special issues of *TriQuarterly*, the *Hudson Review*, the *Drama Review*, and issues of *Mundus Artium* on Latin American poetry and fiction. Examples of anthologies include *An Anthology of Twentieth Century Brazilian Poetry*, edited by Elizabeth Bishop; *The Eye of the Heart*, by Barbara Howes; *Inventing a Word: An Anthology of Twentieth-Century Puerto Rican Poetry*, by Julio Marzán; and José Emilio Pacheco's *Signals from the Flames*. Examples of the bibliographies include *Latin America: Fiction and Poetry in Translation*, by Suzanne Jill Levine, and Marjorie Engber's *Caribbean Fiction and Poetry*.

65. Letter, Bronheim to Hyde.

66. This information was compiled from Shaw's *Latin American Literature in English Translation*.

67. This information was compiled from the ten volumes of Tarbert and Beach's *Book Review Index*.

68. Arnold Belkin, Leonel Góngora, and Rubens Gerchman are the only artists mentioned by name in the article on this conflict, although the article does state that twenty-five artists had been involved in the protest ("Show Is Suspended").

69. Letter, MacLeish to Mr. Stanley, 17 November 1967, *Review* Files, Box 3, Folder 7.

70. MacLeish ruled Neruda out for this task, citing the attack on the poet by Cubans following the PEN congress of 1966 (letter, MacLeish to Stanley).

71. Curiously, the subvention does not appear in the master list of publications subsidized by the Literature program, and the translation does not acknowledge the subsidy. Correspondence between Michael di Capua (an editor at Farrar, Straus and Giroux) and Christ in late 1976, however, does indicate that the payment was made (*Review* Files, Box 20, Folder 11).

72. E-mail, Ronald Christ to author, 3 September 2001.

73. E-mail, King to author, 3 September 2010.

74. The letter from the cultural attaché and Coleman's reaction to it are mentioned in Weinberger's letter to CIAR affiliates, 25 June 1977, KR 544.11, HRHRC.

75. Letter of resignation, Coleman to Stone, dated 21 May 1977 (as the scandal did not erupt until later, the date is probably mistaken, and the letter was probably written in June), Vargas Llosa Papers, Box 6, Folder 8. Letter of resignation, Colchie to Stone, 20 June 1977, KR 544.11, HRHRC. Letter of resignation, Reid to Stone, 21 June 1977, KR 544.11, HRHRC. Letter of resignation, Rodríguez Monegal to Stone, 24 June 1977, Vargas Llosa Papers, Box 8, Folder 18. Colchie's, Coleman's, and Rodríguez Monegal's resignations are also mentioned in statement, Stone, 30 June 1977, Donoso Papers at Princeton, Box 8, Folder 4.

76. I am particularly grateful to John King for his insights into this event and the political context in which it took place.

77. See, for example, letter of resignation, Coleman to Stone, dated 21 May 1977, and letter of resignation, Colchie to Stone, 20 June 1977.

78. Letter of resignation, Reid to Stone, 21 June 1977.

79. Letter of resignation, Rodríguez Monegal to Stone, 24 June 1977.

80. Letter, Weinberger to Laughlin, 16 June 1977, Center for Inter-American Relations, New Directions Publishing Corp. Records (MS Am 2077 [329]), Houghton Library, Harvard University.

81. See statement, Stone, 30 June 1977, and letter, Stone to Rodríguez Monegal, 14 June 1977, Vargas Llosa Papers, Box 6, Folder 8.

82. Letter organized by Weinberger and addressed to "Dear friends," RBF Archives, RG 3.1, Box 193, Folder 1246, RAC, and open letter to CIAR board of directors, 21 July 1977, Vargas Llosa Papers, Box 24, Folder 2.

83. Open letter to CIAR board of directors, 21 July 1977.

84. Ibid.

85. See "Scholar's Colleagues Upset" and "Inter-American Relations Center Torn."

86. Weinberger's letter to CIAR affiliates (25 June 1977), which the *Vuelta* staff presumably had seen, criticized Christ's choice of T. S. Eliot, along with an American musical comedy, for his courses in Chile as being "perfectly suited to such an institution: an Anglo-Catholic Royalist poet, and a minor theatrical genre which is totally alien to the realities of contemporary Chilean life."

87. A copy of the article is preserved in the RBF Archives, RG 3.1, Box 193, Folder 1246, RAC.

88. Statement, Christ, 18 July 1977, Donoso Papers at Princeton, Box 8, Folder 4.

89. Memorandum, Stone to CIAR directors, 20 July 1977, RBF Archives, RG 3.1, Box 193, Folder 1246, RAC.

90. Letter, Rabassa to Stone, 21 June 1977, Vargas Llosa Papers, Box 6, Folder 8.

91. Letter, Martin to Christ, 28 July 1977, Center for Inter-American Relations, New Directions Publishing Corp. Records (MS Am 2077 [329]), Houghton Library, Harvard University.

92. Qtd. in memorandum, Stone to CIAR directors.

93. See, for example, letter, Fuentes to Donoso, 11 October 1977, Donoso Papers at Princeton.

94. I discuss Vargas Llosa's stance on Christ's trip later in this chapter.

95. Letter, Christ to Rodríguez Monegal, 2 March 1977, *Review* Files, Box 26, Folder 6.

96. E-mail, Levine to author, 2 June 2009.

97. Letter, Fuentes to Donoso, 11 October 1977, Donoso Papers at Princeton, Box 8, Folder 7.

98. Christ's supporters, in fact, referred to the contemporary situation using parallel terms such as "el caso Ronald" and "l'affaire Christ" that suggested the critic's political martyrdom.

99. Letter, Vargas Llosa to Rodríguez Monegal, 27 June 1977, Vargas Llosa Papers, Box 6, Folder 8.

100. Letter, Vargas Llosa to Stone, 29 July 1977, Donoso Papers at Princeton, Box 8, Folder 4.

101. Letter, Vargas Llosa to Christ, 18 October 1977, Vargas Llosa Papers, Box 6, Folder 11.

102. When he formally resigned as editor of *Review* for several months, Santos took on that charge as well (e-mail, Santos to author, 15 November 2010).

103. Letter, Arenas to Rama, 27 November 1981, *Review* Files, Box 25, Folder 11.

104. Letter, Rama to Arenas, 30 November 1981, *Review* Files, Box 25, Folder 11.

105. Letter, Rama to Santos, 30 November 1981, *Review* Files, Box 25, Folder 11.

106. I have unfortunately been unable to ascertain why there is such a long gap between the Rama-Arenas correspondence and the open letter.

107. Letter, [Santos] to Rama, 22 September [1982], *Review* Files, Box 25,

Folder 11. (Internal clues identify the author of the letter as Santos; the year is not specified, but a reference to the recent publication of Rama's article in *El Universal* indicates that it was written in 1982.)

108. Letter, Santos to author [2001].

109. Letter, [Santos] to Rama.

110. Handwritten note, Santos to the files, 14 September 1983, *Review* Files, Box 22, Folder 12. Paz had broken with the Literature Department following the Christ uproar but apparently had subsequently re-established relations.

111. The council had, it should be recalled, been proposed in 1965 as a potential partner for the Inter-American Foundation for the Arts.

112. Letter, Santos to author.

113. Letter, [Santos] to Rama. It is interesting to note that the final issue included a focus by José Miguel Oviedo on the state of the Sandino revolution in Nicaragua, with interviews with renowned Nicaraguan writers José Coronel Urtecho and Pablo Antonio Cuadra, both of whom offer support for the revolution and hope for its potential, although Cuadra's is tempered by his experience of government-imposed censorship of the press. The generally positive attitude of both authors toward the possibilities of revolution contrasts starkly with the contemporary political climate in which the United States was at this point funding the Nicaraguan contras.

114. E-mail, Santos to author, 15 November 2010.

115. Even the center has been unable to secure, in the long term, an equal playing field for translations: a 1988 *New York Times* article observed that "big publishers whose books command the most shelf space are leaving translations of works by little-known foreign writers to small presses and university presses with far fewer outlets" (McDowell). Alfred and Blanche Knopf's commitment to bringing Latin American literature to a U.S. audience, all the while knowing that the works they published were more likely to become prestige items than best sellers, remains rare among the larger publishing houses: while several major presses still do make an effort to publish translations, the majority "look mostly for the blockbuster books from overseas, not the steady stream of novels and poetry" (Dennis Kratz, qtd. in McDowell).

CONCLUSION

1. Vargas Llosa, interview by author, tape recording, 21 May 2006, Stratford, UK.

2. Ibid.

3. Ibid.

4. The poem was published in *Starting from San Francisco* (1967), the cover of which bears the image of Machu Picchu. (The poem's spelling of "Machu" reflects Neruda's preference.)

5. Ferlinghetti claims that the trip took place in 1959, but based on a number of other sources focusing on both him and Neruda, as well as his linking of the visit to the first anniversary of the Cuban Revolution, I believe that the visit took place in 1960 instead.

6. See the sections on Ginsberg in Robins, 335–41, and in Mitgang, *Dangerous Dossiers*, 260–64.

7. For Sheldon, "Americanness" explicitly refers to the United States. The travels of the authors whom he studies challenge notions of "Americanness" in a much broader sense as well.

WORKS CITED

Adams, Beverly. "Latin American Art at the Americas Society: A Principality of Its Own." In *A Principality of Its Own: 40 Years of Visual Arts at the Americas Society*, ed. José Luis Falconi and Gabriela Rangel, 24–41. New York: Americas Society, 2006.

Adams, Rachel. "Hipsters and *jipitecas*: Literary Countercultures on Both Sides of the Border." *American Literary History* 16, no. 1 (Spring 2004): 58–84.

"Aide at Columbia Delayed by U.S." *New York Times*, 16 April 1957. ProQuest.

The Americas in a Changing World: A Report of the Commission on United States–Latin American Relations. Preface by Sol Linowitz. New York: Quadrangle Press, 1975.

Arciniegas, Germán. "Public Opinion and McCarran Act." *New York Times*, 22 September 1953. ProQuest.

Arenas, Reinaldo. "Ángel Rama, 'Subversive Agent.'" *Noticias de arte*, special issue (October 1982): 2.

———. "Una Rama entre la delincuencia y el cinismo." *Noticias de arte*, special issue (October 1982): 3–9.

Arnove, Robert F. Introduction to *Philanthropy and Cultural Imperialism: The Foundations at Home and Abroad*. Boston: G. K. Hall, 1980.

"The Assault on Mr. Christ." *Wall Street Journal*, 1 August 1977.

"El aullido vigente." Interview with Allen Ginsberg by Sergio Marras. *Apsi* 206 (22–28 June 1987): 38–40.

"Authors Condemn Immigration Ban." *New York Times*, 12 March 1969. ProQuest.

Balch, Trudy. "Pioneer on the Bridge of Language." *Américas* 50, no. 6 (November–December 1998): 46–51.

Baxandall, Lee. "An Interview with Carlos Fuentes." *Studies on the Left* 3 (1962): 48–56.

Benda, Susan R., and Morton Halperin. "Forbidden Writers: The Foreign Threat in Literary Garb." *College English* 47, no. 7 (November 1985): 690–97.

Bendiner, Robert. "The Diplomacy of Culture." *Show* 2, no. 4 (April 1962): 51–54, 100–101.

Benson, Heidi. "Catching Up with Lawrence Ferlinghetti." *San Francisco Chronicle*, 19 March 2009.

Berger, Mark T. *Under Northern Eyes: Latin American Studies and U.S. Hegemony in the Americas, 1898–1990*. Bloomington: Indiana University Press, 1995.

Berghahn, Volker. *America and the Intellectual Cold Wars in Europe: Shepard Stone between Philanthropy, Academy, and Diplomacy*. Princeton, NJ: Princeton University Press, 2001.

Berman, Edward H. *The Influence of the Carnegie, Ford, and Rockefeller Foundations on American Foreign Policy: The Ideology of Philanthropy*. Albany: State University of New York Press, 1983.

Bérubé, Michael. "American Studies without Exceptions." *PMLA* 118, no. 1 (January 2003): 103–13.

Boldiszar, Ivan. "View from the East." *Nation*, 1 July 1966: 55–59.

Borstelmann, Thomas. *The Cold War and the Color Line: American Race Relations in the Global Arena*. Cambridge, MA: Harvard University Press, 2001.

"Carta abierta de los intelectuales cubanos a Pablo Neruda." *Marcha* 1315 (5 August 1966): 30–31.

Center for Inter-American Relations. *Annual Report*, 1969. New York, 1969.

Center for Inter-American Relations. *Annual Report*, 1970 and 1971. New York, 1971.

Chute, Marchette. *P.E.N. American Center: A History of the First Fifty Years*. New York: PEN American Center, 1972.

Clements, Robert J. "Latin America's Neglected Literature." *Saturday Review* 48 (22 May 1965): 60–61.

Cline, Howard. "The Latin American Studies Association: A Summary with Appendix." *Latin American Research Review* 2, no. 1 (Fall 1966): 57–79.

Cobb, Russell. "Promoting Literature in the Most Dangerous Area in the World: The Cold War, the Boom, and *Mundo Nuevo*." In *Pressing the Fight: Print, Propaganda, and the Cold War*, ed. Greg Barnhisel and Catherine Turner, 231–50. Amherst: University of Massachusetts Press, 2010.

Cobbs, Elizabeth. *The Rich Neighbor Policy: Rockefeller and Kaiser in Brazil*. New Haven, CT: Yale University Press, 1992.

Cohn, Deborah. "Combatting Anti-Americanism during the Cold War: Faulkner, the State Department, and Latin America." *Mississippi Quarterly* 59, nos. 3–4 (Summer–Fall 2006): 396–413.

———. "'He Was One of Us': The Reception of William Faulkner and the U.S. South by Latin American Authors." *Comparative Literature Studies* 34, no. 2 (1997): 149–69.

———. "Retracing *The Lost Steps*: The Cuban Revolution, the Cold War, and Publishing Alejo Carpentier in the United States." *CR: The New Centennial Review* 3, no. 1 (Spring 2003): 81–108.

Coleman, [John] Alexander. "Sunrise with Borges et al." *Review 72*, nos. 4–5 (Winter 1971–Spring 1972): 84–87.

Coleman, Peter. *The Liberal Conspiracy: The Congress for Cultural Freedom and the Struggle for the Mind of Postwar Europe.* New York: Free Press, 1989.

"Con Gabriel García Márquez." Interview by Rosa Castro. *La cultura en México*, 23 August 1967: vi–vii.

Cong. Rec. 82nd Cong., 2d sess., 1952, 98, pt. 6: 8082–8085.

Cong. Rec. 91st Cong., 1st sess., 1969, 115, pt. 15: 19895–19896.

Cong. Rec. 91st Cong., 1st sess., 1969, 115, pt. 17: 22949–22950.

Coombs, Philip. *The Fourth Dimension of Foreign Policy: Educational and Cultural Affairs.* New York: Harper and Row, 1964.

Cortázar, Julio, et al. "USA vs. Foreign Intellectuals." *Index on Censorship* 10, no. 1 (February 1981): 38–41.

Delpar, Helen. *Looking South: The Evolution of Latin Americanist Scholarship in the United States, 1950–1975.* Tuscaloosa: University of Alabama Press, 2008.

de Onís, Harriet. "The Man in the Sulka Shirt." In *Portrait of a Publisher, 1915–1965*, ed. Alfred A. Knopf, 2:201–5. New York: Typophiles, 1965.

Donoso, José. *The Boom in Spanish American Literature: A Personal History.* Translated by G. Kolovakos. New York: Columbia University Press, 1977.

Donoso, María Pilar. *Los de entonces.* Barcelona: Seix Barral, 1987.

Downs, Donald. *Cornell '69: Liberalism and the Crisis of the American University.* Ithaca, NY: Cornell University Press, 1999.

Dudziak, Mary. *Cold War Civil Rights: Race and the Image of American Democracy.* Princeton, NJ: Princeton University Press, 2000.

"Editor's Note." *Review*, no. 30 (September–December 1981): 5.

Edwards, Jorge. *Adiós, Poeta.* Barcelona: Tusquets Editores, 1990.

———. *Persona Non Grata: A Memoir of Disenchantment with the Cuban Revolution.* Translated by Andrew Hurley. New York: Nation Books, 1993.

"Escándalo en el Center for Inter-American Relations." *Vuelta* 10, no. 1 (September 1977): 55.

Esquenazi Mayo, Roberto. "Relato personal." In *Experiencias de toda una vida: Cartas de Germán Arciniegas*, ed. Roberto Esquenazi Mayo, 5–37. Boulder, CO: Society of Spanish and Spanish-American Studies, 1997.

Ferlinghetti, Lawrence. Preface to *The Essential Neruda*, xv. San Francisco: City Lights Books, 2004.

Fernández Retamar, Roberto, Edmundo Desnoes, Lisandro Otero, and Ambrosio Fornet. "Mesa redonda: Sobre la penetración intelectual del imperialismo yanqui en América Latina." *Mundo Nuevo* 6 (November–December 1966): 133–39.

50 Years of Notable Books. Reference and Adult Services Division, American Library Association. Chicago: Booklist Publications, 1996.

Ford Foundation. *Annual Report.* New York, 1968.

Fornet, Ambrosio. "New World en español." *Casa de las Américas* 40 (January–February 1967): 106–15.

Franco, Jean. *The Decline and Fall of the Lettered City: Latin America in the Cold War.* Cambridge, MA: Harvard University Press, 2002.

Frenk, Susan. "Two Cultural Journals of the 1960s: *Casa de las Américas* and *Mundo Nuevo*." *Bulletin of Latin American Research* 3, no. 2 (1984): 83–94.

Freyre, Gilberto. "My Compadre Alfred." In *Portrait of a Publisher, 1915–1965*, ed. Alfred A. Knopf, 2:206–12. New York: Typophiles, 1965.

Frondizi, Risieri. "A Latin American View of U.S. Policy in Latin America." *Cornell Alumni News*, November 1965: 19–23.

Frugé, August. "A Latin American Translation Program." *Scholarly Books in America*, April 1964: 8–10.

———. *A Skeptic among Scholars: August Frugé on University Publishing*. Berkeley: University of California Press, 1993.

Fuentes, Carlos. "Chronologie Personelle (1928–1994)." In *Carlos Fuentes*, ed. Claude Fell and Jorge Volpi, 317–22. Paris: Les Cahiers de L'Herne, 2006.

———. "Correspondance avec Pablo Neruda." In *Carlos Fuentes*, ed. Claude Fell and Jorge Volpi, 72–73. Paris: Les Cahiers de L'Herne, 2006.

———. "Lecture." In *Free Trade in Ideas: A Constitutional Imperative*, 54–63. Washington, DC: Center for National Security Studies, 1984.

———. "Letter from Carlos Fuentes." *PMLA* 83, no. 2 (May 1968): 466.

———. "McCarran-Walter Sadomasochism." *New York Times*, 6 October 1984. ProQuest.

———. "El P.E.N.: Entierro de la Guerra Fría en la Literatura." *"Life" en español* 28, no. 3 (1 August 1966): 54–59.

———. "Mexican Novelist Assails Intervention." *New York Times*, 29 May 1965. ProQuest.

"The Fuentes Incident." *New York Times*, 5 March 1969. ProQuest.

García Márquez, Gabriel. "Con Gabriel García Márquez." Interview by Rosa Castro. *La cultura en México*, 23 August 1967: vi–vii.

Gilman, Claudia. *Entre la pluma y el fusil: Debates y dilemas del escritor revolucionario en América Latina*. Buenos Aires: Siglo Veintiuno Editores Argentina, 2003.

———. "Las revistas y los límites de lo decible: Cartografía de una época." In *La cultura de un siglo: América Latina en sus revistas*, ed. Saúl Sosnowski, 461–68. Madrid: Alianza Editorial, 1999.

Gilroy, Harry. "Ideologies Stir P.E.N. Delegates." *New York Times*, 18 June 1966. ProQuest.

"Gonzalo Rojas: Cronología." *www.gonzalorojas.uchile.cl/cronologia/05.html*.

Greene, Roland. "Inter-American Obversals: Allen Ginsberg and Haroldo de Campos circa 1960." *Xul 5 + 5* (2005). *bc.edu/research/xul/5+5/greene.htm*.

Guibert, Rita. *Seven Voices: Seven Latin American Writers Talk to Rita Guibert*. Translated by Frances Partridge. Introduction by Emir Rodríguez Monegal. New York: Alfred A. Knopf, 1972.

"Habla el poeta." *Marcha* 1315 (5 August 1966): 30–31.

Harss, Luis. "Editor's Note." *Review*, no. 30 (September–December 1981): 5.

Harss, Luis, and Barbara Dohmann. *Into the Mainstream: Conversations with Latin-American Writers*. New York: Harper and Row, 1967.

Herbers, John. "Scholar Facing Ouster by U.S. Gets Hope." *New York Times*, 12 December 1982. ProQuest.

Herrero-Olaizola, Alejandro. *The Censorship Files: Latin American Writers and Franco's Spain*. Albany: State University of New York Press, 2007.

Immigration and Nationality Act, ch. 477, §212(a)(28)(I), 66 Stat. 163, 186 (1952).

"An Immodest Proposal by the Editors." *Show* 2, no. 4 (April 1962): 55.

Indych-López, Anna. "Between the National and Transnational: Aspects of Exhibiting Modern and Contemporary Mexican Art at the Americas Society." In *A Principality of Its Own: 40 Years of Visual Arts at the Americas Society*, ed. José Luis Falconi and Gabriela Rangel, 84–99. New York: Americas Society, 2006.

"Inter-American Blueprint." *New York Times*, 18 November 1974. ProQuest.

"Inter-American Relations Center Torn by Aide's Trip to Chile." *Washington Post*, 31 July 1977. ProQuest.

Joseph, Gilbert. "What We Now Know and Should Know: Bringing Latin America More Meaningfully into Cold War Studies." In *In from the Cold: Latin America's New Encounter with the Cold War*, ed. Gilbert Joseph and Daniela Spenser, 3–46. Durham, NC: Duke University Press, 2008.

Kaplan, Amy. "'Left Alone with America': The Absence of Empire in the Study of American Culture." In *Cultures of United States Imperialism*, 3–21. Durham, NC: Duke University Press, 1993.

Kennedy, Liam, and Scott Lucas. "Enduring Freedom: Public Diplomacy and U.S. Foreign Policy." *American Quarterly* 57, no. 2 (June 2005): 309–33.

Kerr, Lucille. "Writing Donoso behind the Scenes." *Journal of Interdisciplinary Literary Studies* 9, no. 1–2 (2003): 81–100.

King, John. *The Role of Mexico's "Plural" in Latin American Literary and Political Culture: From Tlatelolco to the "Philanthropic Ogre."* New York: Palgrave Macmillan, 2007.

Krenn, Michael L. *Fall-out Shelters for the Human Spirit: American Art and the Cold War*. Chapel Hill: University of North Carolina Press, 2005.

Kryzanek, Michael J. "Political Party Decline and the Failure of Liberal Democracy: The PRD in Dominican Politics." *Journal of Latin American Studies* 9, no. 1 (May 1977): 115–43.

Laber, Jeri. "Writers Not Welcome." *New York Times*, 29 April 1984. ProQuest.

Lask, Thomas. "Poets' Group Here Assails Neruda." *New York Times*, 21 April 1972. ProQuest.

Laughlin, James. "The Function of This Magazine." *Perspectives* 1 (Autumn 1953): 5–8.

"Lawrence Ferlinghetti: A micro-interview with Narlan Matos." *91st Meridian* 7, no. 1 (Spring 2010). Rpt. online at *iwp.uiowa.edu*.

"Legendary Beat Generation Bookseller and Poet Lawrence Ferlinghetti of City Lights Books on the 50th Anniversary of Jack Kerouac's *On the Road*, Allen Ginsberg's 'Howl,' and Poetry as Insurgent Art." Interview with Lawrence Ferlinghetti by Amy Goodman. 24 December 2007. *www.democracynow.org*.

Leonard, John. "Letter from New York." *New York Times*, 30 April 1972. ProQuest.

———. "Myth Is Alive in Latin America." Review of *One Hundred Years of Solitude*. *New York Times*, 3 March 1970. ProQuest.

Levine, Suzanne Jill, ed. *Latin America: Fiction and Poetry in Translation*. New York: Center for Inter-American Relations, 1970.

Levine, Suzanne Jill. "The Latin American Novel in English." In *Cambridge Companion to the Latin American Novel*, ed. Efraín Kristal, 297–317. Cambridge: Cambridge University Press, 2005.

Lewis, Anthony. "Requiem for a Victim." *New York Times*, 1 December 1983. ProQuest.

Lie, Nadia. *Transición y transacción: La revista cubana "Casa de las Américas" (1960–1976)*. Gaithersburg, MD: Ediciones Hispamérica, 1996.

Lowe, Elizabeth, and Earl Fitz. *Translation and the Rise of Inter-American Literature*. Foreword by Ilán Stavans. Gainesville: University Press of Florida, 2007.

Luis, William. *"Lunes de Revolución": Literatura y cultura en los primeros años de la Revolución Cubana*. Madrid: Editorial Verbum, 2003.

Mac Adam, Alfred. "The Boom and Beyond: Latin American Literature and the Americas Society." In *A Hemispheric Venture: Thirty-Five Years of Culture at the Americas Society, 1965–2000*, 179–205. New York: Americas Society, 2000.

MacShane, Frank. "Writers in Calamitous Times." *Columbia Forum* (Fall 1972): 36–38.

Manheim, Jarol. *Strategic Public Diplomacy and American Foreign Policy: The Evolution of Influence*. New York: Oxford University Press, 1994.

Martin, Gerald. "The Boom of Spanish-American Fiction and the 1960s Revolutions (1958–75)." In *A Companion to Latin American Literature and Culture*, ed. Sara Castro-Klarén, 478–94. Oxford, UK: Blackwell Publishing, 2008.

———. "Boom, Yes; 'New' Novel, No: Further Reflections on the Optical Illusions of the 1960s in Latin America." *Bulletin of Latin American Research* 3, no. 2 (1984): 53–63.

———. *Gabriel García Márquez: A Life*. New York: Alfred A. Knopf, 2009.

May, Clifford. "Scholar Will Try to Clear Name from Visa Lists." *New York Times*, 23 August 1986.

"McCarran Act at Work." *New York Times*, 18 September 1953.

"McCarran Redux." *Nation*, 19 June 1982: 737–38.

McCarthy, Kathleen D. "From Cold War to Cultural Development: The International Cultural Activities of the Ford Foundation, 1950–1980." *Daedalus* 116, no. 1 (Winter 1987): 93–117.

———. "The Short and Simple Annals of the Poor: Foundation Funding for the Humanities, 1900–1983." *Proceedings of the American Philosophical Society* 129, no. 1 (March 1985): 3–8.

McDowell, Edwin. "Publishing." *New York Times*, 31 October 1988. ProQuest.

McQuade, Frank. "'Mundo Nuevo': El discurso político en una revista intelectual de los sesenta." *Revista chilena de literatura* 42 (August 1993): 123–30.

———. "*Mundo Nuevo*: La nueva novela y la guerra fría cultural." In *Le discours culturel dans les revues latino-américaines (1940–1970)*, ed. Claude Fell et al., 17–26. Paris: Presses de la Sorbonne Nouvelle, 1992.

Miller, Arthur. *Timebends: A Life*. New York: Harper and Row, 1987.

Miller, Toby, and George Yúdice. *Cultural Policy*. London: Sage Publications, 2002.

Mitgang, Herbert. *Dangerous Dossiers: Exposing the Secret War against America's Greatest Authors*. New York: Donald I. Fine, 1988.

———. "On the 7th Day, the Envoy Writes." *New York Times*, 28 October 1976. ProQuest.

Mudrovcic, María Eugenia. *"Mundo Nuevo": Cultura y Guerra Fría en la década del 60*. Rosario, Argentina: Beatriz Viterbo Editora, 1997.

———. "Reading Latin American Literature Abroad: Agency and Canon Formation in the Sixties and Seventies." In *Voice-Overs: Translation and Latin American Literature*, ed. Daniel Balderston and Marcy Schwartz, 129–43. Albany: State University of New York Press, 2002.

Needler, Martin, and Thomas Walker. "The Current Status of Latin American Studies Programs." *Latin American Research Review* 6, no. 1 (Spring 1971): 119–39.

Neruda, Pablo. *Confieso que he vivido: Memorias*. 2nd ed. Buenos Aires: Editorial Losada, 1974.

Nielsen, Waldemar. *The Big Foundations*. New York: Columbia University Press, 1972.

"1971: A Selection of Noteworthy Titles." *New York Times*, 5 December 1971. ProQuest.

"Octavio Paz en Cornell." *Mundo Nuevo* 3 (September 1966): 73–74.

"Octavio Paz enseña y aprende en Cornell." "*Life*" *en español* 28, no.1 (4 July 1966): 59–62.

Ohmann, Richard. "The Shaping of a Canon: U.S. Fiction, 1960–1975." *Critical Inquiry* 10, no. 1 (September 1983): 199–223.

"Open Letter to the Center for Interamerican Relations." *Noticias de arte*, special issue (October 1982): 1. First published in *El Universal* (Caracas), 1982.

Ortega, Julio. *Retrato de Carlos Fuentes*. Barcelona: Círculo de Lectores, 1995.

Oyarzún, Luis. "Nicanor Parra en Nueva York." *El Mercurio* (Santiago), 14 July 1970: 3. Rpt. in *www.nicanorparra.uchile.cl/prensa/parraenny.html*.

"Papel del escritor en América Latina." *Mundo Nuevo* 5 (November 1966): 25–35.

Parmar, Inderjeet. "American Foundations and Globalisation." Unpublished paper.

———. "Selling Americanism, Combatting Anti-Americanism: The Historical Role of American Foundations." Anti-Americanism Working Papers. Budapest: Center for Policy Studies, Central European University, 2004.

Peyrou, Rosario. "Prologo." In *Ángel Rama: Diario, 1974–1983*, ed. Rosario Peyrou, 5–29. Montevideo: Ediciones Trilce, 2001.

Phillips, McCandlish. "Amid City's Hum, Poetry." *New York Times*, 14 May 1970. ProQuest.

"Professor Freed from Ellis Island." *New York Times*, 18 September 1953. ProQuest.

Rabassa, Gregory. *If This Be Treason: Translation and Its Dyscontents*. New York: New Directions, 2005.

Rama, Ángel. "El 'Boom' en perspectiva." In *Más allá del Boom: Literatura y mercado*, ed. David Viñas, 51–110. México: Marcha Editores, 1981.

———. "Catch 28." *Index on Censorship* 12, no. 4 (August 1983): 7–10.

———. "Las malandanzas de Reinaldo Arenas." *El Universal* (Caracas), 12 September 1982.

Randall, Margaret. "Threatened with Deportation." *Latin American Perspectives* 14, no. 4 (Autumn 1987): 465–80.

———. "When the Imagination of the Writer is Confronted by the Imagination of the State." *Latin American Perspectives* 16, no. 2 (Spring 1989): 115–23.

Raymont, Henry. "Fuentes Incident Revives Dispute." *New York Times*, 3 March 1969. ProQuest.

———. "Fulbright Urges Eased Alien Law." *New York Times*, 9 March 1969. ProQuest.

———. "Immigration Policy." *New York Times*, 9 March 1969. ProQuest.

———. "National Book Awards: The Winners." *New York Times*, 11 March 1969. ProQuest.

———. "Neruda Opens Visit Here with a Plea for Chile's Revolution." *New York Times*, 11 April 1972. ProQuest.

———. "Solzhenitsyn's Nobel Dispute Called 'a Big Bore' by Neruda." *New York Times*, 16 April 1972. ProQuest.

———. "Travel in U.S. Will Be Allowed for Aliens Barred over Politics." *New York Times*, 20 July 1969. ProQuest.

Rexer, Lyle. "Comic Echoes in the Fictional Jungles of the Amazon." *Chicago Tribune*, 15 January 1978. ProQuest.

Riding, Alan. "For García Márquez, Revolution Is a Major Theme." *New York Times*, 22 May 1980. ProQuest.

Rivas, Darlene. *Missionary Capitalist: Nelson Rockefeller in Venezuela*. Chapel Hill: University of North Carolina Press, 2002.

Robin, Ron. *The Making of the Cold War Enemy: Culture and Politics in the Military-Intellectual Complex*. Princeton, NJ: Princeton University Press, 2001.

Robins, Natalie. *Alien Ink: The FBI's War on Freedom of Expression*. New Brunswick, NJ: Rutgers University Press, 1992.

Rockefeller, David. *Memoirs*. New York: Random House, 2002.

Rockefeller Foundation. *Annual Report*. New York, 1960.

Rodman, Selden. "All American." *New York Times*, 10 July 1966. ProQuest.

Rodríguez, José Mario. "Allen Ginsberg en la Habana." *Mundo Nuevo* 34 (April 1969): 48–54.

Rodríguez-Carranza, Luz. "Emir Rodríguez Monegal o la construcción de un mundo (nuevo) posible." *Revista Iberoamericana* 58, nos. 160–61 (July–December 1992): 903–17.

Rodríguez Monegal, Emir. "La CIA y los intelectuales." *Mundo Nuevo* 13 (June 1967): n.p.

———. "Diario del P.E.N. Club." *Mundo Nuevo* 4 (October 1966): 41–51. Rpt. in *www.archivodeprensa.edu.uy/biblioteca/emir_rodriguez_monegal/bibliografia/prensa/artpren/mundo/mundo_046.htm*.

———. "El P.E.N. Club contra la guerra fría." *Mundo Nuevo* 5 (November 1966): 85–90.

———. "Presentación." *Mundo Nuevo* 1 (July 1966): 4.

Rosefelt, Reid. "Harvey and Bob Weinstein: The Early Days." *My Life as a Blog*, 6 February 2011. *my-life-as-a-blog.com*. Reposted at *MovieMaker*, 7 February 2011. *www.moviemaker.com/blog*.

Rostagno, Irene. *Searching for Recognition: The Promotion of Latin American Literature in the United States*. Westport, CT: Greenwood Press, 1997.

"Rules May Be Eased on Aliens' Re-entry." *New York Times*, 2 October 1953. ProQuest.

Santana, Mario. *Foreigners in the Homeland: The Spanish American New Novel in Spain, 1962–1974*. Lewisburg, PA: Bucknell University Press, 2000.

Saunders, Frances S. *Who Paid the Piper? The CIA and the Cultural Cold War*. London: Granta Books, 1999.

Schlesinger, Arthur M., Jr. *Robert Kennedy and His Times*, vol. I. Boston: Houghton Mifflin, 1978.

"Scholar's Colleagues Upset by His Teaching in Chile." *New York Times*, 10 July 1977. ProQuest.

Schreiber, Rebecca. *Cold War Exiles in Mexico: U.S. Dissidents and the Culture of Critical Resistance*. Minneapolis: University of Minnesota Press, 2008.

Schwartz, Abba. *The Open Society*. New York: William Morrow, 1968.

Schwartz, Lawrence H. *Creating Faulkner's Reputation: The Politics of Modern Literary Criticism*. Knoxville: University of Tennessee Press, 1988.

Scott-Smith, Giles. "Building a Community around the Pax Americana: The US Government and Exchange Programmes during the 1950s." In *The US Government, Citizen Groups, and the Cold War: The State-Private Network*, ed. Helen Laville and Hugh Wilford, 83–99. London: Routledge, 2006.

———. *Politics of Apolitical Culture: The Congress for Cultural Freedom, the CIA, and Post-war American Hegemony*. London: Routledge, 2002.

Shanks, Cheryl. *Immigration and the Politics of American Sovereignty, 1890–1990*. Ann Arbor: University of Michigan Press, 2001.

Shapiro, Steven. "Ideological Exclusions: Closing the Border to Political Dissidents." *Harvard Law Review* 100, no. 4 (February 1987): 930–45.

Shaw, Bradley A. *Latin American Literature in English Translation: An Annotated Bibliography*. New York: New York University Press, 1976.

Sheldon, Glenn. *South of Our Selves: Mexico in the Poems of Williams, Kerouac,*

Corso, Ginsberg, Levertov, and Hayden. Jefferson, NC: McFarland and Company, 2004.

"Show Is Suspended as Artists Dissent." *New York Times*, 20 March 1971. ProQuest.

Shumway, David R. *Creating American Civilization: A Genealogy of American Literature as Academic Discipline.* American Culture, vol. 11. Minneapolis: University of Minnesota Press, 1994.

Silesky, Barry. *Ferlinghetti, the Artist in His Time.* New York: Warner Books, 1990.

Sorensen, Diana. *A Turbulent Decade Remembered: Scenes from the Latin American Sixties.* Stanford, CA: Stanford University Press, 2007.

"Soviet Writers Denounce P.E.N." *New York Times*, 29 July 1966. ProQuest.

"A Statement of Aims." *Odyssey Review* 3, no. 2 (June 1963): n.p.

Straus, Roger. "The Fuentes Case." *Publishers Weekly*, 17 March 1969: 37.

Swing, J. M. "Detention of Arciniegas." *New York Times*, 18 April 1957. ProQuest.

Szulc, Tad. "Visa Denial Bars Leftist's Debate." *New York Times*, 7 April 1962. ProQuest.

Tannenbaum, Frank. "Visa Policy Assailed." *New York Times*, 1 May 1962. ProQuest.

Tarbert, Gary C., and Barbara Beach, eds. *Book Review Index: A Master Cumulation, 1965–1984.* 10 volumes. Detroit: Gale Research Company, 1985.

Theberge, James. *The Soviet Presence in Latin America.* New York: Crane, Russak for the National Strategy Information Center, 1974.

———, ed. *Understanding the Allende Revolution and the Fall of Chilean Democracy: A Conference Report.* Washington, DC: Center for Strategic and International Studies, Georgetown University, 1974.

"An Unfortunate Incident." *New York Times*, 16 April 1957. ProQuest.

The United States and Latin America: The Next Steps; A Second Report by the Commission on United States–Latin American Relations. New York: Center for Inter-American Relations, 1976.

"U.S. Eases Visas for Red Delegates to Parleys." *New York Times*, 4 May 1966. ProQuest.

"U.S. Seizes a Columbia Professor for Questioning as 'Security Case.'" *New York Times*, 17 September 1953. ProQuest.

van Delden, Maarten. *Carlos Fuentes, Mexico, and Modernity.* Nashville: Vanderbilt University Press, 1998.

Vargas Llosa, Mario. "Literature Is Fire." In *Making Waves: Essays*, ed. and trans. John King, 70–74. New York: Penguin Books, 1996.

Véjar, Francisco. "El aullido de Nicanor Parra y los beatniks." *El Mercurio* (online), 26 September 1998. Rpt. in *www.emol.com/especiales/nicanor_parra/ articulos26_09_1998.htm.*

Von Eschen, Penny. *Satchmo Blows Up the World: Jazz Ambassadors Play the Cold War.* Cambridge, MA: Harvard University Press, 2004.

Wagley, Charles, and Frank MacShane. "Exclusion of Fuentes." *New York Times*, 30 March 1969. ProQuest.

Wardlaw, Frank. "Jaime García Terrés and the *Lista Negra*." *Harper's Magazine*, January 1965: 16, 22, 25, 26.

Weatherhead, Richard. "Barring Fuentes Protested." *New York Times*, 25 April 1962. ProQuest.

Weiss, Judith. *"Casa de las Américas": An Intellectual Review in the Cuban Revolution.* Chapel Hill, NC: Estudios de Hispanófila, 1977.

Welch, Richard, Jr. *Response to Revolution: The United States and the Cuban Revolution, 1959–1961.* Chapel Hill: University of North Carolina Press, 1985.

Westad, Odd Arne. *The Global Cold War: Third World Interventions and the Making of Our Times.* Cambridge: Cambridge University Press, 2005.

Wilford, Hugh. *The CIA, the British Left, and the Cold War: Calling the Tune?* Foreword by David Caute. London: Frank Cass, 2003.

———. *The Mighty Wurlitzer: How the CIA Played America.* Cambridge, MA: Harvard University Press, 2008.

Williamson, Edwin. *Borges: A Life.* New York: Viking, 2004.

Yglesias, Luis. "Pablo Neruda: The Poet in New York." *Nation*, 1 July 1966: 52–55.

Young, Howard. "Federico de Onís (1888–1966)." *Hispania* 80, no. 2 (May 1997): 268–70.

Zamora, Lois Parkinson. *Writing the Apocalypse: Historical Vision in Contemporary U.S. and Latin American Fiction.* Cambridge: Cambridge University Press, 1989.

Index

The letter "t" following a page number refers to a table.

62: A Model Kit (Cortázar), 225n60

AAUP. *See* Association of American
    University Presses (AAUP)
abstract expressionism, 35
Academy of American Poets, 136, 198
Adams, Rachel, 198–99, 200
Adams, Richard, 162–63
Adán, Martín, 195
Adzhubi, Alexsey, 51, 59–60
Agee, James, 112
agents
    CIAR Literature Department as, 169
    commercial publishers and, 175
    See also Balcells, Carmen; Brandt,
        Carl
Aguilera Malta, Demetrio, 102, 103
Albee, Edward
    IAC and, 149
    IAFA/CIAR and, 154
    Paradise Island symposium and, 145
    PEN congress and, 76, 83
Aldrich Rockefeller, Abby, 158
Alegría, Ciro, 204n14
Alegría, Fernando
    Beat poets and, 193, 194, 196, 197
    CIAR and, 164
    IANP and, 125, 129, 130
    Odyssey Review and, 102
    Paradise Island symposium and, 145
    politics and, 189
    Review and, 186

The Aleph and Other Stories, 1933–1969
    (Borges), 16, 174
Alfred A. Knopf Inc.
    Carpentier and, 130
    cost of translations and, 111–12,
        120–21
    Cumboto and, 126
    H. de Onís and, 104, 132, 171
    Donoso and, 43, 219n87
    Latin American literature and, 9–12
    Lispector and, 215n11
    Mallea and, 126, 219n88
    See also Knopf, Alfred
Algren, Nelson, 107
Alice Tully Hall (New York), 168
Allende, Hortensia, 38
Allende, Salvador, 164, 179–80, 181,
    198
All Fires the Fire (Cortázar), 225n60
All Green Shall Perish (Mallea), 219n88
Alliance for Progress
    CIAR and, 161
    Inter-American Committee of, 150
    political stability and, 25
    W. D. Rogers and, 152, 159
    TV debate and, 49–51
Almeyda, Clodomiro, 164
Alonso, Dámaso, 98
Amado, Jorge, 13, 99, 203n1
Amaru (journal), 195
*América, no en vano invocamos tu
    nombre* (Orrego-Salas), 137

American Association of Teachers of
  Spanish and Portuguese, 214n1
American Civil Liberties Union
  (ACLU), 41, 62–63
American Committee for Cultural
  Freedom (ACCF), 41
American Library Association (ALA),
  174
Americas Society, 188
Antipoems (Parra), 195
Aportes (journal), 21
Arciniegas, Germán
  CLAY and, 138
  Columbia University and, 104
  McCarran-Walter Act and, 40–42,
    210n46
  translations and, 204n14
Arenas, Reinaldo, 187–89
Argentina and Argentine literature
  censorship and, 206n46
  CLAY and, 138–39
  IANP and, 125
  Odyssey Review and, 102, 103
  Rodríguez Monegal and, 17
Arguedas, José María, 125, 131
Arias, Arnulfo, 160–61
Aridjis, Homero
  Christ's trip to Chile and, 182
  Columbia University and, 105
  Galantière and, 212n19
  PEN and, 79, 213n37
Armstrong, Louis, 28
Arnove, Robert F., 28
Arreola, Juan José, 102, 108, 119
Asia Society, 146
Association of American University
    Presses (AAUP)
  vs. CIAR, 175, 176–77, 191–92
  translation subsidy program and,
    15, 113–22, 116–17t, 131, 143
Association of Latin American Studies,
  95
El astillero (Onetti), 125
Asturias, Miguel Ángel
  CIAR and, 178
  IANP and, 125, 129, 131
  McCarran-Walter Act and, 38

Odyssey Review and, 102
PEN and, 72
translations and, 103, 108
Atlantic Monthly Press, 131
Auden, W. H., 102, 112
Aura (Fuentes), 16

Balbontín, Manuel, 79
Balcells, Carmen, 16, 120
Baldwin, James, 150
Ball, George, 52
Bantam, 16
Barlow, William, 150, 152, 153, 157
Barnet, Richard, 163
Barren Lives (Ramos), 125, 131
Barthes, Roland, 19
Barzun, Jacques, 102, 112
Bastos, María Luisa, 169
Battle, Lucius, 146
Baxandall, Lee, 50
The Bay of Silence (Mallea), 219n88
Beat poets, 193–201
Beauvoir, Simone de, 26
Becker, Idel, 218n64
Beckett, Samuel, 15
Beleño, Joaquín, 125, 219n89
Belitt, Ben, 80
Belkin, Arnold, 226n68
Bello, Andrés, 17
Bellow, Saul, 19, 83
Benedetti, Mario, 19, 102
Benítez, Jaime, 150
Berger, Mark T., 95, 143, 162
Berghahn, Volker, 35, 146
Berman, Edward H., 29
Bérubé, Michael, 28–29
Betancourt, Rómulo, 123
Betancur, Belisario, 48
Betrayed by Rita Hayworth (Puig), 174
Bieber, Marion, 68
Big Mama's Funerals (García Márquez),
  218n63
Bioy Casares, Adolfo, 16, 119
Birns, Laurence, 164
Bishop, Elizabeth, 49
Blackburn, Sara, 14, 103, 182. *See also*
  Pantheon

Bled congress (International PEN, 1965), 65, 69, 72, 79
Blumenthal, W. Michael, 224–25n54
Boldiszar, Ivan, 81
Bolivia
    Beat poets and, 195
    CLAY and, 138–39
    Del Greco and, 128
    IANP and, 125
The Book of Imaginary Beings (Borges), 15–16, 177
Books Abroad (journal), 18
the Boom
    Cold War cultural politics and, 7–9
    Cuban Revolution and, 4–5, 24–27, 143, 168
    international mainstream and, 2
    as literary movement and marketing phenomenon, 5–7, 120
    modernism and, 35–36
    See also specific authors
The Boom: A Personal History (Donoso), 24
El Boom de la novela latinoamericana (Rodríguez Monegal), 18
Borges, Jorge Luis
    CIAR and, 179, 189
    Columbia University and, 105, 106
    Harvard and, 15, 98
    International Publishers' Prize and success of, 15–16, 98, 111, 123
    A. Knopf and, 11
    McCarran-Walter Act and, 40
    Mundo Nuevo and, 23
    New York Times and, 174
    Odyssey Review and, 102, 103
    Puterbaugh Conferences and, 100
    reviews and, 177
    Rodríguez Monegal and, 17
    translations and, 13, 108, 119, 175
    University of Texas at Austin and, 98, 119
Borstelmann, Thomas, 7
Borzoi Anthology of Latin American Literature, 17, 104
Bosch, Juan
    Mundo Nuevo and, 23

PEN congress and, 72, 73–74
    PRD and, 53, 140
Botero, Fernando, 168
Botsford, Keith
    CCF and, 20
    National Translation Center and, 113
    PEN and, 68, 71–72
    Rodríguez Monegal and, 69
Bottaro, Raúl Horacio, 218n64
Bourdieu, Pierre, 66, 192
Boyer, Mildred, 119
Brandt, Carl
    Donoso and, 219n87
    Fuentes and, 16–17, 49, 52, 54–55, 57, 120
Brazil and Brazilian literature
    CLAY and, 139
    Nation and, 81
    Odyssey Review and, 102, 103
    Rabassa and, 215n11
    translations and, 13, 104, 119, 175, 203n2
    U.S. academy and, 215n9
Brecht, Bertolt, 19
Brodkey, Harold, 49
Brodsky, Joseph, 106
Bronheim, David, 159
Brooks, Cleanth, 102, 112
Brown, Harrison, 224–25n54
Brown, John L., 212n19
Brown University, 214n6
El buen ladrón (Veloz Maggiolo), 125, 129
Bundy, McGeorge, 29
Bureau of Educational and Cultural Affairs (ECA)
    Christ and, 180
    CLAY and, 135
    cultural diplomacy programs and, 28
    Galantière and, 70
    IAFA/CIAR and, 157
    Iowa Writer's Workshop and, 109
    IWP and, 110–11
    Show and, 146
    Slater and, 156

Cabrera, Sarandy, 47

Cabrera Infante, Guillermo
  Brandt and, 120
  CIAR and, 179
  Cuban Revolution and, 26, 42, 185
  H. de Onís and, 13
  McCarran-Walter Act and, 42
  New York Times and, 174
  Premio Biblioteca Breve and, 123
  Prieto and, 15
  Puterbaugh Conferences and, 100
  Review and, 187–88

Caín, el hombre (Godoy), 219n89

Calder and Boyars, 219n88

Cambio de piel (Fuentes), 123

Cameron, Angus, 11

Campos, Haroldo de, 78

Canfield, Cass, Jr., 14–15, 215–16n29

Canfield, Gabriela, 14–15

Canter, Jacob, 110, 135

Captain Pantoja and the Special Service (Vargas Llosa), 185

Carballido, Emilio, 136

Cardenal, Ernesto
  CIAR and, 178, 179
  IANP and, 124–25

Carlisle Hart, Kitty, 150

Carlo, Omar del, 169

Carnegie Corporation
  CLAY and, 134–35, 138
  cultural diplomacy programs and, 27
  Latin American studies and, 95–96
  Perkins and, 133

Carnegie Endowment for International Peace, 29

Carnegie Hall (New York), 168

Carpentier, Alejo
  Fuentes and, 12, 85, 213n43
  IANP and, 130
  Neruda and, 83, 86
  PEN congress and, 73, 74
  translations and, 13, 14, 108, 132
  Weinstock and, 12

"Carta abierta de los intelectuales cubanos a Pablo Neruda," 26, 83–87, 92

Carter administration, 166–67

Carver, David, 68, 71–72

Casa de las Américas (foundation)
  Boom and, 5, 6, 25
  CIAR and, 155
  literary prizes and, 123–24, 196
  Rama and, 45

Casa de las Américas (journal)
  on CIA and CCF, 20
  Lunes de Revolución and, 204n6
  open letter to Neruda and, 84
  Rama and, 45
  research on, 7

Casa Hispánica (Columbia University), 104

Casanova, Giacomo, 215n12

La casa verde (Vargas Llosa), 43

caso Padilla (Padilla affair, 1971), 26–27, 85

Castellanos, Rosario, 108

Castillo, José Guillermo, 168–69, 175, 186

Castro, Fidel
  Cabrera Infante and, 42
  Khrushchev and, 153
  Padilla and, 26–27
  Soviet Union and, 25
  See also Cuba and the Cuban Revolution

Cates, John, 159, 179–80

Caute, David, 7

Cela, Camilo José, 19

The Censorship Files (Herrero-Olaizola), 7, 185

Center for Inter-American Relations (CIAR)
  Columbia translation center and, 107, 143
  commercial publishers and, 36, 120, 176
  history and fundraising, 152–58, 188–89
  Literature Department, 167–68; Christ's trip to Chile and, 180–88, 189–90; politics and, 177–90; translation subsidy program and, 168–77, 172–73t, 189, 191–92, 219n87

W. MacLeish and, 186
Music and Visual Arts Departments,
    160, 168, 177–78
politics and, 158–60, 177–78
Public Affairs program, 160–67
visiting positions and, 99–100, 105
Chaves and Other Stories (Mallea),
    219n88
Cheuse, Alan, 81
Chicago Tribune, 6
Chile and Chilean literature
Beat poets and, 195
Christ and, 180–88, 189–90
CIAR and, 164–65
CLAY and, 138–39
IANP and, 125
MacShane and, 180, 181, 198
Neruda on, 90–91
See also Allende, Salvador
Choice (journal), 177
Christ, Ronald
CIAR Literature Department and,
    175, 176
trip to Chile, 180–88, 189–90,
    224n53
Christian Science Monitor, 177
Chronicles of Bustos Domecq (Borges and
    Bioy Casares), 16
Chute, Marchette, 81, 211n13
CIA (Central Intelligence Agency)
CCF and, 19–24, 32, 45–46, 83–84,
    150, 154, 190, 191
cultural diplomacy programs and,
    39–40
Ginsberg and, 197
IAC and, 147–48
PEN and, 68, 69
Rama and, 46
Cien años de soledad (García Márquez)
Mundo Nuevo and, 17, 44
reviews and, 177
translation by Rabassa, 1–2, 14–15,
    103, 174, 175
City Lights (San Francisco), 193
La ciudad letrada (Rama), 45
La ciudad y los perros (Vargas Llosa), 123
Clark, Joseph, 58

CLAY (Cornell University's "Latin
    American Year")
conferences and events, 135–38
organization and funding, 133–35
Paz and, 99, 136, 141
student-organized conference,
    138–40
as success, 140–42
Cleveland, Harlan, 74
Cline, Howard, 95–96, 135, 143
Cobb, Russell, 23
Colchie, Thomas, 175, 176, 180
Cold War Exiles in Mexico (Schreiber),
    8–9
Coleman, John Alexander, 169, 175, 176,
    180, 189
Coleman, Peter, 21, 22, 23
Coleridge, Samuel Taylor, 90
Collado, Emilio, 159
Colombia
Arciniegas and, 40–41
CLAY and, 138–39
IANP and, 217n61, 217–18n63
Odyssey Review and, 102–3
Rama and, 48
Colorado State University
Donoso and, 99
Fuentes and, 54–55
Columbia University
Donoso and, 99, 105
Fuentes and, 57–58, 99, 100, 101, 105,
    106
García Márquez and, 44, 105
Hispanic studies at, 104
Neruda and, 91
Odyssey Review, 14, 101–7, 143
Parra and, 99, 105, 106, 197
Puig and, 99
translation center at, 106–7
Vargas Llosa and, 99, 105
Writing Division, 99–100, 105–6,
    143, 169
commercial publishers
AAUP subsidy program and, 175
CIAR and, 36, 120, 176
IAFA and, 150, 151
IANP and, 131–32

commercial publishers, *continued*
    translations and, 111
    vs. university presses, 120–21, 170
    See also specific publishers
Concolorcorvo (Alonso Carrió de la
    Vandera), 119
Confieso que he vivido (Neruda), 179
Configurations (Paz), 174
Congress for Cultural Freedom (CCF)
    American Committee for Cultural
        Freedom and, 41
    CIA and, 19–24, 32, 45–46, 83–84,
        150, 154, 190, 191
    IAC and, 147–48
    Odyssey Review and, 102
    PEN and, 66, 67, 68–69, 89
Coombs, Philip, 28
Copland, Aaron, 145
Corcoran Gallery (Washington, DC), 168
Cordido-Freytes, José Antonio, 126–27
Cornell University, Latin American
    Studies program at, 134. *See also*
    CLAY (Cornell University's "Latin
    American Year")
Cornell University Press, 140
El corno emplumado (literary magazine),
    212n19
Coronación (Donoso), 10, 43, 108, 125, 131
El coronel no tiene quien le escriba (García
    Márquez), 174, 217n63
Coronel Urtecho, José, 228n113
Cortázar, Julio
    CIAR and, 178, 179, 183, 225n60
    Cuban Revolution and, 23, 44, 179,
        189
    Fuentes and, 213n43
    García Márquez and, 5, 171
    MacShane and, 105
    McCarran-Walter Act and, 44, 62
    Mundo Nuevo and, 19, 23
    Puterbaugh Conferences and, 100
    Rabassa and, 14, 103, 104, 171, 208n8
    Review and, 186
    success of *Cien años de soledad* and, 1
    translations and, 175
    visiting positions in the U.S., 100–101
Cortés (López de Gómara), 118, 119

Cosío Villegas, Daniel, 119
Costa Rica, 125, 129
Council on Higher Education in the
    American Republics, 134
Council on Latin America (later Council
    of the Americas), 151–52, 158
Cowley, Malcolm, 112
Creating the Hemispheric Citizen (Fox), 8
"The Crime of the Mathematics
    Professor" (Lispector), 215n11
Crome, Nick, 54–55
Cuadernos (journal), 20, 23, 41, 130
Cuadra, Pablo Antonio, 228n113
Cuba and the Cuban Revolution
    Beat poets and, 194, 195–99
    Boom and, 4–5, 24–27, 143, 168
    Cabrera Infante and, 26, 42, 185
    CIAR and, 159–60, 163–64, 186–88,
        189
    CLAY and, 139
    Cortázar and, 44, 179, 189
    Fuentes and, 26, 49, 50
    IANP and, 125, 129–30
    Latin American studies and, 10, 95–98
    Odyssey Review and, 103
    open letter to Neruda and, 26, 83–87,
        92
    Paz on, 26
    Rama and, 45
    W. D. Rogers and, 159
    Spanish American writers and, 39–40
    Vargas Llosa and, 43, 185
    See also Casa de las Américas
        (foundation); Castro, Fidel
Cuban Affairs office (State Department),
    70, 74
Cuevas, José Luis, 150
cultural diplomacy programs, 27–36
Cumboto (Díaz Sánchez), 125–27, 131,
    132–33

DaCal, Ernesto, 218n64
Daniel, Yuli. *See* Sinyavsky-Daniel trial
    (1966)
Darío, Rubén, 127
Dartmouth College, 54, 99
Davis, Tom, 136

The Death of Artemio Cruz (Fuentes), 16, 52
The Decline and Fall of the Lettered City (Franco), 7
Deep Rivers (Arguedas), 125, 131
Del Greco, Arnold, 123, 124–25, 126–33
Delos (journal), 113
Delpar, Helen, 95, 96
de Onís, Federico, 101, 104
de Onís, Harriet
    Galantière and, 212n19
    on A. Knopf, 10
    on literature and politics, 11–13, 132, 171
    Odyssey Review and, 103, 104
    PEN Translation Prize, 171
Department of Justice. *See* U.S. Department of Justice
Department of State. *See* U.S. Department of State
Los deshabitados (Quiroga), 125
Desnoes, Edmundo, 84
The Devil to Pay in the Backlands (Guimarães Rosa), 225n63
D'Harnoncourt, René, 153
Díaz Ordaz, Gustavo, 100, 210n52
Díaz Sánchez, Ramón, 125–27, 131, 132–33, 219n89
Di Giovanni, Norman Thomas, 98
Doctor Brodie's Report (Borges), 16
Doctorow, E. L., 62
Dohmann, Barbara, 5, 108
Dominican Republic
    CLAY and, 140
    IANP and, 129
    U.S. intervention in, 23, 53, 73, 84, 109, 137, 207n4
Donoso, José
    on the Boom, 24
    Brandt and, 120
    Christ's trip to Chile and, 183
    Crome and, 54
    H. de Onís and, 12, 13
    Fuentes and, 10, 82–83, 120
    IANP and, 125, 131
    McCarran-Walter Act and, 43
    MLA 1968 convention and, 55

New York Times and, 174
    Premio Biblioteca Breve and, 123
    on regionalism, 6, 132
    reviews and, 177
    visiting positions in the U.S., 99, 105, 141; Iowa Writer's Workshop and, 43, 99, 107–10
    Vonnegut on, 11
Donoso, María Pilar, 43, 108, 111
Do Not Enter: The Visa War against Ideas (documentary), 63
Dos Passos, John, 49
Draper, Theodore, 23
Dreamtigers (Borges), 15, 119
Drug Enforcement Agency, 197
Dulles, John Foster, 29, 42
Durrell, Lawrence, 102
Dutton, 14, 15–16, 120–21

Eames, Charles, 150
East German PEN Center, 86
Eco, Umberto, 69
Eder, Ursula, 101
The Edge of the Storm (Yáñez), 118
Editorial Arca, 45
Editorial Jus, 219n89
Edwards, Jorge, 86, 125
Einaudi, Luigi R., 161–62
Eliot, T. S., 183
Ellington, Duke, 28
Elliott, Jorge, 145, 195
Ellison, Ralph, 76, 78
The Emergent Decade (art exhibition), 136
Emmanuel, Pierre, 89
Encounter (journal), 18, 19–20, 84, 206n39
Los enemigos del alma (Mallea), 125, 126, 219n88
Engelbert, Jo Anne, 189
Engle, Paul, 43, 107, 108–11
Enguídanos, Miguel, 119
Entre la pluma y el fusil (Gilman), 7
Érase un hombre pentafácico (Godoy), 125, 131
Eréndira (film), 45
Esau and Jacob (Machado de Assis), 177
Eshelman, Clayton, 182

Espinal, Emmanuel, 140
Esquenazi Mayo, Roberto, 125, 129–30
The Essential Neruda, 196

Face the Nation, 52
Fallas Sibaja, Carlos Luis, 125, 129, 131
The Fall of America (Ginsberg), 196
Farfield Foundation, 150
Farrar, John, 71
Farrar, Straus and Company (later Farrar,
    Straus and Giroux), 14, 16, 49, 52
A Far Rockaway of the Heart (Ferlinghetti),
    196
Faulkner, William
    Boom authors and, 35
    H. de Onís and, 12
    García Márquez and, 44
    Ibero-American Novel Project and,
        123, 124
    Venezuela and, 123
    Weinstock on, 12
    Zavaleta and, 195
Faulkner family, 218n72
Faulkner Foundation, 123, 124, 127, 130
FBI (Federal Bureau of Investigation)
    Ginsberg and, 197
    Neruda and, 75–76
    Rama and, 46–48
    U.S. intellectuals and, 61
Ferlinghetti, Lawrence, 193, 194, 195–96,
    197
Fernández Retamar, Roberto, 19, 24, 83,
    84, 85
Ficciones (Borges), 15
Fielden, William, 218n72
Field Museum of Natural History
    (Chicago), 168
Fiesta in November (Mallea), 219n88
First Amendment, 38, 50
Fisher, John Hurt, 55
Fishlow, Albert, 224–25n54
Fitz, Earl, 103, 120
Fleischmann, Julius, 150, 151
Fleming, Thomas, 89–90
Florit, Eugenio
    IANP and, 125, 129, 130
    Odyssey Review and, 101

Fo, Dario, 38, 62–63
Ford administration, 166
Ford Foundation
    Bundy and, 29
    CCF/IACF and, 19, 21–23, 155
    CIAR and, 162–63
    CLAY and, 135, 138
    cultural diplomacy programs and, 27
    IAC and, 148
    IAFA and, 155–57, 158
    Intercultural Publications and, 112–13
    International Writing Program and,
        111
    Latin American studies and, 95, 96
    National Translation Center and, 113
    open letter to Neruda and, 86
    PEN congress and, 69–70, 76–77
    publishers and, 36
Foreign Leaders program, 28, 128
Fornet, Ambrosio, 84, 213n43
Foucault, Michel, 38
foundations, cultural diplomacy
    programs and, 29–32, 143–44. *See
    also specific foundations*
Fox, Claire, 8
Franco, Jean
    on Casa de las Américas, 5, 123–24
    Christ's trip to Chile and, 182
    on Cuban Revolution, 35
    on *Mundo Nuevo*, 18
    on the promotion of Latin American
        literature, 7
Franco regime (Spain), 7, 185
Frankel, Charles, 72–73, 74
Freedom of Information Act (FOIA),
    46, 60
Free Speech Movement, 133
French PEN center, 72
Freund, Gerald, 115, 118
Freyre, Gilberto, 10, 13
Frondizi, Risieri, 137–38
Frugé, August, 113–14, 119, 121, 177
Fuentes, Carlos
    Brandt and, 16–17, 49, 52, 54–55, 57,
        120
    Carpentier and, 12, 85, 213n43
    Christ's trip to Chile and, 183–85

CIAR and, 159, 178, 225n60
Cuban Revolution and, 26, 84–85, 88
Donoso and, 10, 82–83, 120
García Márquez on, 5
MacShane and, 57–58, 105, 106
McCarran-Walter Act and, 39, 41, 49–61, 62–63, 100, 106, 158, 179
A. Miller and, 49, 77, 78–79, 83, 87–89
MLA 1968 convention and, 55–56
Mundo Nuevo and, 17, 23
open letter to Neruda and, 83–85
Padilla affair and, 26
on PEN congress, 78, 82–83
Premio Biblioteca Breve and, 123
as publicist, 16–17
Puterbaugh Conferences and, 100
translations and, 108, 175
Vargas Llosa and, 56–57, 82, 88–89, 213n43
visiting positions in the U.S., 99, 100; Columbia University and, 57–58, 99, 100, 101, 105, 106; Iowa Writer's Workshop and, 108
Fuera del juego (Padilla), 26
Fulbright, J. W., 58–59
Fulbright Act (1946), 148
Fulbright Program, 28
Fuller, R. Buckminster, 78
Fund for Free Expression, 44, 62–63
Los funerales de la mamá grande (García Márquez), 218n63

Gabriela, Clove and Cinnamon (Amado), 13, 203n1
Galantière, Lewis, 68–71, 72–75, 80
Galin, Saul, 101
Galindo, Sergio, 119, 176
Gallegos, Rómulo, 6, 102, 123, 204n14. See also Rómulo Gallegos Prize
Gamboa Road Gang: Los forzados de Gamboa (Beleño), 125, 219n89
García Lorca, Federico, 198
García Lorca, Francisco, 98
García Márquez, Gabriel
on the Boom, 5

CIAR and, 159, 178, 179
Columbia University and, 44, 105
Cortázar and, 5, 171
Del Greco and, 127
IANP and, 217–18n63
MacShane and, 105
McCarran-Walter Act and, 38, 44–45, 62, 63
Mundo Nuevo and, 23
Neustadt Prize, 123
Odyssey Review and, 102–3
Rabassa and, 104
reviews and, 177
translations and, 14, 15, 175
See also *One Hundred Years of Solitude* (García Márquez)
García Ponce, Juan, 150
García Terrés, Jaime, 43, 150, 151
Garcilaso de la Vega, 119
Gardner, Richard, 224–25n54
Garment, Leonard, 208n8
Garro, Elena, 119, 176
"The General Song of Humanity" (Ferlinghetti), 196
Gerchman, Rubens, 226n68
Gilman, Claudia, 7, 19, 65
Ginsberg, Allen, 193, 194–95, 196–97, 199
Giusti, Roberto, 218n64
The Global Cold War (Westad), 8
Godoy, Emma, 125, 131, 219n89
Goić, Cedomil, 125
The Golden Land, 204n14
Goldmann, Lucien, 69
The Gold of the Tigers (Borges), 16
Góngora, Leonel, 226n68
González Echevarría, Roberto, 98
The Good Conscience (Fuentes), 16, 49, 51
Good Neighbor era, 4, 9, 25, 30–31
Goodrich, Lloyd, 28
Goodwin, Richard, 49–50, 145
Gordon, Lincoln, 153, 178
Goytisolo, Juan, 26, 182
Graves, Robert, 102
Gray, Wallace, 47
The Green Continent (Arciniegas), 204n14
Greene, Graham, 38, 69, 70

Greene, Roland, 198
The Green House (Vargas Llosa), 43
Grossman, William, 101, 103, 119
Grove, 14, 15
Guggenheim Foundation, 109
Guggenheim Museum, 136–37, 168
Guibert, Rita, 81, 82
Guillén, Jorge, 80, 86, 98
Guillén, Nicolás, 83, 86
Guimarães Rosa, João, 13, 78, 132, 171, 225n63
Güiraldes, Ricardo, 6, 204n14
Gurrola, Juan José, 150
Guzmán, Martín Luis, 118–19, 204n14

El hacedor (Borges), 15, 119
Halle, Elinor, 136
Handbook of Latin American Studies, 214n1
Hanke, Lewis, 73, 211n19
Harper and Row
    C. Canfield and, 14–15, 215–16n29
    Klein and, 14, 108
    One Hundred Years of Solitude and, 1
    translations and, 120–21, 131
Harrar, George, 137, 165
Harrison, John P.
    AAUP translation subsidy program and, 113, 115, 122
    Galantière and, 211n19
    IAC and, 149
    IAFA/CIAR and, 175
    Paradise Island symposium and, 145
    Rockefeller Foundation and, 113, 175
Harss, Luis, 5, 108, 186, 188–89
Harvard University
    Borges and, 15, 98
    Fuentes and, 99
    Paz and, 99, 100
    Rodríguez Monegal and, 170
Hauser, Rita, 224–25n54
Heard, Alexander, 224–25n54
Heartbreak Tango (Puig), 174
"The Heights of Macchu Picchu" (Neruda), 195
Heinz, Joan (Mrs. H. J. Heinz II), 150
Heiskell, Andrew

IAC and, 149
IAFA/CIAR and, 152, 153, 155, 165
Heitman, Walter, 165
Hellman, Lillian, 150, 151
Helsinki Accords (1975), 38
Helsinki Watch Committee, 48, 62
Helton, Arthur, 62
Herrera, Felipe, 136
Herrero-Olaizola, Alejandro, 7, 123, 185, 207n3
Hersey, John, 76
Hesburgh, Theodore, 61, 224–25n54
Hills, Lee, 224–25n54
Hispania (journal), 177, 214n1
Hispanic American Historical Review, 214n1
History of My Life (Casanova), 215n12
Hixson, Walter, 7
Hoover, J. Edgar, 61, 75–76, 197
Hopscotch (Cortázar), 14, 103, 108, 171, 225n60
Howell, Richard, 182
"Howl" (Ginsberg), 194
Howl and Other Poems (Ginsberg), 194, 195
Humphrey, Hubert
    CIAR and, 153, 158, 159–60
    Paradise Island symposium and, 146
Hunt, John, 21, 68–69
Huntington, Samuel, 224–25n54
Huxley, Aldous, 102
Hyde, James, 152

I Am Pablo Neruda (film), 179
Ibargüengoitia, Jorge, 48, 111
Ibero-American Novel Project (IANP), 123, 124–33, 142–43
Immigration and Nationality Act. *See* McCarran-Walter Act (1952)
Immigration and Naturalization Service (INS)
    Arciniegas and, 41–42
    Fuentes and, 49, 53, 56–57, 60
    McCarran-Walter Act and, 37, 59
    Rama and, 46, 47–48, 60
Index on Censorship, 62

Indych-López, Anna, 178
Information and Educational Exchange Act (Smith-Mundt Act, 1948), 148
In from the Cold (Joseph and Spenser), 200
In Praise of Darkness (Borges), 16
Instituto Chino-Chileno de Cultura, 43
Instituto de Amistad Chino-Uruguayo, 47
Instituto Internacional de Literatura Iberoamericana, 214n1
Instituto Latinoamericano de Relaciones Internacionales (ILARI), 21–22
Inter-American Committee (IAC), 146–50. *See also* Center for Inter-American Relations (CIAR); Inter-American Foundation for the Arts (IAFA)
Inter-American Development Bank, 161
Inter-American Foundation for the Arts (IAFA)
    Fuentes and, 58
    history and fundraising, 150–52, 154–58, 159
    Iowa Writer's Workshop and, 108, 110
    See also Center for Inter-American Relations (CIAR)
Intercultural Publications Inc. (IPI), 112–13
International Association for Cultural Freedom (IACF), 21–22, 89. *See also* Congress for Cultural Freedom (CCF)
International League for the Rights of Man, 42
International PEN
    1965 Congress (Bled, Yugoslavia), 65, 69, 72, 79
    CCF connections and, 68, 72
    censorship and, 209n29
    centers, 65–66, 72, 87
    Vargas Llosa and, 185, 186
    See also PEN American Center; PEN congress (New York, 1966)
International Publishers' Prize, 15–16, 98, 111, 123, 124
International Writing Program (IWP), 110–11, 143

Into the Mainstream (Harss and Dohmann), 108, 186
Ionesco, Eugène, 19
Iowa Writer's Workshop, 43, 99, 107–11, 143
Irvin, George, 139
Irving, John, 62

Jack Kerouac School of Disembodied Poetics, 197
Javits, Jacob, 153
jazz, 28, 32–33, 35
Johnson administration, 25, 53, 73
Joseph, Gilbert, 4, 26, 200
Josselson, Michael, 19, 20, 21, 72
Jovanovich, William, 78
Justice Department. *See* U.S. Department of Justice
Juventud Revolucionaria Dominicana, 140

Kafka, Franz, 48
Katzenback, Nicholas deB., 224–25n54
Kazin, Alfred, 112
Kennedy, Edward, 128
Kennedy, John F.
    Brazil and, 13
    IAFA and, 151
    McCarran-Walter Act and, 40
    Paradise Island symposium and, 146, 147
Kennedy, Liam, 30
Kennedy, Robert
    CIAR and, 153, 158
    H. de Onís and, 13
    Fuentes and, 52
    McCarran-Walter Act and, 40
    Paradise Island symposium and, 146
Kennedy, William, 176, 189
Kennedy administration, 25, 40
Kenyon Review, 177
Kharlamov, Mikhail, 51–52, 59–60
Khrushchev, Nikita, 153
King, John, 16, 180, 184
The Kingdom of This World (Carpentier), 14
Kissinger, Henry, 44, 164

Kiss of the Spider Woman (Puig), 174
Klein, Roger, 14, 108, 215–16n29
Knopf, Alfred
    H. de Onís and, 10, 216n29
    IAC and, 150
    Latin American literature and, 9–12,
        228n115
    Rabassa and, 104, 216n29
    Rockefeller Foundation and, 114
    Rodríguez Monegal and, 17, 104,
        216n29
    See also Alfred A. Knopf Inc.
Knopf, Blanche, 9, 219n88, 228n115
Kolovakos, Gregory, 169–70
Koshland, William, 126
Krenn, Michael L., 7
Kristol, Irving, 19
Kubitschek, Juscelino, 136, 160
Kunitz, Stanley, 198

Laber, Jeri, 62
Labyrinths (Borges), 15
Lasky, Melvin, 19, 69, 78
Latin American Research Review (journal),
    95–96, 136
Latin American Studies Association
    (LASA), 48, 95
Lattimore, Richmond, 78
Laughlin, James, 112–13, 151, 181–82. *See
    also* New Directions Press
Lawrence, Seymour, 104, 131
El lazarillo (Concolorcorvo), 119
Leaf Storm (García Márquez), 15, 217n63
Lee, Muna, 128
Legters, Lyman, 135
Lenin Peace Prize, 91
Leonard, John, 1–2
Leopardi, Giacomo, 127
Lessing, Doris, 38
The Lettered City (Rama), 45
Levine, Flavián, 149
Levine, Suzanne Jill
    Christ's trip to Chile and, 182, 184
    CIAR and, 107, 169, 170, 171, 175, 176
    Columbia University and, 107
    on commercial publishers, 120–21
    on B. Knopf, 219n88

    on Macrae, 16
    Puig and, 105
Lezama Lima, José, 13
Library Journal (journal), 170, 177
Library of Congress, 81, 100, 198, 214n1
Lida, Raimundo, 101
"Life" en español
    IANP and, 129
    open letter to Neruda and, 84
    on Paz at Cornell, 141
    on PEN congress, 81–82
Lindsay, John, 153
Linowitz, Sol, 165, 167, 178
Lispector, Clarice
    H. de Onís and, 13
    A. Knopf and, 11
    Odyssey Review and, 102
    Rabassa and, 103, 104, 215n11
Listen, Yankee! (Mills), 96, 120
"La literatura es fuego" (Vargas Llosa),
    25, 43, 79
Lleras Restrepo, Carlos, 161
Llosa, Patricia, 193
Lodge, George, 224–25n54
López de Gómara, Francisco, 118, 119
López Mateos, Adolfo, 151
The Lost Steps (Carpentier), 12, 14, 85, 130
Louisiana State University, 99, 197
Lowe, Elizabeth, 103, 120
Lowell, Robert, 80, 102, 103
Lowry, McNeil, 156
Lucas, Scott, 30
Lunes de Revolución (literary supplement),
    26, 195, 204n6

Mac Adam, Alfred, 175, 182, 189
Machado de Assis, Joaquim Maria, 119,
    177
MacLeish, Archibald
    CIAR and, 153, 178
    Neruda and, 77–78, 198
    Odyssey Review and, 102
    PEN congress and, 80
MacLeish, William
    CIAR and, 152, 159, 186
    CLAY and, 133, 137, 141–42, 159
    Galantière and, 212n19

Macomber, William, Jr., 59
Macrae, John, III, 16, 87, 182
MacShane, Frank
  Boom and, 217n49
  Chile and, 180, 181, 198
  CIAR and, 143
  Columbia University and, 99–100,
    101, 105–6, 143, 169
  Fuentes and, 57–58, 105, 106
  PEN conference on translation and,
    87
  Rabassa and, 105
Mades, Leonard, 174
Maggio, Michael, 47, 209n27
Mailer, Norman, 49, 56, 207n2
Mallea, Eduardo, 102, 125, 126, 219n88
Manheim, Jarol, 27–28
Mann, Thomas C.
  CIAR and, 153, 158
  Fuentes and, 49, 51, 52, 158
A Manual for Manuel (Cortázar),
  225n60
Marcha (Uruguayan journal)
  on CIA and CCF, 20
  Rama and, 45–47
  Rodríguez Monegal and, 17, 84
Marcos Ramírez (Fallas Sibaja), 125,
  129, 131
Mariátegui, José Carlos, 119
Marks, Leonard, 109–10
Marqués, René, 125
Martí, José, 119
Martin, Frederick, 183
Martin, Gerald, 1, 16–17, 24, 26
Martínez Moreno, Carlos, 124, 193, 194
Massey, Linton, 130, 218n72
Matthiessen, Peter, 145
McCarran-Walter Act (1952)
  Arciniegas and, 40–42, 210n46
  CIAR and, 165–66
  Cortázar and, 44, 62
  denial of visas and, 34, 37–40, 42–
    43, 61–63
  Fuentes and, 39, 41, 49–61, 62–63,
    100, 106, 158
  García Márquez and, 38, 44–45, 62,
    63

  group waivers for conference
    participants, 56, 75
  Johnson administration and, 53–54
  Neruda and, 38, 54, 62, 70, 75–76,
    89–90
  PEN congress and, 70–71, 72–76, 81
  Rama and, 45–48, 60, 62, 189
  Vargas Llosa and, 38, 43–44, 106
McCarthy, Kathleen D., 69, 154
McDonald, Frank, 164
McGovern Amendment (1977), 38–39
McLuhan, Marshall, 78
McMurtry, Larry, 63
McNamara, Robert, 29
Mead, Robert, 55
Meany, George, 178
Medusa (Carballido), 136
Memoirs (Neruda), 179
Memoirs of Pancho Villa (Guzmán),
  118–19
Mene: A Venezuelan Novel (Díaz
  Sánchez), 219n89
Mercier Vega, Luis, 21
Merwin, W. S., 196
Messer, Thomas, 136, 150, 151, 165
Mexico and Mexican literature
  AAUP translation subsidy program
    and, 216–17n48
  Beat poets and, 194, 195, 198–99
  CLAY and, 138–39
  IAFA conference and, 151
  PEN center in, 87
  U.S. academy and, 98–99
Meyer, Charles, 162, 224–25n54
Meyer, Doris, 183
Michalski, Kirsten, 89
The Mighty Wurlitzer (Wilford), 32
Miller, Arthur
  Fuentes and, 49, 77, 78–79, 83,
    87–89
  McCarran-Walter Act and, 62
  Neruda and, 90
  PEN congress and, 77, 78–79, 80
  as PEN president, 65, 71–72
  Randall and, 207n2
  Translation and, 106
  Vargas Llosa and, 92

Miller, Toby, 31
Mills, C. Wright, 49, 96, 120
Milosz, Czeslaw, 38
Miramax, 45
Mistral, Gabriela, 104
Mitchell, John, 57
Mitgang, Herbert, 197
MLA convention (1968), 55–56
Modern Brazilian Short Stories
    (Grossman), 119
modern dance, 35
Modernism, 34–36
Modern Language Association
    convention (1968), 55–56
Mondragón, Sergio, 54
Montes de Oca, Marco Antonio, 79
Mora, José, 102
Morales-Carrión, Arturo, 224–25n54
Morath, Inge, 81
Morrison, Toni, 207n2
Morse, Richard, 115, 145, 149, 211n19
Moscoso, Teodoro, 146
Movimiento Nacionalista Revolucionario
    (Bolivia), 128
Mowat, Farley, 38
Mudrovcic, María Eugenia, 159, 191
Mundo Nuevo (journal)
    Fornet and, 84
    García Márquez and, 44
    history of, 18–24, 32
    on Paz at Cornell, 141
    PEN congress and, 81, 141
    research on, 7
    Review and, 170, 190–91
    Rodríguez Monegal and, 17, 18, 20–
        24, 190–91
    Weinstock and, 12
Murray, Bill, 107
Murrow, Edward R., 156
Museum of Modern Art (New York),
    148, 158, 168
Mutual Educational and Cultural
    Exchanges Act (1961), 28
Myrdal, Jan, 38

Naropa Institute (Boulder), 197
Nation (journal), 62, 177

National Book Award for Translation,
    103, 127, 171, 225n60
National Council on the Arts (NCA),
    68, 106, 156–57
National Defense Education Act
    (NDEA, 1958), 96
National Endowment for the Arts
    (NEA), 68
National Translation Center, 113
Needler, Martin, 96
Nelson, Alan, 47–48
Neruda, Pablo
    Carpentier and, 86
    CIAR and, 159, 178, 179–80, 226n70
    Columbia University and, 106
    Cuban Revolution and, 195–96
    H. de Onís and, 13
    Fuentes and, 82
    A. Knopf and, 12
    McCarran-Walter Act and, 38, 54,
        62, 70, 75–76, 89–90
    media coverage and, 81–82; *New York
        Times* and, 77–78, 81, 91, 105
    open letter to, 26, 83–87, 92
    Orrego-Salas and, 137
    PEN American Center and, 89–91
    PEN congress and, 72, 73–74, 77–78,
        79, 80–81
    Rockefeller Foundation (RF) and,
        122
    Rodríguez Monegal and, 17, 23
    Silone and, 77, 78, 81
    translations and, 175
    at UC Berkeley, 81, 193
Netherlands PEN Club, 186
Neumann, Hans, 150
Neustadt Prize, 123
New Critics, 12, 34–35, 102
New Directions Press, 15, 179, 196. *See
    also* Laughlin, James
Newman, Paul, 150, 154
"new narrative" (*nueva narrativa*), 114,
    132
New Republic, 176
Newsweek, 177
New World Writing, 122
New Yorker, 169, 176, 177

New York Review of Books, 176
New York State Council on the Arts, 189
New York Times
    on Arciniegas, 41–42
    Christ's trip to Chile and, 182
    on CIA and CCF, 19, 21, 45–46,
       83–84
    on CIAR, 166
    Fuentes and, 50–51, 53, 57, 106
    on Ibero-American Novel Project,
       124
    MacShane and, 105
    on McCarran-Walter Act, 41–42
    on Neruda, 77–78, 81, 91, 105
    on *One Hundred Years of Solitude*,
       1–2, 174
    on PEN congress, 77–78, 81
    on Rama, 48
    reviews in, 174, 176, 177
    on translations, 228n115
New York University, 99, 100, 169, 197
Nicaragua, 124–25, 228n113
Nixon, Patricia, 198
Nixon, Richard, 25, 90
Nixon administration, 58–59, 163–64
Noel, Jesse, 219n89
No One Writes the Colonel (García
    Márquez), 174, 217n63
Norton, 126
Noticias de arte (journal), 188
novela de la tierra (regionalist novels), 6,
    99, 132
nueva narrativa ("new narrative"), 114,
    132
La nueva novela hispanoamericana
    (Fuentes), 17

El obsceno pájaro de la noche (Donoso),
    107, 123, 174, 177
Ocampo, Victoria, 78, 101, 212n19
"Ode to Laziness" (Neruda), 122
Odyssey Review (journal), 14, 101–7, 143
Office for the Coordination of
    Commercial and Cultural Relations
    between the American Republics
    (later, the Office of the Coordinator

    of Inter-American Affairs, OCIAA),
    30–31
Ohmann, Richard, 176, 192
Oliver, Covey, 153
la Onda, 198–99
One Hundred Years of Solitude (García
    Márquez)
    Mundo Nuevo and, 17, 44
    reviews and, 177
    translation by Rabassa, 1–2, 14–15,
       103, 174, 175
"One Thousand Fearful Words for Fidel
    Castro" (Ferlinghetti), 195
Onetti, Juan Carlos, 102, 125, 193
Organization of American States (OAS),
    25
Orozco, José Clemente, 177–78
Orrego-Salas, Juan, 136–37, 168
Ortega, Daniel, 38
Ortega, Julio, 98, 214n6, 217n49
Otero, Lisandro, 84
Other Inquisitions, 1937–1952 (Borges), 15
"Overpopulation" (Ferlinghetti), 194
Oviedo, José Miguel, 98, 228n113

Pacheco, José Emilio, 182
Padilla, Heberto, 13, 26–27, 85
Palés Matos, Luis, 102
Pantaleón y las visitadoras (Vargas Llosa),
    185
Pantheon, 14, 103, 120–21. *See also*
    Blackburn, Sara
Paradise Island symposium, 145–46, 147,
    149
Paris Review, 15
Parmar, Inderjeet, 29–30
Parra, Nicanor
    Beat poets and, 194–95, 196
    faculty positions in the U.S., 99, 141,
       197–98; Columbia University and,
       99, 105, 106, 197; Louisiana State
       University and, 99, 197
    Fuentes on, 82
    MacShane and, 105
    Odyssey Review and, 102
Parrés, Ramón, 78

Partido Revolucionario Dominicano (PRD), 53, 140
Partisan Review (journal), 18, 176
Paso, Fernando del, 111
Pasti, Nino, 38, 62–63
Paz, Octavio
    CIAR and, 179, 182, 188, 189
    on Cuban Revolution, 26
    Mundo Nuevo and, 23
    New York Times and, 174
    Odyssey Review and, 101
    Plural and, 18
    Puterbaugh Conferences and, 100
    translations and, 119, 175
    visiting positions in the U.S., 99, 100; CLAY and, 99, 136, 141
Pedro Páramo (Rulfo), 14
PEN American Center
    censorship and, 209n29
    Columbia University and, 106, 107
    conference on translation and, 87
    Fuentes and, 57
    Latin American literature and, 87
    McCarran-Walter Act and, 62
    Neruda and, 89–91
    Rama and, 48
    Randall and, 207n2
    See also PEN congress (New York, 1966)
PEN congress (New York, 1966)
    backlash and publicity, 80–85
    CCF connections and, 66, 68–69
    conference, 76–80
    consequences, 91–93
    invitations, funding, and visas, 67–76
    as outreach program, 65–67
PEN International. *See* International PEN
Penn State University, 99
PEN Translation Prize, 171, 174
Perkins, James, 133–35, 142
Personal Anthology (Borges), 15
Perspectives, U.S.A. (journal), 112–13
Peru and Peruvian literature
    Beat poets and, 195
    CLAY and, 138–39

Odyssey Review and, 102
    Vargas Llosa on, 79
Peterson, Peter, 224–25n54
Peyrou, Rosario, 47
philanthropies, cultural diplomacy programs and, 29–32, 143–44. *See also specific foundations*
Pinochet regime (Chile), 164, 165, 181
Pinter, Harold, 19
Platero and I . . . (Ramón Jiménez), 114
Plural (journal), 18
PMLA (journal), 56
Podhoretz, Norman, 78, 145
Poems and Antipoems, 196
Poeta en Nueva York (García Lorca), 198
Poetry Society of America, 91
El Popular (Uruguayan weekly), 46
Porgy and Bess, 28
Portuguese literature, 215n9
The Precipice (Galindo), 119, 176
Premio Biblioteca Breve, 123, 124
Premio Rómulo Gallegos, 43, 79
Prieto, Herminia (Pipina), 15, 215–16n29
Princeton University, 99
Publishers Weekly, 57, 170, 174, 177
Puerto Rico
    Fuentes incident in, 56–57, 179
    IAFA symposium in, 150–51
    PEN center in, 87
    U.S. immigration laws and, 208n10
Puig, Manuel, 99, 105, 174, 214n7
Purves, Alan, 101
Puterbaugh Conferences, 100

Queiroz, Rachel de, 119
Quiroga, Horacio, 17
Quiroga Santa Cruz, Marcelo, 125, 128

Rabassa, Gregory
    Boom and, 217n49
    Christ's trip to Chile and, 183
    CIAR and, 107, 143, 169, 170, 175, 189
    Columbia University and, 101, 107, 143
    Cortázar and, 14, 103, 104, 171, 208n8
    H. de Onís and, 104
    A. Knopf and, 104, 216n29

MacShane and, 105
National Book Award for Translation, 171
Odyssey Review and, 14, 101, 103–4
One Hundred Years of Solitude and, 1–2, 14–15, 103, 174, 175
PEN conference on translation and, 87
Rama, Ángel
  McCarran-Walter Act and, 45–48, 60, 62, 189
  politics and, 45, 189
  Review and, 186, 187–88
  Rodríguez Monegal and, 20
  on Zea, 207n4
Rame, Franca, 38
Ramón Jiménez, Juan, 98, 114
Ramos, Graciliano, 119, 125, 129, 131
Ramos, Samuel, 102, 119
Randall, Margaret, 38, 54, 212n19
Ransom, John Crowe, 112
Ravinet, Jaime, 164
Raymont, Henry, 57, 91
Rayuela (Cortázar), 14, 103, 108, 171, 225n60
Reagan, Ronald, 48
Reality Sandwiches, 195
Recollections of Things to Come (Garro), 119, 176
regionalism, 6, 99, 132
Reid, Alastair
  Borges and, 15
  Christ's trip to Chile and, 181
  CIAR and, 169, 170, 180, 189
  Harper and Row and, 215–16n29
Residence on Earth (Neruda), 179
Response to Revolution (Welch), 96
Review (journal)
  Harss and, 186–89
  "Literature and Exile" issue, 186–88, 189
  Mundo Nuevo and, 170, 190
  Rodríguez Monegal and, 184
Review '68 (journal), 18
Revista Hispánica Moderna (journal), 104
Revista Iberoamericana (journal), 18, 214n1

Reyes, Alfonso, 102, 119, 204n14
Reyes, Ramón Emilio, 129
Ribeyro, Julio Ramón, 102
Rich, Adrienne, 207n2
Richardson, Gail, 138, 139
"The Rime of the Ancient Mariner" (Coleridge), 90
Río, Ángel del, 98, 101
Los ríos profundos (Arguedas), 125, 131
Rivera, Diego, 177–78
Rivera, José Eustasio, 6
Roa Bastos, Augusto, 125, 131, 186
Robison, Howard, 135–36
Rockefeller, Abby (née Aldrich), 158
Rockefeller, David
  Council on Latin America and, 151–52, 188
  cultural diplomacy programs and, 31
  IAFA/CIAR and, 148, 152–53, 157–58, 162, 164, 167
Rockefeller, John D., III, 69, 146
Rockefeller, Laurance, 157
Rockefeller, Nelson, 30–31, 153, 162
Rockefeller, Rodman
  cultural diplomacy programs and, 31
  IAC and, 149
  IAFA/CIAR and, 151, 157
Rockefeller Brothers Fund (RBF)
  CIAR and, 225n57
  cultural diplomacy programs and, 31
  IAC and, 148
  IAFA and, 157
  PEN congress and, 69
Rockefeller family, 31, 157–58
Rockefeller Foundation (RF)
  AAUP translation subsidy program and, 15, 113–15, 118, 121–22
  CCF and, 19
  CLAY and, 135
  cultural diplomacy programs and, 27, 31
  Dulles and, 29
  Harrison and, 113, 175
  Latin American studies and, 96
  publishers and, 36
  Rusk and, 29–30, 113
Rockefeller Report on the Americas, 162

Rockefeller Strong de Larraín, Margaret (Marquesa de Cuevas), 153
Rodríguez, Horacio, 22
Rodríguez Monegal, Emir
    Christ's trip to Chile and, 181, 183–84
    CIAR and, 169, 175, 176, 180
    H. de Onís and, 104
    faculty positions in the U.S., 98, 170
    Galantière and, 212n19
    García Márquez and, 44
    IANP and, 124
    Iowa Writer's Workshop and, 108
    as literary ambassador, 17–18
    MLA 1968 convention and, 55
    Mundo Nuevo and, 17, 18, 20–24, 190–91
    open letter to Neruda and, 83–85
    PEN congress and, 69, 79, 80, 81
    Review and, 170, 184
    Weinstock and, 12
Rogers, William D. (CIAR president)
    Alliance for Progress and, 152, 159
    CIAR and, 152–53, 158, 159, 179, 223n39
    Fuentes and, 58, 60–61
Rogers, William P. (Secretary of State), 58, 162
Rojas, Gonzalo, 194
Rómulo Gallegos Prize, 43, 79
Roosevelt administration and Good Neighbor era, 4, 9, 25, 30–31
Rostagno, Irene
    on CIAR, 169, 170
    H. de Onís and, 12–13
    on Fuentes, 50
    on the Knopfs, 9, 11, 132
    on One Hundred Years of Solitude, 14
    on the promotion of Latin American literature, 7
    on Review, 190
Royal Commentaries (Garcilaso de la Vega), 119
Rulfo, Juan, 14, 119
Rusk, Dean
    Fuentes and, 52, 55
    IAC and, 150
    PEN congress and, 71

Rockefeller Foundation and, 29–30, 113
Russell Tribunal II, 189

Sábato, Ernesto, 150–51
Sagarana (Guimarães Rosa), 171
Sáinz, Gustavo, 111
Salazar Bondy, Sebastián, 102, 194, 195
Salinger, Pierre, 52
Salisbury, Harrison, 52
Samuels, Nathaniel, 224–25n54
Santos, Bienvenido (Ben), 107
Santos, Rosario, 186, 188, 189
Sanz de Santamaría, Carlos, 136
Sarduy, Severo, 182, 184, 185
Sartre, Jean-Paul, 19, 23, 26, 196
Saturday Review (journal)
    AAUP translation subsidy program and, 118
    H. de Onís and, 13
    reviews in, 176, 177
Saunders, Frances S., 7, 19, 68, 69, 72
Scheuer, James, 59–60
Schlesinger, Arthur M., Jr., 58, 112, 145, 156
Schreiber, Rebecca, 8–9
Schwartz, Abba, 52, 54, 58
Schwartz, Lawrence H., 7, 34, 122
Scliar, Moacyr, 182
Scorza, Manuel, 48
Scott-Smith, Giles, 23–24
Searching for Recognition (Rostagno), 7
Segovia, Tomás, 111
Seix Barral (publishing house), 6, 123, 124
Selected Poems (Neruda), 179
El señor presidente (Asturias), 125, 131
Shanks, Cheryl, 39
Shannon, Edgar, 130
Shapiro, Steven, 39, 63
Sheldon, Glenn, 198, 199
The Shipyard (Onetti), 125
Show (journal), 145, 146
Silesky, Barry, 196
Silone, Ignazio, 69, 77, 78, 81
Silvert, Kalman, 138
Simpson, Lesley Byrd, 217n48

Sinyavsky-Daniel trial (1966), 77, 81, 83
Siqueiros, David Alfaro, 168, 177–78
Skedgell, Marian, 182
Slater, Joseph, 156
Sloane, William, 115
Smith, David, 159
Smith-Mundt Act (Information and
    Educational Exchange Act, 1948), 148
Solzhenitsyn, Aleksandr, 91
Sommers, Joseph, 182, 217n49
Son of Man (Roa Bastos), 125, 131
Sontag, Susan, 19, 26, 62
Sorensen, Diana, 6, 7, 16, 18
Sosa, Mercedes, 168
Spanish Stories and Tales, 204n14
Spender, Stephen, 19, 84, 102
Squirru, Rafael, 145
Stanford University, 197, 215n14
State Department. *See* U.S. Department
    of State
The State of Latin America (Arciniegas),
    41
Stegner, Wallace, 112
Steinbeck, John, 211n13
Stevens, Roger, 68
St. Martin, Hardie, 174, 179
Stone, Roger, 180, 181–82, 183, 185–86,
    224n53
Strand, Mark, 169, 176, 182
*Strategic Public Diplomacy and American
    Foreign Policy* (Manheim), 27–28
Straus, Roger, 57, 150
Strong Wind (Asturias), 178
structuralist literary criticism, 34–35
Studies on the Left (journal), 50
Styron, Rose, 63, 207n2
Styron, William
    Fuentes and, 49
    IAC and, 149
    IAFA/CIAR and, 154
    McCarran-Walter Act and, 62
    Paradise Island symposium and, 145
    Randall and, 207n2
Sulzberger, Arthur Ochs, 153
Sunrise Semester, 169
Sur group, 15
Swenson, Eric, 126

Szulc, Tad, 51
Szyszlo, Fernando, 145, 168

Tannenbaum, Frank, 50–51
Tarn, Nathaniel, 182
Tarsis, Valery, 77, 81, 83
Tate, Allen, 112
Taylor, Arthur, 150
El testimonio (Reyes), 129
Texas Quarterly (journal), 119
Theberge, James, 163–64
This Sunday (Donoso), 11
Thompson, John, 145
Three Trapped Tigers (Cabrera Infante),
    15, 123, 174
Time, 177
The Time of the Hero (Vargas Llosa), 123
Tinker, Edward Larocque, 153
Tinker Foundation, 105
"To an Old Poet in Peru" (Ginsberg), 195
Tomic, Radomiro, 136, 164
Torre Nilsson, Leopoldo, 149
Torres García, Joaquín, 168
Torres-Rioseco, Arturo, 101
Touraine, Alain, 164
Traba, Marta, 46, 48, 151, 208n20
*Transculturación narrativa en América
    Latina* (Rama), 45
translation
    AAUP subsidy program and, 15, 113–
        22, 116–17t
    CIAR subsidy program, 168–77, 172–
        73t, 189, 191–92, 219n87
    Columbia University center, 106–7
    cost of, 9, 111, 115
    PEN conference on, 87
    See also de Onís, Harriet; Levine,
        Suzanne Jill; *Odyssey Review*
        (journal); Rabassa, Gregory; Reid,
        Alastair; Weinberger, Eliot
Translation (journal), 106–7
Trask, Willard, 215n12
Tres tristes tigres (Cabrera Infante), 15,
    123, 174
The Trial (Kafka), 48
Trillin, Calvin, 49
Trilling, Lionel, 102, 112

TriQuarterly (journal), 18
Trudeau, Pierre, 38
Trujillo, Rafael, 73, 218n76
Truman, Harry S., 37, 61
A Turbulent Decade Remembered (Sorensen), 7

Under Northern Eyes (Berger), 143
UNEAC (Unión de escritores y artistas cubanos), 26
Union of Soviet Writers, 83
United Negro College Fund, 142
The United States and Latin America: Next Steps, 166–67
El Universal (Caracas), 187–88
A Universal History of Infamy (Borges), 16
Universidad Autónoma Nacional de México, 216n32
universities (U.S.)
    faculty positions for Latin American scholars in, 98–101
    Latin American studies and, 95–98, 102, 119–20, 134
    See also CLAY (Cornell University's "Latin American Year"); Ibero-American Novel Project (IANP); university presses; *specific universities*
University of California, Berkeley
    Alegría and, 197
    demonstrations at, 133
    Neruda and, 81, 193
    Vargas Llosa and, 99
University of California Press, 113–14, 118, 177
University of Chicago, 215n14
University of Iowa. *See* Iowa Writer's Workshop
University of Maryland, 45, 47
University of Oklahoma, 100. See also *World Literature Today*
University of Pennsylvania, 99
University of Puerto Rico
    Rama and, 46
    Vargas Llosa and, 56–57, 99
University of Texas at Austin
    Borges and, 98, 119

National Translation Center, 113
    Tinker Foundation and, 215n14
University of Texas Press
    AAUP translation subsidy program and, 15, 113–14, 118–19, 131
    Cumboto and, 126, 127
University of Virginia. *See* Ibero-American Novel Project (IANP)
University of Virginia Press, 126
University of West Indies Press, 219n89
University of Wisconsin–Madison, 215n14
university presses
    AAUP subsidy program and, 15, 113–22, 116–17t, 175, 176–77
    vs. commercial publishers, 120–21, 170
    See also specific university presses
Uruguay and Uruguayan literature
    CLAY and, 138–39
    IANP and, 124, 125
    Rodríguez Monegal and, 17, 184
    See also *Marcha* (Uruguayan journal)
U.S. Agency for International Development (USAID), 135, 154
U.S Department of Justice
    Fuentes and, 50
    McCarran-Walter Act and, 38, 54
    PEN congress and, 75
    See also Immigration and Naturalization Service (INS)
U.S. Department of State
    Arciniegas and, 41
    CIAR and, 158, 161–62
    CLAY and, 138–39, 140
    cultural diplomacy programs and, 27–29, 30–31, 32–33, 39–40, 143–44
    Donoso and, 43
    Foreign Leaders program, 28, 128
    Fuentes and, 50, 51, 54, 55–56, 57–60
    IAC and, 149
    IANP and, 125, 128
    Iowa Writer's Workshop and, 109, 110
    McCarran-Walter Act and, 37–38, 53–54, 62

Neruda and, 89–90
PEN congress and, 70, 72–75, 76–77
Rama and, 46–47
See also Bureau of Educational and Cultural Affairs (ECA)
U.S. Information Agency (USIA)
CLAY and, 135–36
cultural diplomacy programs and, 27, 39–40
IAFA/CIAR and, 154, 167
IANP and, 128
Iowa Writer's Workshop and, 109–10
PEN congress and, 75
Uslar Pietri, Arturo, 104, 204n14

Valenzuela, Arturo, 164
Valenzuela, Luisa, 111, 189
Vallejo, César, 102
Van Doren, Mark, 80
Vargas Llosa, Mario
Chicago Tribune and, 6
Christ's trip to Chile and, 185–86
CIAR and, 178, 184, 189
Cuban Revolution and, 43, 185
faculty positions in the U.S., 99; Columbia University and, 99, 105; University of Puerto Rico and, 56–57, 99; Washington State University and, 43–44, 99
Fuentes and, 56–57, 82, 88–89, 213n43
García Márquez on, 5
on literature as fire, 25
McCarran-Walter Act and, 38, 43–44, 106
Mundo Nuevo and, 23
Neruda and, 193
Padilla affair and, 26
PEN and, 92
Premio Biblioteca Breve and, 123
Puterbaugh Conferences and, 100
Rómulo Gallegos Prize and, 43, 79
translations and, 14, 175
Vasconcelos, José, 119
Vázquez Amaral, José, 211n19
Veloz Maggiolo, Marcio, 125, 128, 129

Venezuela
Faulkner and, 123
Nixon and, 25
PEN center in, 87
Rockefeller family and, 31
Verani, Hugo, 182
Verissimo, Erico, 136
Victor Gollancz, 219n87
Vidal, Gore, 145, 149
Vidas Secas (Ramos), 125, 131
Vietnam War
Fuentes and, 100, 106
Mundo Nuevo and, 12, 23
Neruda and, 78
opposition to, 26, 67
Villaurrutia, Xavier, 102
Visión (newsmagazine), 133, 152
La víspera del hombre (Marqués), 125
Voice of America, 125
Von Eschen, Penny, 7, 32–33, 35
Vonnegut, Kurt, 11, 107, 207n2
Vuelta (journal), 182–83

Wagley, Charles, 57–58, 106
Walker, Alice, 207n2
Walker, Thomas, 96
Wall Street Journal, 183
Wardlaw, Frank, 113–14, 121–22, 126, 127
Warren, Robert Penn, 102, 112
Washington Post
Christ's trip to Chile and, 182
on Ibero-American Novel Project, 124
on Rama, 48
Washington State University, 43–44, 99
Washington University, 52
Weatherhead, Richard W., 50, 51
Webster, William, 47–48
Weinberger, Eliot
Christ's trip to Chile and, 181–82, 183–84
CIAR and, 170, 171
Weinstein, Harvey and Bob, 45
Weinstock, Herbert, 11–12, 13, 17
Welch, Richard, Jr., 33, 96
Wellek, René, 102

West, Robert, 118
Westad, Odd Arne, 8
Wharton, Clifton, Jr., 224–25n54
Where the Air Is Clear (Fuentes), 16
White Museum, 136, 137
Wilder, Thornton, 106
Wilford, Hugh, 32, 147–48, 150, 191
Williams, Tennessee, 112
Williams, William Carlos, 196
Wood, Michael, 176
Woodrow Wilson International Center
    for Scholars, 99
Wool, Robert
    Donoso and, 43
    Fuentes and, 54
    Galantière and, 212n19
    IAC and, 146, 149
    IAFA and, 150–51, 155–58, 168

Iowa Writer's Workshop and, 108–10
    Paradise Island symposium and,
        145–46
    PEN congress and, 73–74, 80
Woolf, Virginia, 35
World Literature Today, 100, 123, 214n7

Yale University, 170, 214n4
Yáñez, Agustín, 108, 118, 119
Yglesias, Luis, 182
Yúdice, George, 31

Zamora, Lois Parkinson, 6
Zavaleta, Carlos, 145, 195
Zea, Leopoldo, 43, 119
Zimbalist, Andrew, 164
Zubiría, Ramón de, 150